How To Choose & Care For A
DOG

BY JOAN PALMER
Consultants
Bruce Sessions
Diane Webb

Illustrated by
John Francis and John Green

English Setter

Gordon Setter

Pharaoh Hound

©1982 HPBooks, Inc.
Printed in U.S.A.
5th Printing

Published in the United States by
HPBooks, A Division of HPBooks, Inc.
P.O. Box 5367
Tucson, AZ 85703
602/888-2150

Publisher: Rick Bailey
Editorial Director: Randy Summerlin
Editor: Judith Schuler
Art Director: Don Burton
Book Design: Dana Martin
Production Coordinator: Cindy J. Coatsworth
Typography: Michelle Carter

ISBN: 0-89586-172-0
Library of Congress Catalog Card Number: 82-81713

Salamander Books, Ltd. (1982)
First produced by Salamander Books Limited of Salamander
House, 27 Old Gloucester St., London WC1N3AF, England.
Not to be sold outside of the United States, and its territories,
and Canada.

DOGS ON COVER:
Top Left: German Shepherd
Bottom Left: Cocker Spaniels
Right: Miniature Poodles

Principal Author

JOAN PALMER has been a committee member of The National Dog Owners' Association of Great Britain for the past 15 years. She has written a number of books on domestic animals. Ms. Palmer and her husband own Chihuahuas and a hairless Chinese Crested female, as well as other animals.

Consultants

BRUCE SESSIONS, formerly Senior Editor and Consultant to *International Dog Fancy Magazine,* is an authority on dogs. He has authored three books on dog care and training. Sessions has hosted an American television series on veterinary care and has trained dogs for the U.S. Navy, the Las Vegas Police Department, and for search and rescue work in Oregon.

DIANE WEBB is the editor of the *American Belgian Tervuren Club Magazine* and the editor/publisher of a monthly tabloid, the *Best In Dogs.* She has raised and shown Belgian Tervurens for 15 years and has had many champions. As an apprentice handler for 2 years, she gained extensive knowledge of many dog breeds.

Contributing Authors

KAY WHITE gained practical experience with dogs from running a large breeding and boarding kennel. She still breeds boxers and has bred 10 generations from her original dogs. She has promoted veterinary education for dog breeders and is now a reporter for a weekly paper and news editor for a veterinary newspaper.

MICHAEL A. FINDLAY is a veterinarian and involved with dog obedience training. He has written or contributed to several books on animal care.

Ibizan Hound

Contents

Beagle

INDEX OF DOG BREEDS

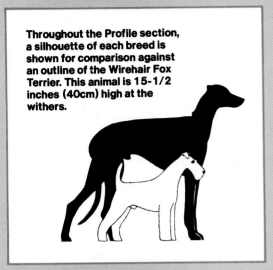

Throughout the Profile section, a silhouette of each breed is shown for comparison against an outline of the Wirehair Fox Terrier. This animal is 15-1/2 inches (40cm) high at the withers.

Parts Of A Dog

This drawing shows the anatomical parts of a dog and the terms used to describe them. For further information on these and other technical terms used in the book, see the Glossary on page 200

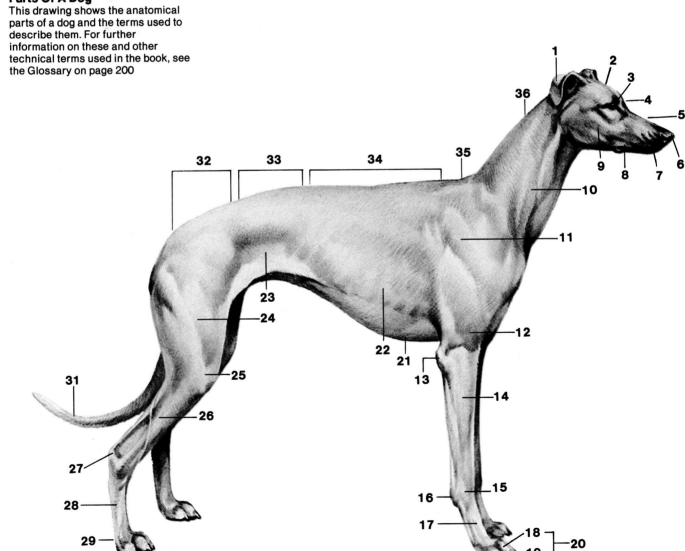

PROFILES

Detailed profiles of more than
200 international breeds, arranged in
order of size.

Parts Of A Dog

1. Ear
2. Skull. The upper, back point of the skull is called the *occiput,* or *peak.* The top of the skull is called the *crown.*
3. Eye
4. Stop
5. Foreface. The foreface, nose and jaws make up the muzzle.
6. Nose
7. Jaws. The fleshy parts of the lips and jaws make up the jowls.
8. Lips. Pendulous upper lips are called *flews.*
9. Cheek
10. Neck
11. Shoulder
12. Upper Arm
13. Elbow
14. Forearm
15. Wrist
16. Stopper pad
17. Pastern
18. Toes
19. Nails
20. Forefoot
21. Sternum, the breastbone
22. Chest
23. Flank
24. Thigh
25. Stifle, the knee
26. Second thigh, the lower thigh
27. Hock, the heel
28. Rear pastern
29. Hind foot
30. Pads
31. Tail. In different types of dogs, the tail is known variously as the brush, flag, rudder and stern.
32. Croup
33. Loin
34. Back
35. Withers, the top of the shoulders
36. Crest of neck

Most dog books present breeds in groups, based on the type of dog or the role it was bred to perform. These groups vary in different parts of the world.

The American Kennel Club (AKC) recognizes seven groups. These are:

1. Sporting breeds
2. Hounds
3. Working breeds
4. Herding breeds
5. Terriers
6. Toys
7. Non-sporting breeds

The Canadian Kennel Club (CKC) recognizes six groups. These are:

1. Sporting breeds
2. Hounds
3. Working breeds
4. Terriers
5. Toys
6. Non-sporting breeds

Throughout most of Europe, the Federation Cynologique Internationale (FCI) recognizes 10 groups. These include:

1. Herding breeds
2. Guard dogs, police dogs and working breeds
3. Terriers
4. Dachshunds
5. Hunting breeds for large game
6. Hunting breeds for small game
7. Pointing gundogs, excluding British breeds
8. Pointing gundogs, British breeds
9. Other British gundogs
10. Toys

The British Kennel Club (BKC) recognizes six groups. These are:

1. Hounds
2. Gundogs
3. Terriers
4. Utility breeds
5. Working breeds
6. Toys

The Scandinavian countries recognize eight groups. These are:

1. Spitz breeds
2. Trailing and hunting breeds
3. Gundogs
4. Guard and working breeds
5. Terriers
6. Sighthounds
7. Non-sporting and companion breeds
8. Toys

In Australia, the following six groups are recognized:

1. Toys
2. Terriers
3. Gundogs
4. Hounds
5. Working breeds
6. Non-sporting breeds

In this book breeds are presented in order of size. This arrangement is helpful to most people, particularly those buying a dog for the first time. The profile section is divided into three parts:

Small Dogs—up to 28 lbs (12kg)
Medium Dogs—28 to 45 lbs (12 to 20kg)
Large Dogs—over 45 lbs (20kg)

Only height standards exist for certain breeds. Some dogs fall between two groups. A few tall, lightweight breeds are large dogs by most standards.

Some breeds have different names listed under the breed name. These indicate another name for the dog, a foreign name for the breed, or a breed or breeds sharing the same characteristics.

The show requirements at the end of each entry are based on official standards of the American Kennel Club. You will also find some standards for the United Kennel Club, the Animal Research Foundation, Federation Cynologique Internationale and the British Kennel Club.

Australian Terrier

Cairn Terrier

SMALL DOGS

Cavalier English Toy Spaniel

Why do you want a small dog? Is it because you have always loved them? Because you live in a small place? Because you think a larger dog might be more than you can handle? Because a small dog is less expensive to feed?

Whatever your reason, you will not regret having a small dog. It can be brave, often foolishly so. It can make a good watchdog and be devoted to you. Often dismissed as lap dogs, small breeds will often walk as far as you wish. A small dog is easier to transport. Chihuahuas and Yorkshire Terriers rarely object to riding in a shopping cart. Smaller breeds may be more acceptable at hotels. Many boarding kennels charge according to a dog's size. Small dogs are intelligent and easy to train. The coat is easier to groom.

Small breeds are not a good choice when there are young children in the house. Toddlers may think they are toys. A good small dog for a family is a Cavalier Spaniel, an English Toy Spaniel or a Miniature Schnauzer.

There is a wide range of small dogs to choose from, of various colors and different types of coat. There are also scaled-down versions of larger breeds, such as the Shetland Sheepdog. Small dogs usually are not less expensive to buy. They do not have large litters.

CHIHUAHUA

Advantages
- **Good traveler**
- **Ideal for city dwellers**
- **Loyal and affectionate**
- **Intelligent**
- **Miniature guard dog**
- **Inexpensive to keep**

Disadvantages
- **May snap at teasing children**
- **Strong-willed**
- **Overly brave**
- **Prefers company of owners**
- **Hates cold**
- **Might become rheumatic**

The Chihuahua is intelligent, protective and inexpensive to own. It is the world's smallest dog. A Chihuahua usually takes a few weeks to reveal its true personality. It will keep its new owner under careful surveillance, perhaps giving the impression it is shy. Actually, it is deciding who is to be master of the house!

Many breeders raise the dog for the pleasure of achieving and showing a perfect specimen. It is not uncommon for a breeder to own 20 or more Chihuahuas.

SIZE
Height—No requirement
Weight—2 to 6 lbs
 (0.9 to 2.7kg)

EXERCISE
The Chihuahua is able to walk as far as most owners wish. Exercise requirements are moderate, which makes this breed ideal for the elderly.

GROOMING
Groom the dog with a soft brush. A rubdown with a velvet glove or pad makes the coat shine. Regularly clip nails and keep ears free of dust.

FEEDING
For daily feeding, 1/2 cup of balanced dry dog food is recommended. Some dogs may prefer 1/2 cup water mixed with each cup of dog food. Add canned dog food for flavor.

HEALTH CARE
Chihuahuas are not delicate dogs. But they dislike cold and need a coat to keep them warm when outside in winter. These dogs should not live in a kennel.

Be careful of the *molera,* a small opening on top of the skull. The Chihuahua's molera, unlike a human baby's, may never fill in. A blow on its head could be fatal. The breed is prone to hiccups. Cure a spasm by lifting the pet up and down. They also have a tendency to shiver. People wrongly imagine the Chihuahua is terrified or cold.

ORIGIN AND HISTORY
Named after the Mexican state of Chihuahua, the dog is believed to have been the sacred dog of the Toltecs and Aztecs. A few may also have been used for food by American Indians. There is a theory that Chihuahuas once lived in holes in the ground. This could account for their inclination to huddle together in a warm place.

The opera singer Adelina Patti publicized the breed. In 1890, she was given a Chihuahua concealed in a bunch of flowers by the President of Mexico. In the 1940s, band leader Xavier Cugat often conducted with a Chihuahua tucked under his arm. For many people this was the first look at this breed.

SHOW REQUIREMENTS
General Appearance—Alert and swift. Small, dainty and compact, with brisk, forceful movement.
Color—Any color or mixture.
Head And Skull—A well-rounded dome skull, with or without molera. Cheeks and jaws lean. Nose moderately short and slightly pointed. Definite stop.
Tail—Medium length, carried up or over the back. Furry and flat in appearance, broadening slightly in the center. Tapers to a point.
Feet—Small, with toes split, but not spread. Pads cushioned. Fine pasterns, not harefooted or catfooted. Nails moderately long.
Teeth—Level or scissors bite. Undershot, overshot or any other distortion of the bite penalized as a serious fault.

There is a longcoat Chihuahua as well as the smoothcoat variety. The only difference is the coat. The longcoat has a long, soft coat, never coarse or rough, and flat or slightly wavy, not tight or curly. There is feathering on the feet and legs. A large ruff on the neck is preferred. The tail is long with a full plume.

YORKSHIRE TERRIER

Advantages
- **Affectionate**
- **Healthy and fearless**
- **Good watchdog**
- **Suitable for apartment living**

Disadvantages
- **Lengthy show preparation**
- **Needs weekly bath**

The Yorkshire Terrier is one of today's most popular breeds. It rivals the Chihuahua for the title of the world's smallest dog. It is unlikely to be intimidated by larger animals and wants to make friends with everybody. It has been described as a large dog in a small dog's body.

SIZE
Height—No requirement
Weight—Up to 7 lbs (3.2kg)

EXERCISE
The Yorkie is well-suited to town and apartment living. It is tireless on a walk.

GROOMING
Many owners are content to allow their pet to have a scruffy, shaggy-dog look. The Yorkshire Terrier may be exhibited on a show box, which displays its coat well. It needs grooming, shampooing and oiling. The show Yorkie spends much of its life away from the ring wearing curlers!

FEEDING
For daily feeding, 1/2 cup of balanced dry dog food is recommended. Some dogs may prefer 1/2 cup water mixed with each cup of dog food. Add canned dog food for flavor.

HEALTH CARE
The Yorkie has strong, terrier-type teeth. Have them scaled by a veterinarian at regular intervals.

ORIGIN AND HISTORY
The Yorkie has been known for more than 100 years. It is believed the breed evolved through crossing a Skye Terrier with the old Black and Tan Terrier. The Maltese Terrier and the Dandie Dinmont Terrier may also have contributed to producing this breed.

SHOW REQUIREMENTS
Consult an expert before buying the first pedigree pup you see. A roachback or swayback Yorkie would be disqualified in the show ring. Too large a specimen would also be disqualified. A breeder cannot guarantee the size of a puppy. A look at the parents can be a useful guide.

Selecting a potential show pup is never easy. Yorkshire Terriers are born black. Not until they are between 3 and 5 months old does the tan begin to show on their legs. The black on the back may take a year to turn to gray.
General Appearance—Long coat hangs straight and evenly down each side. A part extends from the nose to the end of the tail. Compact and neat. Carriage is upright, conveying an important air. The general outline gives the impression of a vigorous, well-proportioned body.
Color—Dark steel-blue, not silver-blue, extending from the nose to the end of the tail. It should not be mingled with fawn, bronze or dark hairs. Hair on the chest is darker at the roots than in the middle. It should shade to a lighter tan at the tips.
Head And Skull—Head small and flat. Not too prominent. Not round in the skull or long in the muzzle. Nose black. The fall of the head is long, tan and deeper in color at the sides above the ear roots. The fall on the muzzle is long. Tan on the head must not extend to the neck. No sooty or dark hair can be intermingled with the tan.
Tail—Cut to medium length, with plenty of hair. Darker blue than the rest of the body, especially at the tip. Carried a little higher than the level of the back.
Feet—Round. Toenails black.
Ears—Small and V-shape. Carried erect and not far apart. Covered with short hair of deep, rich tan.
Teeth—A scissors or level bite.

Longcoat Chihuahua

The Chihuahua is one of the most popular dogs in the world. It has consistently been a well-behaved, successful competitor in the show ring.

Smoothcoat Chihuahua

The Yorkshire Terrier has a keen, intelligent expression. The medium-size, dark eyes look directly forward.

Yorkshire Terrier

PAPILLON
Phalene

Advantages
- **Affectionate**
- **Good housedog**
- **Easily trained**
- **Obedient**
- **Strong and healthy**

Disadvantages
- **Dislikes strangers**
- **Possessive of owners**

The Papillon is a toy spaniel and takes its name from the French word *butterfly*. The breed is often referred to as the *Butterfly Dog* because of the way its ears are set on its head. They are fringed like butterfly wings. The Phalene, or Continental Toy Spaniel, is identical except its ears are dropped. This variety is known as the *moth*.

The Papillon is an affectionate, lively dog. It is resilient, has an easy time giving birth, is a good walker and can adapt to climate extremes. Its attractive appearance and friendly nature make it an ideal family pet. It can be possessive of its owner and may resent visitors in the home.

SIZE
Height — 8 to 11 in (20 to 28cm)

Weight — No requirement

EXERCISE
The Papillon enjoys a walk with its owner. It can go long distances or be content with a walk around the park. You will probably tire before it will!

GROOMING
Daily grooming is necessary.

FEEDING
For daily feeding, 1 to 1-1/2 cups of balanced dry dog food is recommended. Some dogs may prefer 1/2 cup water mixed with each cup of dog food. Add canned dog food for flavor.

ORIGIN AND HISTORY
The Papillon is believed to be a descendant of the Dwarf Spaniel of the 16th century, which originated in Spain. The Papillon has been included in many paintings. The Phalene is identical except for its drop ears. Papillons and Phalenes are judged together as one breed with almost identical standards except for color variations. Specimens over 12 inches tall cannot be shown.

The French Federation Cynologique Internationale separates the breeds by type and weight. Those over 5-1/2 pounds (2.5kg) enter a separate class. Papillons do well in obedience classes.

SHOW REQUIREMENTS
General Appearance — Alert, intelligent and lively. Movement sound, light and free, not cramped or restricted in any way.

Color — White with patches any color except liver. A tricolor must be black and white with tan spots over the eyes, tan inside the ears, under the root of the tail and on the cheeks. The head marking should be symmetrical around a narrow, white, clearly defined blaze.

Head And Skull — Skull slightly rounded between the ears. Muzzle finely pointed and thinner than the skull, accentuating the well-defined stop. Length from the tip of the nose to the stop is about one-third the length of the head. Nose black.

Tail — Long and well-fringed. Set high. Arched over the back with fringes falling to the side to form a plume.

Feet — Harefooted. Tufts of hair should extend beyond toes.

Teeth — Scissors bite.

POMERANIAN

Advantages
- **Adaptable**
- **Devoted to owner**
- **Happy nature**
- **Suitable for apartment living**

Disadvantages
- **Will bark if unchecked**
- **May provoke bigger dogs**

The Pomeranian is a happy, active dog. It will cheerfully adapt to life in a one-room apartment or a spacious home. It enjoys the role of lap dog. It loves to walk with its owner and will amuse itself in a yard. It makes a faithful, devoted companion.

SIZE
Height — No requirement

Weight — Male: 4 to 4-1/2 lbs (1.8 to 2kg)
Female: 4-1/2 to 5-1/2 lbs (2 to 2.5kg)

EXERCISE
The Pomeranian is a lively dog, able to walk as far as you do.

GROOMING
Groom this dog daily. It has two coats to care for: a short, fluffy undercoat and a long, straight topcoat covering the whole body. Daily brushing with a stiff-bristle brush is necessary. Dampen the coat with cold water and rub with your fingertips. Then rub the dog with a towel. Working from the head, part the coat and brush it forward from roots to tips. Make another part and repeat until the dog has been covered.

The Pomeranian requires regular trimming. Seek advice from a breeder or groomer on how to do this.

FEEDING
For daily feeding, 1-1/2 cups of balanced dry dog food is recommended. Some dogs may prefer 1/2 cup water mixed with each cup of dog food. Add canned dog food for flavor.

ORIGIN AND HISTORY
The Pomeranian takes its name from Pomerania, Germany. It is of mid-European origin. As a member of the Spitz family, its history began in the Arctic Circle.

The breed was introduced in several European countries in the mid-18th century. It was popular until about 1860. Some of its popularity waned with the appearance of the Imperial Pekingese.

The Pomeranian once was a larger dog, weighing up to 30 pounds (13.5kg). It was bred down until, by 1896, show classes for Pomeranians were divided into those for exhibits over and under 8 pounds (3.6kg). The British Kennel Club withdrew challenge certificates for the over-8-pound (3.6kg) variety in 1915.

SHOW REQUIREMENTS
General Appearance — Compact, short-coupled and well-knit. Intelligent expression, active and exuberant.

Color — Colors are judged on an equal basis. Any solid color, any solid color with lighter or darker shadings of the same color, any solid color with sable or black shadings, particolor, sable, and black and tan are acceptable. Black and tan is black with sharply defined tan or rust appearing above each eye, on the muzzle, throat and forechest, all legs and feet, and below the tail. Particolor is white with another color distributed in even patches on the body and a white blaze on the head.

Head And Skull — Head and nose have a foxlike outline or wedge shape. Skull slightly flat and large, relative to the muzzle. Hair on the head and face smooth and short. Nose is black in white dogs, orange in shaded sable dogs and brown in chocolate-tipped sable dogs. Nose may be self-colored, but never particolored or white.

Tail — Turned over the back and carried flat and straight. Profusely covered with long, wiry, spreading hair.

Feet — Small and compact.

Teeth — Scissors bite. One tooth out of line does not mean overshot or undershot.

SMALL GERMAN SPITZ
Kleinspitz

Advantages
- **Adaptable to city or country**
- **Excellent guard**
- **Loyal companion**

Disadvantages
- **Likes to bark**
- **Suspicious of strangers**
- **Not common in the United States**

The Small German Spitz is the small variety of the Great German Spitz or *Gross-spitz*. Size is the only difference between the types. Characteristics and conformation are the same.

This is a happy, intelligent dog. It is an excellent companion. A Spitz does not need much exercise and adapts well to city or country life. It loves its owners and does not care for strangers. It likes to bark.

SIZE
Height — 11 in (28cm) at the withers

Weight — Not more than 7-1/2 lbs (3.4kg)

EXERCISE
The Spitz does not need a lot of exercise. It can live happily in a small house or apartment.

GROOMING
Vigorous daily brushing is necessary to remove dead hairs.

Small German Spitz.

FEEDING
For daily feeding, 1-1/2 cups of balanced dry dog food is recommended. Some dogs may prefer 1/2 cup water mixed with each cup of dog food. Add canned dog food for flavor.

ORIGIN AND HISTORY
It is difficult to pinpoint the origin of the Spitz. Prehistoric remains have been found in Asia and on Pacific islands. Drawings of similar dogs were found among the remains of the ancient Pharaohs. There are a number of Spitz varieties, all similar in character and type.

Papillon

Phalene

The Papillon's ears should be large with round tips, heavily fringed, set toward the back of the head, and far enough apart to show the slightly round shape of the skull. When ears are erect, they should be carried like the spread wings of a butterfly.

Pomeranian

MALTESE

Advantages
- *Adaptable about exercise*
- *Wonderful with children*
- *Healthy*
- *Long-lived*
- *Sensitive and sweet*

Disadvantages
- *Needs daily grooming*

The Maltese is good-natured and makes an ideal pet. It is reliable with children, likes to exercise and is healthy. It often remains playful throughout its long life.

SIZE
Height—No requirement
Weight—Under 7 lbs (3.2kg)
4 to 6 lbs preferred

EXERCISE
This dog will enjoy a long walk or be content with a stroll.

GROOMING
Use a stiff-bristle brush every day from puppyhood. Use baby powder on legs and underside to keep it clean between baths. Seek advice about show preparation. This breed may not be the ideal choice for new show aspirants.

FEEDING
For daily feeding, 1 to 1-1/2 cups of balanced dry dog food is recommended. Some dogs may prefer 1/2 cup water mixed with each cup of dog food. Add canned dog food for flavor.

ORIGIN AND HISTORY
The Maltese is described as the oldest European toy breed. There is controversy as to whether it originated in Malta, where the breed has existed for centuries. The dog found its way to China and the Philippines, probably due to Maltese traders.

The Maltese has been drawn by many famous artists, including Francisco Jose de Goya, Peter Paul Rubens and the famous animal painter, Sir Edwin Landseer. In 1930, Landseer produced a portrait entitled *The Lion Dog from Malta—The Last Of His Race.* Maltese were rare on the island at that time. The breed became established in Great Britain during the reign of Henry VIII. It was a popular pet among elegant ladies. It had a class of its own for the first time in England in 1864. It is still a popular breed.

The term *terrier* is applied to the Maltese in the United Kingdom. According to the *American Kennel Club Complete Dog Book,* "they are spaniels, not terriers."

SHOW REQUIREMENTS
General Appearance—Lively and alert. Movement must be free, without extended weaving.
Color—Pure white, but slight lemon markings should not be penalized.

Head And Skull—Stop to center of skull and stop to tip of nose equally balanced. Stop defined. Nose black.
Tail—Arched over the back and feathered.
Feet—Round. Pads black.
Teeth—Even or scissors bite.

BRUSSELS GRIFFON
Griffon Bruxellois,
Griffon Brabancon

Advantages
- *Happy temperament*
- *Hardy*
- *Intelligent*
- *Long-lived*
- *Obedient*

Disadvantages
- *No drawbacks known*

The Griffon is an attractive, happy dog and makes a good family pet. It has a monkeylike face, with a knowing expression. It is hardy and intelligent, with a terrier's temperament. It was orginally used as a vermin catcher and a guard. It captured the interest of royalty and became a fashionable pet.

A pair of Maltese puppies enjoy the sunshine. This good-natured breed has been popular in Europe for centuries. It has been portrayed by several famous artists.

There are two varieties: rough and smooth. The only difference is in the coat. The Bruxellois is a roughcoat and the Brabancon a smoothcoat. Rough and smooth coats can appear in a single litter. The only variation in the breed standard is the coat. Roughs are wiry and free from curl, preferably with an undercoat. Smooths are short and tight.

SIZE
Height—No requirement
Weight—8 to 10 lbs
(3.6 to 4.5kg)
most desirable
Not to exceed 22 lbs
(10kg)

EXERCISE
This dog does not need a lot of exercise, but it enjoys a run in the country.

GROOMING
The roughcoat needs twice-yearly stripping. Have this done by an expert. The smoothcoat should be brushed, toweled and gently rubbed with a velvet glove or chamois cloth. Be sure nails do not grow too long.

FEEDING
For daily feeding, 1 to 1-1/2 cups of balanced dry dog food is recommended. Some dogs may prefer 1/2 cup water mixed with each cup of dog food. Add canned dog food for flavor.

ORIGIN AND HISTORY
The Griffon was first exhibited at the Brussels Exhibition in 1880. It is a Belgian breed. It probably comes from the Affenpinscher, to which it bears a facial resemblance. The introduction of the Pug may be responsible for the Brabancon, or smoothcoat, which in the early days was not a recognized breed.

Queen Astrid of Belgium was an enthusiastic Griffon owner. Before World War I, Griffons were popular in Belgium, but the breeding program was affected by the war.

Griffons have found their way to most countries, but showing differences exist. Different states in the United States have their own show regulations for cropped ears. In Belgium, the Griffon is shown with cropped ears, an illegal practice in the United Kingdom, Scandinavia and Australia.

SHOW REQUIREMENTS
General Appearance—Balanced, lively and alert. Measures the same from withers to tail root as from withers to ground. Action should be free. Well-bent hocks give the correct drive from behind. High-stepping front movement should be discouraged.
Color—Clear-red, black or black and rich tan. In the clear-red, a darker shade on the mask and ears is desirable. Each hair an even red from tip to root. Frosting on the muzzles of mature animals should not be penalized.
Head And Skull—Head large and round but not domed. Wide between the ears. In the rough variety, hair on the skull is coarse. Nose is always black and as short as possible. Large, open nostrils. Deep stop between nose and skull. Muzzle wide with neat lips and good turn-up. Chin prominent and slightly undershot without showing teeth. Bearded in the rough variety.
Tail—Docked, short, carried high, emerging at right angles from a level topline.
Feet—Small, thick, catlike feet with black toenails.
Ears—Often cropped.
Teeth—Chin prominent and slightly undershot, without showing teeth.

The Maltese Terrier's white coat should hang long, flat and silky over the sides of the body. It should reach almost to the ground and be single, without an undercoat.

Maltese Terrier

Smooth Griffon or Brabancon

Not the most attractive breed, the Griffon has won admirers throughout the world with its personality.

Rough Griffon or Bruxellois

ITALIAN GREYHOUND

Advantages
- **Affectionate**
- **Easy to train**
- **Graceful**
- **Intelligent**
- **Obedient**
- **Odorless**
- **Sensitive**
- **Rarely sheds**

Disadvantages
- **Hurt by harsh words**
- **Should not be kept in a kennel**

The Italian Greyhound is a graceful, dainty animal and makes an ideal pet. It needs plenty of exercise and enjoys chasing small animals, such as rabbits.

SIZE
Height—No requirement
Weight—6 to 10 lbs
(2.7 to 4.5kg)

EXERCISE
Do not keep the dog indoors all day. It needs exercise, but can adapt to city living. Provide walks and runs when possible.

GROOMING
The Italian Greyhound benefits from a rubdown with a silk cloth. Regular care and scaling of teeth by a vet is recommended.

FEEDING
For daily feeding, 1 to 1-1/2 cups of balanced dry dog food is recommended. Some dogs may prefer 1/2 cup water mixed with each cup of dog food. Add canned dog food for flavor.

ORIGIN AND HISTORY
This is an obedient, easy-to-train dog. Its ancestors may have been the dogs depicted on the tombs of the Pharaohs. The Italian Greyhound has existed in its present form for centuries. It was favored by Queen Victoria of Great Britain.

Some character was lost through special breeding when reducing the size of the dog. By the early 1950s, only five registrations with the British Kennel Club remained. Fresh stock was imported from Italy and because of the efforts of breeders, the Italian Greyhound was again established by the early 1970s.

SHOW REQUIREMENTS
General Appearance—A miniature Greyhound, more slender in all proportions. It is elegant and graceful in shape, symmetry and action.
Color—All shades of fawn, white, cream, blue, black and fawn, and white pied. Black and tan, such as found in Manchester Terriers, Doberman Pinschers and Rottweilers, are disqualified.
Head And Skull—Skull long, flat and narrow. Muzzle fine. Nose dark in color.
Tail—Long, fine, carried low.
Feet—Long hare feet.

MINIATURE PINSCHER

Advantages
- **Delightful, hackney gait**
- **Easy to care for**
- **Fearless**
- **Intelligent**
- **Rarely sheds**

Disadvantages
- **Easy to overfeed**

The Miniature Pinscher is sometimes called the *King of the Toys*. It is an ideal pet for a city dweller who wants a lively sporting dog. It follows a scent and does well in obedience competitions. The breed has a hackney gait and trots like a horse. It rarely sheds and requires minimal attention to keep its coat in fine condition.

SIZE
Height—11 to 11-1/2 in
(28 to 29cm) at the withers
A dog of either sex, under 10 inches or over 12 inches (25 to 30cm), will be disqualified.
Weight—No requirement

EXERCISE
The Miniature Pinscher exercises itself in a large yard or will accompany you on a daylong hike. This dog is happy living in an apartment or the country.

GROOMING
Daily brushing and rubbing with a chamois cloth keeps the coat gleaming.

FEEDING
For daily feeding, 1 to 1-1/2 cups of balanced dry dog food is recommended. Some dogs may prefer 1/2 cup water mixed with each cup of dog food. Add canned dog food for flavor.

ORIGIN AND HISTORY
The Miniature Pinscher is not a smaller version of the Doberman Pinscher. It is an older breed, descended from the German Smooth-haired Pinscher. The Italian Greyhound and Dachshund may be ancestors. The German Pinscher-Schnauzer Klub awarded it pedigree status in 1895.

SHOW REQUIREMENTS
General Appearance—Balanced and compact. Elegant and smoothcoated. Naturally well-groomed, it is vigorous and alert with animation, spirit and self-possession. It has a hackney gait.
Color—Solid-red or red and black with sharply defined tan. Rust-red markings on cheeks, lips, lower jaw and throat are acceptable. Twin spots above eyes and chest, on lower half of forelegs, inside of hind legs and vent region, and on lower portion of hocks and feet also allowed. Black pencil stripes, solid brown or chocolate with rust or yellow markings allowed on toes. Any color other than these will be faulted. Thumb marks or white on feet and forechest exceeding 1/2 inch (1.25cm) not allowed.
Head And Skull—More elongated than short and round. Narrow, without conspicuous cheek formation. In correct proportion to the body. Skull appears flat when viewed from front. Muzzle must be strong and proportionate to the skull. Nose well-formed, black only, with the exception of chocolates and blues, which may have a self-colored nose.
Tail—A continuation of the top line, carried high and docked short.
Feet—Legs straight. Feet catlike. Elbows close to the body. Nails dark.

TOY MANCHESTER TERRIER
English Toy Terrier

Advantages
- **Affectionate**
- **Easy to care for**
- **Good with children**
- **Intelligent**
- **Lively**
- **Good at catching rodents**

Disadvantages
- **A one-person dog**

The Toy Manchester Terrier, known as the English Toy Terrier in the United Kingdom, is an attractive, affectionate dog. It is intuitive and loyal, but attaches itself to one person. It is usually healthy, easy to keep clean, odorless and gives birth easily.

SIZE
Height—10 to 12 in
(25 to 30cm)
Weight—6 to 8 lbs
(2.7 to 3.6kg)

EXERCISE
This dog adapts to city living if given adequate exercise.

GROOMING
A daily brushing will suffice. Dry the dog with a towel if it gets wet. The coat can be rubbed to give a sheen.

FEEDING
For daily feeding, 1 to 1-1/2 cups of balanced dry dog food is recommended. Some dogs may prefer 1/2 cup water mixed with each cup of dog food. Add canned dog food for flavor. Add a weekly teaspoon of cod liver oil to food.

ORIGIN AND HISTORY
The Toy Manchester is a smaller version of the Manchester Terrier. See page 56. It is descended from the old Black and Tan Roughhair Terrier. Fitness comes from the Italian Greyhound and the Whippet. The breed began in England under the name Toy Manchester Terrier. It was later known as Toy Black and Tan, and Miniature Black and Tan.

SHOW REQUIREMENTS
General Appearance—Balanced, elegant and compact, with terrier temperament and characteristics.
Color—Black and tan. Black should be ebony and tan is a deep, rich chestnut. Colors should not run or blend into each other, but meet abruptly, forming clear and well-defined divisions.
Head And Skull—Head long and narrow with a flat skull. Wedge shape without emphasis of cheek muscles. Filled in under eyes.
Tail—Thick at the root, tapering to a point. Set low, not reaching below the hock. A tail carried up is undesirable if displayed to excess.
Feet—Dainty, compact, split between toes. Arched, with black nails. The two middle toes of the front feet are longer than the others. Hind feet are catlike.
Ears—Naturally carried erect. Cropped or cut are disqualified.
Teeth—Level or scissors bite.

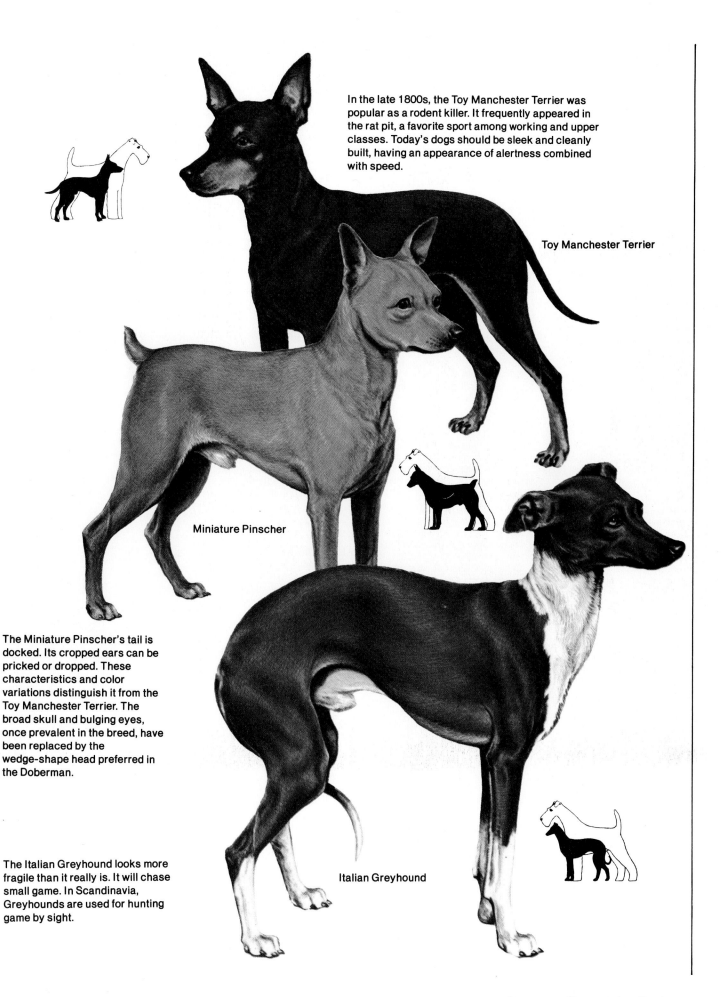

In the late 1800s, the Toy Manchester Terrier was popular as a rodent killer. It frequently appeared in the rat pit, a favorite sport among working and upper classes. Today's dogs should be sleek and cleanly built, having an appearance of alertness combined with speed.

Toy Manchester Terrier

Miniature Pinscher

The Miniature Pinscher's tail is docked. Its cropped ears can be pricked or dropped. These characteristics and color variations distinguish it from the Toy Manchester Terrier. The broad skull and bulging eyes, once prevalent in the breed, have been replaced by the wedge-shape head preferred in the Doberman.

Italian Greyhound

The Italian Greyhound looks more fragile than it really is. It will chase small game. In Scandinavia, Greyhounds are used for hunting game by sight.

BICHON FRISE
Bichon Bolognese

Advantages
- Good pet
- Even-tempered

Disadvantages
- Needs grooming

The Bichon Frise was recognized by the American Kennel Club in the early 1970s. It is an appealing, happy dog, which will become more popular when people become acquainted with the breed.

SIZE
Height—Less than 12 in (30cm) Smallness is highly desirable.
Weight—No requirement

EXERCISE
The Bichon Frise needs plenty of exercise in a yard. It adapts to city living if given regular walks.

GROOMING
This is not the breed for novice exhibitors. You must be willing to spend time grooming, bathing and trimming the dog. When complete, the effect is of a white powder puff. Trim the head and body to give a rounded effect, but show the eyes. Hair around feet should also be trimmed. Ask a groomer for showing and grooming charts, and for a demonstration on trimming.

FEEDING
For daily feeding, 1 to 1-1/2 cups of balanced dry dog food is recommended. Some dogs may prefer 1/2 cup water mixed with each cup of dog food. Add canned dog food for flavor.

An alert and appealing Bichon Frise pup. An older dog's coat falls into corkscrew curls.

ORIGIN AND HISTORY
The Bichon Frise is a descendant of the Barbet, a water spaniel, from which the name Barbichon originates. The name was abbreviated to Bichon.

Bichons originated in the Mediterranean area and were introduced by sailors to the Canary Islands before the 14th century. There were four varieties: Bichon Teneriffe, Bichon Maltaise, Bichon Bolognese and Bichon Havanais. The breed found favor with the French and Spanish nobility and was included in paintings by Goya.

A period of obscurity followed. After World War I, soldiers brought some Bichons home when they left France. A breed standard was written in France in 1933, when the name *Bichon a poil frise*—curly coated Bichon—was adopted.

In 1956, Mr. and Mrs. Francois Picault moved to the United States. They brought the first dogs to have litters here. Two breeders in different parts of the country acquired Bichons and the breed developed. In 1973, the breed was given regular show classification and is shown in the non-sporting group.

The Bichon Bolognese is similar to the Bichon Frise and is registered with the Federation Cynologique Internationale as an Italian breed.

SHOW REQUIREMENTS
General Appearance—Coat falls in soft, corkscrew curls. Head carriage is proud and high. Eyes are alert and expressive.
Color—Solid white or white with cream. Apricot or gray ears. Under the white coat, dark pigment is preferred. Black, blue or beige markings are often found on the skin.

Head And Skull—Head is in proportion to the size of the dog. Skull is broad and round, but not coarse, covered with a topknot. The muzzle is slightly accentuated. Ears are dropped and covered with long, flowing hair. Eyes are large, round and black. The nose is pronounced, round and black.
Feet—Small, round and knuckled. Nails preferably black.

TOY POODLE

Advantages
- Affectionate
- Dainty and appealing
- Excellent retriever
- Intelligent
- Long-lived
- Sense of fun

Disadvantages
- Noisy if unchecked
- Not the best pet for a child
- Sensitive

The Poodle is intelligent and obedient. It is a good swimmer. Poodles are favored for the show ring where they are beautiful when exhibited in the traditional lion clip. It may be the most difficult breed to prepare for the ring, involving time and care.

SIZE
Height—Under 10 in (25cm)
Weight—No requirement

EXERCISE
The Poodle enjoys playing in the yard, practicing obedience exercises or trotting beside you in the park. The toy variety adapts to indoor life and is a good choice for an apartment dweller.

GROOMING
Use a wirepin brush or a wiretooth metal comb for daily grooming. The lion clip is necessary for showing. Pet owners usually give it the more natural lamb clip, with hair a short uniform length. It is possible to clip your own dog with a pair of hairdressers' scissors. Many pet groomers do an excellent job. Regular bathing is essential.

FEEDING
For daily feeding, 1 to 1-1/2 cups of balanced dry dog food is recommended. Some dogs may prefer 1/2 cup water mixed with each cup of dog food. Add canned dog food for flavor.

HEALTH CARE
Purchase your poodle from a breeder who puts quality ahead of daintiness. Watch for signs of ear trouble, nervousness or joint malformations. Teeth need regular scaling.

ORIGIN AND HISTORY
The Poodle was originally a guard dog, retriever and protector of sheep. Its origins are similar to the Irish Water Spaniel. It is probably a common ancestor to the French Barbet and Hungarian Water Hound.

The Poodle is not French. It originated in Germany as a water retriever. The name poodle comes from the German word for puddle, *pudelnass*. From the Standard Poodle—a fairly large and sturdy animal—the Miniature and the Toy have evolved.

The breed has been known since the 17th century. It was favored by Marie Antoinette, who invented the lion clip to match the uniform of her courtiers. With its mane and tufted tail, it has the appearance of a lion in miniature.

SHOW REQUIREMENTS
General Appearance—Active, intelligent, well-balanced and elegant looking. It has a good temperament and carries itself proudly.
Color—All solid colors. White and cream Poodles have black nose, lips, eyerims and toenails. Brown Poodles have dark amber eyes, dark nose, lips, eyerims and toenails. Apricot Poodles have dark eyes with black points or deep amber eyes with liver points. Black, silver and blue Poodles have black nose, lips, eyerims and toenails. Cream, apricot, brown, silver and blue Poodles may show varying shades of the same color. Clear colors preferred.
Head And Skull—Moderately rounded skull with a long, straight, fine muzzle, slight chiseling under the eyes.
Tail—Set high and docked. Carried at a slight angle away from the body. Not curled or carried over the back. Thick at the root.
Feet—Pasterns strong. Tight feet proportionately small, oval in shape, not turning in or out. Toes arched. Pads thick, hard and cushioned.
Teeth—Strong and white, with a scissors bite.

The Bichon Frise was given its offical standard in France in 1933, after almost disappearing during World War I. It was introduced into the United States in 1956 and officially registered in 1972.

Bichon Frise

Toy Poodle,
with an English saddle, or lion, clip

LOWCHEN
Little Lion Dog

Advantages
- Affectionate
- Happy nature
- Intelligent

Disadvantages
- Requires skillful clipping

The Lowchen is a member of the Bichon family. It shares with the Pekingese the title of *little lion dog*, because of the practice of clipping it in the lion clip. It is an affectionate, happy, healthy dog.

SIZE
Height—10 to 13 in (25 to 33cm) at the withers
Weight—4 to 9 lbs (1.8 to 4.1kg)

EXERCISE
This dog enjoys walks in the park or a run in the country.

GROOMING
Clipping should be left to experts. Daily brushing will keep it looking attractive.

FEEDING
For daily feeding, 1 to 1-1/2 cups of balanced dry dog food is recommended. Some dogs may prefer 1/2 cup water mixed with each cup of dog food. Add canned dog food for flavor.

Despite its fragile appearance, the Lowchen is a robust dog that enjoys country walks.

ORIGIN AND HISTORY
The Lowchen is of French origin. It is registered with the Federation Cynologique Internationale under the title *petit chien lion*, little lion dog. It has been known in France and Spain since the late 1500s. A dog similar to the Lowchen appears in a portrait of the Duchess of Alba, painted by Goya. The breed probably evolved in the Mediterranean area about the same time as the Maltese, the Bichon Frise and the Bichon Bolognese.

The Lowchen is a frequent contender in the show ring in many countries. It has not become popular as a pet.

Although not registered by the American Kennel Club, this breed is growing in popularity. The official registration agency for the breed is the Little Lion Club of America.

SHOW REQUIREMENTS
General Appearance—Small and intelligent with an affectionate, lively disposition. The body is clipped in the traditional lion clip. The docked tail is topped with a pompon.
Color—Any color permissible. The most sought-after colors are white, black and lemon.
Head And Skull—Short. Skull relatively wide.
Tail—Medium length, clipped, with a tuft of hair left to form a pompon.
Feet—Small and round.

AFFENPINSCHER

Advantages
- Affectionate
- Cute, monkeylike appearance
- Excellent rat catcher
- Good watchdog

Disadvantages
- No drawbacks known

The Affenpinscher is enchanting, with its monkeylike face. The prefix *Affen* is the German word for monkey. In Germany it is often called the *Zwergaffenpinscher*. *Zwerg* means dwarf. The French call it the *moustached devil*. It is an appealing, comical little dog and is the smallest of the Schnauzers and Pinschers. It is alert, gentle and affectionate, but always ready to defend.

An adult Affenpinscher, showing the round, monkeylike face typical of this breed.

SIZE
Height—9-1/2 to 11 in (24 to 28cm)
Weight—6-1/2 to 9 lbs (3 to 4.1kg)

EXERCISE
Like most toy dogs, the Affenpinscher is content with short walks.

GROOMING
Regular brushing keeps the coat in condition.

FEEDING
For daily feeding, 1 to 1-1/2 cups of balanced dry dog food is recommended. Some dogs may prefer 1/2 cup water mixed with each cup of dog food. Add canned dog food for flavor.

ORIGIN AND HISTORY
Until 1896, Affenpinschers and Miniature Pinschers were classified as one breed. At the Berlin show that year, it was decided the longcoat variety should be known as the Affenpinscher.

The Affenpinscher is an ancient German breed depicted by 15th century artists Jan van Eyck and Albrecht Durer. There is some controversy as to its origin, though not its nationality. Some believe it is related to the Brussels Griffon. Others attribute the Brussels Griffon to the Affenpinscher. A third school of thought claims the Affenpinscher is a toy version of the German coarsehair terrier, the *Zwergschnauzer*. This breed was recognized by the American Kennel Club in 1936.

SHOW REQUIREMENTS
General Appearance—Wire hair

An Affenpinscher pup is a small bundle of fur with a hint of the comic expression of the adult dog.

---

and stout, with monkeylike expressions. Small and sturdy build.
Color—Black, although dark gray and black with gray, rich tan or brown markings are permissible.
Head And Skull—Head is small in proportion to the body, with a domed forehead, broad brow and marked stop. Muzzle blunt and short, but not flattened to cause wrinkling of the skin or difficulty in breathing. Chin prominent with a good turn-up. Distance between the eyes and nose form an equal-sided triangle.
Tail—Carried high. It can be left a natural length or docked to the third dock.
Feet—Small, round and compact. Not turned in or out. Pads and nails dark.
Teeth—Upper jaw is shorter than lower jaw. Teeth close together. A slight undershot condition is not important. Teeth should not show.

The Lowchen has not been officially recognized by the American Kennel Club. After a period of obscurity during the early 1900s, the breed is enjoying a revival of interest in many countries.

Lowchen

The coat is an important factor in the Affenpinscher. It should be short and dense in certain parts and shaggy and longer in others, especially around the eyes, nose and chin. It gives the breed a monkeylike appearance.

Affenpinscher

SILKY TERRIER
Australian Silky Terrier or Sydney Silky Terrier, Australian Terrier

Advantages
- **Alert**
- **Affectionate**
- **Dainty**
- **Excellent rat catcher**
- **Hardy**
- **Good pet**

Disadvantages
- **No drawbacks known**

The Silky Terrier is known in Australia as the Australian Silky Terrier or the Silky. It is a dainty dog and looks like a Yorkshire Terrier. It is alert and hardy with a happy, affectionate nature.

SIZE
Height—9 in (23cm)
at the withers
Weight—8 to 10 lbs
(3.6 to 4.5kg)

EXERCISE
Despite its small stature, the Silky has well-developed terrier instincts. It adapts to apartment living and enjoys walking, running and chasing.

GROOMING
The Silky Terrier should be well-groomed. This calls for a coat length of 5 to 6 inches (12.5 to 15cm) from behind the ears to the set on of the tail. Legs from knees and hocks to feet free of long hair.

FEEDING
For daily feeding, 1 to 1-1/2 cups of balanced dry dog food is recommended. Some dogs may prefer 1/2 cup water mixed with each cup of dog food. Add canned dog food for flavor.

ORIGIN AND HISTORY
The Silky Terrier was derived from crossing Yorkshire Terriers with Skye Terriers. Some say it was crossbred with the Australian Terrier, which has Norwich and

The Australian Silky Terrier is an alert dog. It enjoys running in fields.

Cairn Terrier blood. It probably also has some Dandie Dinmont in its ancestry.

The breed has been recognized since 1959. It is a relative newcomer to the United States. In Great Britain standards exist for the Australian Terrier and the Australian Silky Terrier.

SHOW REQUIREMENTS
General Appearance—Compact and set moderately low. Body is medium length, with a refined structure and sufficient substance to suggest the ability to hunt and kill rodents. It should display terrier characteristics, with alertness, activity and soundness. The parted, straight silky hair must look well-groomed.
Color—Blue and tan or gray-blue and tan—the richer the better. Dark blue on tail. The distribution of the blue and tan as follows: Silver-blue or fawn topknot; tan around the base of the ears, the muzzle and on side of cheeks; blue from base of skull to tip of tail, running down the forelegs to the knees and down the thighs to the hocks; tan line showing down the stifles; tan from the knees and hocks to the toes and around the vent.
Head And Skull—Moderately long, and slightly shorter from the top of the nose to between the eyes than from the same position to the top rear of the skull. Strong, with terrier character. Broad between the ears. Skull flat, without fullness between the eyes. Long fall of hair on foreface and cheeks objectionable. Fine silky topknot, not falling over the eyes. Nose black.
Tail—Docked and carried erect.
Feet—Small, padded, catlike. Closely knit toes with black or dark nails.

TIBETAN SPANIEL

Advantages
- **Confident**
- **Easy to train**
- **Happy nature**
- **Intelligent**
- **Good pet**
- **Suitable for city or country**

Disadvantages
- **No drawbacks known**

The Tibetan Spaniel is an attractive dog with a happy, independent nature. It is easy to train and makes an ideal pet because it is reliable with children. It looks like a large Pekingese and is an enjoyable dog to show.

SIZE
Height—10 in (25cm)
Weight—9 to 15 lbs (4 to 6.8kg)

EXERCISE
Requires walks and runs.

GROOMING
Brush the dog daily.

FEEDING
For daily feeding, 1 to 1-1/2 cups balanced dry dog food is recommended. Some dogs may prefer 1/2 cup water mixed with each cup of dog food. Add canned dog food for flavor.

ORIGIN AND HISTORY
The Tibetan Spaniel was first discovered in Tibetan monasteries. G. Harrap writes in *Champion Dogs of the World:* "Reports indicate that it still turns the prayerwheel of Tibetans who seek to reap the rewards of a devout life without the inconvenience of physical exertion." This practice may have ceased when the Chinese outlawed dogs. It is a close relative of the Tibetan Terrier and Lhasa Apso, both originating in Tibet. The Tibetan Spaniel was first seen in England in 1905.

The dog is eligible for American Kennel Club obedience classes and miscellaneous classes. The official breed registry is the Tibetan Spaniel Club of the United States.

SHOW REQUIREMENTS
General Appearance—Small, active and alert. Outline gives a balanced appearance, slightly longer in body than height at withers.
Color—All colors and mixtures allowed.
Head And Skull—Small in proportion to body and carried

First discovered in the monasteries of Tibet, the Tibetan Spaniel makes an ideal pet.

proudly, giving impression of quality. Masculine, but free from coarseness. Skull slightly domed, of moderate width and length. Stop slight, but defined. Medium-length muzzle, blunt with cushioning. Free from wrinkle. Chin shows depth and width. Black nose.
Tail—Set high, richly plumed and carried in a curl over the back when moving. Should not be penalized for dropping tail when standing.
Feet—Harefooted, small and neat with feathering between toes often extending beyond the feet. White markings allowed.

Two delightful Tibetan Spaniel puppies, only a few weeks old. These dogs are easy to train and happily adapt to city life.

The Australian Silky Terrier's attractive coat should be fine, glossy and have a silky texture. It is usually parted on the head and down the back to the root of the tail. On the top of the head, the hair forms a topknot. Groomed carefully for the show ring, the Australian Silky Terrier is beautiful.

Australian Silky Terrier

Short-nose specimens of the Tibetan Spaniel were once compared to the Pekingese. Careful breeding has produced an unmistakable, popular breed.

Tibetan Spaniel

MEXICAN HAIRLESS
Xoloitzcuintli

Advantages
- **Even-tempered**
- **Intelligent**
- **Affectionate**
- **Does not shed**

Disadvantages
- **Must live in a warm climate**
- **Cries instead of barking**
- **Not common in the United States**

The Mexican Hairless is one of the oldest and most endangered breeds in the world. These animals have been seen wandering along the waterfront in Hong Kong. Efforts are now being made to protect the breed in its native Mexico.

This breed is totally hairless except for a tuft of short, coarse hair on its skull. It is a quiet, reserved animal, growling only when provoked. It is described as happy and intelligent, yet dignified and unaggressive. Young pups tend to be snub-nosed and short-legged. They do not conform to their adult appearance until late in their development.

SIZE
Height—19 in (48cm)
Weight—30 to 35 lbs
(13.6 to 15.9kg)

FEEDING
For daily feeding, 3 cups of balanced dry dog food is recommended. Some dogs may prefer 1/2 cup water mixed with each cup of dog food. Add canned dog food for flavor.

HEALTH CARE
The Mexican Hairless perspires through its skin. Other breeds perspire through respiration. These dogs need a warm environment because their body temperature is about 105F (40.5C) compared to a normal canine temperature of 101.4F (38.5C). They have no premolar teeth.

ORIGIN AND HISTORY
The Mexican Hairless did not originate in Mexico. It was brought there by nomadic tribes of Indians. It may originally have come from as far away as Turkey.

The naked *Xoloitzcuintli,* as it was named, was considered a gift from the gods by the Aztecs. When anyone was sick, the dog warmed the patient with its naked body.

The earliest inhabitants of Mexico, the Toltecs, kept the blue Chihuahua in their temples for religious purposes. When the Aztecs conquered the Toltecs, dogs of both breeds were kept inside the temples. It is possible interbreeding of the Mexican Hairless with the Chihuahua may have produced today's Chinese Crested dog.

SHOW REQUIREMENTS
The following characteristics are from the *Associacion Canofila Mexicana,* the Mexican Kennel Club.
Color—Dark bronze, elephant gray, gray-black or black. Animals with pink or brown blotches, or areas without pigmentation, are acceptable. Lack of pigment on an exaggerated scale is undesirable. Hair on head and tail, if present, is black in dark animals. In lighter animals, hair may be of any harmonizing color.
Skin—Soft and smooth to the touch, particularly in areas less exposed to the sun. Accidental scars are not penalized, because skin is sensitive.
Tail—Long, tapering to a fine point.
Feet—Hare feet, with toes retracted. Claws black in dark animals, light in those with unpigmented feet.
Undesirable Points—A timid character. Ears not entirely erect. Hair growing elsewhere than where mentioned. Exaggerated depigmentation. Skin excessively loose, forming folds and creases. The presence of dewclaws.

CHINESE CRESTED

Advantages
- **Does not shed**
- **Intelligent**
- **Devoted companion**
- **Good with children**

Disadvantages
- **Greedy**
- **Skin looks reptilian**

The Chinese Crested is a fascinating pet and show dog. It is small, clean, odorless and does not shed. It is dainty, alert, intelligent, courageous and gentle. It seldom requires veterinary care and is an easy whelper. It adjusts to cold or warm climates. Its body temperature is 4F (2.2C) higher than a human's. It has its own heating system. The body feels hotter to the touch after the animal has eaten. It can grip with its paws in an almost-human fashion.

In almost every litter there are one or two pups with hair, known as powder puffs. Although these haired pups have been excluded from selective breeding over the years, they still appear. Many believe a powder puff is nature's way of keeping the hairless pup warm. Some think breeding a hairless dog with a powder puff results in healthier stock, because the powder puff is stronger. If you breed this species, you can get a good price for a powder puff female because she is likely to produce hairless pups. The powder puff commands a moderate price as a pet.

SIZE
Height—No requirement
Weight—12 lbs (5.4kg.)

EXERCISE
The Chinese Crested enjoys walks. It will work off surplus energy running and playing with toys.

GROOMING
The Chinese Crested needs frequent bathing. Regularly rub the skin with baby oil to prevent cracking and to keep it smooth. Prevent sunburn. Keep the skin free of blackheads and other blemishes. Facial hair and whiskers are usually removed.

FEEDING
For daily feeding, 1 to 1-1/2 cups of balanced dry dog food is recommended. Some dogs may prefer 1/2 cup water mixed with each cup of dog food. Add canned dog food for flavor.

HEALTH CARE
These dogs lack premolar teeth. Do not give them bones. They are allergic to wool.

ORIGIN AND HISTORY
Until 1966, an elderly lady in the United States owned the only Chinese Crested dogs in the world. With controlled breeding, the breed came back and is now thriving. Classes for the breed are being introduced in many dog shows.

The dog is considered a purebred but not registerable by the American Kennel Club. The organization responsible for registration is the American Chinese Crested Club.

SHOW REQUIREMENTS
General Appearance—Small, active and graceful. Medium to fine bones. Smooth, hairless body, with hair on feet, head and tail.
Crest—Flat, high or long-flowing. Sparse crest acceptable, but full crest preferred.
Color—Any color, plain or spotted.
Head And Skull—Long skull, slightly rounded. Slight stop. Moderately long muzzle. Lean cheeks.
Tail—Carried up and over the back, looped, but never curled. Plume on the lower two-thirds of the tail. Sparse plume acceptable, but full plume preferred.
Feet—Hare feet. Nails moderately long. Hair should not come above the first joint from the floor.

In almost every litter of Chinese Crested pups, there is one with hair, known as a powder puff.

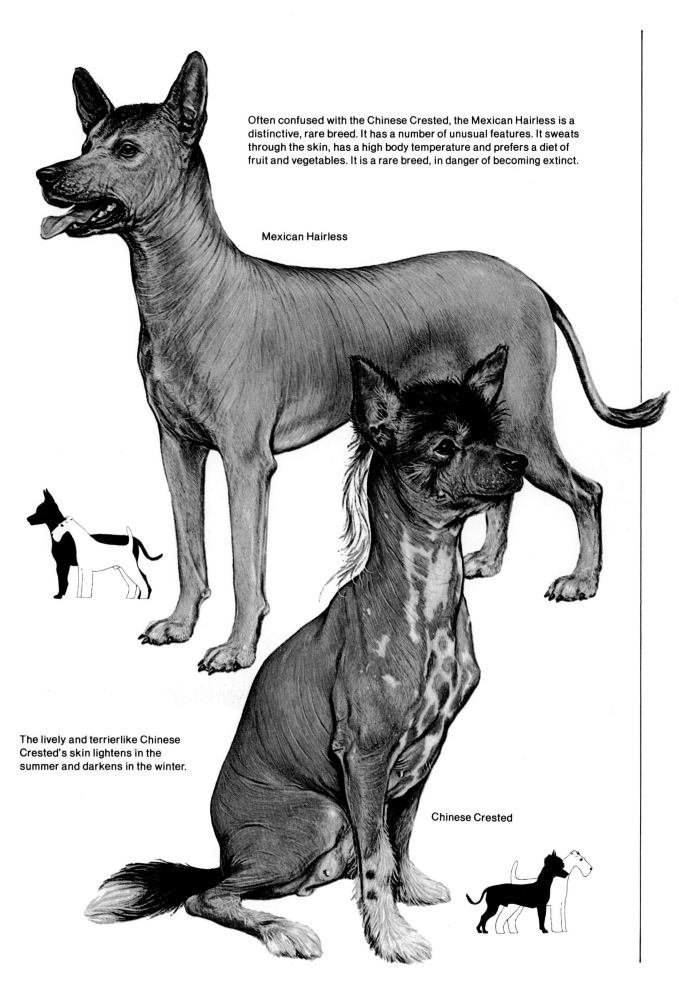

Often confused with the Chinese Crested, the Mexican Hairless is a distinctive, rare breed. It has a number of unusual features. It sweats through the skin, has a high body temperature and prefers a diet of fruit and vegetables. It is a rare breed, in danger of becoming extinct.

Mexican Hairless

The lively and terrierlike Chinese Crested's skin lightens in the summer and darkens in the winter.

Chinese Crested

ENGLISH TOY SPANIEL

Advantages
- *Hardy*
- *Clean*
- *Loves children*
- *Compatible with other pets*

Disadvantages
- *Needs monthly bath*
- *May get sores in ears*
- *Needs daily grooming*
- *Not suited to outdoor kennels*

The English Toy Spaniel is good with other animals and children. Despite its small stature, it is healthy. It requires daily grooming, regular bathing and eye cleaning every day. Be careful with ears—canker sores develop in them.

The English Toy Spaniel is known in the United Kingdom as the King Charles Spaniel, Black and Tan variety. Varieties include the Prince Charles, a tricolor, the Ruby and the Blenheim.

In 1903, an attempt was made in Great Britain to change the breed name to English Toy Spaniel. The change was opposed by King Edward VII, a devotee of the breed.

SIZE
Height—No requirement
Weight—9 to 12 lbs
(4.1 to 5.4kg)

EXERCISE
The English Toy Spaniel enjoys daily outings.

GROOMING
Regular brushing with a stiff-bristle brush is essential. Examine paws for interdigital cysts. Check ears for cankers, often detectable by an unpleasant odor. Wipe eyes with cotton dipped in a weak saline solution to keep them clear of unsightly tear streaks.

FEEDING
For daily feeding, 1 to 1-1/2 cups of balanced dry dog food is recommended. Some dogs may prefer 1/2 cup water mixed with each cup of dog food. Add canned dog food for flavor.

ORIGIN AND HISTORY
The English Toy Spaniel is thought of as a British breed, but can be traced to Japan in 2000 B.C. The breed was found at the English 16th-century court. As short-nose dogs became fashionable, this spaniel evolved.

The breed has many royal associations. One was found hidden in the folded gown of Mary, Queen of Scots after her execution.

An English Toy Spaniel pup with black, white and tan markings.

SHOW REQUIREMENTS
General Appearance—Compact and short-bodied with refined lines. Chest wide and deep. Legs short and straight. Back short and level. Movement free, active and elegant.
Color—The only recognized colors follow.
English Toy Spaniel: Black and tan. Glossy black, with bright, mahogany tan markings on muzzle, legs, chest, linings of ears, under tail and spots over the eyes.
Tricolor: Ground white, with well-distributed black patches. Tan markings on cheeks and linings of ears, under tail and spots over the eyes. A wide white blaze between the eyes and up the forehead. Also known as the Prince Charles variety.
Blenheim: Ground white with well-distributed chestnut red patches. A wide clear blaze with a clear chestnut red mark in the center of skull.
Ruby: Whole colored, a rich chestnut red.
Head And Skull—Skull massive relative to body. Well-domed, full over the eyes. Nose black and large, open nostrils, short and turned up to meet the skull. Stop between skull and nose defined. Muzzle square, wide, deep and well-turned up. Lower jaw wide. Lips meet exactly, giving a nice finish. Cheeks should not fall away under the eyes but be cushioned up. A protruding tongue is objectionable, but does not disqualify.
Tail—Flagged and not carried over the level of the back.

CAVALIER ENGLISH TOY SPANIEL

Advantages
- *Hardy*
- *Clean*
- *Good with children*
- *Gets along with other pets*

Disadvantages
- *Needs monthly bath*
- *May get sores in ears*
- *Needs daily grooming*
- *Not suited to outdoor kennels*

Many people find it hard to distinguish between the English Toy and the Cavalier Spaniels. The Cavalier is larger with a different head formation. The skull is almost flat between the ears and its stop is shallower than the English Toy's. It has the same characteristics of courage, hardiness and good nature.

SIZE
Height—No requirement
Weight—12 to 18 lbs
(5.4 to 8.2kg)

EXERCISE
This dog needs normal exercise. It adapts to city or country living. It should not be kenneled outdoors.

GROOMING
Same as for the English Toy Spaniel.

FEEDING
For daily feeding, 1-1/2 cups of balanced dry dog food is recommended. Some dogs may prefer 1/2 cup water mixed with each cup of dog food. Add canned dog food for flavor.

ORIGIN AND HISTORY
Samuel Pepys and other British diarists report King Charles II spent more time playing with his toy spaniels during meetings than he did dealing with matters of state. He even took his dogs into his bedchamber.

The Cavalier is purebred, but not registered by the American Kennel Club. It is currently shown in miscellaneous and obedience classes.

SHOW REQUIREMENTS
General Appearance—Active, graceful, well-balanced. Fearless and sporting in character. Free in action.
Color—The only recognized colors follow. Any other color or combination of colors is undesirable.
Cavalier: Black and tan. Black with tan markings above the eyes, on cheeks, inside ears, on chest, legs and underside of tail. Tan is bright.
Tricolor: Black and white, well-spaced and broken up. Tan markings over the eyes, on cheeks, inside ears and legs, and on underside of tail.
Blenheim: Rich chestnut marking, broken up on a white ground. Markings should be evenly divided on the head, leaving room between the ears for the valued lozenge mark or spot. It is a unique characteristic of the breed.
Ruby: Whole-colored rich red.
Head And Skull—Head almost flat between the ears, without dome. Stop is shallow. Length from base of stop to tip about 1 to 1-1/2 inches (2.5 to 3.5cm). Nostrils developed and black. Muzzle tapered. Lips not houndlike. Face filled out underneath the eyes.
Tail—Tail docking is optional. No more than one-third can be removed. Length of the tail in balance with the body.
Feet—Compact, cushioned and feathered.

Cavalier pups, showing the Blenheim markings, left, and tricolor markings, right.

English Toy Spaniel (Ruby)

English Toy Spaniel (Tricolor)

Cavalier English Toy Spaniel (Blenheim)

The Cavalier English Toy Spaniel is larger than the English Toy. It has a longer nose, but it is still difficult to distinguish between the two breeds.

TOY FOX TERRIER

Advantages
- *Fits well into a household*
- *Hardy, healthy and spirited*
- *Good watchdog*

Disadvantages
- *No drawbacks known*

This playful breed is popular because of its hardiness and guarding capabilities. Its size has made it adaptable to city life. The breed is recognized and registered by the United Kennel Club. The National Toy Fox Terrier Association is the official breed organization that sanctions state and national shows.

SIZE
Height—No requirement
Weight—3-1/2 to 7 lbs
(1.6 to 3.2kg)

EXERCISE
These dogs are self-exercisers. They require space for daily exercise.

GROOMING
The short coat of the Toy Fox Terrier requires no special grooming other than an occasional bath and brushing.

ORIGIN AND HISTORY
In 1912, the United Kennel Club began registering the Smooth Fox Terrier. Between 1912 and the mid-1920s, a miniature variety was developed. These dogs were almost identical to the modern Toy Fox Terrier, but were still registered by UKC as Smooth Fox Terriers. In 1936, the UKC began registering the Toy Fox Terrier as a separate breed. In 1948, fanciers who had spent years breeding the small terrier met to form the National Toy Fox Terrier Association.

SHOW REQUIREMENTS
General Appearance—Bright and energetic, with great spirit and animation. Appearance of a miniature Smooth Fox Terrier. Length of body is equal to height. Movement is smooth and flowing. When moving, the back should remain straight, the head and tail carried erect.
Coat—Short, satiny and slightly longer at the ruff. The body is predominately white and can have black or tan spots. White is free of ticking, although some speckling is permissible. Tan points appear on the cheeks and above the eyes. In white and tan dogs, points are a lighter or darker shade of tan.
Head And Skull—Skull is slightly rounded with a medium stop. The pointed muzzle is medium length.

A Toy Fox Terrier is a hardy dog and an excellent guard. Its body is white and can have tan or black spots.

Nose is black. Eyes are round, dark and expressive, never bulgy. V-shape ears carried erect.
Tail—Carried erect and set high. Docked, with about three-fifths taken off.
Feet—Compact, oval rather than round.
Teeth—Tight scissors bite. Overshot or undershot bites faulted.

TOY HAVANESE

Advantages
- *Loves children*
- *Quick learner*
- *Good watchdog*
- *Non-shedding and odorless*
- *Obedient*

Disadvantages
- *No drawbacks known*

The Havanese is a rare breed, even though its numbers are growing. The breed is not recognized by the American Kennel Club but has its own registry and an active national club, The Havanese Club of America. The club is working toward recognition for the breed.

The Havanese is an intelligent and charming breed. It becomes a full-fledged member of the family.

SIZE
Height—10-1/2 in (27cm)
Weight—13-1/2 lbs (6.2kg)

EXERCISE
This dog adapts to apartment living or suburban life. Daily walks are necessary if a fenced yard is not available for exercise.

GROOMING
This dog needs daily brushing. Curly coated dogs can be trimmed for neatness.

ORIGIN AND HISTORY
The breed originated in the Western Mediterranean area and found its way to Cuba with Italian sea captains. Sailors presented the small dogs to the Cuban women. Many wealthy Cuban homes extended a warm reception to the sailors on receiving such a charming gift.

The breed was reintroduced to Europe where it became popular. In the following years, the breed lost status and became nearly extinct. Due to efforts of a few devoted Cuban families who emigrated to the United States, the breed was saved.

In Cuba, these dogs often helped with daily plantation life, herding cattle and other barnyard animals.

They entertained children with games and protected the family with devotion and courage in the face of danger.

The Toy Havanese is a family member and companion. Constantly busy and always curious, it is intelligent and quick witted. It has a natural ability to please owners.

SHOW REQUIREMENTS
Color—Shades of white, cream, gold, chocolate, silver, blue and black or combinations of these. Pure white is rare.
Coat—Soft, ranging from slightly wavy to curly. May be clipped to give a neat appearance, but a natural coat is preferred.
Head And Skull—Skull is broad with the front rising slightly to a moderate stop. Muzzle is not sharp or blunt. Cheeks are flat and lips clean. Lips and nose preferably black. Brown pigment is permitted in chocolate dogs. Pointed ears are dropped, forming a gentle raised fold. Eyes are large, dark and almond shape. Eyelids are dark, giving the eye a soft, expressive look. The body is longer than high, with rounded ribs and well-raised flanks. The line of the back ends with a dropped croup.
Tail—Carried over the back and plumed with long, silky hair.

The Toy Havanese found its way from Europe to Cuba; it came with Cuban families when they emigrated to the United States. It is growing more popular as the breed becomes more widely known.

Toy Havanese

Toy Fox Terrier

JAPANESE SPANIEL
Japanese Chin

Advantages
- *Affectionate*
- *Loyal family dog*
- *Hardy*
- *Good with children*

Disadvantages
- *Sheds*
- *Avoid vigorous exertion*
- *Breathing difficulties*

At first glance, the Japanese Spaniel might be mistaken for a Pekingese. It is possible the two breeds may have had common ancestors. The Japanese Spaniel is a highstepping, graceful dog. It is longer in the leg and has a lighter body than a Pekingese.

It is a lively, dignified dog that likes to be the center of attention and is miserable when ignored. The Japanese Spaniel shares some similarities with the English Toy Spaniel, whose origin can also be traced to Japan.

SIZE
Height—No requirement
Weight—4 to 7 lbs
 (1.8 to 3.2kg)
The daintier the better, providing type, quality and soundness are not sacrificed.

EXERCISE
This dog enjoys walks and playing games with the family. It will walk a long distance or be happy with a short run. The Japanese Spaniel is tough, despite its delicate structure. It likes to climb, so be careful it does not fall and injure itself. Young pups should not be taken for long walks when muscles can be strained or overdeveloped.

Japanese Chin puppy shows the most common colors.

GROOMING
Daily grooming with a stiff-bristle brush maintains its silky coat. Bathe this breed before a show.

FEEDING
For daily feeding, 1 to 1-1/2 cups of balanced dry dog food is recommended. Some dogs may prefer 1/2 cup water mixed with each cup of dog food. Add canned dog food for flavor.

ORIGIN AND HISTORY
For more than 1,000 years, this breed was a favorite of Japanese emperors. One emperor decreed all Japanese Spaniels should be worshipped. Some small dogs were kept in hanging cages like birds.

The breed found its way to medieval Europe with returning seamen. It did not make its appearance in the British show ring until 1862. It is not on record as being shown in the United States until 20 years later.

Two Japanese Spaniels were presented to Queen Victoria by Commodore Perry on his return from the Far East in 1853. This helped promote the breed. Although they never were as popular as the Pekingese, they had a steady following. During World War I, their numbers diminished. Registrations have been increasing in recent years. The Japanese Spaniel is a dependable show dog.

SHOW REQUIREMENTS
General Appearance—Lively and dainty, with a compact carriage and profuse coat. It should lift its feet high when moving. The heavily feathered tail should be carried closely curved or plumed over the back.
Color—Black and white or red and white. Red includes all shades: sable, brindle, lemon or orange. The brighter and clearer the red, the better. Color evenly distributed on cheeks, ears and as patches on the body. Not too heavily marked. White should be clear, not flecked.
Head And Skull—Large, with a broad skull, rounded in front.
Tail—Twisted to either right or left. Carried over the back. Profusely covered with long hair. Ring tails not desirable.
Feet—Slender, harefooted and feathered at tips.

PEKINGESE
Little Lion Dog

Advantages
- *Loyal*
- *Affectionate*
- *Brave guard dog*
- *Healthy*
- *Intelligent*

Disadvantages
- *Aloof*
- *Subject to eye trouble*
- *Needs daily grooming*
- *Best for adults*
- *Avoid vigorous exertion*
- *Breathing difficulties*
- *Independent*

A Pekingese breeder once said, "You have to say please to a Pekingese." Yell at it and it will sulk until you feel you are wrong! The Pekingese expects to be petted and pampered, but it is not a delicate creature. It is fearless and loves to play.

A Peke is good with children, but is best as an adult's companion. It likes being the center of attention and having the run of the house. A restricted or neglected Peke may become destructive because of boredom. It has a mind of its own and is condescending by nature. When it offers you its affection, it is a loyal and loving companion.

SIZE
Height—No requirement
Weight—Not over 14 lbs (6.2kg)

EXERCISE
The Pekingese enjoys a walk in the country or is content with a walk in the park.

GROOMING
Brush daily with a soft-bristle brush. Groom the underside with the Peke lying on its back. Do the rest of the job with the pet standing on a table or in your lap. It is not necessary to bathe a Peke frequently. As an alternative, apply talcum powder to the coat and brush it thoroughly.

A sleeve Peke. A smaller than usual specimen.

FEEDING
For daily feeding, 1 to 1-1/2 cups of balanced dry dog food is recommended. Some dogs may prefer 1/2 cup water mixed with each cup of dog food. Add canned dog food for flavor.

ORIGIN AND HISTORY
This *little lion dog* came to Europe following the Chinese Boxer Rebellion in 1860. The British invaded the Summer Palace in Peking and stole five Imperial Pekingese from the women's apartments. Before this, it was forbidden for anyone other than a Chinese royal family member to own a Peke. Theft was punishable by death.

One of the Pekes taken by the British was presented to Queen Victoria. It was named Looty. It lived until 1872, and was the subject of a painting by Landseer.

After being imported to the United States, the breed quickly became popular. In 1909, the Pekingese Club of America was formed.

SHOW REQUIREMENTS
General Appearance—Small, well-balanced and thickset. Has great dignity and quality. Carries itself fearlessly in the ring with an alert, intelligent expression.
Color—All colors and markings are permissible and equally desirable, except albino or liver. Particolors should be evenly broken.
Head And Skull—Massive head. Skull broad, wide and flat between the ears, not domed. Wide between the eyes. Nose short and broad, nostrils large, open and black. Muzzle wide, wrinkled, with firm underjaw. Profile looks flat with nose up between the eyes. Deep stop.
Feet—Large and flat, not round. Stands up on its feet, not on pasterns. Front feet turned slightly out. Soundness essential.

The eyes are a distinctive feature of the Japanese Chin. They should be large, dark and set far apart. White shows in the inner corners, giving the breed a look of astonishment, or making it appear cross-eyed.

Japanese Chin

Pekingese

The Pekingese, for many centuries a royal dog in China, was first exhibited in Europe in the late 1800s. The Pekingese Club of America was formed in 1909.

MINIATURE DACHSHUND

Longhair, Smooth-hair and Wirehair Dachshund, Teckel, Dachel, Dacksel and Badger Hound

Advantages
- *Affectionate*
- *Courageous*
- *Easy to care for*
- *Loyal family pet*
- *Great sense of fun*
- *Good watchdog*

Disadvantages
- *Prone to disc trouble*
- *Self-willed*
- *Can be aggressive*

The Dachshund was bred as a badger hound in Germany. Badger hunting required a short-legged hound, with a keen sense of smell coupled with courage and gameness. Its body was bred to burrow well. Your dog may want to do this in your yard. The dog loves to dig.

Some Dachshunds are still bred as hunting dogs. They will attack an opponent larger than themselves, such as a badger. They will also defend their owner. Today, they are companions and good with children. They are affectionate and full of fun, but can be aggressive with strangers. Despite their short legs, they like as much exercise as you can give them. They have a loud bark for their size and are good watchdogs.

SIZE
Height—No requirement
Weight—10 lbs (4.5kg)

These Smooth Miniature Dachshund pups are full of fun and make excellent pets.

EXERCISE
Because the dog can get fat, regular exercise is important. Short, frequent walks or plenty of exercise in a fenced yard are all that is necessary.

GROOMING
The Dachshund's coat is easy to care for. The Smooth-hair needs only a few minutes of attention every day with a hound glove and soft cloth. Use a stiff-bristle brush and comb on the Longhair and Wirehair varieties.

FEEDING
For daily feeding, 1 to 1-1/2 cups of balanced dry dog food is recommended. Some dogs may prefer 1/2 cup water mixed with each cup of dog food. Add canned dog food for flavor.

ORIGIN AND HISTORY
The Dachshund was bred as a hunting dog. It existed before the 16th century and was derived from the oldest breeds of German hunting dog, such as the Bibarhund.

When the German Dachshund Club was formed in 1888, there was only one variety, the Smooth-hair Dachshund. This dog had wrinkled paws, a characteristic that has been almost bred out. Today there are three varieties, with miniatures of each type—the Smooth-hair, Wirehair and Longhair. The Wirehair Dachshund came from crossing the Scottish Dandie Dinmont with

other terriers. The Longhair was produced by crossing the Smooth-hair with the spaniel and a German gundog, the Stoberhund.

Bandiness, due to weakness in the tendons, and exaggerated body length have been bred out.

Miniatures, like standards, were introduced for a reason. At the end of the 19th century, German sportsmen required a hound to dig after rabbits. Some were produced by chance—the smaller, weaker members of a litter. A miniature type, known as the *Kaninchenteckel*, was intentionally produced by mating lightweight Dachshunds to toy terriers or Pinschers. Early miniatures had little show quality. Selective breeding produced a better type, for many years known as the *dwarf Teckel*. It had the shallow chest, short head and full eye characteristics of its predecessor.

SHOW REQUIREMENTS
The following descriptions apply to all three varieties.
General Appearance—Compact, with short legs and a long body. Muscular and strong, with a bold, intelligent expression. The body should not be plump and look like a short-body, or slender and look like a weasel. Shoulder height is half the length of the body measured from the breast bone to the base of the tail. The girth of the chest is double the height at the shoulder. The length from the tip of the nose to the eyes equals the length from eyes to base of skull.
Color—Any color except white. No white is permissible, except for a small spot on the breast but this is undesirable. Nose black. In dapples and chocolates, nose may be flesh-color or brown. Coat color bright and clearly defined. In black and tans, the tan is sharply divided from black. Dapples free from large unbroken patches, dappling evenly distributed over the whole body.
Head And Skull—Long and conical when seen from above. Sharp in profile and finely modeled. Skull not too broad or narrow, only slightly arched without prominent stop. Foreface long and narrow, finely modeled.

Longhair Miniature Dachshunds are well-mannered, friendly and good with children.

Lips tightly drawn but covering the lower jaw. Not heavy or sharply cut away. Corners of the mouth slightly marked.
Tail—Set in a continuation of the spine. Not too long. Tapers, without a marked curve. Not carried too high and never curled over the back.
Feet—Broad and large, relative to the size of the dog. Straight or turned only slightly outward. Hind feet smaller than forefeet. Must stand equally on all parts of the foot. Toes close together with each toe arched. Nails strong.
Teeth—Powerful teeth. Scissors bite.

The Wirehair Dachshund, most recent of the varieties, has a thick coat for hunting through undergrowth.

The Smooth Miniature Dachshund has achieved consistently high ratings in the show ring because of its self-confidence and happy, lively manner. It is also popular as a pet, especially for people living in apartments.

Smooth Miniature Dachshund

Longhair Miniature Dachshund

The coat of the Wirehair Miniature Dachshund is short and wiry, with a dense, soft undercoat to keep out cold and rain.

Wirehair Miniature Dachshund

NORFOLK TERRIER

Advantages
- *Adaptable to most lifestyles*
- *Even-tempered*
- *Fearless*
- *Good with children*
- *Hardy*
- *Lovable*

Disadvantages
- *No drawbacks known*

The Norfolk Terrier coexisted as one breed with the Norwich Terrier for more than a century. In 1979, the breeds were officially separated by the American Kennel Club. The AKC separated the breeds according to ear type—drop ears and erect ears. The breed with drop ears became the Norfolk Terrier. The erect-ear variety became known as the Norwich Terrier. The appearance and size of the dogs are the same. They are hardy dogs with an even temperament. They adapt to almost any lifestyle and are fearless and sporty.

SIZE
Height—10 in (25cm)
Weight—11 to 12 lbs
(5 to 5.3kg)

EXERCISE
The Norfolk Terrier will settle for regular walks, but enjoys runs in a park or country. It will chase small animals.

GROOMING
Little grooming or trimming is required.

FEEDING
For daily feeding, 1-1/2 cups of balanced dry dog food is recommended. Some dogs may prefer 1/2 cup water mixed with each cup of dog food. Add canned dog food for flavor.

ORIGIN AND HISTORY
These sporty terriers came from England. The dogs were red, rarely weighed more than 10 pounds and included both type of ears. They have been shown at dog shows since 1870.

SHOW REQUIREMENTS
General Appearance—Small, low, compact and strong, with a short back, good substance and bone.
Color—All shades of red, red-wheat, black and tan, or grizzle. White marks or patches are undesirable but do not disqualify.
Head And Skull—Skull wide and slightly rounded with good width between ears. Muzzle wedge shape and strong. Length of muzzle slightly less than half the length of the skull. Stop well-defined.
Tail—Medium docked.
Feet—Round, with thick pads.
Teeth—Scissors bite.

Norfolk Terriers play by the river.

NORWICH TERRIER

Advantages
- *Adaptable to most lifestyles*
- *Even-tempered*
- *Fearless*
- *Good with children*
- *Hardy*
- *Lovable*

Disadvantages
- *No drawbacks known*

Prior to 1979, the Norwich Terrier and the Norfolk Terrier were recognized as one breed by the American Kennel Club. The Norwich gained independent status as the erect-ear variety. Its appearance and characteristics are otherwise identical to its Norfolk kin.

SIZE
Height—10 in (25cm)
Weight—No requirement

EXERCISE
The Norwich Terrier will settle for regular walks. It is happiest when allowed to run in the country. It enjoys chasing small animals.

GROOMING
Little grooming or trimming is required.

FEEDING
For daily feeding, 1-1/2 cups of balanced dry dog food is recommended. Some dogs may prefer 1/2 cup water mixed with each cup of dog food. Add canned dog food for flavor.

ORIGIN AND HISTORY
There is controversy as to whether Col. Vaughan of Southern Ireland or Jodrell Hopkins, a horse dealer

The Norwich Terrier will prick up its ears when alerted.

---

from England, deserves credit for first developing the Norwich Terrier breed.

In the 1860s, Col. Vaughan hunted with a pack of small red terriers that evolved from the Irish Terrier. There were many outcrosses and terriers with drop and erect ears were produced. Breeders cropped the ears of drop-ear animals until it became illegal. When it did, the Norwich Terrier Club protested about the admittance of the drop-ear variety. When the breed was recognized by the British Kennel Club, the Norwich Terrier Club requested the standard call for only those with erect ears.

Hopkins owned a female. Many of her pups were owned by an employee, Frank Jones. Jones crossed them with other terriers, including the Irish and the Glen of Imaal terriers, using only small dogs of these breeds. The offspring were known as Trumpington or Jones Terriers. One breeder claims a direct line from Jones' dogs to the Norwich of today.

SHOW REQUIREMENTS
General Appearance—Small, low, compact and strong. Good substance and bone. Excessive trimming is undesirable. Honorable scars from wear and tear are not unduly penalized.
Color—All shades of red, straw-yellow, black and tan, and grizzle. White marks or patches undesirable.
Head And Skull—Muzzle foxlike and strong. Length about one-third less than the measurement from the rear skull to the bottom of the stop. Stop well-defined. Skull has good width between ears and is slightly rounded.
Tail—Medium docked, set on high to complete a perfectly level back. Carried erect.
Feet—Round, with thick pads.
Teeth—Scissors bite.

The Norfolk and Norwich Terriers, among the smallest terriers, are strong and sturdy for their size. They are fearless working dogs, originally bred to hunt rats, rabbits, fox and badgers. They do not fight and have a lovable disposition.

Norfolk Terrier

The hard, wiry coat of the Norfolk and Norwich Terriers lies close to the body and has a thick protective undercoat.

Norwich Terrier

SHIH TZU
Chrysanthemum Dog

Advantages
- *Adores human company*
- *Affectionate*
- *Hardy*
- *Intelligent*
- *Loves children and animals*
- *Suitable for city or country*

Disadvantages
- *Can have eye trouble*
- *Arrogant*

The Shih Tzu is a happy, attractive pet. It loves human company and hates neglect. It is an intelligent, arrogant animal. It enjoys daily grooming sessions, which are necessary.

SIZE
Height—10-1/2 in (27cm)
Weight—Male 10 to 18 lbs
(4.5 to 8.2kg)
Female: 10 to 16 lbs
(4.5 to 7.2kg)

EXERCISE
Short, regular walks are necessary.

GROOMING
Brush with a pure-bristle brush. If you neglect this, combing out tangles will be painful for the dog. Keep the topknot from getting into the eyes. Be sure ears are free of matted hair and other objects.

FEEDING
For daily feeding, 1-1/2 cups of balanced dry dog food is recommended. Some dogs may prefer 1/2 cup water mixed with each cup of dog food. Add canned dog food for flavor.

ORIGIN AND HISTORY
The Chinese may have crossed the Pekingese with the Lhasa Apso to develop the Shih Tzu. Export of the Shih Tzu from China was forbidden. Not until the death of the Empress Tzu-hsi, in 1908, were dogs smuggled to the United States and Europe.

SHOW REQUIREMENTS
General Appearance—Active, lively and alert. Arrogant carriage.
Color—All colors permissible, but a white blaze on the forehead and a white tip on the tail are highly prized. Dogs with liver markings may have dark liver-colored noses and slightly lighter eyes. Pigmentation on muzzle as unbroken as possible.
Head And Skull—Head broad and round. Wide between the eyes. Hair falling over the eyes. Good beard and whiskers. Hair growing up on the nose gives a chrysanthemum effect. Muzzle square and short, but not wrinkled like a Pekingese. Muzzle flat and hairy. Nose black, 1 inch (2.5cm) from tip to stop.
Tail—Heavily plumed and curled over back.
Feet—Firm and padded. Appear big because of the amount of hair.

Two beautifully groomed Shih Tzus. These are popular show dogs.

LHASA APSO

Advantages
- *Affectionate*
- *Confident*
- *Good with children*
- *Hardy*
- *Suitable for city or country*

Disadvantages
- *Needs regular grooming*
- *Not fond of strangers*

The Lhasa Apso, like the Tibetan Terrier and Tibetan Spaniel, comes from the mountains of Tibet. It is a shaggy dog that looks like a miniature Old English Sheepdog. It makes an excellent pet but is suspicious of strangers.

SIZE
Height—Male: 10 in (25cm)
Female: Slightly smaller
Weight—No requirement

EXERCISE
This breed needs plenty of walks.

GROOMING
Thorough brushing and combing daily will keep the coat in condition.

FEEDING
For daily feeding, 1-1/2 cups of balanced dry dog food is recommended. Some dogs may prefer 1/2 cup water mixed with each cup of dog food. Add canned dog food for flavor.

ORIGIN AND HISTORY
This dog was offered by the Dalai Lama of Tibet to the Chinese emperors. It existed for centuries in Tibetan mountains until it was brought to Europe by early explorers and missionaries. The Tibetan words *Lhasa Apso* mean *goatlike*. It may have first found favor as a guard and protector of wild Tibetan goats.

SHOW REQUIREMENTS
General Appearance—Well-balanced, solid and assertive. Free-moving.
Color—Gold, sand, honey, slate, smoke, particolor, black, white or brown.
Head And Skull—Heavy head fur with good fall over the eyes. Good whiskers and beard. Skull narrow, falling away behind the eyes. Not quite flat, but not domed or apple shape. Straight foreface, with medium stop. Nose black. Muzzle about 1-1/2 inches (3.5cm) long, but not square. Length from tip of nose to end is roughly one-third the total length from nose to back of skull.
Tail—High set, carried over back in a screw. Often a kink at the end. Feathered.
Feet—Round and catlike, with good pads and feathers.
Teeth—Mouth level, otherwise slightly undershot preferred.

A Lhasa Apso with pup. A glamorous show dog, this breed is also an excellent pet.

The Shih Tzu arrived in America in 1938 and was given show classification in the Toy Group in 1969. In 1940, the breed was registered separately from the Lhasa Apso.

Shih Tzu

The Lhasa Apso is the most recent Tibetan dog to become popular in the Western World.

Lhasa Apso

BEDLINGTON TERRIER

Advantages
- *Adores children*
- *Good family pet*
- *Behaves well*
- *Good watchdog*
- *Obedient*

Disadvantages
- *Could be dangerous in a pack*
- *Formidable fighter*

The Bedlington Terrier is an attractive, hardy dog. When trimmed, it resembles a shorn lamb. Its dainty appearance and love of children belies its first-rate watchdog qualities. It is smart and trains easily. Many have been used successfully in obedience competitions.

SIZE
Height—Male: 16-1/2 in (42cm)
Female: 15-1/2 in (39cm)
Weight—Male: 23 lbs (11kg)
Female: 17 lbs (7.6kg)

EXERCISE
The Bedlington enjoys an energetic ball game or exercise in a fenced area. It can easily adapt to city life if given regular walks.

GROOMING
This dog does not shed. Dead hairs stay in the coat until you comb them out. Trim the dog regularly or the coat will become tangled. Brush it every day with a stiff-bristle brush. Do not bathe the animal too often or the coat may weaken. Remove hair from inside the dog's ears regularly with fingers or tweezers.

FEEDING
For daily feeding, 1-1/2 cups of balanced dry dog food is recommended. Some dogs may prefer 1/2 cup water mixed with each cup of dog food. Add canned dog food for flavor.

ORIGIN AND HISTORY
It is possible the Greyhound or Whippet played a part in the origin of the Bedlington Terrier. The soft topknot suggests it may also share common ancestry with the Dandie Dinmont Terrier. A strain of similar terriers existed in England in the 18th century. In 1820, J. Howe came to Bedlington with a female. This dog whelped the first named Bedlington Terrier. From 1825, systematic breeding of the Bedlington began. The breed was shown during the 1860s. The first Bedlington Terrier Club was formed in 1875.

SHOW REQUIREMENTS
General Appearance—Graceful, lithe and muscular. No sign of weakness or coarseness.
Color—Blue, blue and tan, liver or sandy. Darker pigment encouraged.
Head And Skull—Skull narrow, but deep and round. Covered with a silky topknot a lighter color than the body. Jaw long and tapering. No stop.
Tail—Moderate length. Thick at the root, tapering to a point. Gracefully curved. Set on low, never carried over the back.
Feet—Long hare feet with thick, closed pads.
Teeth—Large, strong and white. Level or scissors bite.

MINIATURE POODLE

Advantages
- *Affectionate*
- *Dainty and appealing*
- *Excellent retriever*
- *Good sense of fun*
- *Intelligent*
- *Long-lived*
- *Obedient*

Disadvantages
- *Noisy if unchecked*
- *May not be good child's pet*
- *Sensitive*

The Poodle is fun, intelligent and obedient. It performs well in obedience competitions. It is favored for the show ring, where it is beautiful when exhibited in the traditional lion clip.

SIZE
Height—Male: 15 in (38cm)
Female: 11 in (28cm)
Weight—10 to 11 lbs (4.5 to 5kg)

EXERCISE
The Poodle enjoys games, practicing obedience exercises or running in the park. It also likes to swim.

GROOMING
Use a wire brush and a metal comb for daily grooming. The lion clip is essential for the show ring. Pet owners usually prefer the more natural lamb clip, with hair a short uniform length. It is possible to clip your dog with a pair of scissors. Or take your dog to a groomer. It needs clipping no more than once every six weeks. Bathe regularly.

FEEDING
For daily feeding, 1-1/2 cups of balanced dry dog food is recommended. Some dogs may prefer 1/2 cup water mixed with each cup of dog food. Add canned dog food for flavor.

HEALTH CARE
Purchase a Miniature Poodle from a breeder who emphasizes quality animals. Watch for signs of ear trouble, nervousness or joint malformations. Teeth need regular scaling.

ORIGIN AND HISTORY
The Poodle was originally a guard, retriever and protector of sheep. Its origins are similar to the Irish Water Spaniel. It may be a common ancestor to the French Barbet and Hungarian Water Hound.

The Poodle originated in Germany as a water retriever. The word *poodle* comes from the German *pudelnass*, or puddle. The Miniature and Toy have evolved from the Standard Poodle.

The breed has been known in England since Prince Rupert of the Rhine, accompanied by his Poodle, came to the aid of Charles I in battle. The breed was favored by Marie Antoinette, who invented the lion clip. She devised the style to match the uniform of her courtiers.

SHOW REQUIREMENTS
Same as for Toy Poodle. See page 18.

PUG

Advantages
- *Happy disposition*
- *Good with children*
- *Affectionate*
- *Intelligent*

Disadvantages
- *Overfeeding makes it fat*
- *Lungs may be delicate*
- *Avoid vigorous exertion*

A Pug can look elegant and will make a charming family pet. It can develop respiratory trouble from overheating or vigorous exercise. With its flat, squashed-looking face it may have breathing difficulties.

SIZE
Height—No requirement
Weight—Male: 18 lbs (8.2kg)
Female: 14 lbs (6.4kg)

EXERCISE
The Pug enjoys more exercise than many breeds of similar size. It can become fat. It will walk best on a leash. Do not give it vigorous exercise because of potential respiratory problems.

GROOMING
A good daily brushing is sufficient.

FEEDING
For daily feeding, 1 cup of balanced dry dog food is recommended. Some dogs may prefer 1/2 cup water mixed with each cup of dog food. Add canned dog food for flavor.

ORIGIN AND HISTORY
The Pug arrived in France with the Turkish Fleet in 1553. It found favor in Holland, where the color of its coat was compared to the color of the House of Orange. When William and Mary journeyed to Britain to take the throne in 1689, some Pugs accompanied them. For 300 years, the breed enjoyed a popularity similar to today's Poodle.

They gradually declined in numbers. In 1864, Queen Victoria had difficulty locating one to add to her kennels. Twenty years later the Pug Dog Club in England was formed. Efforts were made to improve and standardize the breed, resulting in the elegant, solid Pug of today.

SHOW REQUIREMENTS
General Appearance—Compact form, well-knit proportions and developed muscles.
Color—Silver, apricot, fawn or black. Each color should be clearly defined to contrast color, trace and mask.
Head And Skull—Head large, massive and round. Not apple shape. No indentation of the skull. Muzzle short, blunt, square, but not upfaced. Wrinkles large and deep.
Tail—Curled as tightly as possible over the hip. Double curl is perfect.
Feet—Not harefooted or catfooted. Well-split toes. Nails black.

The Bedlington Terrier is a livelier dog than its elegance suggests. When aroused, its eyes sparkle and the dog looks full of courage. Bedlingtons are capable of great speed and have the appearance of being able to move quickly. Their movements are distinctively mincing, light and springy in the slower paces. They have a slight roll when in full stride. When galloping, the animal uses its whole body.

Bedlington Terrier

Miniature Poodle with a lamb clip

The Pug uses attack as the best form of defense. Like the Bulldog, the Pug has a tendency to snore and may experience breathing difficulties in warm weather or during vigorous exercise.

Pug

BORDER TERRIER

Advantages
- **Good-natured**
- **Hardy**
- **Reliable**
- **Sporty working dog**

Disadvantages
- **Needs space for exercise**

The Border Terrier is the smallest working terrier. It is a natural breed that evolved in the border counties of England and Scotland. Its task was to flush foxes from their lairs.

It is a hardy dog with an even temperament. It is compatible with people and other animals.

SIZE
Height—No requirement
Weight—Male: 13 to 15-1/2 lbs
(5.9 to 7kg)
Female: 11-1/2 to 14 lbs
(5.2 to 6.4kg)

EXERCISE
The Border Terrier has vitality. Do not keep one unless you can give it adequate exercise.

GROOMING
The coat needs little trimming for the show ring. It requires minimal grooming.

FEEDING
For daily feeding, 1-1/2 cups of balanced dry dog food is recommended. Some dogs may prefer 1/2 cup water mixed with each cup of dog food. Add canned dog food for flavor.

ORIGIN AND HISTORY
The Border Terrier developed in the border counties of England and Scotland in the mid-19th century. It was the practice to produce a terrier for certain tasks. Sportsmen wanted a hardy dog able to run with hounds and foxes.

The Border Terrier, with its otterlike head, still works with hounds. It has been changed less to meet the dictates of the show ring than almost any other breed. It was recognized in 1920.

SHOW REQUIREMENTS
Color—Red, straw-yellow, grizzle and tan, or blue and tan.
Head And Skull—Head like an otter's. Moderately broad skull, with a short strong muzzle and black nose.
Tail—Moderately short and thick at the base, then tapering. Set high, but not curled over the back.
Feet—Small, with thick pads.

AUSTRALIAN TERRIER

Advantages
- **Courageous**
- **Devoted**
- **Hardy**
- **Keen watchdog**

Disadvantages
- **Aggressive**

The Australian Terrier is a loyal, devoted dog and an excellent companion. Its alertness and speed make it an excellent rodent catcher. The Aussie's coat is weather-resistant, so you can keep it in the house or an outdoor kennel.

SIZE
Height—10 in (25cm)
Weight—12 to 14 lbs
(5.4 to 6.3kg)

EXERCISE
This is an active dog. Give it regular walks and runs in a fenced area. It can adapt to apartment living.

GROOMING
Regular grooming with a stiff-bristle brush stimulates the skin and encourages good coat growth. If you show your Aussie, bathe it at least two weeks before the show. During spring and summer, when show dates may be close together, do not bathe on each occasion. Frequent washing softens the coat.

FEEDING
For daily feeding, 1-1/2 cups of balanced dry dog food is recommended. Some dogs may prefer 1/2 cup water mixed with each cup of dog food. Add canned dog food for flavor.

ORIGIN AND HISTORY
The Australian Terrier evolved from several varieties of British terriers brought to Australia by settlers. It was known by various names until 1889. In that year, a club was formed in Melbourne to foster the breed.

The purebred Australian Terrier evolved from the offspring of a Yorkshire Terrier female smuggled aboard a sailing ship. It was mated to a dog resembling a Cairn Terrier.

SHOW REQUIREMENTS
General Appearance—Low set, compact and active.
Color—Blue-black or silver-black body, tan color on legs and face. The richer the tan the better. Topknot blue or silver. Also, clear sandy or red, with a soft topknot.
Head And Skull—Head long. Skull flat and full between the eyes, with a soft-hair topknot. Long powerful jaw. Nose black.
Tail—Docked.
Feet—Clean, small and padded with no tendency to spread. Black toenails.

CAIRN TERRIER

Advantages
- **Intelligent**
- **Hardy**
- **Happy disposition**
- **Can live indoors or outside**
- **Family companion**

Disadvantages
- **May be too energetic**

The Cairn Terrier comes from Scotland. The word *cairn* means a heap of stones. It is a suitable name for a terrier that digs. It is an affectionate, sporty dog with an almost rain-resistant coat. It is active, obedient and makes an ideal pet.

SIZE
Height—No requirement
Weight—14 lbs (6.4kg)

EXERCISE
The Cairn is energetic and likes to run and play ball. It will adapt to walks on a leash and sedate city living if it has a yard to play in.

GROOMING
The Cairn is an easy dog to groom or prepare for the show ring. It is shown in a natural condition. Brush and comb it. Remove excess feathering from behind front legs and tail. Any long hairs on the ears and the underside must also be removed.

FEEDING
For daily feeding, 1-1/2 cups of balanced dry dog food is recommended. Some dogs may prefer 1/2 cup water mixed with each cup of dog food. Add canned dog food for flavor.

ORIGIN AND HISTORY
More than 300 years ago, a working terrier of this type was used in Scotland. J.W.H. Beynon in his work, *The Popular Cairn Terrier,* says every Highland chieftain had his pack of terriers to chase fox, badgers and other animals.

The oldest known strain of Cairns was developed by Capt. MacLeod of Drynoch, Isle of Skye. It goes back over 150 years. John MacDonald, gamekeeper for over 40 years of Macleod, Denvegan Castle, kept this strain alive. The Cairn was then known as a Shorthair Skye Terrier. Interbreeding of the Cairn with the West Highland was permitted until 1924.

The Cairn Terrier became popular during the 1930s.

SHOW REQUIREMENTS
General Appearance—Active, hardy and shaggy. Strong and compactly built. Stands forward on its forepaws. Strong quarters, with deep ribs. Free in movement. Coat hard enough to resist rain. Head small, but in proportion to body. A foxlike expression is the chief characteristic of this dog.
Color—Red, sandy, gray, brindled or nearly black. Dark points such as ears and muzzle are typical. Solid white or white on chest or feet is not permitted.
Head And Skull—Skull broad. Strong, but not too long or heavy a jaw. Prominent indentation between the eyes. Hair should be full on the forehead. Muzzle powerful but not heavy. Strong jaw.
Tail—Short, furnished with hair, but not feathery. Carried upward but not turned down toward back.
Feet—Forefeet larger than hind feet. May be slightly turned out. Pads thick and strong. Thin, ferretlike feet are objectionable.
Teeth—Not undershot or overshot.

The Border Terrier is a working terrier. It is able to follow a horse and combine activity with gameness. The coat is wiry and dense, with a close undercoat. This keeps out cold and wet when the dog is running down a fox in thick undergrowth. The breed also makes a fine pet and is good with children.

Border Terrier

The Australian Terrier is supposed to have a hard-bitten appearance. Do not brush the hair forward on the muzzle because it gives the dog a Yorkshire Terrier appearance, which is wrong for this breed.

Australian Terrier

The Cairn Terrier is a hardy working dog. Cairn Terrier Clubs throughout the world have preserved the essential nature of the breed.

Cairn Terrier

IRISH TERRIER

Advantages
- *Alert*
- *Courageous*
- *Excellent rat catcher*
- *Good with children*
- *Not snappy*
- *Good protector*

Disadvantages
- *Prone to fighting*

The Irish Terrier looks like a small Airedale with a self-colored yellow coat. It is a fine watchdog, loyal protector and excellent family pet. It is courageous. Stories of faithfulness to its master are well-known. Its only drawback is its tendency to fight other dogs.

SIZE
Height—18 in (46cm)
Weight—Male: 27 lbs (12.5kg)
　　　　　Female: 25 lbs (11.5kg)

EXERCISE
The Irish Terrier has been trained to hunt and is good at chasing and killing rodents. It performs well in obedience competitions. It adapts to life as a pet and should have regular exercise and a yard to play in.

GROOMING
The Irish Terrier needs stripping several times a year. Have this done professionally until you learn how to do it. An inexperienced attempt at stripping could be painful for the dog. It might harm its temperament. Some owners clip the dog. This is permissible with an elderly animal but causes loss of color and condition in the coat. Normally, brushing keeps the dog in condition. Allow it to keep its thick coat after the show season is over.

FEEDING
For daily feeding, 3 cups of balanced dry dog food is recommended. Some dogs may prefer 1/2 cup water mixed with each cup of dog food. Add canned dog food for flavor.

ORIGIN AND HISTORY
The Irish Terrier was established in Ireland before the arrival of St. Patrick. Some say it is a smaller version of the Irish Wolfhound. The relationship seems remote. It is more likely the Irish Terrier is a descendant of the Black and Tan Wirehair Terriers, used to hunt fox in Britain for more than 200 years. Studies of Welsh and Lakeland Terriers show a similarity between the breeds. It seems they all have the Black and Tan Terrier as a common ancestor. In the area around County Cork, Ireland, a large Wheaten Terrier existed that could have been the forerunner of the Irish Terrier.

Standard breeding of the Irish Terrier did not take place until 1879. Before that year there was considerable variation in type, size and color. The Irish Terrier in Antrim was black, brown and white. In Whitley, it was red. The ones in Kerry were black or black-brown.

In 1879, a specialist Breed Club was formed. Later, the Irish Terrier in its present form and color became popular.

SHOW REQUIREMENTS
General Appearance—Active, lively, lithe and wiry, with lots of substance. Free of clumsiness. Speed and endurance, as well as power, are essential. Graceful racing outline.
Color—Self-colored, the most preferable colors being bright red, rust or yellow-red. White sometimes appears on the chest and feet. More objectionable on the chest than the feet. A speck of white on the chest is frequently seen in all self-colored breeds.
Head And Skull—Head long. Skull flat and narrow between ears, getting slightly narrower toward the eye. Free from wrinkles. Stop barely visible except in profile. Jaw strong and muscular, not too full in the cheek and a good length. Nose black.
Tail—Docked to three-quarters. Free of fringe or feather, but covered with rough hair. Set high, carried gaily, but not over the back or curled.
Feet—Strong, round and moderately small. Toes arched and straight. Black toenails desirable. Pads sound and free from cracks or horny outgrowths.
Teeth—Strong, white and even, not undershot or overshot.

SHETLAND SHEEPDOG

Advantages
- *Intelligent*
- *Faithful*
- *Obedient*

Disadvantages
- *Not a good kennel dog*
- *Suspicious of strangers*

The Shetland Sheepdog is the perfect Rough Collie in miniature. It is a good size for the owner who thinks the Rough Collie is too large for his home.

The Sheltie is a good family dog, but wary of strangers. It does not like to be petted by people it does not know. It is faithful, intelligent and easy to train. It is good with other animals, such as horses. Some are still used as sheepdogs.

SIZE
Height—13 to 16 in
　　　　　(33 to 41cm)
Weight—No requirement

EXERCISE
The Sheltie will be happy if it has a large yard and daily walks.

GROOMING
It is difficult to keep clean. Brush regularly with a stiff-bristle brush and use a comb to avoid tangles, particularly behind the ears. Frequent bathing is unnecessary. Bathe the animal when it loses its winter coat. The Sheltie is meticulous about its appearance. You will often find it cleaning itself.

FEEDING
For daily feeding, 3 cups of balanced dry dog food is recommended. Some dogs may prefer 1/2 cup water mixed with each cup of dog food. Add canned dog food for flavor.

ORIGIN AND HISTORY
The Sheltie originated in the Shetland Islands off the north coast of Scotland. The island is also famous for Shetland ponies. Both have been bred with thick coats to protect them against the harsh climate.

The dog has bred true for 125 years and has generated controversy. The ideals of the breed club formed at Lerwick in 1908 conflicted with the desires of the Shetland Collie Club. Their desire was to produce a miniature Collie. Agreement was reached in 1914, when the English Shetland Sheepdog Club was formed. The Sheltie received separate classification. Today the breed's popularity is universal.

SHOW REQUIREMENTS
General Appearance—Intelligent and alert. Action is lithe and graceful with great speed and jumping power. Outline symmetrical so no part appears out of proportion. An abundance of coat, mane and frill, with shapeliness of head and sweetness of expression.
Color—Tricolors have intense black with no signs of ticking. Rich tan markings on tricolor are preferred. Sables may be clear or shaded, any color from gold to deep mahogany. In its shade, the color should be rich in tones. Wolf-sable and gray colors are undesirable. In blue-merles, a clear silver-blue is desired, splashed and marbled with black. Rich tan markings and a slate-color or rusty tinge in either topcoat or undercoat are undesirable. The general effect is blue. White markings may be shown in a blaze, collar, chest frill, legs, stifle and tip of tail. Tan markings may be shown on eyebrows, cheeks, legs, stifles and undertail. Nose black.
Head And Skull—Head refined. When viewed from the top or side, it is a long blunt wedge, tapering from ear to nose. The width of skull depends on the combined length of skull and muzzle. The whole must be considered in connection with the size of the dog.
Tail—Set on low. Tapering bone must reach at least to the hock joint, with abundant hair and slight upward sweep.
Feet—Oval. Soles padded. Toes arched and close together.
Teeth—Scissors or level bite. Teeth evenly spaced.

Irish Terrier

The Irish Terrier is good-natured, especially with humans. It develops an extraordinary devotion for its master and has been known to track its master for incredible distances.

The Shetland Sheepdog's eyes are an important feature, giving expression to the dog. Eyes should be medium size, obliquely set and almond shape. Color is dark brown, except in the case of merles, when blue is permissible.

Shetland Sheepdog

GERMAN HUNT TERRIER
Deutscher Jagdterrier

Advantages
- *Excellent hunter*
- *Good gundog*
- *Good traveler*
- *Robust*
- *Good retriever*

Disadvantages
- *Needs a lot of exercise*
- *Can be aggressive*

The German Hunt Terrier is popular in Germany, Austria and other German-speaking regions. It is not recognized by the American Kennel Club. It can be kept as a pet, but is a worker. It needs plenty of exercise and has an aggressive temperament.

SIZE
Height—16 in (41cm)
Weight—Male: 19-1/2 to 22 lbs
(8.8 to 10kg)
Female: 16 to 18 lbs
(7.2 to 8.2kg)

EXERCISE
This dog needs plenty of exercise.

GROOMING
Daily brushing is required.

FEEDING
For daily feeding, 1-1/2 cups of balanced dry dog food is recommended. Some dogs may prefer 1/2 cup water mixed with each cup of dog food. Add canned dog food for flavor.

ORIGIN AND HISTORY
This German breed derived from crossing the English Fox Terrier with the Lakeland Terrier and other dogs. The goal was to create a hardy, dark-coated terrier. The first results were not encouraging, although good working terriers were produced. By 1925, a satisfactory German Hunt Terrier had evolved, able to go to earth and retrieve small game from land or water. It is courageous, willing to take on fox and boar, as well as rats and small rodents.

The Association of the German Hunt Terrier has a list of work-tests designed specifically for the breed. It accepts for breeding only Hunt Terriers that have achieved high marks.

LAKELAND TERRIER

Advantages
- *Fine guard*
- *Good family dog*
- *Adapts to home life*

Disadvantages
- *May be too energetic*

The Lakeland Terrier is similar to Welsh and Airedale Terriers. It is a good family pet, because of its temperament and small size. The dog guards well, too. In the past it has been used for fox and badger hunting. Today, it is kept mainly as a pet and in recent years has been a successful contender in the show ring.

SIZE
Height—14-1/2 in (37cm)
at the shoulder
Weight—Male: 17 lbs (7.7kg)
Female: 15 lbs (6.8kg)

EXERCISE
Do not choose a terrier unless you want an animal with plenty of energy. The Lakeland Terrier is fearless and always ready for a game or walk. It is suitable for apartment living if you can give it regular exercise.

GROOMING
Trimming the Lakeland for the show ring requires skill. Daily brushing helps keep the coat tidy. Stripping in spring, summer and autumn is recommended.

The compact, sturdy Lakeland Terrier is a lively pet. It needs plenty of vigorous exercise to stay in top condition. Originally bred for hunting, the Lakeland Terrier has become a favorite in the show ring.

FEEDING
For daily feeding, 1-1/2 cups of balanced dry dog food is recommended. Some dogs may prefer 1/2 cup water mixed with each cup of dog food. Add canned dog food for flavor.

ORIGIN AND HISTORY
The Lakeland Terrier originated in the Lake District of England. It was originally known as the Patterdale Terrier and worked with the local hunts. The Lakeland did not make an appearance in the show ring until a Breed Club was formed in 1932.

SHOW REQUIREMENTS
General Appearance—Smart and workmanlike, with fearless demeanor.
Color—Black and tan, blue and tan, red, wheat, red-grizzle, liver, blue or black. Mahogany or deep tan is not typical.
Head And Skull—Balanced. Skull flat and refined. Jaws powerful. Muzzle broad but not too long. Length of the head from the stop to the nose not to exceed that from the occiput to the stop. Nose black.
Tail—Carried up, but not curling over the back.
Feet—Small, compact, round and padded.
Teeth—Meet in level edge-to-edge bite or slightly overlapping scissors bite. Overshot or undershot are disqualifying.

WELSH TERRIER

Advantages
- *Affectionate*
- *Bold*
- *Even-tempered*
- *Obedient*

Disadvantages
- *No drawbacks known*

The Welsh Terrier has much in common with the Airedale, Irish and Lakeland Terriers. It looks like a small Airedale. It makes a good pet with its even temperament, affection and obedience.

SIZE
Height—15-1/2 in (39.5cm)
Weight—20 to 21 lbs
(9 to 9.5kg)

EXERCISE
Give this dog regular daily walks. Like most terriers, it enjoys a run in open spaces.

GROOMING
The Welsh Terrier's coat needs stripping twice a year. Regular brushing keeps it in show condition. Many owners clip their terriers. Leave the coat on in winter to provide extra warmth.

FEEDING
For daily feeding, 3 cups of balanced dry dog food is recommended. Some dogs may prefer 1/2 cup water mixed with each cup of dog food. Add canned dog food for flavor.

ORIGIN AND HISTORY
The Welsh Terrier is of Celtic origin. Two strains once existed together. One was bred from a Coarsehair Black and Tan Terrier. The other was an English variety achieved through crossing an Airedale with a Fox Terrier. These two types caused dissent while recognition for the breed was being sought. The English variety appears to have died out. The true Celtic strain was presented in 1885. The Welsh Terrier Club was founded a year later. In 1886, the Welsh Terrier was awarded championship status by the British Kennel Club. The first Welsh Terriers were taken to the United States in 1888, but not in large numbers until after 1901.

SHOW REQUIREMENTS
Color—Black and tan or black-grizzle and tan. Free from black penciling on the toes. Black below the hocks or white is a fault.
Head And Skull—Skull flat and wide between the ears. Jaw powerful, clean cut and deep. This gives a masculine appearance. Stop not too defined. Fair length from stop to end of black nose.
Tail—Not carried up.
Feet—Small, round and catlike.
Teeth—Undershot or pig-jaw mouth is disqualifying.

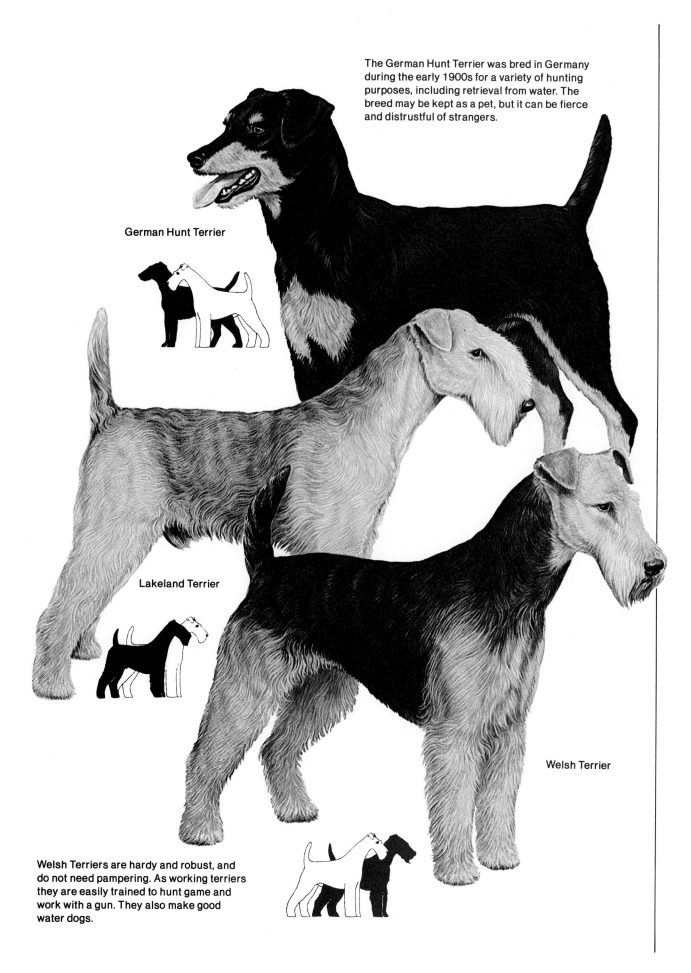

The German Hunt Terrier was bred in Germany during the early 1900s for a variety of hunting purposes, including retrieval from water. The breed may be kept as a pet, but it can be fierce and distrustful of strangers.

German Hunt Terrier

Lakeland Terrier

Welsh Terrier

Welsh Terriers are hardy and robust, and do not need pampering. As working terriers they are easily trained to hunt game and work with a gun. They also make good water dogs.

TELOMIAN DOG

Advantages
- **Loyal and affectionate**
- **Excellent health**
- **Quiet**
- **Little odor**

Disadvantages
- **May have behavior problems**

The Telomian Dog, a rare Malaysian breed, was saved from extinction by the efforts of fanciers. The Telomian Dog Club of America maintains a Stud Book and is responsible for registration. Club activities are geared toward American Kennel Club, Federation Cynologique Internationale and Malaysian Kennel Club registration. Each year the club sponsors a rare-breeds show. A continuing search for Telomians in the jungles of Malaysia is financially assisted by the club.

SIZE
Height—15 to 17 in
(38 to 43cm)
at the shoulder
Weight—18 to 28 lbs
(8.2 to 12.5kg)

EXERCISE
Telomians need exercise in a large fenced area. Some Telomians have been clocked running at 30 to 40mph (78 to 105kph).

GROOMING
Telomians keep themselves clean and require little grooming. An occasional bath, brushing with a soft-bristle brush or the use of a hand glove are all that is necessary.

ORIGIN AND HISTORY
Ancient Malaysian legends tell of a small breed of dog protected by the aborigines deep in Malaysian jungles. They were so highly regarded they shared their owner's beds and tables.

In 1963, after traveling thousands of miles, Dr. Orville Elliot found a pair of dogs he believed to be those described in legends. The dogs were found at the Telom River near the equator and became known as Telomians.

Their similarity to the Basenji and Dingo was remarkable. Dr. Elliot sent the pair to Dr. J.P. Scott, a reknowned dog expert, for evaluation. Dr. Scott suggests the Telomian is the genetic and geographic missing link between the Basenji and the Dingo. See page 56.

SHOW REQUIREMENTS
General Appearance—Small and muscular, with a slightly elongated back. The wrinkled head is carried proudly with alertness and poise. When moving, it should single track.
Coat—Short and smooth with pliant skin. Color any shade of sable, blond to deep red, with white ticking. A black mask is not unusual.
Head And Skull—Skull is medium wide, flat and chiseled. Wrinkles on the forehead. The muzzle is not snipy or coarse. Nose is black, but a pink tinge will not penalize an otherwise excellent specimen.
Tail—Long and carried up over the back when alert. It may drop at rest. A tight curl is a fault.
Feet—Compact with arched toes and tough pads.
Teeth—Level or scissors bite.

AMERICAN ESKIMO

Advantages
- **Good with children**
- **Excellent guard**
- **Intelligent**
- **Good in obedience training**
- **White coat resists soiling**
- **Odorless**

Disadvantages
- **Wary of strangers**
- **Enjoys barking**

This dog is called *the dog beautiful* by enthusiasts. The American Eskimo is becoming more popular. It is recognized and registered by the United Kennel Club. The American Eskimo Dog Association is the national organization that sanctions breed activities. There are numerous state associations, affiliated with the national club, which host specialty shows and activities.

SIZE
Miniature
Height—No requirement
Weight—Male: 12 to 20 lbs
(5.4 to 9kg)
Female: 10 to 18 lbs
(4.5 to 8.2kg)
Standard
Height—No requirement
Weight—Male: 20 to 35 lbs
(9 to 16kg)
Female: 18 to 32 lbs
(8.2 to 14.5kg)

EXERCISE
This dog adapts to apartment or city living. If a fenced yard is not available for exercise, daily walks are needed.

GROOMING
Daily brushing and an occasional bath will keep an American Eskimo shining. Once a year, usually in the spring, Eskimos shed their coats.

ORIGIN AND HISTORY
The Peat Dog of the New Stone Age was probably the early ancestor of the American Eskimo. Remains of this dog were found in Scandinavia. The modern breed most closely associated with the American Eskimo is the Great German Spitz. Although somewhat larger, the Spitz closely resembles the American Eskimo. All Spitz breeds resemble each other in character, showing intelligence and devotion to their owners. A strong hunting instinct has been replaced by a guarding instinct in the American Eskimo.

SHOW REQUIREMENTS
General Appearance—Proportioned and well-balanced. Back length from point of shoulder to root of tail equals the height from pad to top of withers. Carriage alert and movement smooth, with good reach in the forequarters and driving action in the rear. The face is Nordic with triangular ears. Coat is thick with longer hair forming a ruff or mane. The richly plumed tail is carried over the back.
Color—Any color other than white or biscuit will be disqualified.
Coat—Thick, short undercoat and longer guard hair. No curls or waves. A ruff around the neck is noticeable. Males have a more pronounced ruff. Quality is more important than quantity.
Head And Skull—Wedge-shape head, with a broad, slightly crowned skull, is in proportion to the size of the dog. Stop defined, but not abrupt. Muzzle in proportion to the head, medium in length and covered with short, smooth hair. Eyes are slightly oval, but not slanted. Eyes brown to black. Nose, eyerims and lips black or dark brown.
Tail—Set moderately high and carried over the back. Covered with long, thick hair. Dropped at rest. When down, the tail should reach the hock.
Feet—Oval, with tough, deeply cushioned pads. In a normal stance, feet should not toe in or out.
Teeth—Level or scissors bite.

The American Eskimo has a short white or biscuit-color undercoat and longer guard hairs. Its odorless coat resists soiling.

Telomian Dog

Telomians look like Basenjis
with their similarly shaped
heads. Telomians are native to
the jungles of Malaysia.

American Eskimo

STANDARD DACHSHUND

Teckel, Dachel, Dacksel, Badger Hound

Advantages
- **Affectionate**
- **Brave watchdog**
- **Easy to look after**
- **Loyal family pet**
- **Sense of fun**

Disadvantages
- **Prone to back trouble**
- **Self-willed**
- **Can be aggressive**

The Dachshund, or Teckel, was bred as a badger hound in Germany. A short-legged hound was needed that had a keen sense of smell, courage and gameness. The dog also needed to be able to burrow. If unchecked, the Dachshund will burrow and dig up your yard.

Some Dachshunds are still bred as hunting dogs. They will tackle an opponent larger than themselves, such as a badger. They will also defend their master to the death. Their role today is mainly as a companion. They may be aggressive with strangers, but can also be affectionate and full of fun. Despite their short legs they can take as much exercise as you want to give them. They have a loud bark and are excellent watchdogs.

SIZE
Longhair
Height—No requirement
Weight—Male: 18 lbs (8.2kg)
     Female: 17 lbs (7.7kg)

Smooth-hair
Height—No requirement
Weight—Male: 25 lbs (11.3kg)
     Female: 23 lbs (10.4kg)

Wirehair
Height—No requirement
Weight—Male: 20 to 22 lbs
     (9 to 10kg)
     Female: 18 to 20 lbs
     (8.2 to 9kg)

EXERCISE
Regular exercise is important. They have a tendency to put on weight. Short, frequent walks are advisable, with plenty of runs in a fenced yard.

GROOMING
The Dachshund's coat is easy to keep clean. The Smooth-hair needs only a few minutes' attention every day with a hound glove and soft cloth. Use a stiff-bristle brush and comb on the Longhair and the Wirehair.

FEEDING
For daily feeding, 1-1/2 cups of balanced dry dog food is recommended. Some dogs may prefer 1/2 cup water mixed with each cup of dog food. Add canned dog food for flavor.

HEALTH CARE
A Dachshund can suffer from disc trouble because of its long back and stubby legs. Anyone who has seen a dog paralyzed will realize the need to keep the pet's weight within the breed standard. Treatment varies from injections of cortisone to an operation. Do not let your dog leap.

The Dachshund's teeth are prone to tartar. Regular scaling is recommended. Remove stains with a paste of water and cream of tartar, applied with cotton.

ORIGIN AND HISTORY
The Dachshund was bred as a badger hound and hunting dog. It is derived from the oldest breeds of German hunting dog, such as the Bibarhund. It existed before the 16th century.

When the German Dachshund Club was formed in 1888, there was only one variety, the Smooth-hair Dachshund. Its wrinkled paws, then a characteristic, have now been nearly bred out. Today, there are three varieties, with miniatures of each type—the Smooth-hair, Wirehair and Longhair. The Wirehair was introduced through crossing with the Scottish Dandie Dinmont and other terriers. The Longhair was a cross of the Smooth-hair with a spaniel and an old German gundog, the Stoberhund. Bandy legs in the breed, due to weak tendons, have been eliminated. Exaggerated length has also been bred out. The American Kennel Club standard allows for a larger dog than European clubs.

The Longhair Dachshund's coat is easy to look after.

SHOW REQUIREMENTS
The following applies to the Longhair.
General Appearance—Form, color, size and character are similar in all respects to those of the Smooth-hair Dachshund, except for the long, soft hair. Form is compact, short legged and long. Sinewy and muscular. Bold head carriage and intelligent expression. Body not too plump or too slender. Height at shoulder should be half the length of the body measured from the breast bone to the tail. Girth of the chest double the height at the shoulder. Length from the tip of the nose to the eyes equal to the length from the eyes to the base of the skull. Tail should not touch the ground when at rest. The ears should not extend beyond the nose when pulled to the front.
Color—Black and tan, dark brown with lighter shadings, dark red, light red, dappled, tiger-marked or brindle. In black and tan, red and dappled dogs, the nose and nails are black. In chocolate ones, it is often brown.
Head And Skull—Long and conical when seen from above. In profile, sharp and finely modeled. Skull not too broad or too narrow, only slightly arched. No prominent stop. Foreface long and narrow, finely modeled. Lips tightly drawn, covering the lower jaw. Lips not heavy or sharply cut away. Corners of the mouth slightly marked.
Tail—Set in a continuation of the spine, not too long. Tapering, without a marked curve. Not carried high. Fully feathered.
Feet—Broad and large, straight or turned slightly outward. Hind feet smaller and narrower than forefeet. Toes close together, with a distinct arch to each toe. Nails strong. The dog must stand equally on all parts of the foot.
Teeth—Powerful canine teeth fit closely together in a scissors bite.

A Smooth Dachshund, carrying its head erect.

The following applies to the Smooth-hair.
General Appearance—Long and low, with a compact, muscular body. Not crippled, cloddy or clumsy. Bold head carriage and an intelligent expression.
Color—Any color except white. A white spot on the breast is permitted. Nose and nails are black. In red dogs, a red nose is permissible but not desirable. In chocolate and dapple dogs, the nose may be brown or flesh-color. In dapples, large spots of color are undesirable. The dog should be evenly dappled all over.

Head And Skull—Long and conical when seen from above. From a side view, tapering to the point of the muzzle.
Tail—Set in a continuation of the spine. Strong and tapering, but not too long, curved or carried too high.
Feet—Front feet full, broad, close knit and straight or turned slightly outward. Hind feet are smaller and narrower.

The Wirehair Dachshund has a distinctive beard.

The following applies to the Wirehair.
General Appearance—Low to the ground and short legged. Body long, but compact and muscular. Head carried boldly, with an intelligent expression. Not awkward, cramped, crippled or lacking in substance.
Color—All colors are allowed. A white patch on the chest, though not a fault, is not desirable. Nose is black, except in chocolates, when it may be brown or flesh-color.
Head And Skull—Looked at from above or the side, the head should taper uniformly to the tip of the nose and be clean cut. Skull is only slightly arched. Not too broad or too narrow. It slopes gradually, without marked stop, to a finely formed, slightly arched muzzle. Nasal bones and cartilage long and narrow. Ridges of the frontal bones developed, giving prominence to the nerve bosses over the eyes. Jaw has strong bones, is long and opens wide. Not too square.
Tail—Continues line of the spine, slightly curved. Must not be carried up or reach the ground when at rest.
Feet—Front feet are full, broad in front, straight or turned a bit outward. Toes are compact, arched and have tough pads. The dewclaw is left alone. Nails are strong and short. The dog must stand true and equally on all parts of the foot. Hind feet smaller and narrower than forefeet. They are placed straight, with no dewclaw.

A sporting dog, the Smooth Dachshund is versatile. It is adaptable as a pet. The smooth, close coat is not affected by rain or mud. The breed's temperament and intelligence make it an ideal companion for city or country. It loves exercise.

Smooth Dachshund

Wirehair Dachshund

The Longhair Dachshund's thick, soft hair protects it against thorns, enables it to endure cold and heat, and is rainproof. The breed is suited to water work.

Longhair Dachshund

WIREHAIRED FOX TERRIER

Advantages
- **Excellent companion**
- **Good with children**
- **Intelligent**
- **Good rat catcher**
- **Easy to train**

Disadvantages
- **Needs plenty of exercise**
- **Defends itself if provoked**

When groomed, the Wirehaired Fox Terrier is beautiful. It is intelligent, cheerful and easy to train. It makes a good children's pet with lots of energy. It is more common today than the smooth variety.

SIZE
Height—Male: 15-1/2 in (39cm) at the withers
Female: 12 in (30cm)
Weight—Male: 18 lbs (8.2kg)
Female: 16 lbs (7.2kg)
A margin of 1 lb (0.45kg) either way is allowed.

EXERCISE
The Wirehaired Fox Terrier enjoys hunting. It will sniff out rodents and is not afraid to fight, despite its usual good nature. It is happiest in the country.

GROOMING
Daily brushing will usually suffice. Stripping is required in spring, summer and autumn. Do it more frequently if you show the dog. Chalking is usual for a show. Watch the coat carefully because terriers are susceptible to eczema.

FEEDING
For daily feeding, 1-1/2 cups of balanced dry dog food is recommended. Some dogs may prefer 1/2 cup water mixed with each cup of dog food. Add canned dog food for flavor.

ORIGIN AND HISTORY
The Wirehaired Fox Terrier is a separate breed from the Smoothcoated Fox Terrier. The breeds have the same conformation. The Wirehaired probably came from terriers in the British coal mining areas of Durham, Wales and Derbyshire. It existed there before gaining attention. It did not appear in the show ring until 1872. For a number of years it was less popular than the smooth variety, but now the position has been reversed.

SHOW REQUIREMENTS
General Appearance—Balanced. Skull and foreface, head and back are symmetrical. Height at the withers and the length of the body from shoulder-point to buttock also symmetrical. Ideal proportion is reached when the last two measurements are the same.
Color—Predominately white. Brindle, red, liver or slate-blue objectionable. Otherwise, color is not important.
Head And Skull—Top of the skull almost flat, sloping slightly. Gradually decreases in width toward the eyes. Little difference in length between skull and foreface in a well-balanced head. If foreface is noticeably shorter, it is a fault. Nose black.
Tail—Set high and carried up but not curled. Strong and fair length. A three-quarters dock is correct. It allows a safe grip when handling a working terrier. A short tail is not suitable for work or show.
Feet—Round, compact and small. Pads tough and cushioned. Toes moderately arched and straight. A dog with well-shaped forelegs and feet will wear its nails down through contact with the ground. Body weight distributed between toepads and heels.
Teeth—Even or scissors bite. Overshot or undershot is disqualifying.

SMOOTHCOATED FOX TERRIER

Advantages
- **Alert**
- **Intelligent family pet**
- **Good rat catcher**

Disadvantages
- **Needs plenty of exercise**

Terrier comes from the Latin word *terra* meaning earth. The job of a terrier was to kill vermin and scare a fox from its lair. The Smoothcoated Fox Terrier may be the smartest terrier bred for this purpose. It is popular in the show ring. Its elegance perhaps was attained at the expense of its hunting ability. It is an ideal pet.

SIZE
Height—No requirement
Weight—Male: 16 to 18 lbs (7.3 to 8.2kg)
Female: 15 to 17 lbs (6.8 to 7.7kg)

EXERCISE
The terrier, called the *little athlete of the dog world,* needs plenty of exercise. It adjusts to regular walks on a leash, but it needs frequent runs.

GROOMING
Brush the dog daily with a stiff-bristle brush. Trimming is required a few weeks before a show. Give attention to the inside and outside of ears, jaw and muzzle. A chalk block is often used to make the coat snowy white.

FEEDING
For daily feeding, 1-1/2 cups of balanced dry dog food is recommended. Some dogs may prefer 1/2 cup water mixed with each cup of dog food. Add canned dog food for flavor.

ORIGIN AND HISTORY
Smoothcoated Fox Terriers have existed for about 100 years. Before then, nearly all terriers that hunted were known as fox terriers. Its ancestors probably were the Beagle and other terriers. In 1862, the breed made its debut in the show ring at the Birmingham, England National Dog Show.

SHOW REQUIREMENTS
General Appearance—Lively and active. Strength is essential. Not cloddy or coarse. Speed and endurance considered, as well as power. Not too long or too short in the leg.
Color—Predominately white. Brindle, red or liver markings objectionable. Otherwise, color is unimportant.
Head And Skull—Skull flat and moderately narrow. Gradually decreases in width toward the eyes. Stop not apparent. Dip in the profile between the forehead and top jaw. Muzzle gradually tapers to a black nose.
Tail—Set high and carried up, not over the back or curled. Strong.
Feet—Round, compact and not large. Soles hard and tough. Toes moderately arched and straight.
Teeth—Even or scissors bite. Severe overshot or undershot is disqualifying.

JACK RUSSELL TERRIER

Advantages
- **Affectionate**
- **Sporting companion**

Disadvantages
- **Excitable in a pack**
- **Not a pedigree breed**

The Jack Russell Terrier has become popular in recent years. It is not registered with the American Kennel Club, but there is a growing interest in the dog.

In the United Kingdom, fanciers are working to standardize the breed. The British Kennel Club will not accept it as long as there is extensive variation in color, size and form.

SIZE
The Jack Russell Terrier Club of the United Kingdom has drawn up a provisional breed standard for a uniform type of terrier for two different heights.

Height—at the shoulder
Variety #1 11 to 15 in (28 to 38cm)
Variety #2 Under 11 in (28cm)
Weight—No requirement

EXERCISE
The Jack Russell Terrier adapts to city life if you give it regular walks. It is most suited to the country, where it can chase animals and run.

GROOMING
Brush it daily with a stiff-bristle brush.

FEEDING
Same as for Wirehaired Fox Terrier. Increase the amount if the dog is active.

ORIGIN AND HISTORY
The Rev. Jack Russell was a minister in Devonshire, England. He bred a strain of Wirehaired Fox Terriers to hunt with his hounds and chase fox. The dogs were hunt terriers. Russell not only bred his unique hunt terriers but also judged terriers at West Country shows. He was one of the earliest members of the British Kennel Club.

SHOW REQUIREMENTS
The following is from the Jack Russell Terrier Club.
Color—Basically white with black, tan or traditional hound markings.
Coat—Smooth but woolly.
Head And Skull—Strong-boned with powerful jaws, level bite and strong cheek muscles. Eyes almond shape. Small V-shape, dropped ears carried close to the head. Back straight with a high-set tail. Hindquarters strong and angular.

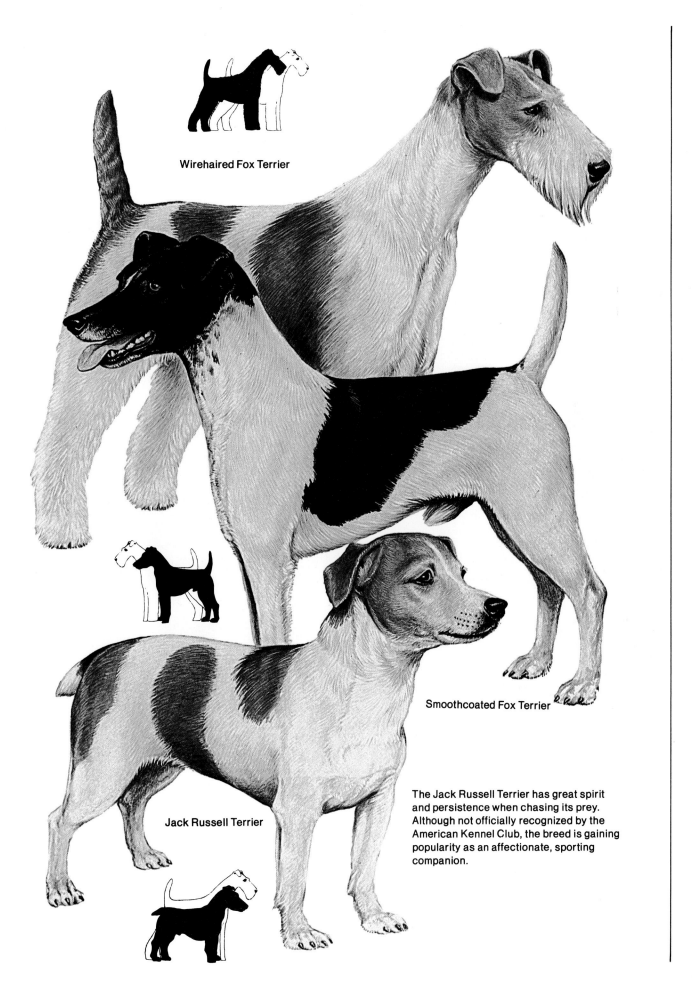

Wirehaired Fox Terrier

Smoothcoated Fox Terrier

Jack Russell Terrier

The Jack Russell Terrier has great spirit and persistence when chasing its prey. Although not officially recognized by the American Kennel Club, the breed is gaining popularity as an affectionate, sporting companion.

DANDIE DINMONT TERRIER

Advantages
- *Courageous*
- *Intelligent*
- *Good sense of humor*
- *Excellent watchdog*

Disadvantages
- *A one-person dog*
- *Do not kennel*

Although once popular as a badger and fox hunter, the Dandie Dinmont is now kept as a pet. It likes living indoors better than living in kennels. It is suspicious of strangers, giving its devotion to one owner. An excellent guard dog, it has a loud bark.

SIZE
Height—8 to 11 in (20 to 28cm) at the top of the shoulder
Length from top of shoulder to root of tail should be no more than twice the dog's height, but preferably 1 to 2 inches (2.5 to 5cm) less.
Weight—18 to 24 lbs (8.2 to 11kg)

EXERCISE
This is an adaptable dog. It is happy whether put to work on the farm or kept as a city pet. Do not keep this active dog in a home without a yard.

GROOMING
Grooming is not difficult. Use a stiff-bristle brush and comb. Remove old hair with your fingers, allowing the undercoat to come through. Do not use a trimming knife because it will ruin the coat. Daily brushing will keep it immaculate.

FEEDING
For daily feeding, 1-1/2 cups of balanced dry dog food is recommended. Some dogs may prefer 1/2 cup water mixed with each cup of dog food. Add canned dog food for flavor.

ORIGIN AND HISTORY
Most Dandie Dinmonts can be traced back to the late 1700s. James Davidson was renowned for his pepper and mustard terriers, named because of their color. It was from Davidson that Sir Walter Scott acquired his dogs. The breed received its name from a character in Scott's novel *Guy Mannering*.

SHOW REQUIREMENTS
Color—Pepper or mustard. Peppers range from a dark blue-black to a light silver-gray. Intermediate shades are preferred. Body color extends down the shoulder and hips, gradually merging into the leg color. Mustards vary from red-brown to pale fawn. Head is creamy white, legs and feet a shade darker than the head. Claws are dark, as in other colors. Nearly all have some white on the chest. Some have white claws. White feet are objectionable.
Head And Skull—Head strong and large, but not out of proportion. Muscles show development, especially the macillary. Skull broad between the ears, narrowing gradually toward the eye. It measures the same from the inner corner of the eye to the back of the skull as it does from ear to ear. Forehead domed. Head covered with soft silky hair, not confined to a topknot. The lighter in color and the silkier, the better. Nose black.
Tail—Short, about 8 to 10 inches (20 to 25cm). Covered on the upper side with wiry hair, darker in color than the body. Hair on the underside is lighter in color and not as wiry. A feather about 2 inches (5cm) long gets shorter near the tip.
Feet—Flat feet are objectionable. Whole claws should be dark. Claws vary in shade according to the color of the dog's body. Feet of a pepper dog should be tan, varying from a rich tan to a pale fawn. Those of a mustard dog are a darker shade than the head. Hind feet smaller than forefeet.
Teeth—Large, strong, meeting in a tight scissors bite.

SKYE TERRIER

Advantages
- *Pleasant disposition*
- *Patient*

Disadvantages
- *Needs grooming*
- *Does not like strangers*

The Skye Terrier originated on the Isle of Skye in the Hebrides. It can be a relentless fighter. It is a valiant hunter, bred to hunt fox, otter and badger. A Skye Terrier is not vicious, but tends to trust and give devotion to its owner with little time for strangers. Take considerable care grooming this breed.

SIZE
Height—Male: 10 in (25cm)
Female: Slightly smaller
Total length 41-1/2 in (105cm)
Weight—Male: 25 lbs (11.3kg)
Female: Slightly smaller

EXERCISE
This dog is tireless and enjoys long walks and playing outdoors.

GROOMING
Brush the dog daily and comb it once a week with a widetooth comb. The coat does not reach full beauty until the third year.

FEEDING
For daily feeding, 3 cups of balanced dry dog food is recommended. Some dogs may prefer 1/2 cup water mixed with each cup of dog food. Add canned dog food for flavor.

ORIGIN AND HISTORY
The Skye Terrier is known all over the world from the tale of Greyfriar's Bobby. His statue stands near Greyfriars Church in Edinburgh, Scotland. Following his master's death, each day for 14 years Bobby visited the cafe he had gone to with his master. There he was given a bun. Then he retraced his steps to his master's grave. He spent each day this way until his own death from old age. A statue was erected in his memory.

Although the Cairn and other breeds existed in the Highlands, the Skye owes its appearance to none of these breeds. The Skye evolved from the small terriers kept in Scotland that were used to hunt foxes, badgers and other small animals. Highland terriers in early days were not separate breeds.

SHOW REQUIREMENTS
General Appearance—Elegant, with style and dignity. Agile and strong with sturdy bones and hard muscles. Twice as long as high. Covered with a heavy coat falling straight on either side of its body.
Color—Dark or light gray, fawn, cream or black, with black points. Any self color allowed if shading of the same color and lighter undercoat are present. Ears black. A small white spot on the chest is allowed.
Head And Skull—Head long, with powerful jaws. Nose black.
Tail—When hanging, upper part pendulous and lower half thrown back in a curve. When raised, follows the incline of the back, not rising or curling up.
Feet—Large and pointing forward.
Teeth—Level or scissors bite.

GLEN OF IMAAL TERRIER

Advantages
- *Affectionate*
- *Courageous*
- *Excellent with children*
- *Good working dog*
- *Loyal*
- *Playful*

Disadvantages
- *Not a show dog*

The Glen of Imaal Terrier originated in Ireland. It is still used as a working terrier to hunt fox and badger.

SIZE
Height—14 in (35.5cm)
Weight—Male: up to 35 lbs (15.9kg)
Female: Slightly smaller

EXERCISE
The dog is happiest when able to run in open spaces. The Glen of Imaal Terrier is an adaptable dog that enjoys household life if it has a yard to play in. Give it regular walks.

GROOMING
A daily brushing is necessary.

FEEDING
Same as Skye Terrier.

ORIGIN AND HISTORY
The Glen of Imaal Terrier is an Irish working terrier. It is still popular in Ireland. Although its fame has spread outside Ireland, it is not often seen in the show ring. It is recognized by the British Kennel Club and the Federation Cynologique Internationale, but not by the American Kennel Club.

SHOW REQUIREMENTS
This standard is taken from the Federation Cynologique Internationale.
General Appearance—Long-coated, strong, active, agile and low to the ground. Movement free, not hackney, covering the ground effortlessly.
Color—Blue-brindle or wheat but not toning to black.
Head And Skull—Head wide and of fair length, with a foreface of power bearing to the nose. Not bottle-headed. A pronounced stop.
Tail—Strong at the root and carried up.
Feet—Compact, with strong, rounded pads.

CESKY TERRIER

The Cesky Terrier, also known as the Bohemian Terrier, comes from Czechoslovakia. It is not widely known, but it is a short-legged dog that is hardy, healthy and adaptable. It make an excellent pet.

SIZE
Height—Male: 11 to 14 in (28 to 35.5cm)
Female: Slightly smaller
Weight—No requirement

FEEDING
For daily feeding, 1-1/2 cups of balanced dry dog food is recommended. Some dogs may prefer 1/2 cup water mixed with each cup of dog food. Add canned dog food for flavor.

COLOR
The Cesky comes in two colors, blue-gray and light coffee-brown.

The coat of the Dandie Dinmont Terrier should be a mixture of hard and soft hair, which gives it a crisp feel. Hair on the under part of the body is lighter in color and softer in texture.

Cesky Terrier

Dandie Dinmont Terrier

Glen of Imaal Terriers meeting the high standard of gameness set by the Breed Club receive an award known as *Teastors Misneac.*

Glen of Imaal Terrier

Skye Terrier

FRENCH BULLDOG

Advantages
- **Affectionate and devoted**
- **Loves human company**

Disadvantages
- **Lubricate facial crease**

The French Bulldog is an ideal family pet. It has a clownish sense of humor, is intelligent and adapts to city or country living. It may be the healthiest of the Bulldogs because it does not suffer from the nasal difficulties of the Boston Terrier and English Bulldog.

SIZE
Height—No requirement
Weight—*Heavyweights*
    Male: 28 lbs (12.7kg)
    Female: 24 lbs (10.9kg)
    Lightweights
    Under 22 pounds
Soundness must not be sacrificed for smallness.

EXERCISE
Give this dog short, regular walks and runs.

GROOMING
Normal daily brushing will keep the coat in condition. Lubricate facial crease with petroleum jelly.

FEEDING
For daily feeding, 3 cups of balanced dry dog food is recommended. Some dogs may prefer 1/2 cup water mixed with each cup of dog food. Add canned dog food for flavor.

ORIGIN AND HISTORY
This animal is the descendant of small Bulldogs. The French developed this breed. It is uncertain whether it comes from English Bulldogs taken to France by Nottingham laceworkers in the 19th century or from crossings with dogs imported to France from Spain. By the beginning of this century it had become popular in the United States.

SHOW REQUIREMENTS
General Appearance—Sound, active and intelligent, with a compact, medium or small build. Short, smooth coat. Various points evenly balanced so the dog does not look out of proportion.
Color—Brindle, pied or fawn. Brindle is a mixture of black and colors. May contain white if brindle predominates. The pied is predominately white over brindle. White dogs are classified with pieds, but eyelashes and eyerims are black. A fawn dog may contain brindle hairs but must have black eyerims and eyelashes.

French Bulldogs love people and have a sense of fun.

Head And Skull—Head massive, square and broad. Skull nearly flat between the ears, with a domed forehead. Loose skin forms symmetrical wrinkles. Muzzle broad, deep and laid back with the muscles of the cheek well-developed. Nose and lips black. Stop well-defined. Lower jaw deep, square, broad, slightly undershot and turned up. Nose short, black and wide. Nostrils open and the line between them defined. The upper lip covers the lower lip on each side with plenty of cushion. Does not hang below the level of the lower jaw.
Tail—Short and set low. Thick at the root, tapering quickly to the tip. Straight or kinked, but not curling over the back. Not carried up.
Feet—Moderate size and compact. Placed in continuation of the line of the leg, with sound pasterns. Hind feet are longer than forefeet. Toes compact. Knuckles high. Nails short, thick and black.
Teeth—Lips thick. Lower lip meets upper lips in the middle, completely hiding the teeth.

MINIATURE BULL TERRIER

Except for size, the Miniature Bull Terrier is a replica of the Bull Terrier. See page 76. It is more suited to apartment dwelling than the Bull Terrier. Miniatures are not easy to breed and are rare. It is a purebred, currently shown in the Miscellaneous Class at American Kennel Club shows. Headings relating to the Bull Terrier are identical for the Miniature except for the following.

SIZE
Height—Not more than
    14 in (35.5cm)
Weight—Not more than
    than 20 lbs (9kg)

FEEDING
For daily feeding, 1-1/2 cups of balanced dry dog food is recommended. Some dogs may prefer 1/2 cup water mixed with each cup of dog food. Add canned dog food for flavor.

BOSTON TERRIER
Formerly American Bull Terrier

Advantages
- **Affectionate and playful**
- **Easy to look after**
- **Excellent guard**
- **Good with people**
- **Obedient**
- **Rarely sheds**

Disadvantages
- **Sensitive to drafts**
- **Not a good kennel dog**
- **Not easy to breed**
- **Watch for eye trouble**

The Boston Terrier is lively, attractive, intelligent and trainable. This American breed is a delightful companion, always ready for a walk or game. Achieving desired markings can be difficult. Females may require Caesarean sections when giving birth.

SIZE
Height—No requirement
Weight—Not more than
    25 lbs (11.3kg)

EXERCISE
This breed enjoys a walk on a leash if you do not have a yard. It should not be kept outside in a kennel.

GROOMING
Daily brushing is necessary. The coat rarely sheds. Ears are cropped.

FEEDING
For daily feeding, 1-1/2 cups of a balanced dry dog food is recommended. Some dogs may prefer 1/2 cup water mixed with each cup of dog food. Add canned dog food for flavor.

HEALTH CARE
Watch for dust and foreign bodies in the eyes.

ORIGIN AND HISTORY
The Boston Terrier, sometimes called *the American gentleman,* traces its ancestry to 1865. The offspring of a Bulldog-Terrier named Judge were mated with English and Staffordshire Bull Terriers, until today's Bulldog evolved. It was first known as the American Bull Terrier. Because of objections from other Bull Terrier clubs, it was renamed the Boston Terrier, after the city of its origin.

SHOW REQUIREMENTS
General Appearance—Lively and intelligent. Smooth coat. Short head and tail, and compactly built. Well-balanced and medium size. Body short and well-knit. Limbs strong and neatly turned. No feature so prominent the dog appears out of proportion. Determined, strong and active. Carriage easy and graceful. Surefooted and straight gaited. Forelegs and hind legs move ahead with perfect rhythm, each step indicating grace and power.
Color—Brindle with white marking. Brindle shows distinctly. Black and white markings permissible, but brindles with white markings preferred. Brindle coloring evenly distributed over the body. Best markings are white muzzle, even-white blaze over head, collar, breast, part or whole of forelegs and hind legs below hocks.
Head And Skull—Head in proportion to size of dog. Skull square, flat on top and free of wrinkles. Cheeks flat, brow abrupt, stop well-defined. Muzzle short, square, wide, deep and in proportion to the skull. Free of wrinkles. Shorter in length than width and depth. Does not exceed one-third of skull length. Width and depth carried to the end. Muzzle from stop to end of nose on a line parallel to the top of the skull. Nose black, wide with well-defined line between nostrils. Jaws broad and square with chops of good depth but not pendulous. Lips completely cover the teeth when mouth is closed.
Tail—Short, fine and tapering. Straight or screw. Devoid of fringes or coarse hair. Not carried above horizontal.
Feet—Round, small and compact. Not turned in or out. Toes arched.
Teeth—Even or undershot to sufficiently square mouth.

Boston Terrier pups should live indoors out of drafts.

A distinctive feature of the French Bulldog is its bat ears. They should be medium size, wide at the base, round at the top, set high and carried upright and parallel.

French Bulldog

Miniature Bull Terrier

Boston Terriers were first exhibited at the Boston Show in 1878. It was not until 1893 that the Breed Club was officially recognized, after changing its name from the American Bull Terrier Club of Boston to the Boston Terrier Club.

Boston Terrier

MANCHESTER TERRIER

Advantages
- **Clean**
- **Good family dog**
- **Great sporting dog**
- **Long-lived**
- **Suitable for city or country**

Disadvantages
- **Tends to be a one-person dog**

The Manchester Terrier is a small, hardy dog. It makes a great sporting companion. It fits into family life, but tends to attach itself to one person. It is long-lived and seldom ill. It can live indoors or outside in a heated kennel, but is happiest if given a place inside.

SIZE
Height—Male: 16 in (40.5cm)
Female: 15 in (38cm)
Weight—*Toy Variety*
not over
12 lbs (5.4kg)
Standard Variety
12 to 22 lbs
(5.4 to 10kg)

EXERCISE
This dog loves to run outside. It can live in the city if kept in a fenced yard and given regular walks.

GROOMING
Manchesters do not like rain. They should be dried with a towel if they get wet. A daily brushing will keep the coat clean. Its coat condition is an indication of health.

FEEDING
For daily feeding, 1-1/2 cups of balanced dry dog food is recommended. Some dogs may prefer 1/2 cup water mixed with each cup of dog food. Add canned dog food for flavor.

ORIGIN AND HISTORY
The Manchester Terrier can trace its lineage back to the hunting Black and Tan Terrier. The Manchester Terrier was once related to a white English terrier that has disappeared.

The Manchester Terrier has evolved into a reliable pet. It has retained its sporting instincts while fitting happily into a home. It is usually good with children.

At one time, the Manchester Terrier and the Toy Manchester Terrier were shown as Black and Tan Terriers in a certain weight division. There is a Toy variety and a Standard variety. The Toy Manchester Terrier is classified separately in the United Kingdom. See page 16.

Many Manchesters were exported from Great Britain to the United States, Canada and Germany in the 1800s. Some think the Manchester is an ancestor of the Doberman, because of its short, shiny black and tan coat. See Doberman Pinscher, page 128.

SHOW REQUIREMENTS
General Appearance—Compact, with good bone.
Color—Black and mahogany tan distributed on the head. Muzzle tan to the nose. Nose and nasal bone black. Small tan spot on each cheek and above each eye. Underjaw and throat marked with a distinct tan V. Divisions between colors clearly defined.
Head And Skull—Long, narrow, flat skull. Level and wedge shape.
Tail—Short. Set on where the arch of the back ends.
Feet—Small hare feet. Strong, with arched toes.
Ears—Erect or button ears. If cropped, they should have long points and be carried erect.
Teeth—Level or scissors bite.

TIBETAN TERRIER

Advantages
- **Happy disposition**

Disadvantages
- **No drawbacks known**

The Tibetan Terrier is one of three small Tibetan breeds. The others are the Tibetan Spaniel and the Lhasa Apso. There is also a Tibetan Mastiff, which is larger. The Tibetan Terrier resembles a small Old English Sheepdog. It is not a terrier because it has no history of digging or chasing small animals.

SIZE
Height—Male: 14 to 16 in (35.5 to 40.5cm)
at the shoulder
Female: Slightly smaller
Weight—No requirement

EXERCISE
The Tibetan Terrier enjoys running and the freedom of a yard. Otherwise, normal walks suffice.

GROOMING
This dog needs thorough brushing daily.

FEEDING
Same as for Manchester Terrier.

ORIGIN AND HISTORY
Bred in the monasteries of Tibet, the Tibetan Terrier has a history of farm work. Tibetan breeds first reached Europe at the beginning of this century. At that time, both the Lhasa Apso and the Tibetan Terrier were referred to as Lhasa Terriers. Because it was confusing, in 1934 the British Kennel Club formed the Tibetan Breeds Association.

The first officially recorded Tibetan Terriers arrived in the United States in 1956. Tibetan Terriers were recognized by the American Kennel Club and admitted to regular dog show classes in 1973. Since then, the breed has attracted many enthusiasts.

SHOW REQUIREMENTS
General Appearance—Muscular. Medium size. General appearance of a miniature Old English Sheepdog.
Color—White, gold, cream, gray or smoke, black, particolor and tricolor preferred. Any color except chocolate or liver.
Head And Skull—Skull medium length, not broad or coarse. Narrows slightly from ear to eye. Not domed, but not flat between the ears. Nose black.
Tail—Medium length, set on high and carried in a curl over the back. Feathered. There may be a kink near the tip.
Feet—Large and round, with hair between toes and pads.
Teeth—Level preferred, but slight undershot not penalized.

BASENJI
Zande Dog, Belgian Congo Dog, Congo Bush Dog, Bongo Terrier, Congo Terrier or Nyam-Nyam Terrier

Advantages
- **Adaptable to most climates**
- **Has no bark**
- **Clean**
- **Gentle with children**
- **Intelligent**

Disadvantages
- **Does not like rain**
- **Mischievous**
- **Females may come into season only once a year**

Basenji is the translation of an African word meaning *bush thing*. It is an interesting and attractive breed. The Basenji has no bark, but it growls and whines like other breeds. It can express itself with a distinctive chortle or yodel. It has vocal cords, but some think years of training to hunt game silently may account for its quietness.

It is known for its gentle disposition and love of children. It can be aloof with strangers and is mischievous and curious. An appealing feature is its curling tail, high set and lying over to one side of the back. It has a habit of washing with its paw like a cat. Its forehead wrinkles are also appealing.

SIZE
Height—Male: 17 in (43cm)
at the shoulder
Female: 16 in (40.5cm)
An inch (2.5cm) either way should not penalize a balanced dog.
Weight—Male: 24 lbs (10.9kg)
Female: 21 lbs (9.5kg)

EXERCISE
The Basenji is a great hunter, but if not exercised, it puts on weight. It is fast, tireless and enjoys a daily walk or jog. The breed is particularly good with horses.

Do not keep this dog in a kennel. It is suitable for apartment living if it has plenty of exercise.

GROOMING
Regular use of a hound glove is recommended.

FEEDING
For daily feeding, 3 cups of balanced dry dog food is recommended. Some dogs may prefer 1/2 cup water mixed with each cup of dog food. Add canned dog food for flavor. Add green vegetables to the Basenji diet. They like to eat grass and should have access to it.

ORIGIN AND HISTORY
Basenji-type dogs are depicted in carvings in the tombs of pharaohs. It is believed they were brought as precious gifts by travelers from the lower regions of the Nile. The Basenji almost disappeared until the mid-19th century, when it was discovered by explorers in the Congo and Southern Sudan.

The foundation stock recognized today came from the Belgian Congo, with other imports from Sudan and Liberia. Similar dogs are found in the Malayan jungle and north of Katmandu. These do not appear to have been taken from their homeland.

In 1942, the Basenji Club of America was formed. In 1943, the American Kennel Club accepted the breed for registration in its stud book.

SHOW REQUIREMENTS
General Appearance—Lightly built, finely boned and aristocratic. Long legs compared with its length. Always poised, alert and intelligent.
Color—Pure red, black or black and tan. All with white feet, chest and tail tip.
Head And Skull—Skull flat, chiseled and medium width. Tapers toward the nose with only a slight stop. Black nose is desirable.
Tail—High set with the posterior curve of the buttock extending beyond the root.
Feet—Small, narrow and compact, with deep pads. Arched toes.
Teeth—Level, with a scissors bite.

Tibetan Terrier

Manchester Terrier

Basenji

Successful breeding of
imported Basenjis began in the
United States in 1941. The
breed first appeared as the
Congo Terrier or Bush Dog.

WEST HIGHLAND WHITE TERRIER

Advantages
- *Easy to train*
- *Friendly with other dogs*
- *Good with children*
- *Suitable for city or country*

Disadvantages
- *No drawbacks known*

The West Highland White Terrier is a sturdy dog originating in Scotland. In recent years it has gained popularity because of its attractive appearance and sporting instincts. It gets along with children and other dogs, making it an ideal family pet.

SIZE
Height—11 in (28cm)
 at the withers
Weight—No requirement

EXERCISE
The Westie adapts to town or country. It will live indoors or in a kennel, but will be happiest as a family pet living in the house. It was originally used as a working terrier and needs exercise. This breed enjoys energetic game playing.

GROOMING
The Westie is an ideal choice for someone who wants a healthy, active dog. It may not be the ideal dog for a show aspirant who does not want to spend time grooming. Brush and comb the Westie's coat daily. Surplus hair must be stripped twice a year. Straggly hairs should be removed from ears and tail. The Westie's coat should be about 2 inches (5cm) long, with neck and throat hair shorter. Ask the breeder to demonstrate grooming before you make your purchase. Ask for a grooming chart with full instructions or go to a dog grooming shop.

FEEDING
For daily feeding, 3 cups of balanced dry dog food is recommended. Some dogs may prefer 1/2 cup water mixed with each cup of dog food. Add canned dog food for flavor.

ORIGIN AND HISTORY
The first West Highland White Terrier club was formed in 1905. Breeds such as the Cairn Terrier and Skye Terrier, which had been classified as Small Highland Working Terriers, attained individual status.

In the late 1800s, there was a white Scottish Terrier strain bred by Col. Malcolm of Poltalloch. From this the name Poltalloch Terrier was derived. They were also known as Roseneath Terriers.

SHOW REQUIREMENTS
General Appearance—Small and hardy. Strongly built, deep in chest and back ribs. A level back and powerful quarters on muscular legs.
Color—Pure white.
Head And Skull—Skull slightly domed. When gripped across the forehead it should present a smooth contour. Only a slight tapering from the skull at the level of the ears to the eyes. The distance from the occiput to the eyes should be slightly greater than the length of the foreface. Jaws strong and level. Nose black and large, forming a smooth contour with the muzzle.
Tail—About 5 to 6 inches (12.5 to 15cm) long, covered with hard hair, not feathers. As straight as possible. Carried jauntily, not over the back. Long tail objectionable, but must not be docked.
Feet—Forefeet larger than hind feet. Round, proportionate, strong, thickly padded and covered with short, hard hair. Hind feet are smaller and thickly padded.
Teeth—Tight scissors bite.

SCOTTISH TERRIER

Advantages
- *Even-tempered*
- *Fine guard dog*
- *Loyal*
- *Home-loving*

Disadvantages
- *Not friendly with strangers*

The Scottish Terrier is a devoted companion, but has little time for strangers. It is not the most suitable dog for a family with children. It will fight small animals and enjoys an energetic ball game. It is an attractive, sporty animal.

SIZE
Height—10 to 11 in
 (25 to 28cm)
Weight—19 to 23 lbs
 (8.6 to 10.4kg)

EXERCISE
The Scottie loves to be outdoors, so do not deprive it of playing in the yard. Give it regular walks several times a day. It can live happily indoors or in an outside kennel that is heated in winter.

GROOMING
The Scottie needs daily brushing and combing, particularly its fine beard. This should be trimmed in spring and autumn.

FEEDING
For daily feeding, 3 cups of balanced dry dog food is recommended. Some dogs may prefer 1/2 cup water mixed with each cup of dog food. Add canned dog food for flavor.

ORIGIN AND HISTORY
The Scottish Terrier was once known as the Aberdeen Terrier. Today, it is generally known as the Scottie. It has existed in various forms for many centuries. The first Scottish Terrier Club was formed in Scotland in 1882, when a standard was established for the breed. It has changed little since then.

SHOW REQUIREMENTS
General Appearance—Sturdy, thickset and short-legged. Able to go to ground. Alert in carriage, suggesting great power and activity in a small compass.
Color—Black, wheat or brindle of any color. White markings objectionable, permitted only slightly on chest.
Head And Skull—Head long, without being out of proportion to the size of the dog. Length of skull enables it to be wide, yet retain a narrow appearance.
Tail—Moderate length to give general balance to the dog. Thick at the root and tapering toward the tip. Set on with an upright carriage or slight bend.
Feet—Large and padded. Toes arched and close knit.
Teeth—Scissors or level bite.

SEALYHAM TERRIER

Advantages
- *Devoted*
- *Good with children*
- *Sporting*

Disadvantages
- *Enjoys a fight*
- *Needs lots of grooming*
- *Obstinate*

The Sealyham was bred as a rat and badger hunter, but has evolved into a pet and show dog. If you want to show the dog, you must devote time to its coat. It is a lovable dog, devoted to its owners. It can be obstinate and snappy if not disciplined when young.

SIZE
Height—Not to exceed 12 in
 (30cm) at the shoulder
Weight—Male: 20 lbs (9kg)
 Female: 18 lbs (8.2kg)

EXERCISE
This dog will happily adapt to walks in the park and fenced runs.

GROOMING
Strip the dog twice a year. Daily combing with a wire comb to remove surplus hair is necessary. Stripping by an inexperienced person can be disastrous for the owner and dog. Have the job done professionally or ask an expert to show you how. Clipping is allowed for an older dog, but will ruin its coat for showing.

FEEDING
For daily feeding, 1-1/2 cups of balanced dry dog food is recommended. Some dogs may prefer 1/2 cup water mixed with each cup of dog food. Add canned dog food for flavor.

ORIGIN AND HISTORY
The Sealyham takes its name from Sealyham, Wales, where the breed was created in the mid-1800s. Its ancestors were other terriers with proven hunting ability. Some say the Sealyham owes its existence to a terrier imported to Wales from Belgium in the 15th century. The first Sealyham Terrier Club was formed in 1908 by Fred Lewis. Lewis improved the strain. The American Kennel Club recognized the breed in 1911.

SHOW REQUIREMENTS
General Appearance—Powerful and determined. Keen, alert and free of clumsiness.
Color—Mostly white, or white with lemon, brown or badger pied markings on head and ears.
Head And Skull—Skull slightly domed. Wide between the ears. Head powerful and long, with a punishing, square jaw. Nose black.
Tail—Docked and carried upright.
Feet—Round and catlike, with thick pads.
Teeth—Sound, strong and white with canines fitting close together.

The West Highland White Terrier's white coat is one of its most striking features. The outer coat consists of hard hair, free from curl. The undercoat, which resembles fur, is short, soft and close. The coat may be whitened with powder for showing.

West Highland White Terrier

Scottish Terrier

The Sealyham Terrier has been a successful show dog around the world. It made its show debut in California in 1911.

Sealyham Terrier

MINIATURE SCHNAUZER

Advantages
- *Intelligent*
- *Obedient*
- *Long-lived*
- *Good with children*

Disadvantages
- *Indoor animal*

The Miniature Schnauzer is an attractive dog with appealing bushy eyebrows. It is good-natured and adores children. Schnauzers are happiest living indoors. It is long-lived, easy to train and does well in obedience competitions.

SIZE
Height—12 to 14 in
　　　　(30 to 36cm)
Weight—No requirement

EXERCISE
The Miniature Schnauzer is a city or country dog. It does not require a lot of space, although it enjoys a yard to run in and likes long walks.

GROOMING
This dog needs to be stripped in spring and summer, more often if it has a show career. Have this done professionally or get instructions from the breeder. Clumsy, inexperienced hands can ruin a good temperament. A weekly brushing is essential to remove dead hair from the undercoat.

FEEDING
For daily feeding, 1-1/2 cups of balanced dry dog food is recommended. Some dogs may prefer food mixed 1 cup of dog food to 1/2 cup water. Add canned dog food for flavor.

ORIGIN AND HISTORY
The Miniature Schnauzer is a smaller replica of the Standard Schnauzer. See page 92. There is a 4 inch (10cm) difference in height between them. Many think the Miniature Schnauzer evolved by crossing the Standard Schnauzer with the Affenpinscher. A Pomeranian or a Fox Terrier may have been used.

This miniature variety was bred in Germany for a century before finding its way to the United States, where it has been bred since 1925. The American Miniature Schnauzer Club has been active since the early 1930s. The breed is still popular today. Its popularity among British fanciers has been slower, but the breed has been awarded Challenge Certificates since 1935.

The Miniature Schnauzer is an appealing, good-natured breed.

SHOW REQUIREMENTS
General Appearance—Powerfully built and muscular. Almost square. The length of its body is equal to its height at the shoulder. It has high spirits, reliability, strength, endurance and vigor. Its expression is keen and its attitude alert. Correct conformation is more important than color.
Color—Pure black or salt-and-pepper colors in even proportions.
Head And Skull—Head strong and elongated. Gradually narrows from ears to eyes, toward the tip of the nose. Upper part of the head moderately broad between the ears, with flat, creaseless forehead. Well-muscled but not too strongly developed cheeks. Medium-stop accentuates prominent eyebrows. Powerful muzzle formed by the upper and lower jaws ends in a moderately blunt line. Bristly, stubby moustache and chin whiskers. Nose ridge straight, running almost parallel to the extension of the forehead. Nose black and full. Lips tight and not overlapping.
Tail—Set on and carried high. Cut to three joints.
Feet—Short, round and compact, with close-arched toes. Deep or thickly padded, pointing forward. Dark nails and hard soles.
Ears—May be cropped or natural.
Teeth—Scissors bite.

LUNDEHUND
Puffin Dog, Puffin Hound

Advantages
- *Alert*
- *Active*
- *Excellent hunter*
- *Faithful companion*

Disadvantages
- *Not common in the United States*

The Lundehund has existed for centuries on two islands off the coast of Northern Norway. Little is known about it outside Scandinavia. For many years it was impossible to export them. The breed is derived from the Miniature Elkhound.

SIZE
Height—Male: 12-1/2 to 14 in
　　　　(31.5 to 35.5cm)
　　　　Female: 12 to 13-1/2 in
　　　　(30 to 34cm)
Weight—13 to 14 lbs
　　　　(5.9 to 6.4kg)

EXERCISE
This dog is a hunter, skillful at scaling rocks and precipices. It is happiest if exercised a lot.

GROOMING
Daily brushing with a stiff-bristle brush should be sufficient.

FEEDING
For daily feeding, 1-1/2 cups of balanced dry dog food is recommended. Some dogs may prefer 1/2 cup water mixed with each cup of dog food. Add canned dog food for flavor.

ORIGIN AND HISTORY
The Lundehund, or Puffin Dog, is a Spitz variety that received recognition in Scandinavia in 1943. Its job is to locate puffins' nests in rocks and crevices, and to retrieve the eggs and birds. Puffin hunting is an art that has existed in Scandinavia for at least 400 years.

This dog has five functional toes on each foot. Most dogs have four. In the upper part of the ears, the cartilage ends meet and can shut when the ears are partly raised. This may prevent water from penetrating and damaging the ear.

SHOW REQUIREMENTS
This breed is not recognized in the United States. It is a small variety of Spitz.
Colors—Black, gray and various shades of brown with white.
Coat—Rough, dense and close to the body.
Tail—Set on high. Has a short dense coat, but no flag.

SCHIPPERKE

Advantages
- *Affectionate*
- *Excellent guard*
- *Good with children*
- *Hardy*

Disadvantages
- *Indoor dog*
- *Needs affection*
- *Needs attention*

The Schipperke originated in Belgium. Its job was to guard canal barges when they tied up for the night. The name Schipperke is Flemish for *little captain.*

Besides being an excellent guard dog, the Schipperke is an affectionate animal. It is good with children, hardy and long-lived. It needs individual attention and likes to be treated as a member of the family. It takes time to accept strangers.

SIZE
Height—No requirement
Weight—12 to 16 lbs
　　　　(5.4 to 7.3kg)

EXERCISE
This dog can walk up to 6 miles or more without any sign of fatigue. It can manage with less exercise if its owner lives in a city.

GROOMING
The Schipperke has a dense, hard coat that needs little regular grooming.

FEEDING
For daily feeding, 1-1/2 cups of balanced dry dog food is recommended. Some dogs may prefer food mixed 1 cup of dog food to 1/2 cup water. Add canned dog food for flavor.

ORIGIN AND HISTORY
This dog originated in Belgium, but is often thought to be a Dutch dog. The breed is over 100 years old. Some claim it is nearer 200 years old, but there are no records to support this theory.

Evolution of the breed is subject to conjecture. Some classify it as a member of the Spitz family, others as the result of a cross between a Terrier and Pomeranian. The Schipperke and the Groenendael probably have a common ancestor. The Schipperke closely resembles a small Groenendael.

SHOW REQUIREMENTS
General Appearance—Small and cobby, with a sharp expression. Lively, giving the appearance of being on the alert. Muscular, developed thighs. Well-rounded, tailless rump. Legs strong and muscular, hocks let down.
Color—Black is the only permissible color.
Head And Skull—Foxlike head. Skull not round, but broad, flat and with little stop. Muzzle moderately long, fine but not weak. Filled out under the eyes. Nose black and small.
Feet—Small and catlike. Stands on its toes.
Teeth—Even or scissors bite. Overshot or undershot disqualified.

The Miniature Schnauzer's coat should be hard, wiry and short. It must be clean on the neck, shoulders, ears and skull, with plenty of hard hair on the front legs.

Lundehund or Puffin Dog

Miniature Schnauzer

Schipperke

The Schipperke's coat should be dense and rough. It must be smooth on the head, ears and legs, lying close on the back and sides. It should be erect and thick around the neck, forming a mane and frill. There should be a good culotte on the back of the thighs.

AMERICAN COCKER SPANIEL

Advantages
- **Suitable for city or country**
- **Excellent family pet**
- **Intelligent**
- **Obedient**

Disadvantages
- **Needs grooming**

The American Cocker Spaniel is an excellent hunter. It excels in flushing and retrieving birds. It is also popular as a pet. Cocker Spaniels are attractive, affectionate, adaptable and make excellent companions.

SIZE
Height—Male: 15 in (38cm) at the withers
Female: 14 in (35.5cm)
Height may vary 1/2 inch (1.25cm) above or below this height without penalty.
Weight—No requirement

EXERCISE
The Cocker Spaniel was originally bred for hunting. Although it adapts happily to the role of companion and family pet, it will enjoy two walks a day. It should have a yard to play in.

GROOMING
The American Cocker Spaniel has a luxurious coat that needs daily brushing and combing. Give it a bath and trim every 8 to 10 weeks. Ask the breeder for advice or visit a professional dog groomer. Trim skull and muzzle hair with electric clippers. The neck and shoulders must be carefully scissored. Leave feathering on the legs, ears and belly. Feet must also be trimmed. You may do this yourself, but learn from an expert first.

FEEDING
For daily feeding, 3 cups of balanced dry dog food is recommended. Some dogs may prefer 1/2 cup water mixed with each cup of dog food. Add canned dog food for flavor.

ORIGIN AND HISTORY
The American Cocker is smaller than the English Cocker. The American Cocker has a thicker coat and has been bred along different lines than the English Cocker. Its elegant trousers and coat length are the easiest means of identification.

An American Cocker was first shown in New Hampshire, in September 1883. Permission was given by the American Kennel Club for the American and English Cocker Spaniel varieties to be shown. The American Cocker Spaniel created much enthusiasm.

SHOW REQUIREMENTS
General Appearance—Refined head. Straight legs. Compact body with wide, muscular hindquarters. Sturdy, with powerful quarters and strong, well-boned legs. Capable of considerable speed and endurance. Free, sound, well-balanced and, keen to work. Even-tempered, with no timidity.
Color—Black. Shadings of brown or liver in the sheen of the coat are not desirable. Black and tan, classified under solid colors, have definite tan markings on a black body. Tan markings are distinct and plainly visible. Tan color may be from the lightest cream to the darkest red. Tan markings restricted to 10% or less of the color of the animal. Tan markings in excess of 10% are disqualified. Tan markings not readily visible in the ring, or the absence of tan markings in any of the specified locations, will be disqualified. In solid colors, a small amount of white on chest and throat is allowed. White in any other location will be penalized. Particolors are two or more definite colors appearing in clearly defined markings. Primary color of 90% or more will be penalized. Secondary color or colors limited to one location will also be penalized. Roans are classified as particolors and may be any of the usual roaning patterns. Tricolors are any of the above colors combined with tan markings. Tan markings should be in the same pattern as for black and tan.
Head And Skull—Square muzzle with a distinct stop midway between the tip of the nose and the occiput. Skull developed and cleanly chiseled. Not too fine or too coarse. Cheek bones not prominent. Nose wide enough to allow for acute scenting power.
Tail—Set on slightly lower than the line of the back. Carried in line with the back, never cocked up. Not docked too long or too short to interfere with its action.
Feet—Compact but large. Round and firm with thick pads.
Teeth—Scissors bite.

ENGLISH COCKER SPANIEL
Merry Cocker

Advantages
- **Affectionate**
- **Excellent hunting dog**
- **Good with children**
- **Long-lived**
- **Gentle**

Disadvantages
- **May have a weight problem**
- **Keep ears out of feed bowl**

The *merry cocker,* as it is called, is an ideal family pet. It is a dog for the children to play with or for hunting. It is manageable, intelligent and an all-purpose gundog.

SIZE
Height—Male: 16 to 17 in (41 to 43cm) at the withers
Female: 15 to 16 in (38 to 41cm)
Weight—28 to 32 lbs (12.7 to 14.5kg)

EXERCISE
This dog needs regular exercise. It loves the country and may not be the ideal choice for city dwellers. It enjoys home comforts.

GROOMING
The Cocker requires daily brushing and combing. Be sure its coat does not become matted. Watch that ears do not flop into the feed bowl.

ORIGIN AND HISTORY
In the United States, this dog is known as the English Cocker. In the United Kingdom, it is known as the Cocker Spaniel. It is also referred to as the merry cocker because of its happy, lively temperament and wagging tail. Other names given it have been the Cocking Spaniel because of its prowess at flushing out woodcock.

The Cocker Spaniel originated in 14th century Spain. The name *spaniel* comes from the word Spain. The breed was used in various countries for falconry. Today it enjoys rabbit hunting and flushing other game. It is also able to retrieve and is an ideal choice for both working trials and dog training competitions.

The English Cocker Spaniel, here with pup, makes a gentle pet.

FEEDING
For daily feeding, 3 cups of balanced dry dog food is recommended. Some dogs may prefer 1/2 cup water mixed with each cup of dog food. Add canned dog food for flavor.

SHOW REQUIREMENTS
General Appearance—Sturdy, well-balanced and compact. It measures about the same from the withers to the ground as from the withers to the root of the tail.
Color—Various colors are permissible, such as self-colors, particolors, black and tan, and roan. In self-colors, a white frill is desirable.
Head And Skull—Square muzzle. A distinct stop occurs midway between the tip of the nose and the occiput. Skull developed and cleanly chiseled. Not too fine or too coarse. Cheek bones not prominent. Nose wide enough to allow for its acute scenting power.
Tail—Set on slightly lower than the line of the back. Carried in line with the back and never cocked up. Tail not docked too long or too short to interfere with action.
Feet—Firm, thickly padded and catlike.

The most noticeable difference between the American and English Cocker Spaniels is size. Bred to flush and retrieve smaller game in America, the American Cocker Spaniel is a smaller breed. Both breeds have achieved great success in the show ring. The American Cocker Spaniel is usually shown with a more profuse coat than the English breed.

American Cocker Spaniel

English Cocker Spaniel

BEAGLE

Advantages
- **Adores children**
- **Good with other pets**
- **Intelligent**
- **Happy and affectionate**

Disadvantages
- **Curious**
- **May gain weight**

The Beagle is a happy, affectionate dog that loves humans and other pets. It adores children and is a wonderful companion. It will guard its home and owner faithfully. It is not a barker. It wanders, so do not leave gates open.

SIZE
There are 2 varieties of Beagle.
Height—
Variety # 1 13 to 15 in (33 to 38cm) at the withers
Variety # 2 13 in (33cm) or under at the withers
Weight—No requirement

EXERCISE
Beagles keep themselves fit as easily in a small yard as on a farm. Take your dog for a walk every day. Because they are healthy, you will rarely need a veterinarian.

GROOMING
Its short coat is tough, weatherproof and needs no grooming. After a muddy walk, leave a Beagle alone for an hour to clean itself up.

These Beagle pups, playing with their master's slipper, may one day be heard in full cry on the scent of a rabbit.

Beagles enjoy daily walks and a chance to explore.

FEEDING
For daily feeding, 3 cups of balanced dry dog food is recommended. Some dogs may prefer 1/2 cup water mixed with each cup of dog food. Add canned dog food for flavor.

ORIGIN AND HISTORY
The Beagle is one of the smallest hounds. It has all their virtues in a small body. An ancient breed, it has proven a joy to sportsmen for hundreds of years. Beagles were first mentioned by name in writing in 1475.

They have hunted in packs after rabbits. They were first used for this purpose. Beagles have hunted many different animals in many climates. They have hunted jackal in the Sudan and Palestine, wild pig in Ceylon and deer in Scandinavia.

They are used as gundogs to seek out and retrieve game and to hunt by scent in competitive Field Trials.

SHOW REQUIREMENTS
General Appearance—Sturdy and compactly built. Quality without coarseness.
Color—Any recognized hound color other than liver.
Head And Skull—Head fair length. Powerful in the male without being coarse. Finer in the female. Free from frown and excessive wrinkle. Skull slightly domed, moderately wide, with indication of a peak. Stop well-defined and dividing length between occiput and top of nose as equally as possible. Muzzle not snipy, lips well-flewed. Nose broad and nostrils expanded. Preferably black, but less pigmentation permissible in lighter-colored hounds.
Tail—Sturdy and moderate length. Set on high and carried up, but not curled over the back or inclined forward from the root. Covered with hair, especially on the underside.
Feet—Tight and firm. Knuckled up and strongly padded. Not harefooted. Nails short.
Teeth—Jaws level.

DREVER

Advantages
- **Even-tempered**
- **Keen sense of smell**
- **Steady worker**

Disadvantages
- **Not common in the United States**

The Drever is little-known outside Scandinavia, where it is one of Sweden's most popular dogs. It is a steady, slow worker and has a good nose for following animals. It will drive them toward the gun. It is also a popular pet. A similar dog, the Strellufsstovare, is bred in Denmark.

SIZE
Height—Male: 12-1/2 to 15 in (31.5 to 38cm)
Female: 11-1/2 to 14 in (29 to 35.5cm)
Weight—No requirement

EXERCISE
This dog needs plenty of exercise. It is happiest when hunting.

GROOMING
Give this dog normal daily brushing.

FEEDING
For daily feeding, 3 cups of balanced dry dog food is recommended. Some dogs may prefer 1/2 cup water mixed with each cup of dog food. Add canned dog food for flavor.

ORIGIN AND HISTORY
The Drever is a product of other Swedish hunting dogs mated with Dachshunds. There is something of the Dachshund and Beagle in its appearance.

At the beginning of the century, the breed was known by the German name of *Dachsbracke*. As it began to change to meet Swedish requirements, the name was changed and recognition sought with the Swedish Kennel Club under the new name of Drever. This was achieved in 1949. Recognition by the Federation Cynologique Internationale followed in 1953. This breed is not recognized by the American Kennel Club. It is a strong, muscular dog, like a Dachshund. Colors are red and white, yellow and white, or tricolor. White must not predominate but must be apparent from all angles.

DACHSBRACKE

Advantages
- **Brave**
- **Dedicated hunter**
- **Even-tempered**

Disadvantages
- **Not common in the United States**

The Dachsbracke is little known outside Germany. It is a close relative of the Swedish Drever. Many refer to the Dachsbracke and Drever as one. There are three varieties: the Westphalian, the Erz Mountains and the Alpine. The Westphalian, the smallest of the three, is almost extinct.

The breed stands between 13-1/2 and 16-1/2 inches (34 and 42cm). It has a short, dense coat and bears a slight resemblance to the Dachshund. A litter was bred in Britain in 1949. The Dachsbracke is not recognized by the American Kennel Club. It gained recognition in Germany in 1896.

The Beagle is known throughout the world for its hunting qualities. Beagles are used for hunting rabbits. Two size varieties are recognized. One must not exceed 13 inches (33cm) at the shoulder. The other must be over 13 inches (33cm) but not exceed 15 inches (38cm).

The patches of white on the Drever's coat help make the dog more visible when it is tracking deer in the thick forests of Sweden.

Beagle

Drever

Dachsbracke

In its native Germany, the Dachsbracke excels at tracking prey by scent in rugged country. Its slow but steady progress is the best method of hunting animals such as deer.

SWEDISH VALLHUND
Vastgotaspets

Advantages
- *Active*
- *Excellent with cattle*
- *Loyal*

Disadvantages
- *Not common in the United States*

The Vallhund is a Swedish breed. It is similar in appearance to the Welsh Corgi. It is an active, intelligent worker and is gaining popularity in many parts of the world.

SIZE
Height—Male: 13 in (33cm)
Female: 12-1/3 in (31.2cm)
Weight—No requirement

EXERCISE
Give this dog plenty of exercise.

GROOMING
Normal daily brushing is all that is necessary.

FEEDING
For daily feeding, 3 cups of balanced dry dog food is recommended. Some dogs may prefer 1/2 cup water mixed with each cup of dog food. Add canned dog food for flavor.

ORIGIN AND HISTORY
The *Vastgotaspets,* its Swedish name, looks like a cross between a Cardigan and a Pembroke Corgi. There is a connection between the Corgi and this breed. It is unknown whether it evolved as the result of Vikings taking Corgis to Sweden or if Swedish dogs brought to Great Britain developed into the Corgi. The Swedes claim credit for this fine cattle dog. It owes its present development and recognition to Swedish breeder Bjorn von Rosen.

The Vallhund closely resembles the Welsh Corgi. It was developed in Sweden as a cattle dog.

PEMBROKE WELSH CORGI

Advantages
- *Devoted companion*
- *Excellent guard*
- *Fond of children*
- *Hardy*
- *Tireless*

Disadvantages
- *Needs training when young*

The Pembroke Welsh Corgi has worked in South Wales for many centuries. It has evolved as a popular, affectionate pet. It is favored by the British royal family.

SIZE
Height—10 to 12 in (25 to 30cm) at the shoulder
Weight—Male: not over 30 lbs (12.5kg)
Female: not over 28 lbs (11.7kg)

EXERCISE
This dog is a worker. It will adapt to life as a pet, if given daily walks. Without enough exercise, this dog can become fat.

GROOMING
Brush daily. The breed has a water-resistant coat.

FEEDING
For daily feeding, 1-1/2 cups of balanced dry dog food is recommended. Some dogs may prefer 1/2 cup water mixed with each cup of dog food. Add canned dog food for flavor.

ORIGIN AND HISTORY
The Pembroke has worked in South Wales since the Domesday Book survey was instigated by William the Conqueror in the 11th century. Its task was to control cattle by nipping at their ankles, then getting quickly out of range. It is bolder than the Cardigan Welsh Corgi.

Some say the Pembroke comes from stock brought to Wales by Flemish weavers who settled in the area. They crossed their dogs with Welsh native stock. Others say the similarities between the Pembroke and the Swedish Vastgotaspets suggest crossbreeding. They think trading between Wales and Sweden introduced the breed to Wales.

SHOW REQUIREMENTS
General Appearance—Low-set, strong, sturdily built. Alert and active, giving an impression of substance and stamina in a small body. Outlook bold, expression intelligent and workmanlike. Movement free and active. Elbows fit closely to the sides, not loose or tied. Forelegs move forward, without too much lift, in unison with the thrusting action of the hind legs.

Pembroke Welsh Corgis make affectionate pets.

Color—Self-colors in red, sable, fawn, black and tan, or with white markings on legs, chest and neck. Some white on head and foreface is permissible.
Head And Skull—Head foxlike in shape and appearance. An alert and intelligent expression. Skull fairly wide and flat between the ears. Moderate amount of stop. Length of foreface in proportion to the skull in a ratio of 3 to 5. Muzzle tapers slightly. Nose black.
Tail—Short, preferably natural. Otherwise docked as short as possible without being indented.
Feet—Oval. Two center toes slightly extended beyond the two outer ones. Pads strong and arched. Nails short.
Teeth—Scissors bite.

CARDIGAN WELSH CORGI

Advantages
- *Devoted companion*
- *Excellent guard*
- *Fond of children*
- *Hardy*
- *Quieter than the Pembroke*
- *Tireless*

Disadvantages
- *Prone to eye defects*

The Cardigan Welsh Corgi has been working in South Wales for centuries. It is hardy, fond of children and tireless. Despite its original task of nipping the heels of cattle to bring them into line, it is more even-tempered than the Pembroke. It is less likely to nip the heels of unsuspecting visitors.

SIZE
Height—12 in (30cm) at the shoulder
Weight—Male: 22 to 26 lbs (10.9 to 11.8kg)
Female: 20 to 24 lbs (9 to 10.9kg)

EXERCISE
Although traditionally a worker, the Cardigan adapts to domestic life. Give it daily walks of average length. Without enough exercise, the dog will get fat.

GROOMING
Daily brushing is needed. The breed has a water-resistant coat.

FEEDING
For daily feeding, 1-1/2 cups of a balanced dry dog food is recommended. Some dogs may prefer 1/2 cup water mixed with each cup of dog food. Add canned dog food for flavor.

HEALTH CARE
Avoid letting your pet jump from heights, especially if overweight. This could lead to painful spine trouble. Many eye defects have been eradicated from the breed, but have your dog checked by a vet before buying.

ORIGIN AND HISTORY
In South Wales, the Cardigan Welsh Corgi has worked for centuries controlling the movement of cattle by nipping at their ankles. It made its first appearance in the British show ring in 1925, and was classified as one breed with the Pembroke Welsh Corgi. It received separate classification in 1934. Welsh folklore contains many references to this dependable breed. It may have missed out on popularity due to the British royal family's particular fondness for its Pembroke cousin.

SHOW REQUIREMENTS
General Appearance—Expression foxlike. Alertness essential. Body measures about 36 inches (91.5cm) from point of nose to tip of tail.
Color—Red, sable, red-brindle, black-brindle, tricolored, black, blue-merle. Usually with white flashings on chest, neck, feet, face or tip of tail. Pure white is a disqualification.
Head And Skull—Head foxlike in shape and appearance. Skull wide and flat between the ears, tapering toward the eyes, above which it is slightly domed. Muzzle should measure about 3 inches (7.5cm) or in a ratio of 3 to 5 in proportion to the skull. Tapers toward the snout. Nose black, except in blue-merles, slightly projecting and not blunt. Moderate-size nostrils. Underjaw clean cut and strong, without prominence.
Tail—Moderately long and set in line with the body, not curled over the back. Resembles a foxtail.
Feet—Round and padded. All dewclaws removed.
Teeth—Scissors bite preferred but level permitted.

An ancient breed, the Swedish Vallhund is an integral part of the agricultural scene in Sweden. It was taken so much for granted at the beginning of this century it almost disappeared as a pure breed. Although it resembles the Pembroke Corgi, this dog has a gray, brown-yellow or brindle coat.

Swedish Vallhund

Pembroke Welsh Corgi

Cardigan Welsh Corgi

Lapphund

Iceland Dog

MEDIUM DOGS

Border Collie

Medium-size dogs are the most popular. They are not as showy as small or large animals. They are more acceptable as part of a household. A family with a medium-size house and yard often choose a dog to conform to its lifestyle. The dog is not too small or too large. It is easy to exercise and not too expensive to feed. The medium-size dog can play with children when fully grown. It can be a companion and a protector.

Dogs of this size are easiest to find and care for. Because people want medium-size puppies, breeders are rarely in short supply. Pet accessories are usually made with the average, or medium-size, pet in mind.

There is a medium-size breed to suit almost everyone. Those who want to enter their pet in obedience competitions can choose a Border Collie. A Whippet will satisfy the buyer who wants an elegant animal that can share sporting interests. There is a type of spaniel suitable for almost any hunter. A Bulldog is a wonderful choice for someone who wants a dog that does not need much exercise. The Beagle or Basset Hound is ideal for someone who wants an amusing, affectionate pet, but who understands the dog may wander off.

BRITTANY SPANIEL

Advantages
- *Affectionate*
- *Excellent pointer*
- *Keen sense of smell*
- *Tireless*
- *Loyal*

Disadvantages
- *Sensitive*
- *Needs kind handling*

The Brittany Spaniel combines the roles of hunter and companion. It has a natural talent for pointing and has been described as more of a setter than a spaniel. It has a keen sense of smell and can cope with difficult terrain. It is a sensitive animal that needs kind handling from its master. It is easily distinguishable by its short, stumpy tail. This breed has been successful in field trials.

SIZE
Height—17-1/2 to 20-1/2 in (45 to 53cm)
Weight—30 to 40 lbs (13.5 to 17kg)

EXERCISE
This dog needs plenty of exercise.

GROOMING
Brush the dog daily. Be careful nothing lodges in ears, eyes or paws.

FEEDING
For daily feeding, 3 cups of balanced dry dog food is recommended. Some dogs may prefer 1/2 cup water mixed with each cup of dog food. Add canned dog food for flavor.

ORIGIN AND HISTORY
The Brittany originated in Spain or the Argoat Forests of Brittany. A red and white English Setter probably mated with a Breton female, which started the development of the Brittany Spaniel. The first Brittany Spaniels were imported to the United States in 1931. They have been exhibited since then.

SHOW REQUIREMENTS
General Appearance—Small and elegant. Vigorous, compact and stocky. Movement is energetic, with an intelligent expression.
Color—Orange and white or liver and white. Tricolors—orange, liver and white—severely penalized. Any black in the coat, or a nose so dark as to appear black, is disqualified.

Head And Skull—Skull average length and round. Hollow stop obvious, lightly falling in or sloping. Forehead shorter than the larger axis of the skull. Forehead straight or slightly curved, in a ratio of 3 to 2 to the skull. Nose a deep shade, according to the color of the dog. Nostrils open. Nose angular. Lips thin and receding. Upper lip slightly overlaps lower.
Tail—Naturally tailless or not over 4 inches (10cm) long. Can be natural or docked. Set on high as an extension of the spine.
Feet—Closed toes, with little hair between them.
Teeth—Scissors bite.

WELSH SPRINGER SPANIEL

Advantages
- *Loyal*
- *Fine gundog*
- *Keen sense of smell*
- *Good water dog*
- *Good pet*

Disadvantages
- *Needs training*

The Welsh Springer Spaniel is a lively dog with enthusiasm and endurance. It needs training when young. In stature, it stands between the Cocker Spaniel and the English Springer. It is a tireless breed and if given exercise and correct feeding, will live a long life.

SIZE
Height—Male: 19 in (48cm) at the shoulder
Female: 18 in (46cm)
Weight—No requirement

EXERCISE
Like most spaniels, the Welsh Springer is a working animal. It is not suited for apartment life or for people who cannot take it for long walks.

GROOMING
Regular brushing and combing are necessary.

FEEDING
For daily feeding, 3 cups of balanced dry dog food is recommended. Some dogs may prefer 1/2 cup water mixed with each cup of dog food. Add canned dog food for flavor.

ORIGIN AND HISTORY
An ancestor of the Welsh Springer Spaniel is mentioned in records of the Laws of Wales, 1300 A.D. Before then, a similiar white spaniel with red markings had been associated with the region. The Welsh Springer Spaniel is similar to the Brittany Spaniel. It makes an excellent gundog and pet.

SHOW REQUIREMENTS
General Appearance—Compact, symmetrical and strong. Happy and active. Not stiff in appearance. Built for endurance and hard work. A quick, active mover, displaying push and drive.
Color—Red and white only.
Head And Skull—Skull proportionate and moderate length. Slightly domed, with a clearly defined stop. Well-chiseled below the eyes. Muzzle medium length, straight and square. Nostrils flesh-color or dark. A short, chubby head is objectionable.
Tail—Set on low. Never carried above the level of the back. Lightly feathered and lively in action.
Feet—Round, with thick pads.
Teeth—Jaw not overshot or undershot.

WETTERHOUN
Dutch Water Spaniel

Advantages
- *Excellent watchdog*
- *Fearless*
- *Hardworking*
- *Intelligent*

Disadvantages
- *Aggressive*
- *Needs firm handling*
- *Not common in the United States*

The Wetterhoun, or Dutch Water Spaniel, was registered in Holland in 1942. It was known for many years before then, but almost exclusively in Holland. It is an intelligent, fearless hunter and often kept as a pet. Its aggressive nature, inherited from years of hunting, makes firm handling and early training necessary.

SIZE
Height—Male: 21-1/2 in (54.5cm) at the withers
Female: Slightly smaller
Weight—No requirement

EXERCISE
This dog needs plenty of exercise.

GROOMING
Regular brushing is necessary.

FEEDING
For daily feeding, 3 cups of balanced dry dog food is recommended. Some dogs may prefer 1/2 cup water mixed with each cup of dog food. Add canned dog food for flavor.

ORIGIN AND HISTORY
Bred from dogs used for otter hunting, the Wetterhoun has evolved as a strong and fearless hunter. It is prized as a guard dog. In the past it was crossed with the Stabyhoun. See page 80. The Wetterhoun is a larger, sturdier dog.

SHOW REQUIREMENTS
General Appearance—Solid build, without being coarse or heavy. Strong and compact. Its skin fits close to the body without forming wrinkles, even at the throat. Lips are not pendulous. It is courageous on the attack.
Color—Black, brown-white and blue-white.
Head And Skull—Lean and strong. Size in proportion to body. Skull and muzzle of equal length. Skull slightly rounded and wider than long. Merges with the cheeks. Nose is large, with open nostrils and no cleft. It is black in black or black-and-white dogs, brown in brown dogs. Blunt muzzle narrows gradually toward the nose without being pointed. The nasal bridge is straight, not arched or hollow. Broad seen from above. Lips are close fitting, not pendulous. Stop is not accentuated. The passage from skull to muzzle is gradual.
Tail—Set on at moderate height, curled in a spiral over the croup. The spiral is the chief ornament and typical of the breed.
Feet—Rounded, with well-developed pads.
Teeth—Strong and meet in a scissors bite.

The Wetterhoun is a popular guard and farm dog in Holland. Its dense curly coat is not affected by bad weather.

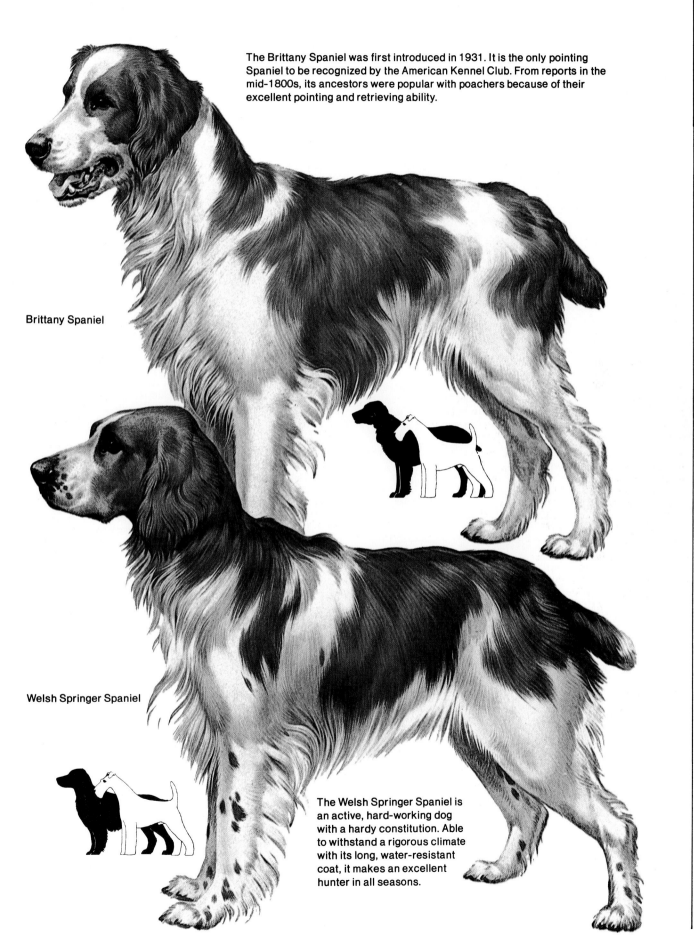

The Brittany Spaniel was first introduced in 1931. It is the only pointing Spaniel to be recognized by the American Kennel Club. From reports in the mid-1800s, its ancestors were popular with poachers because of their excellent pointing and retrieving ability.

Brittany Spaniel

Welsh Springer Spaniel

The Welsh Springer Spaniel is an active, hard-working dog with a hardy constitution. Able to withstand a rigorous climate with its long, water-resistant coat, it makes an excellent hunter in all seasons.

FIELD SPANIEL

Advantages
- *Intelligent*
- *Excellent in the field*
- *Affectionate*
- *Docile*
- *Keen sense of smell*

Disadvantages
- *Not common in the United States*

The Field Spaniel has an origin similar to the Cocker's. In 1892, they were divided into separate breeds. After 1892, the Cocker Spaniel improved dramatically and the Field Spaniel did not. It became long-bodied and short-legged. The Field Spaniel Society was formed in the United Kingdom in 1948 and a standard type has evolved which is breeding true. Although recognized, the dog is little known. The Field Spaniel is a docile animal, excellent in the field and a good pet. It is intelligent and has an even temperament.

SIZE
Height—18 in (46cm) at the shoulder
Weight—35 to 50 lbs (15.9 to 22.7kg)

EXERCISE
A Field Spaniel should not be kept in an apartment. It needs lengthy walks and a yard in which to run.

GROOMING
Daily brushing and combing will suffice. Be sure the coat does not get tangled or matted and nothing lodges between the toes.

FEEDING
For daily feeding, 3 cups of balanced dry dog food is recommended. Some dogs may prefer 1/2 cup water mixed with each cup of dog food. Add canned dog food for flavor.

The Field Spaniel is a willing and tireless worker.

ORIGIN AND HISTORY
The history of the Field Spaniel runs parallel to the Cocker. See page 62. Until the breeds were separated in 1892, they were shown as Field Spaniels under and over 25 pounds (11.3kg). The Field Spaniel is recognized by the American Kennel Club, but there are few registrations.

SHOW REQUIREMENTS
General Appearance—Well-balanced, built for activity and endurance. A combination of beauty and utility. Docile.
Color—Self-colored in black, liver, golden liver, mahogany red, roan or any of these colors with tan over the eyes and on the cheeks, feet and pasterns. Other colors, such as black and white, liver and white, or orange and white are a fault.
Head And Skull—Skull developed, with a distinct occipital protuberance. Not too wide across the muzzle. Muzzle long and lean, not squarely cut, curving gradually from nose to throat. Lean beneath the eyes. Thickness here gives coarseness to the head. The length of the muzzle gives the highest possible scenting powers. Nose developed, with open nostrils.
Tail—Carried low. If possible, carried below the level of the back in a straight line or with a slight downward inclination. Never elevated above the back. In action, always kept low. Fringed with wavy feather of silky texture.
Feet—Not too small. Round with short, soft hair between the toes. Strong pads.

WACHTELHUND
German Spaniel,
German Quail Dog

Advantages
- *Keen sense of smell*
- *Good in water*
- *Fine retriever and gundog*
- *Hardy*

Disadvantages
- *Not common in the United States*

The Wachtelhund is a hardy breed that bears some resemblance to the English Springer Spaniel. It is little known outside Germany, where it has a reputation as a gundog and retriever.

SIZE
Height—15-1/2 to 19-1/2in (39.5 to 49.5cm)
Weight—No requirement

EXERCISE
This dog needs plenty of exercise.

GROOMING
Normal daily brushing is necessary.

FEEDING
For daily feeding, 3 cups of balanced dry dog food is recommended. Some dogs may prefer 1/2 cup water mixed with each cup of dog food. Add canned dog food for flavor.

ORIGIN AND HISTORY
When they bred the Wachtelhund, the Germans wanted to create a breed to cope with water and forest, and to flush and retrieve game. The breed was produced by crossing a number of small dogs. Harrap's *Champion Dogs of the World* credits the German Stober with the Wachtelhund's excellent nose. The now-extinct Stober had tracking ability similar to the Bloodhound's.

The Wachtelhund is usually dark brown. There can be white marks on chest and toes. It can also be white with brown spots, white and brown, or solid white.

SUSSEX SPANIEL

Advantages
- *Loyal*
- *Tireless worker*
- *Intelligent*
- *Alert*

Disadvantages
- *A one-person dog*

The Sussex Spaniel has been known in Southern England for more than a century. It was popular with Sussex farmers, where the name comes from. It was first recognized in 1795, when the breed was larger. Later, the Harvieston appeared with traits of the Bloodhound and the Clumber.

Today the Sussex Spaniel is in danger of becoming extinct.

It is a loyal companion, active, alert and has a good nose. It has a rich liver coat, which loses some of its golden color and darkness if the animal is kept indoors as a pet.

SIZE
Height—15 to 16 in (38 to 40.5cm)
Weight—Male: 45 lbs (20.5kg) Female: 40 lbs (18.1kg)

EXERCISE
The Sussex is a working animal and not suited for apartment life. It is not for those who do not have time to take it for long walks.

GROOMING
Daily brushing and combing is necessary. Be sure the ears do not get tangled and mud does not get caked between paws or in the coat.

FEEDING
For daily feeding, 3 cups of balanced dry dog food is recommended. Some dogs may prefer 1/2 cup water mixed with each cup of dog food. Add canned dog food for flavor.

ORIGIN AND HISTORY
The Sussex is an English breed. It has been shown since 1862, when it was exhibited at Crystal Palace, in London. The breed was bred between World War I and World War II by Fourclovers Kennels. They are given credit for the survival of the breed. In the mid-1950s, the Sussex was crossed with the Clumber, resulting in improved bone size and temperament.

SHOW REQUIREMENTS
General Appearance—Massive and strongly built. Active, energetic and strong. Its characteristic movement is rolling, unlike any other spaniel.
Color—Rich golden liver, hair shading to gold at the tips, with gold predominating. Dark liver or gray-purple is objectionable.
Head And Skull—Skull wide, showing a moderate curve from ear to ear. Not flat or apple-headed. It has a center indentation and a pronounced stop. Brows frowning. Occiput decided, but not pointed. Nostrils developed and liver color. A well-balanced head.
Tail—Set low and carried above the level of the back. Free action. Thickly clothed with hair, but no feather. Docked 5 to 7 inches (12.5 to 18cm).
Feet—Circular, padded and feathered between toes.

The coat of the Field Spaniel should be flat or slightly wavy, silky in texture but dense enough to be weather resistant. It must be glossy. The chest, underbelly and behind the legs should be feathered. Any curl or wiriness is a show fault.

Field Spaniel

Wachtelhund Or German Spaniel

Sussex Spaniel

PORTUGUESE WARREN HOUND
Podengo Portugues

Advantages
- *Three sizes*
- *Good hunter*

Disadvantages
- *Not common in the United States*

In Portugal, the Portuguese Warren Hound is known as the *Podengo*. It is rare outside of Portugal, where it is popular as a companion and hunter of rabbits and deer. It is bred in three sizes—the Podengo Pequeño, which resembles a large Chihuahua; a larger variety, the Medio; and the largest, the Podengo Ibicenco, which resembles the Spanish Ibizan Hound.

SIZE
Height—at the shoulder
Podengo Pequeño 8 to 12 in
(20 to 30cm)
Podengo Medio: 20 to 22 in
(51 to 56cm)
Podengo Grande: 22 to 27 in
(56 to 68.5cm)
Weight—No requirement

EXERCISE
This dog is happiest when given plenty of exercise.

GROOMING
Regular brushing is needed. A velvet pad will improve the coat's appearance.

FEEDING
For daily feeding, 1-1/2 cups of balanced dry dog food is recommended for a small Podengo, 3 cups for a medium Podengo and 5 cups for a large Podengo. Some dogs may prefer 1/2 cup water mixed with each cup of dog food. Add canned dog food for flavor.

ORIGIN AND HISTORY
The Podengo is well-established in Portugal. It is usually fawn color and can have a rough or smooth coat. The small and medium sizes are used for hunting rabbits. The largest dog is used for hunting deer. It has been crossed with gazehounds. The Pequeño is closely allied to the Chihuahua. None of the dogs are currently recognized by the American Kennel Club, the United Kennel Club, the British Kennel Club or the Federation Cynologique Internationale.

The Portuguese Water Dog is an unusual breed, little known outside its native country.

PORTUGUESE WATER DOG
Cao d'Agua

Advantages
- *Excellent retriever*
- *Good swimmer*
- *Good watchdog*
- *Loyal*

Disadvantages
- *Suspicious of strangers*

The Portuguese Water Dog is commonly found in the Algarve area of Portugal. It is a fisherman's dog, acting as a member of the crew and performing many tasks. It guards nets, dives and retrieves. It can catch fish in its jaws and swim back with it to the boat. It is loyal to its master, but not trustworthy with strangers.

SIZE
Height—Male: 20 to 22-1/2 in
(51 to 57cm)
Female: 17 to 20-1/2 in
(43 to 52cm)
Weight—Male: 42 to 55 lbs
(19 to 25kg)
Female: 35 to 48-1/2 lbs
(15.9 to 22kg)

EXERCISE
This dog enjoys an active, outdoor life.

GROOMING
The Portuguese Water Dog has two coat types. Because this is the only difference between them, there is only one standard for the breed. There is a long-coat variety, which has a lion show-trim like a Poodle. The short, curly coat variety is an appealing animal because of its scruffy appearance. Regular brushing is advised.

FEEDING
For daily feeding, 3 cups of balanced dry dog food is recommended. Some dogs may prefer 1/2 cup water mixed with each cup of dog food. Add canned dog food for flavor.

ORIGIN AND HISTORY
This dog not only catches fish, but can also catch rabbits. It has been known for centuries around the Iberian Peninsula, where it was bred for retrieving fish and guarding nets. Formerly used throughout Portugal, it is limited today to the Algarve region. It is little known outside its country of origin. This breed should not be confused with the Portuguese Warren Hound, which is found in Northern Portugal and used for rabbit hunting.

This breed is currently shown in the Miscellaneous class at American Kennel Club shows. Although still a rare breed, it has a growing number of fanciers.

SHOW REQUIREMENTS
General Appearance—Medium size, well-proportioned, rugged and muscular. Its use as a water retriever accounts for its muscular development.

Color—Black, white, various shades of brown and combinations of black or brown with white. A white coat does not indicate albinism if the nose, mouth and eyelids are black.

Head And Skull—Head is well-proportioned and massive. Viewed in profile, the skull is slightly longer than the muzzle. The curve of the skull is more accentuated at the back than in front. The occiput is well-defined. Viewed from the front, the skull is domed, concaving slightly in the middle. The forehead is furrowed for two-thirds the length of the parietal bones. Frontal bones are prominent. The muzzle tapers from base to nose. The stop lies slightly farther back than the inner corner of the eyes. Nose is wide, with open, finely pigmented nostrils. Nose color varies with coat color. Lips are thick, especially in front. The inner mouth is black. Jaws are not undershot or overshot.

Tail—Not docked. Thick at the base, tapering gradually to the tip. Not set on too high or too low. Extended, it should not reach below the hock. When the dog is on the alert, the tail is held in a ring. The forepart does not lie beyond the rear limit of the loin. The tail is used actively in swimming and diving.

Feet—Round and flat. Toes not too long or knuckled up. Webbed to their tips with a soft membrane covered with hair. Black nails preferred but nails of other colors permitted in conformity with coat color. Nails are held slightly off the ground. The central pad is thick.

Teeth—Not visible when the mouth is closed.

The Portuguese Warren Hound is an elegant, muscular dog, short and rectangular in build. The fine head is wedge shape, flat in the skull with pronounced eyebrow ridges. The tail is medium length and often carried vertically or curled slightly over the back. Although fawn is the most common color, the coat may be yellow, brown, gray-black or sooty, with or without white patches and spots.

Portuguese Warren Hound (Medio)

The Portuguese Water Dog was once common in Portuguese and Spanish seaports. Used as a working dog on fishing boats, it had a reputation as a formidable fighter.

Portuguese Water Dog

BULL TERRIER

Advantages
- *Affectionate*
- *Can live in most climates*
- *Good with children*
- *Good guard*
- *Healthy*
- *Hardy*

Disadvantages
- *Suited to country life*
- *Needs discipline*
- *Needs plenty of exercise*
- *Powerful*

Despite its fierce appearance, the Bull Terrier is gentle and reliable with children. Although the female will let children climb all over her, if provoked by another dog, it will fight to the death. The Bull Terrier never lets go. It is a fine guard. It is not a beautiful breed, but has an attraction of its own.

SIZE
Height—No requirement
Weight—No requirement
The Bull Terrier can be 70 pounds (31.75kg) or half that. Substance is required according to the size of the dog.

EXERCISE
The Bull Terrier is a powerful dog with boundless energy. It should not be confined to an apartment with only a run in the back yard. Country life with plenty of exercise is better for the animal.

GROOMING
Normal daily brushing is necessary.

FEEDING
For daily feeding of an animal of 20 to 50 pounds, 3 cups of balanced dry dog food is recommended. For an animal of 50 to 100 pounds, 5 cups of balanced dry dog food is recommended. Some dogs may prefer 1/2 cup water mixed with each cup of dog food. Add canned dog food for flavor.

HEALTH CARE
The Bull Terrier is a healthy, hardy dog. Do not buy a white one without checking its hearing. Some have congenital hearing problems.

ORIGIN AND HISTORY
This terrier began as a fighting dog, until bull baiting was outlawed in 1835. Fanciers decided to preserve the breed and refine it, while preserving its strength and tenacity. James Hinks of England crossed the White English Terrier with the Bulldog and Dalmatian. This produced a new strain of white dogs he called English Bull Terriers. Following World War II, colored Bull Terriers made their appearance. The breed never regained the popularity it enjoyed in the 1940s as a companion and friend. Today there are few breeders producing sound, attractive stock.

SHOW REQUIREMENTS
General Appearance—Strongly built, muscular, symmetrical and active. It must have a keen, determined and intelligent expression. Courageous but even-tempered, willing to be disciplined. Males should look masculine and females feminine.
Color—For white, a pure white coat. Skin pigmentation and markings on the head should not be penalized. For colored, the color should predominate. Brindle is preferred.
Head And Skull—Long, strong and deep to the end of the muzzle. Not coarse. Viewed from the front, it is egg-shape and completely filled. Nose black and bent down at the tip. Nostrils developed. Underjaw strong.
Tail—Short, set on low and carried horizontally. Thick at the root, tapering to a fine point.
Feet—Round and compact, with arched toes.
Teeth—A level or scissors bite.

AMERICAN STAFFORDSHIRE TERRIER

Advantages
- *Good guard*
- *Fearless*
- *Excellent rat catcher*
- *Good with children*

Disadvantages
- *Needs discipline*
- *Stubborn*

Do not confuse the American Staffordshire Terrier with the Staffordshire Bull Terrier, a lighter dog with smaller bones. At one time the American Kennel Club allowed the American Staffordshire Terrier to be shown with the Staffordshire Bull Terrier. Crossbreeding of the two was also allowed. Although the American Staffordshire's ancestry originates in England, it has evolved as an independent breed.

SIZE
Height—Male: 18 to 19 in (46 to 48cm) at the shoulder
Female: 17 to 18 in (43 to 46cm)
Weight—No requirement
Height and weight should be proportionate.

EXERCISE
As for Staffordshire Bull Terrier.

GROOMING
As for Staffordshire Bull Terrier.

ORIGIN AND HISTORY
The American Staffordshire Terrier came from the English Bulldog and an English terrier. It was also known as the Pit Bull Terrier, later the Staffordshire Bull Terrier. In 1870, it became known under the names Pit Dog, Yankee Terrier and American Bull Terrier. The breed was recognized by the American Kennel Club in 1935, under the name of Staffordshire Terrier. It was changed in 1972 to American Staffordshire Terrier.

SHOW REQUIREMENTS
General Appearance—Muscular, agile and graceful. Aware of its surroundings. Stocky, but not long-legged or racy in outline.
Color—Any color and pattern, such as solid, particolor or patched permissible. Black, tan and liver, all white or more than 80% white are not encouraged.
Head And Skull—Head medium length. Broad skull. Pronounced cheek muscles. Distinct stop. Ears set high. Jaws defined. Nose black.
Tail—Short in comparison to size. Low set, tapering to a fine point. Not curled or held over back. Not docked.
Feet—Moderate, arched and compact.
Teeth—Upper teeth meet tightly outside lower teeth in front.

STAFFORDSHIRE BULL TERRIER

Advantages
- *Good guard*
- *Fearless*
- *Excellent rat catcher*
- *Good with children*

Disadvantages
- *Needs discipline*
- *Stubborn*

The Staffordshire Bull Terrier is a sound breed and excellent family dog. It resulted from crossing a Bulldog with a terrier breed sometime in the 1800s. The Old English Bulldog's partner was probably the Old English Black and Tan Terrier, which preceded the Manchester Terrier. The Staffordshire Bull Terrier is an English breed, first recognized by the British Kennel Club in 1935.

The Staffordshire Bull Terrier is a gentle dog. It is reliable with young children. It is a good guard and adores its family.

SIZE
Height—14 to 16 in (35.5 to 40.5cm) at the shoulder
Weight—Male: 28 to 38 lbs (12.7 to 17.2kg)
Female: 24 to 34 lbs (11 to 15.4kg)

EXERCISE
The Staffordshire Bull Terrier cannot resist a fight with another dog if given the chance. Keep this breed on a leash when walking in public. It is a good rat catcher and field companion. It adapts to life in a yard if given regular walks.

GROOMING
This breed requires little attention other than a daily brushing.

FEEDING
For daily feeding, 3 cups of balanced dry dog food is recommended. Some dogs may prefer 1/2 cup water mixed with each cup of dog food. Add canned dog food for flavor.

ORIGIN AND HISTORY
The Staffordshire Bull Terrier was bred for bull and bear baiting and later for dog fighting. With the banning of these sports, the Staffordshire was developed as a companion dog. It was recognized by the British Kennel Club as a purebred in the mid-1930s.

The Staffordshire Bull Terrier was admitted to the American Kennel Club stud book in 1974. In 1975, it was granted regular show classification in the Terrier group.

SHOW REQUIREMENTS
General Appearance—Smooth coat, with great strength. Although muscular, it is active and agile.
Color—Red, fawn, white, black, blue or any of these colors with white. Any shade of brindle or brindle with white.
Head And Skull—Short, broad skull. Pronounced cheek muscles. Distinct stop. Short foreface. Black nose.
Tail—Medium length, low set, tapering to a point. Carried low, not curled.
Feet—Padded, strong and medium size.

The ideal Bull Terrier is well-rounded in the body, with a short, strong back and a marked spring to the ribs. The shoulders, though powerful, must not be heavy. The legs must be strong-boned but not coarse. Forelegs are straight, hind legs muscular in the thighs. The overall impression should be one of immense power and strength, combined with supple agility.

Bull Terrier

American Staffordshire Terrier

The modern Staffordshire Bull Terrier draws its courage, intelligence and tenacity from its history as a fighter. With its affectionate and trustworthy nature, it makes an excellent family pet.

Staffordshire Bull Terrier

KERRY BLUE TERRIER
Irish Blue Terrier

Advantages
- *Good guard*
- *Good sporting dog*
- *Excellent with children*

Disadvantages
- *Enjoys fights*

The Kerry Blue Terrier loves children and makes an ideal pet. It has a temper and needs firm, gentle training.

SIZE
Height—No requirement
Weight—33 to 37 lbs
(15 to 16.8kg)

EXERCISE
Bred as a working dog, it needs plenty of exercise.

GROOMING
Daily brushing with a stiff-bristle brush and metal comb is necessary. You can learn to scissor trim the pet yourself. If you plan to show the dog, there is a lot of work involved in show preparation.

FEEDING
For daily feeding, 3 cups of balanced dry dog food is recommended. Some dogs may prefer 1/2 cup water mixed with each cup of dog food. Add canned dog food for flavor.

ORIGIN AND HISTORY
The Kerry Blue originated in the county of Kerry, Southern Ireland. The Irish Terrier is an ancestor, as are the Bedlington Terrier and Bull Terrier.

The Kerry Blue was a hunter of badger and fox. It has hunted otter and it is a keen, strong swimmer. It guarded livestock, too. During World War II, it served with the military. Now, it is kept as a pet and show dog.

SHOW REQUIREMENTS
General Appearance—Compact, upstanding and well-proportioned. A developed, muscular body.
Color—Any shade of blue, with or without black points. Kerry color, in its process of clearing from black at birth to mature color, passes through several transitions. These involve dark blue, tinges of brown and a mixture of these. Until the dog is 18 months old, these deviations are permitted. Solid black is disqualifying. A small white patch on the chest is not penalized.
Head And Skull—Head is balanced and long. It is proportionately lean, with slight

Above: The Kromfohrlander is little known outside Germany.

Left: The Kerry Blue Terrier is a beautiful, well-proportioned dog. It is a popular pet and show dog.

stop, and flat over the skull. Foreface and jaw strong, deep and punishing. Nose black.
Tail—Set on high to complete a straight back. Carried erect. Moderate length.
Feet—Round and small. Toenails black.
Teeth—Level or scissors bite.

KROMFOHR-LANDER

Advantages
- *Even-tempered*
- *Good companion*
- *Good guard*
- *Good hunter*
- *Intelligent*

Disadvantages
- *Not common in the United States*

This is a faithful, intelligent dog with guarding and hunting instincts. It is little known outside Germany.

SIZE
Height—15 to 18 in
(38 to 46cm)
at the withers
Weight—No requirement

EXERCISE
This terrier has a lot of energy, so give it plenty of exercise.

GROOMING
Normal daily brushing is recommended.

FEEDING
For daily feeding, 3 cups of balanced dry dog food is recommended. Some dogs may prefer 1/2 cup water mixed with each cup of dog food. Add canned dog food for flavor.

ORIGIN AND HISTORY
The Kromfohrlander has been known only since the end of World War II. A group of American soldiers, accompanied by a medium-size dog, passed through the Siegen area of Germany. The dog found a new home with Frau Schleifenbaum, who owned a female English Wirehair Terrier. Their puppies were so pleasing, she decided to develop a specific type. It became known as the Kromfohrlander. In 1953, it received recognition from the German Kennel Club.

There are three varieties of this terrier: shorthair roughcoat, roughcoat and longhair roughcoat. The roughcoat is the most popular. Colors are white, with markings ranging from light to dark brown on the head or with a white star on a brown head. Markings should be regular.

An all-purpose dog, the Kerry Blue Terrier makes an excellent pet or working dog. It can be trained easily to the gun and will track and retrieve like a gundog. Affectionate and gentle with its friends, it is a fearsome adversary. As a companion and watchdog, it is unequaled.

Kerry Blue Terrier

Kromfohrlander

The Kromfohrlander is a powerful dog with a long, wedge-shape head, rectangular body and strong, sturdy legs. A cross between a Griffon and a Terrier, it makes a lively, affectionate pet.

SOFTCOATED WHEATEN TERRIER

Advantages
- *Hardy*
- *Will eat most foods*
- *Intelligent*
- *Excellent guard*
- *Good with children*

Disadvantages
- *Not suited to outdoor kennels*

The Softcoated Wheaten Terrier is intelligent and defensive without being aggressive. It is an excellent guard, but gentle with children. The Wheaten has strong sporting instincts. Some dogs have been successfully trained for the gun.

SIZE
Height—Male: 18 to 19-1/2 in
(46 to 50.5cm)
at the withers
Female: Slightly smaller
Weight—35 to 45 lbs
(15.9 to 20.5kg)

EXERCISE
The Wheaten loves exercise. It has excelled as a hunter of rats, rabbits, otters and badgers. It will work any kind of cover. Its soft coat is ample protection against the densest undergrowth.

GROOMING
The Wheaten does not shed. Daily combing should start in puppyhood. Regular grooming will keep the coat clean and tanglefree.

Fuzziness, not natural to the breed, can be caused by the use of a wire or plastic brush. A medium-tooth metal comb should be used instead.

Bathe as necessary. If showing, bathe the dog about three days before the event to avoid a fly-away appearance. Ears, tail and feet need to be tidied. Any long, straggly hairs underneath the body should be trimmed.

FEEDING
For daily feeding, 3 cups of balanced dry dog food is recommended. Some dogs may prefer 1/2 cup water mixed with each cup of dog food. Add canned dog food for flavor.

ORIGIN AND HISTORY
The origin of the Softcoated Wheaten is unknown. From pictures and records, the breed can be traced back 200 years in Ireland. For many generations, there were few farms that did not have a Wheaten.

The Softcoated Wheaten Terrier is the oldest Irish terrier breed. It may be an ancestor of the Kerry Blue and Irish Terrier. Legend says a blue dog swam ashore from a ship wrecked near Ireland about 1800. This dog mated with a Wheaten and from this originated the Kerry Blue. Wheat-color pups pups appear in Kerry Blue litters from time to time. There is no record of crossbreeding in the Wheaten. It appears today as it always has.

The breed was given American Kennel Club regular show classification in the Terrier group in 1972.

SHOW REQUIREMENTS
General Appearance—Medium size and compact. It is covered with a soft, wheat-color natural coat that falls in loose curls or waves.
Color—A clear wheat, the shade of ripening wheat. A white or red coat is objectionable. Dark shading on the ears is not unusual. Dark overall color and darker markings, often present in the immature coat, should clear by about 18 months.
Head And Skull—Head moderately long. Covered with a coat that falls forward over the eyes. The skull, while not coarse, is narrow. Nose black and large. Head powerful without being coarse.
Tail—Docked. Tail of a fully grown dog should be about 4 to 5 inches (10 to 12.5cm) long. Set on high, carried up, but never over the back. Not curled or thick.
Feet—Strong and compact, not turned in or out. Deep pads. Toenails dark.
Teeth—Level or scissors bite.

BORDER COLLIE

Advantages
- *Intelligent*
- *Loyal*
- *Obedient*
- *Good family dog*
- *Good worker*

Disadvantages
- *Will herd anything*

The Border Collie is an excellent working dog. It is famous for herding cattle and rounding up sheep. It has won numerous obedience competitions and sheepdog trials. It is a breed favored by those who want a working dog.

The name Border Collie refers to the English-Scottish border. The dog was bred for speed, stamina and intelligence. It makes a first-class companion, is good with children and is one of the most trainable medium-size dogs.

SIZE
Height—Male: 21 in (53.5cm)
Female: Slightly smaller
Weight—No requirement

EXERCISE
This working dog enjoys being outdoors. It likes to exercise at a dog training class or work on a farm. It is adaptable, but not ideally suited to city life.

GROOMING
Brush regularly with a comb and stiff-bristle brush. Inspect the ears for signs of cankers. Keep ears and feet free of foreign matter. Remove dead fur when grooming.

FEEDING
For daily feeding, 3 cups of balanced dry dog food is recommended. Some dogs may prefer 1/2 cup water mixed with each cup of dog food. Add canned dog food for flavor.

ORIGIN AND HISTORY
The Border Collie is a modern strain descended from the collies of the lowland and border counties of England and Scotland. It is a working sheepdog and has been exported to many countries of the world where sheep are raised. It is an excellent guide-dog for the blind.

This breed is currently shown in the Miscellaneous class at American Kennel Club shows. Its popularity is growing steadily, especially among stock-trial enthusiasts.

In July 1976, a standard for the breed was approved by the British Kennel Club. This came from a combination of several proposed standards, including the recognized one from the Australian Kennel Club.

SHOW REQUIREMENTS
General Appearance—Well-proportioned. The smooth outline shows gracefulness and perfect balance, combined with substance. Capable of enduring long periods of active duty.
Color—A variety of colors is permissible.
Head And Skull—Skull broad, occiput not pronounced. Cheeks not full or round. Muzzle tapers to the nose, is moderately short and strong. Skull and foreface approximately the same length. Nose black. Nostrils developed. Stop distinct.
Tail—Moderately long. The bone reaches at least to the hock joint. Set on low. Furnished with an upward swirl toward the end.
Feet—Oval. Pads deep, strong and sound. Toes moderately arched and close together. Nails short and strong.

STABYHOUN

Advantages
- *Affectionate*
- *Easily trained*
- *Good guard*
- *All-purpose sporting dog*

Disadvantages
- *Not common in the United States*

The Stabyhoun is one of the most popular dogs in Holland. Little is known about it elsewhere in the world. It is an all-purpose sporting dog. As a pet, it is reliable with children, has an affectionate nature and is easy to train. It has an even temperament. It is an excellent retriever, with a keen sense of smell.

SIZE
Height—Male: 19-1/2 in (49.5cm)
at the withers
Female: Slightly smaller
Weight—No requirement

EXERCISE
The Stabyhoun excels at working in the field as a retriever. It adapts to town life if given exercise.

GROOMING
Regular brushing keeps the coat in condition.

FEEDING
For daily feeding, 3 cups of balanced dry dog food is recommended. Some dogs may prefer 1/2 cup water mixed with each cup of dog food. Add canned dog food for flavor.

ORIGIN AND HISTORY
The Stabyhoun was recognized by the Dutch Kennel Club in 1942. It has existed in the Netherlands since around 1800. At that time, it was bred as an all-purpose gundog, but primarily as a rodent catcher. It was crossed with the Wetterhoun.

Stabyhoun.

SHOW REQUIREMENTS
General Appearance—Simple, robust pointer, whose body is longer than high. Not too massive or fragile.
Color—Dappled black, dappled blue, dappled brown, dappled orange.
Head And Skull—Head is lean in proportion to the rest of the body. Longer than broad. Skull and muzzle of equal length. Skull slightly rounded, not narrow. Nose black for brown and orange dogs, not divided. Nostrils open and large.
Tail—Long, reaching to the hocks. Set on at medium height. Hangs straight. The last third turns upward. In action, the tail is raised. Covered with long hair, not curled, wavy or thick.
Feet—Hind feet are round, with strong pads.

Softcoated Wheaten Terrier

As its name suggests, the coat of the Softcoated Wheaten Terrier is soft and silky, loosely waved or curly. It should be abundant on the head and legs. The length and texture of the coat remains the same throughout the year.

Because the Border Collie's ancestry is a mixture of sheepdogs, there has been considerable individual variation in type. Only recently, a standard for the breed was established and official recognition granted.

Border Collie

SHAR-PEI
Chinese Fighting Dog

Advantages
- *Excellent watchdog*
- *Loyal*
- *Amiable unless provoked*
- *Intelligent*
- *Good with children*

Disadvantages
- *Susceptible to eye disease*

The Chinese Shar-Pei is currently listed in the *Guinness Book of World Records* as the rarest dog in the world. Interest in the breed is steadily rising. Descriptions of it vary from a dog that looks as if its skin is several sizes too big, to a Bloodhound with wrinkles all over.

SIZE
Height — 18 to 20 in
(46 to 51cm)
at the withers
Weight — 40 to 50 lbs
(18.1 to 22.7kg)

EXERCISE
The Shar-Pei was used to hunt wild boar and herd flocks. It needs a large yard where it can exercise, and daily walks and runs.

FEEDING
For daily feeding, 3 cups of balanced dry dog food is recommended. Some dogs may prefer 1/2 cup water mixed with each cup of dog food. Add canned dog food for flavor.

HEALTH CARE
The breed is susceptible to *entropion,* an eye disease causing blindness if lashes penetrate the cornea. Entropion is curable. Consult your veterinarian at the first sign of eye irritation.

The female's season can be at irregular intervals. With some females, the season may not occur until she is 15 months or older. When the Shar-Pei is in season, she will not attract the attention of males of other breeds. She will attract only certain members of her own breed.

ORIGIN AND HISTORY
Works of art depicting a likeness to the Shar-Pei survive from the Han Dynasty, 206 B.C. to 220 A.D. It is possible the Shar-Pei originated in Tibet or the Northern Province of China about 20 centuries ago. It was probably a larger dog than it is now, weighing 85 to 165 pounds (38.6 to 74.8kg).

The Shar-Pei may be a descendant of the Service Dogs. For thousands of years, they lived in the Southern Province near the South China Sea.

The Shar-Pei was also named the Chinese Fighting Dog. It was provoked, then matched against other dogs for the owner's profit. The loose skin of the Shar-Pei made it difficult for its opponent to get a firm grip on its body. Drugs were used to heighten the breed's aggressiveness; it is basically a loving and gentle animal.

The Shar-Pei has small, rectangular ears that point toward the eyes. Its tail forms a circle, its tip touching the base. Its stiff short hair stands up. Its rarity will probably not last — 14 Shar-Peis were counted in the kennels of Ernest Albright in California. He is largely responsible for saving the Shar-Pei from extinction. There are also other Shar-Peis throughout the United States and Canada.

The future of the Shar-Pei was in peril in 1947, when the tax on dogs in the People's Republic of China rose steeply. Few people could afford to keep them. Many were eaten. The Shar-Pei may have survived because it was not tasty!

It is an intelligent dog, friendly unless provoked and enjoys human company. Chin, a Shar-Pei trained by Albright, has won three ribbons in obedience trials. An added advantage is Shar-Pei pups are said to housetrain themselves!

SHOW REQUIREMENTS
The Shar-Pei Club of America was formed to adopt a breed standard. The dog is a purebred, although not recognized by the American Kennel Club. Its popularity is rapidly growing and several of its strongest supporters are well-known dog fanciers. The following are from the tentative standard:

General Appearance — Active, compact, short-coupled and squarely built. Stands firmly on the ground with the posture of a warrior.

Color — Self-colored. May be black, dark fawn, light fawn or cream. Fawn with dark eyes, blue-gray mask and black nose preferable.

Head And Skull — Skull flat, broad and large, with little stop. Occiput not pronounced. Profuse wrinkles on forehead and cheeks. Heavy dewlaps. Muzzle moderately long and broad with no tapering toward the nose.

Tail — Set high. Thick and round at the base. Tapers to a fine point at the tip. Tail curled tightly in a circle or loosely in a semicircle. Carried to one side.

Feet — Compact and firm. Toes separated. Knuckles high.

Teeth — Level or scissors bite. Tongue, roof of the mouth and gums are blue-black.

BULLDOG

Advantages
- *Courageous*
- *Intelligent*
- *Even-tempered*
- *Loves children*
- *Easy to groom*

Disadvantages
- *Cannot tolerate heat*
- *Snores*
- *Cannot take exercise*

Despite its ferocious appearance, the Bulldog has a docile temperament and usually loves children. It is quick to learn and enjoys games. Its build does not permit fast running and it should not be allowed to overexert itself in hot weather. Its nose is not equipped for rapid breathing. Do not leave it in a car or other confined space without plenty of fresh air.

This breed is not known for long life. It can be a loyal guard and lovable family pet.

SIZE
Height — No requirement
Weight — Male: 55 lbs (25kg)
Female: 50 lbs (22.7kg)

EXERCISE
The Bulldog enjoys a daily walk on a loose leash. The dog will amble at its own pace. Do not drag it or let it overexert itself. Experience will show how much exercise it enjoys without tiring. A Bulldog is not the breed for those who like all-day hiking.

GROOMING
Daily brushing with a stiff-bristle brush and a rubdown with a hound glove will keep the Bulldog in good condition. Choose a warm day for its annual bath.

FEEDING
For daily feeding, 3 cups of balanced dry dog food is recommended. Some dogs may prefer 1/2 cup water mixed with each cup of dry food. Add canned dog food for flavor. A daily teaspoon of cod liver oil is recommended in winter as a body builder.

ORIGIN AND HISTORY
This breed can be traced back to the Molossus, a fighting dog of the ancient Greeks. The Mastiff, Bulldog and Boxer may have been common ancestors.

The Bulldog is often associated with the sport of bull baiting. The dog seized the bull by the nose and held on until the bull fell. It was promoted by the Earl Warren of Stamford, Lincolnshire. After enjoying the sight of two dogs fighting bulls in 1209, he tried to bring the sport to a wider audience.

Bull baiting became illegal in 1838. The Bulldog was in danger of extinction because it appeared to have no further purpose. Breeders continued to breed Bulldogs and developed it into a reliable pet. The Bulldog Club, established in 1875, was the first specialist breed club set up in Great Britain. At the beginning of the 20th century, New Yorkers paid large sums of money for Bulldogs, when the breed became fashionable.

SHOW REQUIREMENTS
General Appearance — Thickset and low in stature. Broad, powerful and compact. Head is strikingly massive and large in proportion to dog's size. Face short and muzzle broad, blunt and inclined upward.

Color — Whole or smut, a whole color with a black mask or muzzle. The only colors are whole colors, such as brindles, red, fawn, fallow, white and pied.

Head And Skull — Skull large; the larger the better. In circumference it should measure at least the height of the dog at the shoulders. Black nose. A flesh-color nose is disqualifying.

Tail — Straight or screwed, but never curly or curved. Short and hung low with a decided downward carriage. Thick at the root and fine at the tip.

Feet — Hind feet and forefeet round and compact. Knuckles prominent. Forefeet straight, turning slightly outward, moderately round. Toes compact, thick and split up.

Teeth — Jaws massive, broad and undershot. Teeth large and strong.

Now perhaps the world's rarest dog, the Shar-Pei originated in the Orient. For centuries, it was bred and trained as a fighting dog. It is believed drugs were used to provoke the Shar-Pei to aggression, because it is basically a friendly, gentle dog.

Shar-Pei

The Bulldog should give an impression of strength, determination and activity.

Bulldog

CANAAN DOG

Advantages
- **Good guard**
- **Intelligent**

Disadvantages
- **Distrusts strangers**

This dog is a native of Israel, where it is used as a guard and protector of livestock. It is alert, intelligent and home-loving. Although distrustful of strangers, it does not look for trouble.

SIZE
Height—19-1/2 to 23-1/2 in
(49.5 to 60cm)
Weight—40 to 55 lbs
(18.1 to 25kg)

EXERCISE
Regular walks are necessary.

GROOMING
Normal daily brushing keeps the coat in condition.

FEEDING
For daily feeding, 5 cups of balanced dry dog food is recommended. Some dogs may prefer 1/2 cup water mixed with each cup of dog food. Add canned dog food for flavor.

ORIGIN AND HISTORY
During the Middle East wars of the 1960s and 1970s, the Canaan Dog was used as a messenger and guard. Enough interest was created for some dogs to be exported to the United States and other countries. It is recognized by the Federation Cynologique Internationale and the American Kennel Club, but not the United Kennel Club or the British Kennel Club.

SHOW REQUIREMENTS
There are two types: the Collie and the Dingo. The Dingo is heavier.
Color—Sandy to red-brown, white or black. Large white markings desirable. Harlequins acceptable.
Tail—Curled over the back when the dog is alerted. Set on high and bushy.

WIREHAIRED POINTING GRIFFON

Advantages
- **Easy to train**
- **Even-tempered**
- **Good companion**
- **Intelligent**
- **A reliable, careful gundog**

Disadvantages
- **Can be slow**

The Wirehaired Pointing Griffon is an intelligent dog that points and does well in water. It is an attractive, good-natured animal and performs its task slowly but surely. It is easy to train.

SIZE
Height—Male: 21-1/2 to 23-1/2 in
(54.5 to 60cm)
Female: 19-1/2 to
21-1/2 in (49.5 to 54.5cm)
Weight—No requirement

EXERCISE
This dog needs vigorous exercise.

GROOMING
Regular brushing will keep the coat in condition.

FEEDING
For daily feeding, 3 cups of balanced dry dog food is recommended. Some dogs may prefer 1/2 cup water mixed with each cup of dog food. Add canned dog food for flavor.

ORIGIN AND HISTORY
The Wirehaired Pointing Griffon was developed in the 1870s by a Dutch sportsman, Edward Korthals. Korthals managed the kennels of a German prince for many years. He wanted to produce a dog with courage and hunting ability. He achieved this by crossing French, Belgian and German gundogs. A reliable and plucky worker resulted. Some say it is the ideal gundog for the older sportsman. It was first shown in Great Britain in 1888.

The first dog of the breed registered by the American Kennel Club was Zoelette. She was registered as a Russian Setter (Griffon) in 1887.

SHOW REQUIREMENTS
These standards are from the Federation Cynologique Internationale.
Color—Steel-gray, with chestnut markings, or uniformly red chestnut or roan.
Head And Skull—Head large with rough, tufted hair. Thick but not long. Pronounced moustache and eyebrows. Skull not wide. Muzzle long, strong and square. Facial angle not pronounced. Nose brown.
Tail—Carried horizontally or with the tip slightly raised. Hair abundant but not plumed. Usually docked.
Feet—Round and well-formed.

These Wirehaired Pointing Griffons are slow but reliable.

The Canaan Dog has only recently become known outside Israel. Its origin is uncertain. It may have evolved from selective breeding of Middle Eastern Pariah Dogs, domestic dogs that have regressed to a wild state.

Canaan Dog

The Wirehaired Pointing Griffon was first registered with the American Kennel Club as the Russian Setter (Griffon) in 1887. It was not shown in the United States until about 1900.

Wirehaired Pointing Griffon

BEAUCERON
**Beauce Shepherd,
French Shorthair Shepherd,
Berger de la Beauce,
Bas-rouge**

Advantages
- **Brave**
- **Faithful**
- **Good guard**
- **Intelligent**

Disadvantages
- **Ferocious if roused**
- **Not common in the United States**

The Beauceron is a guard and herder, intelligent and loyal. It resembles the Doberman in appearance.

SIZE
Height—Male: 25 to 28 in
(63.5 to 71cm)
at the shoulder
Female: 24 to 27 in
(61 to 68.5cm)
Weight—No requirement

EXERCISE
This dog is happiest when working. It needs plenty of exercise.

GROOMING
Regular brushing keeps the coat in condition.

FEEDING
For daily feeding, 5 cups of balanced dry dog food is recommended. Some dogs may prefer 1/2 cup water mixed with each cup of dog food. Add canned dog food for flavor.

ORIGIN AND HISTORY
The Beauceron is one of the four best-known herding breeds of France. All are from different areas. The others are the Briard, Picardy and The Great Pyrenees Dog. See pages 154 and 168.

The Beauceron resembles the Doberman in color and appearance. It comes from an old, less-refined shepherd dog, probably used for hunting. It has been established in its present form only since the end of the 19th century. It is a natural herder and in recent years its temperament has been greatly improved.

It is not registered with the American Kennel Club. It is considered a rare breed. Interest in it is constantly growing.

SHOW REQUIREMENTS
General Appearance—Big, robust and powerful. Muscular but not heavy.
Color—Black, gray, gray with black-and-tan markings called red stockings, fawn, fawn and black. A white spot on the chest is tolerated but objectionable. For a working dog, darker coats are preferred.

Head And Skull—Long, with a flat or slightly domed skull. Medial furrow is not prominent. The occipital protuberance is visible. Stop not pronounced, lying at midpoint between occiput and tip of nose. The bridge is not arched, except slightly toward the extremity. Muzzle long, but not narrow or pointed. Nose black. Lower lips slightly let down, not heavy.
Tail—Not docked. Carried low, reaching to the hocks. Hangs straight. May be slightly curved or hooked at the end.
Feet—Strong. Round, with black nails and hard pads. Double dewclaws on the hind legs. Dogs without dewclaws can take only a mention.
Teeth—White, well-adapted to their purpose.

PUMI

Advantages
- **Good watchdog**
- **Intelligent**
- **Even-tempered**
- **Useful farm dog**

Disadvantages
- **Does not like strangers**
- **Not common in the United States**

The Pumi is a pleasant companion and guard. It prefers its owner's company and will bark at strangers. It has an unkempt appearance which can be appealing. It is not often seen outside its native Hungary, where it is a farm dog.

SIZE
Height—13 to 17-1/2 in
(33 to 44.5cm)
at the withers
Weight—17-1/2 to 28-1/2 lbs
(8 to 13kg)

EXERCISE
This dog is happiest running outdoors.

GROOMING
Brushing will help keep the coat in condition.

FEEDING
For daily feeding, 3 cups of balanced dry dog food is recommended. Some dogs may prefer 1/2 cup water mixed with each cup of dog food. Add canned dog food for flavor.

ORIGIN AND HISTORY
The Pumi is a sheepdog. In recent years it has been employed as an all-purpose farm dog and cattle herder in Hungary. It excels at police and guard work. Its history is obscure, but the Puli and the Poodle are probably ancestors.

SHOW REQUIREMENTS
General Appearance—Medium size, vigorous, with terrier characteristics. Head long, with the muzzle more developed. Ears are

semierect. Coat is medium length and free from matting. Tail erect. Eyes and muzzle barely visible because of the long coat.
Color—Many colors occur: dove-gray, silver-gray and slate-gray are common. Black, light gray, white and chestnut are also found. Particolored but never brindle. Coat must not be mottled or have any markings.
Head And Skull—Elongated muzzle. The bridge is straight. Muzzle narrows gradually from the skull to the nose, which is pointed. Top of the nose is also narrow. Lips fit closely over the gums. The stop is not pronounced. The occiput is narrow but slightly rounded and long. Development of the supraorbital ridges is moderate.
Tail—Set on high, carried out or slightly lowered. Docked to two-thirds of its length.
Teeth—Scissors bite.

PULI
**Hungarian Puli,
Hungarian Water Dog**

Advantages
- **Easily trained**
- **Fine guard**
- **Intelligent**
- **Loyal**

Disadvantages
- **A one-person dog**

The Hungarian Puli is a loyal, obedient dog. It may be the best-known Hungarian sheepdog. It is distinguishable by its long, dark, corded coat, which is not as difficult to groom as you might think.

SIZE
Height—Male: 16 to 18 in
(41 to 46cm)
Female: 14 to 16 in
(36 to 41cm)
Weight—Male: 29 to 33 lbs
(13.1 to 15kg)
Female: 22 to 29 lbs
(10 to 13.1kg)

EXERCISE
Plenty of exercise is needed. This dog will fit into city life if given long walks.

GROOMING
The coat hangs in long black cords, which in the adult dog reach to the ground. It gives a tousled, unkempt look. Cords must be separated by hand and regularly brushed and combed. Cleanliness is essential.

FEEDING
For daily feeding, 3 cups of balanced dry dog food is recommended. Some dogs may prefer 1/2 cup water mixed with each cup of dog food. Add canned dog food for flavor.

ORIGIN AND HISTORY
The Puli is better known than other Hungarian sheepdogs. In Hungary, it directs a flock by jumping on or over the sheep's backs. It has existed for 1000 years and is a descendant of sheepdogs brought to Hungary by the Magyars. It has proven to be a fine water retriever and does well in obedience and police work. Hungarian shepherds favor their dark color, which is easily picked out among a flock.

SHOW REQUIREMENTS
General Appearance—Lively, agile, intelligent and medium size. Solid, lean and muscular. Body outline is square. Examination of individual parts of the body is difficult. It is completely covered with a thick, long, wavy coat that mats. Head gives the impression of being round because the long hair comes down over the eyes, concealing its shape. The shaggy tail, long and curled up to the loins, makes hindquarters appear to slope upward. Precise body lines are hard to follow.
Color—Black or black with red or white ticking, and several varieties of gray.
Head And Skull—Medium size, in proportion to the dog. Skull is slightly domed and not too broad. A strong muzzle of medium length.
Tail—May be born with bobtails. This is acceptable, but the tail is never docked. Carried low with the end curled up at rest.
Teeth—Strong and large, meeting in a level or scissors bite. An undershot or overshot bite is a serious fault.

This Puli was photographed in Hungary. The cords of its coat are thick.

Despite its name, the Beauceron comes from the Brie region of France rather than Beauce. Its name was probably given to avoid confusion with the Briard herding breed. Less popular than the Briard, the Beauceron is still a working dog. It is not often seen outside of France.

Beauceron

Pumi

Hungarian Puli

FINNISH SPITZ
Suomenpystykorva

Advantages
- Brave
- Good guard
- Good housedog
- Faithful
- Good with children
- Good hunter
- Home-loving

Disadvantages
- No drawbacks known

The Finnish Spitz is Finland's national dog. It is popular as a bird hunter. It is also kept as a pet and show dog. It is a beautiful animal that cleans itself like a cat.

SIZE
Height—Male: 17-1/2 in (44.5cm)
Female: 15-1/2 in (39.5cm)
Weight—No requirement

EXERCISE
This is an outdoor dog and likes to run free when possible. It also enjoys its place in the home, so it should not be kenneled.

GROOMING
Normal daily brushing is necessary.

FEEDING
For daily feeding, 3 cups of balanced dry dog food is recommended. Some dogs may prefer 1/2 cup water mixed with each cup of dog food. Add canned dog food for flavor.

HEALTH CARE
The Finnish Spitz is a hardy, healthy dog in adulthood. It can prove delicate as a pup. This Spitz type is not the easiest to breed.

ORIGIN AND HISTORY
The Finnish Spitz was known for centuries in Finland before receiving official recognition. It originated in Finland and is mentioned in the country's literature.

It was called the *Finkie* by Lady Kitty Ritson, who pioneered the breed in Great Britain in the 1920s. It is related to the Russian Laika. It is a descendant of the earliest known hunting dogs of Lapland and Scandinavia.

This breed is a purebred, but not registered by the American Kennel Club. It is growing in popularity.

SHOW REQUIREMENTS
General Appearance—Body almost square. Bearing bold. Appearance, particularly eyes, ears and tail, indicates liveliness.
Color—On the back, red-brown or yellow-red, preferably bright. Hairs on the inner sides of the ears, on cheeks, under the muzzle, on the breast and abdomen, inside the legs, at the back of the thighs and under the tail are a lighter shade. White markings on feet and a narrow white stripe on the breast

---

Finnish Spitz puppies enjoy the sun. They can be delicate as puppies, but grow into beautiful pets or show dogs.

permitted. Some black hairs on lips and sparse separate hairs with black points along the back acceptable.
Head And Skull—Medium size and clean cut. Forehead slightly arched and stop pronounced. Muzzle narrow and clean cut when seen from above. Evenly tapering from the sides. Nose black. Lips tightly closed and thin.
Tail—Curves forward, downward and backward, then presses down against the thigh. Tip extends to the middle part of the thigh. When extended, tail vertebrae usually reach to the hock joint.
Feet—Round.

NORRBOTTEN SPITZ
Norrbottenspets

Advantages
- Good guard
- Good with children
- Strong herding instinct

Disadvantages
- Not common in the United States

The Norrbotten Spitz is named after the Northern region of Sweden, Norrbotten, from which it originates. It is Sweden's answer to the Finnish Spitz and the Norwegian Buhund. It is smaller and lighter. It is an excellent companion, pet and farmyard protector.

SIZE
Height—16 in (40.5cm)
Weight—No requirement

EXERCISE
This dog is a natural herder and enjoys its freedom. It adapts to life as a pet, with regular walks.

GROOMING
Normal daily brushing is necessary.

FEEDING
For daily feeding, 3 cups of balanced dry dog food is recommended. Some dogs may prefer 1/2 cup water mixed with each cup of dog food. Add canned dog food for flavor.

ORIGIN AND HISTORY
The Norbotten Spitz is not well-known outside Sweden. It was declared extinct by the Swedish Kennel Club in 1948. This was untrue. There was an upsurge of interest in the 1960s. It resulted in enough registrations for the breed to become re-established. Its Spitz origin probably comes from Finnish Spitz or Norwegian Buhund ancestry. The Norrbotten Spitz is not recognized in the United States.

SHOW REQUIREMENTS
General Appearance—Small and compact. Light build. Good carriage.

Color—All colors permissible. Preference is given to white as the base color with russet or yellow markings. Each color area distinct from the others.
Tail—Set on high. Curved, generally carried on the side. When down, the tip reaches to mid-thigh. Tail joints do not reach below the hock. A docked tail is permissible, but not desirable.

JAPANESE SPITZ

Advantages
- Courageous
- Intelligent
- Loyal

Disadvantages
- A one-person dog
- Distrusts strangers
- Not common in the United States

The Japanese Spitz is a close relation of the Norrbotten Spitz. It was developed as a separate breed in Japan. Only recently has it come on the international scene. It is still rare.

SIZE
Height—Male: 12 to 16 in (38 to 40.5cm)
Female: 10 to 14 in (25 to 35.5cm)
Weight—No requirement

EXERCISE
This dog is a natural herder. It enjoys its freedom but adapts to life as a pet when walked regularly.

GROOMING
Normal daily brushing is required.

FEEDING
For daily feeding, 5 cups of balanced dry dog food is recommended. Some dogs may prefer 1/2 cup water mixed with each cup of dog food. Add canned dog food for flavor.

SHOW REQUIREMENTS
General Appearance—Profuse white coat. A sharply pointed muzzle. Triangular ears stand erect. Tail is carried over the back. Body firm, strong and flexible. Forequarters and hindquarters balanced and well-proportioned.
Color—Pure white.
Head And Skull—Head medium size, without coarseness. Moderately broad and slightly round. Skull broadest at occiput. Well-defined stop. Cheeks rounded. Muzzle sharply pointed, not too thin or too long. Lips firm and tightly closed. Nose round, small and black.
Tail—Set on high. Carried over the back.
Feet—Toes small, round and catlike. Padded, with good pigment. Nails hard and black or dark.

The Finnish Spitz is characterized by its courage, fidelity and eagerness to hunt. Its coat is short and close lying on the head and legs; on the backs of thighs, it is long and dense. The outer coat on the shoulders is longer and coarser, particularly in males. The undercoat is short, soft and dense.

Finnish Spitz

Originally bred as a hunting dog, the Norrbotten Spitz is an affectionate and lively pet. It is little known outside Sweden, where it was bred during the 1960s.

Norrbotten Spitz

It is possible the Japanese Spitz is from the family known as Japanese Dogs. It is seldom seen outside Japan.

Japanese Spitz

BASSET HOUND

Advantages
- *Even-tempered*
- *Good with children*
- *Good family pet*

Disadvantages
- *Needs exercise*
- *Likes to wander*
- *Needs discipline*

The Basset Hound is a lovable dog that gets along with most people. It is an ideal family pet. It retains strong hound instincts and will wander away if a gate is left open. The Basset has a mind of its own. It is lovable, but not always obedient. It needs discipline.

SIZE
Height—15 in (38cm)
Weight—No requirement

EXERCISE
If you cannot give a Basset Hound plenty of exercise do not have one.

GROOMING
Daily brushing and combing are necessary. Pay attention to ears and toenails.

FEEDING
For daily feeding, 3 cups of balanced dry dog food is recommended. Some dogs may prefer 1/2 cup water mixed with each cup of dog food. Add canned

Lovable pets, Basset Hounds can be willful at times.

dog food for flavor. Careful feeding in puppyhood is necessary for this fast-growing breed.

HEALTH CARE
Choose a pup with the straightest limbs, even if knobby knees seem attractive.

ORIGIN AND HISTORY
The Basset Hound is of French origin. It was bred from the French Basset Artesien Normand, imported to England and crossed with the Bloodhound. The first Bassets appeared in a litter of normal long-legged hounds. In breeding from these, the Basset Hound appeared. It is a slow, sure tracker and still used to hunt rabbits. It is also kept as a pet.

SHOW REQUIREMENTS
General Appearance—Short legged, with considerable substance. Balanced and full of quality. Action is important. A smooth, free action—forelegs reach forward and hind legs show powerful thrust. Moves true both front and rear. Hocks and stifles not stiff in movement. Toes must not drag.
Color—Generally black, white and tan, or lemon and white. Any recognized hound color is acceptable.
Head And Skull—Domed, with some stop. The occipital bone prominent. Medium width at the brow, tapering slightly to the muzzle. Foreface is lean. The top

of the muzzle is almost parallel with the line from stop to occiput. Muzzle not longer than the head from stop to occiput. A moderate amount of wrinkle at the brows and beside the eyes allowed. Head skin loose enough to wrinkle noticeably when drawn forward or when the head is lowered. Flews of the upper lip overlap the lower substantially.
Tail—Long, strong at the base. Tapering, with a moderate amount of coarse hair underneath. When moving, the stern is carried up and curves gently over the back. Never curled.
Feet—Massive, knuckled up and padded. Forefeet may point straight ahead or turn slightly outward. Weight must be borne equally by toes with pads together, so feet leave the imprint of a large hound. No unpadded areas in contact with the ground.
Teeth—Large, sound and regular. Meet in a scissors or even bite.

BASSET GRIFFON VENDEEN

Advantages
- *Good family pet*
- *Friendly*
- *Likes human company*
- *Bark deters strangers*

Disadvantages
- *Needs exercise*
- *Not suitable for apartments*
- *Not common in the United States*

The Basset Griffon Vendeen is an ancient French hunting breed. It is a combination of short-legged, roughcoat hound. It originated in the Vendee district. It is one of the four breeds of Basset Hound found in France. The others are the Basset Artesien Normand, the Basset Blue de Gascogne and the Basset Fauve de Bretagne.

The Basset Griffon Vendeen is a cheerful, active, busy hound. It is intelligent and inquisitive. Its friendly nature and liking for human companionship make it an excellent family pet. Its deep resonant voice is a deterrent to unwelcome callers.

SIZE
Height—13-1/3 to 15 in
(34 to 38cm)
A tolerance of 2/5 inch (1cm) is allowed.
Weight—No requirement

EXERCISE
The Basset Griffon Vendeen is active and energetic. It needs plenty of exercise. Do not keep it in a small apartment or house with a small yard unless you can give it care and time.

GROOMING
Its rough coat needs little attention.

FEEDING
For daily feeding, 3 cups of balanced dry dog food is recommended. Some dogs may prefer 1/2 cup water mixed with each cup of dog food. Add canned dog food for flavor.

ORIGIN AND HISTORY
According to Monsieur Doubigne, an expert on the breed, the Griffon Vendeen is a miniature Basset in size and proportion. It retains all the qualities of the breed—passion for hunting, fearlessness in the densest covers, activity and vigor. It was bred down from a larger variety, the Grand Basset Griffon Vendeen. It was originally used for wolf hunting and is now used for hunting wild boar in France.

SHOW REQUIREMENTS
General Appearance—Small, lively and vigorous, with a medium-length body. Tail carried proudly. Coat rough and long, without exaggeration. Expressive head. Ears turned, garnished with long hair and attached below the line of the eye. Not too long.
Color—
Unicolor: Grizzle, gray or fawn, although fawn is not encouraged.
Bicolor: Orange and white or tan and white.
Tricolor: Black, white and tan; brown, white and tan; white, gray and tan.
Head And Skull—Skull slightly convex and moderately long. Not too wide. Narrow below the eyes. Stop marked. Occipital bone showing.
Tail—Set high, strong at base and gradually tapering. Not too long. Carried saber fashion. Lively.
Feet—Not too strong. Hard, with tight pads. Nails solid.

BASSET ARTESIEN NORMAND

The Basset Artesien Normand is nearly identical to the Basset Hound. It has the same feeding and grooming requirements, and general characteristics. It is of French origin, descended from the old French Bloodhound and the St. Hubert Hound. Its job was to tail deer and small game.

This breed found favor as a hunting dog in France, but was adopted by the British. They crossed it with the Bloodhound to develop the Basset Hound, now popular as a pet.

The breed stands 10 to 13 inches (25 to 33cm) high. Colors are white or white and orange. A tricolor dog must be widely marked, with tan on the head and a mantle of black or badger color specks.

The long ears of the Basset Hound should be set on low but not excessively so. They must never be above the line of the eye. Narrow and curling inward, ears should reach at least to the end of the muzzle. They should be supple and velvety in texture.

Basset Hound

Basset Griffon Vendeen

Basset Artesien Normand

WHIPPET

Advantages
- **Clean**
- **Gentle**
- **Good with children**
- **Affectionate**

Disadvantages
- **Strong hunting instincts**

The Whippet is an excellent choice for those who want a gentle, affectionate pet. Some like its ability to perform on the track or in the show ring. It has a peaceful temperament, but can be nervous in strange surroundings.

SIZE
Height—Male: 19 to 22 in
(48 to 55.5cm)
Female: 18 to 21 in
(45.5 to 53cm)
Judges use discretion and do not unduly penalize an otherwise good specimen.
Weight—No requirement

EXERCISE
The Whippet is a racer, capable of running 35 to 40 miles per hour (56 to 64kph). It must be given plenty of exercise.

GROOMING
This dog needs little grooming, but its tail usually needs to be cleaned for show. Teeth should be scaled regularly. Nails need clipping.

FEEDING
For daily feeding, 1-1/2 cups of balanced dry dog food is recommended. Some dogs may prefer 1/2 cup water mixed with each cup of dog food. Add canned dog food for flavor.

HEALTH CARE
Whippets are hardy, despite their delicate appearance, but they should sleep indoors and be kept out of drafts.

ORIGIN AND HISTORY
The Greyhound is an ancestor of the Whippet. There is controversy as to whether the cross was with a terrier, a Pharaoh Hound or other imported hound. The breed has been popular since the beginning of the century. It was exhibited at Crufts in 1897 and was recognized by the British Kennel Club five years later.

The Whippet was originally brought to the United States by English mill operators in Massachusetts. The dogs were used for racing. Many Whippet owners get great pleasure from keeping a dog that satisfies their sporting interests and is also a popular show contender and loving pet.

SHOW REQUIREMENTS
General Appearance—Balanced muscular power and strength, combining elegance and grace. Symmetrical outline, muscular development and powerful gait. Freedom of action. Forelegs thrown forward and low over the ground. Hind legs come under the body, giving great propelling power. Movement not stilted, high stepping or mincing.
Color—Any color or mixture of colors.
Head And Skull—Head long and lean. Flat on top, tapering to the muzzle. Wide between the eyes. Jaws powerful and clean cut. Nose black. In blues, a blue color is permitted, and in livers a nose of the same color. In whites or particolors, a butterfly nose is permissible.
Tail—No feathering. Long and tapering. When in action, carried in a delicate curve up but not over the back.
Feet—Neat, split between the toes. Knuckles highly arched. Pads thick and strong.

AUSTRALIAN KELPIE

Advantages
- **Brave**
- **Excellent working dog**
- **Good companion**
- **Loyal**

Disadvantages
- **No drawbacks known**

The Australian Kelpie is an excellent sheepdog. It is descended from Scottish stock. It runs along the backs of sheep to reach the head of the flock. It is fast and can go without water for long periods. It is attractive, intelligent and loyal to its master.

The breed has been shown in the miscellaneous group at American Kennel Club-sanctioned shows.

SIZE
Height—18 to 20 in
(45.5 to 50.5cm)
at the shoulder
Weight—30 lbs (13.6kg)

EXERCISE
This dog needs plenty of exercise.

GROOMING
This breed will benefit from regular, vigorous brushing.

FEEDING
For daily feeding, 3 cups of balanced dry dog food is recommended. Some dogs may prefer 1/2 cup water mixed with each cup of dog food. Add canned dog food for flavor.

ORIGIN AND HISTORY
The Kelpie comes from Collies brought to Australia by early settlers. Its ancestry can be traced to a pup named Caesar, later mated to a female named Kelpie. Her offspring included the famous King's Kelpie, winner of the first sheepdog trials in Australia in 1872. The Scottish writer Robert Louis Stevenson refers to the Water Kelpie in his story *Kidnapped,* giving credence to the suggestion that Kelpies came from working Scottish Collies.

STANDARD SCHNAUZER

Advantages
- **Affectionate**
- **Lively and playful**
- **Good with children**
- **Intelligent**
- **Good watchdog**

Disadvantages
- **Distrusts strangers**

The Schnauzer is a good-natured, lively dog that loves children and games. It does not trust strangers. It is terrierlike, intelligent and makes an excellent guard.

SIZE
Height—Male: 18-1/2 to 19-1/2 in
(46 to 49cm)
Female: 17-1/2 to
18-1/2 in (44 to 46cm)
Weight—No requirement

EXERCISE
This dog enjoys regular walks and ball games. It will adapt to country or city living.

GROOMING
Brush the dog daily and trim in spring and autumn.

FEEDING
For daily feeding, 3 cups of balanced dry dog food is recommended. Some dogs may prefer 1/2 cup water mixed with each cup of dog food. Add canned dog food for flavor.

ORIGIN AND HISTORY
The Schnauzer is of German origin. In Stuttgart, there is a statue dated 1620 that shows a dog similar in appearance to today's Schnauzer.

The breed originated in Bavaria and Wurttemberg, where it was a rodent catcher and cattle driver. When cattle-driving died out, the breed found its way to the city. There it gained popularity. It came to the attention of serious fanciers in the late 1800s.

Standard Schnauzers were shown in the Miscellaneous class in an American Kennel Club-sanctioned show in 1899. The breed was then classified as a terrier. Later it was moved into the working group.

SHOW REQUIREMENTS
General Appearance—Powerfully built, robust, sinewy and almost square. Body length is equal to its height at the shoulder. High spirited, reliable, strong and vigorous. Expression keen and attitude alert.
Color—All salt-and-pepper colors in even proportions or pure black.
Head And Skull—Head strong and elongated. Gradually narrows from ears to eyes and forward to the tip of the nose. Occiput to base of the forehead moderately broad between the ears. Flat, creaseless forehead. Muscular cheeks but not strongly developed. Slight stop accentuates prominent eyebrows. Muzzle formed by the upper and lower jaws ends in a moderately blunt line. Bristly, stubby moustache and chin whiskers. Nose-ridge straight and running almost parallel to the extension of the forehead. Nose black and full. Lips tight.
Tail—Set moderately high and carried erect. Docked to not less than 1 inch or more than 2 inches (2.5 to 5cm).
Feet—Short, round, extremely compact. Close-arched toes. Dark nails and hard soles. Feet deep or thickly padded, pointed forward.
Teeth—Strong. Meet in a scissors bite.

MEDIUM PINSCHER
German Pinscher

Advantages
- **Good guard**
- **Loyal**

Disadvantages
- **Aggressive**
- **Fiery temperament**
- **Not common in the United States**

The Medium Pinscher, known in the past as the German Pinscher, is an old breed. It is almost unknown outside Germany. This Pinscher bears more similarity to the Doberman than the Miniature Pinscher. Like the Doberman, its ears are cropped. The tail is docked and the coat is smooth and glossy. Color is usually black with small tan markings or self-red. There is also a distinctive harlequin Pinscher.

The Medium Pinscher was bred as a rodent catcher. Today it is kept as an alert, lively pet. Height is 16 to 19 inches (40.5 to 48cm).

The coat of the Whippet should be short and finely textured. Its chest should be deep, its back broad, well-muscled and arched over the loin.

Whippet

Medium Pinscher

Australian Kelpie

The Schnauzer breed was first shown in the United States at the beginning of the 20th century. Confusion resulted because Schnauzers and Dobermans were generally called Pinschers.

Standard Schnauzer

AUSTRALIAN SHEPHERD

Advantages
- **Excellent working breed**
- **Exceptional companion**

Disadvantages
- **Reserved with strangers**

The Australian Shepherd may be the most popular breed in the United States not recognized by the American Kennel Club. A well-balanced dog with remarkable agility, it has strength and stamina. The Aussie is primarily a working dog with herding and guarding instincts. Once assigned a task, it performs with great enthusiasm. Aussies come in a variety of colors and patterns.

SIZE
Height—Male: 20 to 23 in (50.5 to 58cm) at the withers
Female: 18 to 21 in (46 to 53cm)
Weight—No requirement

EXERCISE
This working breed requires daily exercise. When not working, exercise in a large fenced area is preferred. Aussies adapt readily to rural or urban living.

GROOMING
Daily brushing and an occasional bath will keep an Aussie neat and clean. For shows, whiskers, hocks and pads may be trimmed.

ORIGIN AND HISTORY
Three distinct breeds developed in Australia during the 1800s. The two breeds considered to be true Australians are the Australian Kelpie and the Australian Cattle Dog.

The ancestor of today's Australian Shepherd was known as the Spanish Shepherd. It originated in the Basque areas of France and Spain. The dog was brought to Australia with Marino sheepherders and their sheep. Spanish Shepherds were interbred with Dingos. Some of those traits are still carried in the modern Aussie.

The dog was imported from Spain to California during the 1800s. Its last port of call was Australia, so it received the name Australian Shepherd.

The dog is registered by the United Kennel Club and the Animal Research Foundation.

SHOW REQUIREMENTS
General Appearance—Attentive and animated, with a natural or docked bobtail. It is slightly longer than tall, with a deep chest. Its gait is fluid with a well-balanced, ground-covering stride. Coat is moderate in length and coarseness. It is easily trained and a good worker.

The Australian Shepherd, an excellent companion, is one of the most popular breeds in the United States.

Color—Clear and rich. Recognized are blue-merle, red or liver-merle, solid black and solid red-liver, with or without white or tan points. Area surrounding ears and eyes dominated by a color other than white.
Coat—Medium texture, straight or slightly wavy. Weather resistant. Moderate length with an undercoat. Climate may affect the quantity of undercoat. Backs of forelegs feathered. Backs of rear legs have moderately full breeches. Mane is more pronounced in males.
Head And Skull—Head in proportion to the body. Clean cut with a flat skull. Stop well-defined. Muzzle tapers to a rounded tip. Ears set high on the head. At full attention, they tip forward one-fourth to one-half above the base. Prick or hound ears are severe faults. Eyes are expressive, clear and almond shape. Color may be brown, blue, amber or any variation, including flecks and marbling.
Tail—Straight, not to exceed 4 inches (10cm). Natural or docked.
Feet—Compact and oval with arched toes and thick pads. Dewclaws removed.
Teeth—Strong white teeth meet in a scissors bite. Level bites faulted. Overshot or undershot bites are disqualifying.

CATAHOULA LEOPARD DOG
Louisiana Hog Dog, Texas Catch Dog

Advantages
- **Good working dog**
- **Natural herder**
- **Good hunter**

Disadvantages
- **No drawbacks known**

The Catahoula Leopard Dog is growing in popularity. Known for its ability to drive wild cattle and hogs, it has become a favorite in the bushland of Texas and Louisiana. It is used to hunt game and is an excellent watchdog and family pet. A purebred, it is registered with the Animal Research Foundation. It is also known as the Louisiana Hog Dog and the Texas Catch Dog. Although it is not shown in conformation classes, it is entered in competitive classes at stockdog trials.

ORIGIN AND HISTORY
Theories about the development of the Catahoula vary. The most widely accepted is that it originally was a cross between the Beauceron Shepherd and the Plott Hound. See pages 86 and 118. Beauceron Shepherds were brought to the area of Catahoula Lake, Louisiana by French explorers as early as 1540. The Plott Hound was bred for hunting bear and wild hogs by a German family residing in the Great Smoky Mountains in Tennessee and North Carolina.

SHOW REQUIREMENTS
General Appearance—Medium to large. Streamlined but muscular. Chest broad and muscular, thick through the rib cage. Back is long and slopes gently from the withers. A deep, carrying voice.
Color—Solid color or spotted with white on the chest.
Head And Skull—Head wide. Muzzle medium length and slightly dished. Nose preferably dark. Eyes range in color from yellow to dark.
Coat—Short, thick and glossy. White on the chest is the dominant characteristic, but color varies. Can be spotted or solid. Color is not the most important point.
Tail—Long, with a hook.

ENGLISH SHEPHERD

Advantages
- **Intelligent**
- **Excellent companion**
- **Courageous worker**
- **Good watchdog**

Disadvantages
- **Uses its teeth when working**

The English Shepherd is one of the most common breeds in the United States. Owners and fanciers appreciate the breeding that has produced this excellent herder-farm worker, obedience competitor and wonderful companion.

SIZE
Height—18 to 22 in (45.5 to 55.5cm) at the shoulder
Weight—Male: 40 to 50 lbs (18 to 22.5kg)
Female: 35 to 45 lbs (16 to 20.5kg)

EXERCISE
This working dog needs exercise.

GROOMING
Daily brushing with a stiff-bristle brush keeps the coat tanglefree and eliminates constant shedding. An occasional bath to remove dirt will keep the dog in good condition.

ORIGIN AND HISTORY
The English Shepherd may be the descendant of dogs brought to England by Romans. Used to drive cattle and sheep, they were similar to the ancestors of the Rottweiler. The English Shepherd first traveled to America with the Pilgrims.

The dog is registered by the United Kennel Club and the Animal Research Foundation.

SHOW REQUIREMENTS
General Appearance—Solid, energetic, intelligent and courageous. Deep in the chest with wide muscular shoulders. Medium size. Coat shines, giving an impression of good health and heartiness. Head is carried slightly raised. It has a kind expression.
Color—Sable; black and white; black and tan; black, tan and white. A white ring around the neck, a white tail tip, white chest, white on lower legs and a face blaze are permitted. Tan dots are permitted over eyes and on feet.
Head And Skull—Skull wide and flat above the eyes. Broad between the ears. Muzzle heavy, but not pugged or pointed. Ears wide, tapering to a point. Carried slightly raised.
Coat—Straight or curly, covering the body from ears to feet. It is excessive over the main body, but not maned.
Tail—Heavily haired. Carried slightly higher than the back with a slight curve. May be white tipped.
Feet—Large, padded and round.

Australian Shepherd

English Shepherd

Catahoula Leopard Dog

The Catahoula Leopard Dog
is popular in the Southern
United States. It serves as a
watchdog and family pet, as
well as a hunting dog.

SWISS HUNTING DOGS

**Schweizer Laufhund,
Bruno de Jura, Lucernese,
Bernese**

Advantages
- *Active*
- *Friendly*
- *Good hunters*

Disadvantages
- *Not suitable as pets*
- *Not common in the United States*

There are four varieties of the Swiss Hunting Dog. Do not confuse them with the smaller types. With the exception of the Jura, they all have the same standard in Switzerland. They are friendly, active and powerfully built. They hunt rabbit and are excellent, speedy trackers with good noses. Their lively dispositions and strong hunting instincts do not make them good pets.

SIZE
Height—17-1/2 in (43cm)
Weight—No requirement

EXERCISE
These dogs need plenty of vigorous exercise for full fitness.

GROOMING
Regular brushing is necessary.

FEEDING
For daily feeding, 3 cups of balanced dry dog food is recommended. Some dogs may prefer 1/2 cup water mixed with each cup of dog food. Add canned dog food for flavor. This amount should be increased when the hound is exercising a lot.

ORIGIN AND HISTORY
The Swiss Hound, particularly the Laufhund, is gaining international recognition. The origin of the Swiss Hound can be traced to the pre-Christian era. Similar hunting dogs were introduced into Egypt by the Phoenicians and Greeks. They found their way to Switzerland when it was under Roman rule. The age of the breed is verified by illustrations in Zurich Cathedral made during the 12th century.

The heaviest of the four is the Jura, similar to the St. Hubert and the French Ardennes Hound. When it gets a scent, it will bay with a drawn-out note heard for many miles. It is similar to the English Bloodhound. The Bruno de Jura is about the same size, but appears sleeker and faster.

A powerfully built Bernese Swiss Hound, with tan markings on its cheek and above the eye.

SHOW REQUIREMENTS
These standards are for the Swiss, Lucernese and Bernese.
General Appearance—Medium size and long. Lively and intelligent, with enthusiasm for the hunt. Forelegs are strong and vertical, hind legs powerful. Back is long and straight. Loins are muscular, shoulders long and sloping. The rib cage is deep. A keen sense of smell. Self-reliance in the field and a powerful voice.
Color—
Swiss: White coat, with large markings of yellow-orange or orange. Dogs with red coats are admissible. An occasional small red spot is not considered a fault.
Lucernese: White background with gray or blue specklings and broad dark or black markings. Tan markings or yellow-brown areas of color on the head, body and feet. Beneath the white hair, skin is speckled with dark markings. When the coat is wet, the white disappears and the dog seems to be slate-gray or blue.
Bernese: Tricolor—white, black and intense tan markings. Background is white, with huge black markings and small spots. Tan markings above the eyes, on cheeks, inner part of the ears and at the root of the tail.

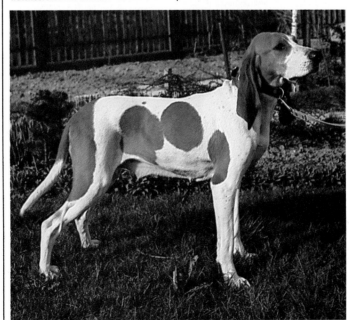

Lively and intelligent, the Schweizer Laufhund is one of four varieties of the Swiss Hunting Dog.

Head And Skull—Head lean and long. In proportion to the size of the dog. Stop well-defined. Nose black and large, with broad, open nostrils. Bridge slightly arched. Lips not heavy. Muzzle long. Jaws strong.
Tail—Not too long. Carried horizontally or slightly curved, never curled. Pointed at the tip. Feathered, smooth in smooth-hair dogs and thicker in coarsehair dogs. Not tufted.
Feet—Round, with hard, wrinkled pads and solid nails.
Teeth—Pincer or scissors bite.

This standard is for the Bruno de Jura.
General Appearance—Strong. Back is long and broad. Distinguishing features include the dewlap, the heavy, massive head with its long muzzle, lips, wrinkles on the forehead and its melancholy expression.
Color—Solid brown-yellow or red-brown. May have a black saddle on the back. May be black with tan markings above eyes, on cheeks and underparts of the body. There may be a white mark on the chest.
Head And Skull—Powerful and massive. Skull broad and round. Forehead wrinkled. Pronounced occipital protuberance. Long, folded ears set low.
Tail—Medium length. Ends in a pointed tip. Strong and feathered. Never tufted. Carried high, without curving. Never carried above the back.
Feet—Round, closed, with hard, wrinkled pads. Nails strong and black.
Teeth—Pincer or scissors bite.

The Bruno de Jura, a keen, clear-voice hound, has only one type of coat—short, dense and hard. The Bruno should not be below 17-1/2 inches (44.5cm) high. The lighter Shortlegged Jura Hound, resembling the Basset Artesien Normand, is not more than 15 inches (38cm) at the shoulder.

Bruno de Jura

Lucernese

The Lucernese is a medium-size hound with a graceful build. Its narrow ears, set back and low, should reach the tip of its muzzle. A smaller variety, the Shortlegged Lucernese, stands 11-1/2 to 15 inches (29 to 38cm) at the shoulder.

Schweizer Laufhund

LAPPHUND
Lapland Spitz

Advantages
- *Easy to train*
- *Friendly*

Disadvantages
- *Suspicious of strangers*
- *Not common in the United States*

The Lapphund was bred to hunt reindeer. Because this activity has ceased, the breed has been adopted as a cattle dog and pet. It makes a good pet, is friendly and easy to train.

SIZE
Height—Male: 17-1/2 to 19-1/2 in (44.5 to 9.5cm) at the shoulder
Female: 15-1/2 to 17-1/2 in (39.5 to 44.5cm)
Weight—No requirement

EXERCISE
This dog needs regular walks and runs for fitness.

GROOMING
Regular brushing keeps the coat in condition.

FEEDING
For daily feeding, 3 cups of balanced dry dog food is recommended. Some dogs may prefer 1/2 cup water mixed with each cup of dog food. Add canned dog food for flavor.

ORIGIN AND HISTORY
The Lapphund was bred as a hunter and herder of reindeer. When reindeer became farm animals, the Lapphund was given a new role as a cattle dog. Many found their way to Southern Sweden, where they were kept as family pets. The breed is becoming popular in Sweden.

SHOW REQUIREMENTS
General Appearance—Medium size, tall, with strong jaws and prick ears.
Color—Dark brown, black or brown-white. Solid colors preferred, but not required. A white spot on the chest, a white collar, white chest and markings on the feet and nape of the neck allowed.
Head And Skull—Conical, with a straight bridge and black nose. Lips fit over the gums. Muzzle short and cone shape. Broad at the base and narrowing to a point at the nose. Stop well-defined. Skull is domed and broad between the ears. The ridge above the eyes is prominent.
Tail—A ring or docked tail. Curled up on the back, with thick feathering. Normally long. A natural short tail or a docked tail is acceptable.
Feet—Long and powerful. Closed toes. Arched, with hair between them.

LAPPISH VALLHUND
Laplandic Herder

Advantages
- *Fine herder*
- *Good pet*
- *Good guard*

Disadvantages
- *Not common in the United States*

The Lappish Vallhund is similar to the Swedish Lapphund. It is a Finnish Spitz, used mainly for herding reindeer. It makes a good pet and companion.

SIZE
Height—Male: 19 to 22-1/2 in (48 to 56.5cm)
Female: 17 to 19 in (43 to 48cm)
Weight—No requirement

EXERCISE
Provide this dog lots of vigorous exercise for good health.

GROOMING
Regular brushing keeps the coat looking healthy.

FEEDING
For daily feeding, 5 cups of balanced dry dog food is recommended. Some dogs may prefer 1/2 cup water mixed with each cup of dog food. Add canned dog food for flavor.

ORIGIN AND HISTORY
In *Dogs of the World*, Bengtson and Wintzell suggest that when contact between the people of Lapland in Northern Scandinavia increased, their dogs interbred with various Southern Scandinavian breeds. Southern breeders preserved the pure strain of the original Lapphund. The Laplanders' dogs were ruined for reindeer herding because of crosses with unsuitable dogs of other breeds. They set about breeding out imported, undesirable traits. The result is the Lappish Vallhund.

ICELAND DOG
Icelandic Sheepdog

Advantages
- *Faithful*
- *Intelligent*
- *Trustworthy*

Disadvantages
- *Not common in the United States*

The Iceland Dog has been known since the 19th century. It is a reliable sheepdog, similar in appearance to the Finnish Spitz and Norwegian Buhund. See pages 88 and 100.

SIZE
Height—19 in (48cm)
Weight—No requirement

EXERCISE
This dog needs plenty of exercise.

GROOMING
Normal daily brushing is necessary.

FEEDING
For daily feeding, 3 cups of balanced dry dog food is recommended. Some dogs may prefer 1/2 cup water mixed with each cup of dog food. Add canned dog food for flavor.

ORIGIN AND HISTORY
A standard was introduced for the Iceland Dog in Denmark in 1898. It is not recognized in the United States. The breed is rarely exhibited. The role of the Iceland Dog, like the Norwegian Buhund, is as a reliable, all-purpose farm animal.

The faithful Iceland Dog resembles the Finnish Spitz and Norwegian Buhund.

Strongly built with an alert, intelligent appearance, the Lappish Vallhund shares many of the features of the Spitz family, but is longer in the back. The loosely curling tail is sometimes carried over the back and sometimes droops over one thigh. The Federation Cynologique Internationale approved this dog as a separate breed in 1946.

Lappish Vallhund

Lapphund

Iceland Dog

Although the Lapphund is no longer used as a herder, it is popular as a pet. The Swedish Army uses Lapphunds as guard dogs.

KEESHOND

Advantages
- **Even-tempered**
- **Good watchdog**
- **Long-lived**

Disadvantages
- **Needs lots of grooming**

The Keeshond, Holland's national dog, was a barge dog. It is loyal with an even temperament. It needs a great deal of grooming. It usually attaches itself to one member of the family. This long-lived dog is an excellent watchdog.

SIZE
Height—Male: 18 in (46cm)
Female: 17 in (43cm)
Weight—No requirement

This dog needs average exercise.

GROOMING
Groom the Keeshond regularly with a brush. Do not use a choke chain on this breed or it will spoil the ruff.

FEEDING
For daily feeding, 3 cups of balanced dry dog food is recommended. Some dogs may prefer 1/2 cup water mixed with each cup of dog food. Add canned dog food for flavor.

A Keeshond and her pup. Note the ruff on the adult dog. This breed needs regular grooming.

ORIGIN AND HISTORY
The Keeshond, pronounced *kayshond,* has an unusual history. Preceding the French Revolution, patriots were led by a man named Kees de Gyselaer. He owned a dog of this type. The dog, named Kees, became the symbol of the patriots and gave the breed its name.

The Keeshond has been bred for soundness and quality. It may have evolved in the Arctic Circle. It has a traditional Spitz tail, tightly curled over the back.

SHOW REQUIREMENTS
General Appearance—Short, compact body. Alert carriage and foxlike head. Small pointed ears. Feathered tail, carried over the back. Hair thick on the neck, forming a large ruff. Head, ears and legs covered with short, thick hair. Moves cleanly and briskly. Movement straight and sharp.
Color—A mixture of gray and black. Not all black or all white. Markings definite.
Head And Skull—Head well-proportioned to the body. Wedge shape when seen from above. From the side, shows a definite stop. Muzzle medium length, not coarse or snipy.
Tail—Tightly curled. A double curl at the end is desirable. White plume on the top where curled, with a black tip.
Feet—Round and catlike, with black nails.

NORWEGIAN BUHUND
Norsk Buhund

Advantages
- **Friendly**
- **Good with children**
- **Good guard**

Disadvantages
- **Natural herder**
- **Not common in the United States**

The Norwegian Buhund is a lively, alert dog. It is a natural herder and will round up anything—poultry, cattle or people. It needs lots of exercise and makes an ideal playmate for children.

SIZE
Height—Male: 17-3/4 in (44cm)
Female: Slightly smaller
Weight—No requirement

EXERCISE
This dog needs plenty of exercise.

A young Norwegian Buhund adopts his favorite position, typical of Spitz dogs.

GROOMING
Regular brushing and combing is necessary. It is an easy dog to prepare for showing.

FEEDING
For daily feeding, 3 cups of balanced dry dog food is recommended. Some dogs may prefer 1/2 cup water mixed with each cup of dog food. Add canned dog food for flavor.

ORIGIN AND HISTORY
The Buhund is one of Norway's national dogs. It was developed as an all-purpose farm dog to control sheep and cattle. In the 1920s, the breed became known outside Norway. The word *buhund* is Norwegian for farm dog. The Buhund is a farm dog, still used occasionally for herding.

SHOW REQUIREMENTS
General Appearance—Lightly built, with a short compact body. Smooth coat and erect, pointed ears. Tail carried curled over the back. Well-balanced, free of exaggeration and capable of arduous work.
Color—Wheat, black, red, if not too dark, or wolf-sable. Preferably self-colored but small symmetrical markings, such as white on chest and legs, blaze on head, narrow ring on neck, black mask and black tip on the tail allowed.
Head And Skull—Head lean, light and broad between the ears. Wedge shape, narrowing toward the point of the nose. Skull and back of head almost flat. Marked, but not sharp stop. Muzzle medium length, tapering evenly from above. Straight bridge. Lips tightly closed.
Tail—Short, thick and hairy, without long hair. Tightly curled.
Feet—Small and oval. Closed toes.

The body of the Norwegian Buhund is short, strong but light, with a straight back and a deep chest with good ribs. Its erect, sharply pointed, mobile ears should have a height greater than their width at the base.

Norwegian Buhund

Keeshond

The re-establishment of the Keeshond's popularity, after a decline during the 19th century, was largely due to breeding and public relations by Baroness van Hardenbroek during the 1920s and 1930s.

SIBERIAN HUSKY

Advantages
- *Adaptable*
- *Friendly*
- *Good with children*
- *Intelligent*
- *Reliable*

Disadvantages
- *Needs lots of exercise*

The Siberian Husky may be the most friendly of all Arctic Spitz breeds. It has a long history of friendship with man. It has been a pet and worker, hauling the sled or herding. It is faithful and reliable.

SIZE
Height—Male: 21 to 23-1/2 in
(53 to 59cm)
at the withers
Female: 20 to 22 in
(50.5 to 55.5cm)
Weight—Male: 45 to 60 lbs
(20.5 to 27.2kg)
Female: 35 to 50 lbs
(15.9 to 22.7kg)
Weight proportionate to height.

EXERCISE
This dog must not be confined in a small yard.

GROOMING
Regular brushing will keep the coat in condition.

FEEDING
For daily feeding, 5 cups of balanced dry dog food is recommended. Some dogs may prefer 1/2 cup water mixed with each cup of dog food. Add canned dog food for flavor.

ORIGIN AND HISTORY
The Siberian Husky was bred by the nomadic Chukchi tribe of Northeast Asia. Their purpose in breeding the Husky was to produce a hardy animal to combine the roles of companion and hunter with that of a speedy sled dog. At times, the animal would be their only means of transport.

More recently, the Siberian Husky has been recognized as a show dog. It has performed well as a Search and Rescue dog for the Air Force in World War II.

The Siberian Husky is a graceful dog with speed and endurance. It was bred to hunt and pull sleds in Northeast Asia, and to provide reliable companionship. It is famed for sled racing.

SHOW REQUIREMENTS
General Appearance—Medium size, quick and light on its feet. Free and graceful in action. Compact, well-furred body. Erect ears and brush tail. Its body proportions reflect speed and endurance. Males masculine, but never coarse. Females feminine, but without weakness of structure. Both capable of endurance. It is undesirable for the animal to appear to have excessive weight; clumsy gait; straight or loose shoulders; weak pasterns; weak, sloping or roach back; straight stifles; soft or splayed feet; feet too large and clumsy or too small and delicate.
Color—All colors. All markings permissible. A variety of markings on the head is common, including many striking patterns not found in other breeds.
Head And Skull—Head medium size, in proportion to the body. Not clumsy or fine. Slightly round on top, tapering gradually from the widest point to the eyes. Muzzle medium length and width, but not snipy or coarse. Tapers gradually to a round nose. Distance from the tip of the nose to the stop equal to the distance from the the stop to the occiput. Stop clearly defined but not excessive. Line of the nose straight from the stop to the tip. Nose black in gray, tan or black dogs; liver in copper dogs; flesh-color in white dogs.

Tail—Well-furred, round, foxlike. Set on below the level of the top line. Carried over the back in a graceful curve when the dog is at attention. When carried up, the tail does not curl too tightly, curl to either side of the body or snap flat against the back. Hair medium length, about the same length all around. A trailing tail is normal for the dog when it is working or in repose.

SAMOYED

Advantages
- *Devoted to owner*
- *Obedient*
- *Intelligent*

Disadvantages
- *Independent*
- *White coat sheds*

The Samoyed, or Sammy as it is often called, is a beautiful, independent breed. According to its standard, it should show "marked affection for all mankind." These dogs love the snow and are happiest in open spaces. It can also be happy as a family pet.

SIZE
Height—Male: 21 to 23-1/2 in
(53 to 59m)
at the shoulder
Female: 18 to 20 in
(46 to 50.5cm)
Weight—In proportion to height

EXERCISE
This dog needs a great deal of exercise. Include obedience work, even if only weekly attendance at a dog training class.

GROOMING
Regular brushing and combing are necessary. The undercoat sheds once a year. Comb out as much surplus hair as possible. Bathing helps loosen the hair.

FEEDING
For daily feeding, 5 cups of balanced dry dog food is recommended. Some dogs may prefer 1/2 cup water mixed with each cup of dog food. Add canned dog food for flavor.

ORIGIN AND HISTORY
The Samoyed is a beautiful Spitz-type. It takes its name from the Siberian tribe, the Samoyedes. A sled dog in its native country, it is also used to guard and herd reindeer. Some Sammies were used by the explorer Nansen on his journey to the North Pole.

The breed was brought to Britain in 1889. Today's stock can be traced to the original pair. British stock has popularized the breed in other countries of the world.

The Samoyed is a beautiful, devoted dog and is becoming more popular. Coming from a cold climate, its heavy, weather-resistant coat needs regular brushing and combing. This dog needs plenty of exercise and should attend obedience classes.

The breed found favor with Queen Alexandra. The descendants of her dogs are found today in many American and British kennels.

SHOW REQUIREMENTS
General Appearance—Strong, active and graceful. Coat is weather resistant. Not too long in the back. A weak back makes a dog useless for work. Body muscular. A deep chest and well-sprung ribs. Strong neck, proudly arched. Straight front and strong loins. Male and female free from coarseness. Legs moderately long. Hindquarters developed, stifles angular. Unsound stifles or cow hocks severely penalized.
Color—White, white and biscuit or cream.
Head And Skull—Head powerful and wedge shape. A broad, flat skull. Muzzle medium length. Foreface not too sharply defined. Lips black. Hair short and smooth at the ears. Nose preferably black. May be brown or flesh-color. Strong jaws.
Tail—Long and profuse, carried over the back when alert. Sometimes dropped when at rest.
Feet—Long, flat and slightly spread out. Soles cushioned with hair.

It is said the Samoyed is closer than any other modern breed to the primitive dog, with no trace of fox or wolf. The Samoyed's popularity was boosted when 28 Sammies helped Amundsen reach the South Pole in 1911.

Samoyed

Siberian Husky

The coat of the Siberian Husky is double and medium length, giving a well-furred appearance. It should never obscure the clean-cut outline of the dog. The undercoat, normally absent during the shedding season, is soft and dense.

Bull Mastiff

Neopolitan Mastiff

LARGE DOGS

Irish Wolfhound

Large dogs are magnificent and impressive. They can be useful. They can also attract the wrong owners. You may want a large dog because you like and admire them, you want one for a particular task, you want one as a guard, you want to enter it in obedience competitions or you want a large, lovable family pet. A large dog is a good choice if you select a breed carefully, have adequate space and can give the dog the feeding and exercise it needs.

Do not buy a large animal such as a German Shepherd because you feel it will make you safe. A German Shepherd is not an unbeatable burglar alarm. It is an intelligent animal that needs a job to do. It is loyal and affectionate, but it also has strong protective and guarding instincts. Do not leave it alone at home all day to get bored.

The Rottweiler and Doberman also make excellent guards. But get a female Airedale if you want your guard dog to be a children's playmate. Or leave the kids with a lovable, reliable St. Bernard.

Large dogs whelp easier than small ones and usually have large litters. Most large dogs are good-natured, but benefit from discipline in puppyhood. They should attend dog training classes.

With a few exceptions, large dogs love companionship and attention almost as much as vigorous outdoor activity. Many breeds mentioned in this section have reputations of being gentle when stroked, fierce when provoked.

STANDARD POODLE

Advantages
- **Even-tempered**
- **Intelligent**
- **Good pet**
- **Excellent retriever**
- **Stamina**
- **Obedient**
- **Good with other animals**

Disadvantages
- **An outdoor dog**

The Standard Poodle is intelligent and obedient. It is a good competitor in obedience competitions and is favored for showing. It is beautiful when exhibited in the traditional lion clip. It is also one of the most difficult breeds to prepare for the ring. Preparation involves a full day's canine beauty treatment.

SIZE
Height—15 in (38cm)
Weight—No requirement

EXERCISE
This is a robust, healthy dog that loves the outdoors. It has plenty of stamina and retains retrieving sporting instincts. It enjoys water and plenty of exercise.

GROOMING
Use a wire-pin pneumatic brush and a wide-tooth metal comb for daily grooming. The lion clip is essential for the show ring. Owners usually resort to the more natural lamb clip with the hair a uniform short length. It is possible to clip your own dog with a pair of hairdresser's scissors. If you find the task tedious, there are pet groomers who can do the job. Bathe the dog regularly.

FEEDING
For daily feeding, 3 cups of balanced dry dog food is recommended. Some dogs may prefer 1/2 cup water mixed with each cup of dog food. Add canned dog food for flavor.

ORIGIN AND HISTORY
The Poodle was used originally as a guard, retriever and protector of sheep. Its origins are similar to the Irish Water Spaniel. Common ancestors could be the French Barbet and Hungarian Water Hound.

The Poodle originated in Germany as a water retriever. Even the word Poodle comes from the German *pudelnass*, meaning puddle. The Miniature and Toy have evolved from the large sturdy Standard Poodle.

The breed has been known in England since Prince Rupert of the Rhine, accompanied by his Poodle, came to the aid of Charles I in battle. The breed was favored by Marie Antoinette, who developed the lion clip to match the uniform of her courtiers.

SHOW REQUIREMENTS
General Appearance—Active, intelligent, well-balanced and elegant. Even-tempered. Carries itself proudly.
Color—Any solid color. White and cream Poodles have black nose, lips and eyerims. Brown Poodles have dark amber eyes dark liver nose, lips, eyerims and toenails. Apricot Poodles have dark eyes with black points or deep amber eyes with liver points. Black, silver and blue Poodles have black nose, lips, eyerims and toenails. Cream, apricot, brown, silver and blue Poodles may show varying shades of the same color. Clear colors preferred.
Head And Skull—Rounded skull with a long, straight, fine muzzle. Slight chiseling under the eyes. Chin definite enough to preclude snipiness.
Tail—Set on high. Carried at a slight angle away from the body. Never curled over the back. Thick at the root.
Feet—Pasterns strong. Feet small and oval, not turning in or out. Toes arched. Pads thick, hard and cushioned.
Teeth—Strong, with a scissors bite.

IRISH WATER SPANIEL

Advantages
- **Brave**
- **Easily trained**
- **Even-tempered**
- **Intelligent**
- **Loving**

Disadvantages
- **No drawbacks known**

The Irish Water Spaniel is attractive, loyal, intelligent and has an affectionate nature. It is an excellent retriever and a strong, fearless swimmer. It is useful for wild fowl hunting.

SIZE
Height—Male: 22 to 24 in
(55.5 to 60.5cm)
Female: 21 to 23 in
(53 to 58cm)

Weight—Male: 55 to 65 lbs
(25 to 32kg)
Female: 45 to 58 lbs
(21 to 26kg)

EXERCISE
This dog needs plenty of exercise.

GROOMING
Daily brushing and weekly combing will keep the coat in condition. Seek advice on stripping the coat. Be careful mud does not become caked between toes.

FEEDING
For daily feeding, 3 cups of balanced dry dog food is recommended. Some dogs may prefer 1/2 cup water mixed with each cup of dog food. Add canned dog food for flavor.

ORIGIN AND HISTORY
There is a resemblance between the Standard Poodle and the Irish Water Spaniel. They are both good water retrievers. The Irish Water Spaniel is a gundog bred for work in all types of shooting. It is suited for wild fowl hunting. Its fitness is evident by its appearance.

The Irish Water Spaniel was developed from several spaniel breeds near the end of the 19th century.

SHOW REQUIREMENTS
General Appearance—Strong, compact, intelligent and eager.
Color—Dark liver, with a purple tint or bloom, sometimes referred to as puce-liver.
Head And Skull—Head well-chiseled. High skull with dome, good length and width. Muzzle long, strong and square with a gradual stop. Face smooth. Skull covered with long curls in a topknot, growing in a well-defined peak to a point between the eyes. Nose large and developed. Nose dark liver color.
Tail—Thick at the root and covered with 2 to 3 inches (5 to 7.5cm) of short curls. Tapers to a fine point covered with smooth hair. Looks clipped. Does not reach the hock joint.
Feet—Large, round and spreading. Covered with hair.

AMERICAN WATER SPANIEL

Advantages
- **Even-tempered**
- **Good worker**
- **Hardy**

Disadvantages
- **No drawbacks known**

The American Water Spaniel is little known outside the United States. It is popular as a working gundog. It is a strong swimmer and an excellent retriever.

SIZE
Height—15 to 18 in
(38 to 46cm)
Weight—Male: 28 to 45 lbs
(12.7 to 20.5kg)
Female: 25 to 40 lbs
(11.3 to 18.1kg)

EXERCISE
This dog needs plenty of exercise.

GROOMING
Daily brushing and weekly combing is necessary. Seek advice on stripping the coat. Be careful mud does not become caked between toes.

FEEDING
For daily feeding, 3 cups of balanced dry dog food is recommended. Some dogs may prefer 1/2 cup water mixed with each cup of dog food. Add canned dog food for flavor.

ORIGIN AND HISTORY
The American Water Spaniel may have come from crossing an Irish Water Spaniel with a smaller spaniel breed or a Curly Coated Retriever. In some parts of the country, it is still known as the Boykin Spaniel, named after Whit Boykin, a pioneer breeder in South Carolina. The breed was recognized by the American Kennel Club in 1940, but has still not been recognized in the United Kingdom.

SHOW REQUIREMENTS
General Appearance—Medium size, sturdy spaniel. Curly coat. Active and muscular. Emphasis on size and conformation, texture of coat and color. Intelligent and strong, with stamina. Good disposition.
Color—Solid liver or dark chocolate. A little white on toes or chest permissible.
Head And Skull—Moderate in length. Skull broad and full. Stop moderately defined, but not too pronounced. Forehead covered with short, smooth hair, without tuft or topknot. Muzzle medium length and square. No inclination to snipiness. Jaws strong and long. Nose wide, with well-developed nostrils for scenting power.
Tail—Moderate length. Curved in a slight rocker shape. Carried below level of back. Tapered and covered with hair to tip.
Feet—Padded, closed toes.
Teeth—Straight. Not undershot or overshot.

The Poodle's potential for glamor has sometimes obscured its active, sporting character. Because it is intelligent, can be trained to perform complex tricks, and can be attractively clipped, it has been employed as a circus dog.

Standard Poodle

Irish Water Spaniel

American Water Spaniel

ENGLISH SPRINGER SPANIEL

Advantages
- **Good with children**
- **Good worker**
- **Intelligent**
- **Loyal**
- **Good pet**
- **Obedient**

Disadvantages
- **Can put on weight**

The English Springer Spaniel is an excellent gundog and pet. It does well in obedience competitions and is a happy, efficient retriever.

SIZE
Height—20 in (50.5cm)
Weight—50 lbs (22.7kg)

EXERCISE
This dog needs exercise or it will put on weight.

GROOMING
Daily brushing is necessary. Be careful mud does not become caked in the paws. Keep ears clean and tanglefree to prevent infection.

FEEDING
For daily feeding, 3 cups of balanced dry dog food is recommended. Some dogs may prefer 1/2 cup water mixed with each cup of dog food. Add canned dog food for flavor.

ORIGIN AND HISTORY
The English Springer is one of the oldest British spaniels. It has never been as popular as the smaller Cocker Spaniel. It is usually favored by those interested in shooting and field trials.

The English Springer was valued by Americans as a bird dog before it was recognized by the British Kennel Club. There is controversy as to whether the dog, originally called a Norfolk Spaniel, came from the county of Norfolk, England or took its name from the famous Norfolk family. The name *springer* comes from its early task of springing game for the hunter's nets.

SHOW REQUIREMENTS
General Appearance—Symmetrical, compact, strong and upstanding. Happy and active. Built for endurance. High on the leg and racy in build.
Color—Liver and white, black and white or either of these with tan markings.
Head And Skull—Skull medium length, broad and slightly round. Rises from the foreface, making a brow or stop. Divided by a fluting between the eyes gradually receding along the forehead toward the occiput bone, which is not peaked. Cheeks flat, not round or full. Foreface proportionate to the

The English Springer Spaniel needs regular grooming and plenty of long walks.

skull, broad and deep without being coarse. Well-chiseled below the eyes. Deep and square in flew, but not interfering with comfort when retrieving. Nostrils developed.
Tail—Set low, following the natural line of the croup. Docked and fringed with wavy feathering.
Feet—Tight, compact and round, with strong full pads.
Teeth—A level or scissors bite.

CLUMBER SPANIEL

Advantages
- **Even-tempered**
- **Intelligent**
- **Reliable**

Disadvantages
- **Slow, steady worker**

The Clumber is the heaviest spaniel. It is of French origin and may have come from crossing a Basset Hound with the Alpine Spaniel, which is now extinct. It is a brave, attractive, reliable dog. It is a slow, steady worker and excels in hunting. The Clumber Spaniel is an excellent retriever.

SIZE
Height—No requirement
Weight—Male: 55 to 70 lbs
(25 to 32kg)
Female: 45 to 60 lbs
(20.5 to 27kg)

EXERCISE
This is a working dog, suited to country life. It needs plenty of exercise.

GROOMING
Routine brushing to keep coat tanglefree is necessary. Be careful mud does not become caked between the toes.

FEEDING
For daily feeding, 3 cups of balanced dry dog food is recommended. Some dogs may prefer 1/2 cup water mixed with each cup of dog food. Add canned dog food for flavor. Adjust rations according to the amount of work the dog does.

ORIGIN AND HISTORY
The Clumber Spaniel was developed by the Duc de Noailles before the French Revolution. The breed became renowned as retrievers in the field. When the war started, the Duc brought his dogs to England. He gave them to the Duke of Newcastle at Clumber Park, from which the name comes. The spaniels were left to develop in England.

SHOW REQUIREMENTS
General Appearance—Massive, but active. It moves with a rolling gait characteristic of the breed.
Color—White, with lemon markings. Orange permissible. Slight head markings and freckled muzzle. White body preferred.
Head And Skull—Head large, square and massive. Medium length, broad on top, with a decided occiput. Brow has a deep top. Heavy muzzle, well-developed flew. Pendulous upper lip. Level jaw and mouth. Nose square and flesh-colored.
Tail—Set level. Carried low.
Feet—Large and round, covered with hair.

Attractive and large, Clumbers make reliable workers.

The coat of the English Springer Spaniel should be close, straight and weather resistant without being coarse. The dog's ears, which must be given special attention in grooming, are lobular in shape and set close to the head in line with the eye. They are a good length and width, but not exaggerated.

English Springer Spaniel

Clumber Spaniel

KARELIAN BEAR DOG

Advantages
- *Brave*
- *Fine hunter*
- *Hardy*
- *Loyal*

Disadvantages
- *Dislikes other dogs*
- *Unsuitable as a family pet*
- *Needs exercise*
- *Not common in the United States*

The Karelian Bear Dog is a hunter of bear and elk. It is brave and loyal to its master. Because it does not get along with other dogs, it is not recommended as a family pet.

SIZE
Height—Male: 21 to 24 in (53 to 61cm) at the shoulder Female: 19 to 21 in (48 to 53cm)
Weight—No requirement

EXERCISE
This dog needs plenty of exercise.

GROOMING
Daily brushing will keep the coat in condition.

FEEDING
For daily feeding, 3 cups of balanced dry dog food is recommended. Some dogs may prefer 1/2 cup water mixed with each cup of dog food. Add canned dog food for flavor.

ORIGIN AND HISTORY
The Karelian Bear Dog is a Spitz, belonging to the family of Russian Laikas. This type evolved in Finland. It is known throughout Scandinavia as a fearless hunter of bear and elk. In 1947, the Russians decreed only four distinct types of Spitz should be referred to as Laikas. They are little known and rarely exported outside the USSR.

SHOW REQUIREMENTS
General Appearance—Medium size, robust and strong. Slightly longer than high. Thick coat, cocked ears and an introverted nature. Brave and persistent. Its senses are keen.
Color—Black, preferably slightly brown or dull. White markings or spots on the head, neck, chest, belly and legs.
Head And Skull—Wedge shape. Broad at the forehead and cheeks. Forehead slightly arched. Stop slopes gently. Slight protuberance above the eyes. Muzzle is high and bridge is straight, tapering slightly toward the nose. Nose black and well-developed.
Tail—Medium length, usually arched. A full arch is desirable.
Feet—Hind feet slightly longer and lower than forefeet. Paws thick, high and round.

ELKHOUND
Norwegian Elkhound

Advantages
- *Good pet*
- *Odorless*
- *Reliable with children*
- *Good guard*

Disadvantages
- *Needs firm, gentle discipline*

The Elkhound is a happy breed, devoted to its master and reliable with children. It loves the outdoors and is energetic. The Elkhound is not recommended for those unable to provide exercise.

SIZE
Height—Male: 20-1/2 in (52cm) at the shoulder Female: 19-1/2 in (49.5cm)
Weight—Male: 50 lbs (22.7kg) Female: 48 lbs (19.5kg)

EXERCISE
This dog needs plenty of exercise.

GROOMING
Daily brushing and combing will keep the coat in condition.

FEEDING
For daily feeding, 3 cups of balanced dry dog food is recommended. Some dogs may prefer 1/2 cup water mixed with each cup of dog food. Add canned dog food for flavor.

ORIGIN AND HISTORY
The job of the Elkhound once was to seek out an elk and hold it at bay until its master moved in for the kill. It has existed in Norway for centuries, but was not considered a show prospect until 1877. That year the Norwegian Hunters' Association held its first show.

Today's Elkhound has been bred to meet standards of various

The powerful Elkhound has a thick, weather-resistant coat that looks good in the show ring.

Scandinavian clubs and societies. Other Spitz breeds died out while a Norwegian breed standard emerged for this dog which has become the national breed.

SHOW REQUIREMENTS
General Appearance—Compact, short body. Thick coat and prick ears.
Color—Gray of various shades, with black tips on the long outer coat. Lighter on the chest, stomach, legs and underside of the tail. Any distinct variation from gray is undesirable. Too dark or too light a color avoided. Pronounced markings on legs and feet also undesirable.
Head And Skull—Broad between the ears. Forehead and back of head slightly arched with a clearly marked stop. Muzzle moderately long, broader at the base. Gradually tapers but not pointed. Bridge of the nose straight. Jaw strong with lips tightly closed.
Tail—Set high. Tightly curled over the back but not carried on either side. Hair thick and close.
Feet—Compact, oval shape, not turning outward. Closed toes. Toenails firm and strong.

SWEDISH ELKHOUND
Jamthund

Advantages
- *Brave*
- *Even-tempered*
- *Good hunter*

Disadvantages
- *Not common in the United States*

The Swedish Elkhound is a hunting dog. It is not well-known outside Sweden. Its popularity surpasses the Norwegian Elkhound because of its stamina. It is a bold and energetic hunter. An excellent guard and loyal to its master, it has a calm temperament.

SIZE
Height—Male: 23 to 25 in (58.5 to 63.5cm) at the shoulder Female: 21 to 23 in (53 to 58.5cm)
Weight—No requirement

EXERCISE
This dog needs plenty of exercise.

GROOMING
Brush and comb the dog daily to keep coat in condition.

FEEDING
For daily feeding, 3 cups of balanced dry dog food is recommended. Some dogs may prefer 1/2 cup water mixed with each cup of dog food. Add canned dog food for flavor.

ORIGIN AND HISTORY
The Swedish Elkhound is similar in appearance and performance to the Norwegian Elkhound. Despite its popularity in Sweden, it is little known elsewhere. The dog has had success in the show ring.

The breed was developed by Swedish huntsmen who considered their local Spitz breeds superior to the Norwegian Elkhound for hunting. It is taller than the Norwegian dog. The Swedes think it is a better hunter.

SHOW REQUIREMENTS
General Appearance—Large Spitz type, with erect ears. Robust, compact and lean without heaviness. Courageous, energetic and calm.
Color—Dark or light gray. Parts of the muzzle, cheeks and throat are light gray or cream. These are characteristic of the breed. Varicolor on legs, chest, belly and around the vent is allowed.
Head And Skull—Long, lean, broad between the eyes. Skull slightly round. Stop clearly defined but not pronounced. Nose broad. Bridge straight, wide and strong. Lips fit close over jaws. Muzzle slightly shorter than the skull, tapering gently and uniformly to the nose. Not pointed when seen from above or in profile. Cheeks flat.
Tail—Set on high. Medium length. Uniform thickness. Feathered without fringe. Carried curled up over the back, not to the side.
Feet—Not turned out. Slightly elliptical. Closed toes.
Teeth—Level bite.

The Elkhound has a long, coarse topcoat, dark at the tips, with a soft, woolly undercoat. Around the neck and front of the chest, where the coat is longest, it forms a ruff. With the dog's pointed, mobile ears, expressive eyes and tightly curled tail, it has an alert, energetic appearance.

Elkhound

The Karelian Bear Dog, named for the Karelen province in Eastern Finland, was recognized as a pure breed in 1935. It was officially recognized by the Federation Cynologique Internationale in 1946. With its striking, attractive appearance, it is popular in Finland.

Karelian Bear Dog

The Swedish Elkhound survived the adoption of the Norwegian Elkhound as the offical Scandinavian elk-hunting Spitz at the turn of the century. It was recognized as a separate breed in 1946.

Swedish Elkhound

ENGLISH FOXHOUND

Advantages
- Good hunter
- Lively

Disadvantages
- Noisy
- Not a suitable family pet

The Foxhound is not a good pet. It is usually part of a foxhunting pack. Foxhounds are attractive, vivacious pups, but are too active and destructive for the average household.

SIZE
Height—Male: 23 in (58.5cm)
Female: Slightly smaller
Weight—No requirement

EXERCISE
Vigorous exercise is necessary. Foxhounds should be able to spend all day running foxes with the hunt or similar activities.

GROOMING
Use a hound glove for grooming.

FEEDING
For daily feeding, 3 cups of balanced dry dog food is recommended. Some dogs may prefer 1/2 cup water mixed with each cup of dog food. Add canned dog food for flavor.

ORIGIN AND HISTORY
The Foxhound is descended from the now-extinct Talbot Hounds and the St. Hubert Hounds, brought to England by Norman invaders. The Foxhound is never exhibited at ordinary dog shows. It has its own events in the United Kingdom held by the Association of Masters of Foxhounds.

SHOW REQUIREMENTS
Color—Any color.
Head And Skull—Skull broad.
Feet—Toes close together and not open.
Tail—Quarters should not end abruptly or be chopped off. A curly stern, although unsightly, is not detrimental to the hound's hunting qualities.

AMERICAN FOXHOUND

Advantages
- Good hunter
- Lively

Disadvantages
- Noisy

The American Foxhound is a lighter, racier dog than the English Foxhound. It is exhibited in the show ring.

SIZE
Height—Male: 22 to 25 in
(56cm to 63.5cm)
Female: 21 to 24 in
(53 to 61cm)
Measurements made at the withers, with the hound standing in a natural position, its feet under it.
Weight—No requirement

EXERCISE
This dog needs vigorous exercise.

GROOMING
Use a hound glove for grooming.

FEEDING
For daily feeding, 3 cups of balanced dry dog food is recommended. Some dogs may prefer 1/2 cup water mixed with each cup of dog food. Add canned dog food for flavor.

ORIGIN AND HISTORY
The ancestors of today's American Foxhound were a pack of Foxhounds brought to America by Robert Brooke in 1650. They needed to be fast because their quarry, the American red fox, was speedy.

In 1770, George Washington imported Foxhounds from Great Britain. He also received a gift from Lafayette of French hounds in 1785. The French and English breeds were crossbred, producing the Virginia Hounds. They were crossed with the hounds that existed at that time to form today's American Foxhound.

SHOW REQUIREMENTS
Color—Any color.
Head And Skull—Skull fairly long. Slightly domed at occiput, with cranium broad and full. Ears set on moderately low and long, reaching nearly to the tip of the nose when drawn out. Ears are fine textured, broad, with little erectile power. Set close to the head, with the forward edge slightly turning to the cheek. Round at tip.
Feet—Foxlike. Pad full and hard. Arched toes. Strong nails.
Tail—Set on moderately high. Carried up, but not turned forward over the back. Slight curve and slight brush.

HAMILTON HOUND
Stovare

Advantages
- Good hunter

Disadvantages
- Noisy
- Not common in the United States

This medium-size hound was named after Count Hamilton, the founder of the Swedish Kennel Club. He created the breed by crossing English Foxhounds with German hounds, including the Holstein Hound and the Hanoverian Haidbracke. It is the most popular hunting hound in Sweden.

SIZE
Height—Male: 19-1/2 to 23 in
(49.5 to 58.5cm)
Female: 18 to 22-1/2 in
(46 to 57cm)
Weight—No requirement

EXERCISE
This dog requires strenuous exercise.

GROOMING
Use a hound glove for grooming.

FEEDING
Same as for the American Foxhound.

SHOW REQUIREMENTS
General Appearance—Well-built, giving an impression of strength and ruggedness. Tricolor coat.
Head And Skull—Head long, rectangular and lean. Skull moderately arched and broad. The occipital protuberance is not prominent. Stop not pronounced. Nose always black. Fairly large, with wide nostrils. Bridge is straight and parallel to the line of the skull. Upper lips full but not excessively pendulous. Muzzle is robust, rectangular and long. The zygomatic arch is not prominent.
Tail—Set on high, almost as a continuation of the backline. When down, it reaches the hocks. Thick at the root, tapering toward the tip. Carried straight out or slightly curved.
Feet—Strong and directed forward. Elastic, closed toes and large pads. Wolf feet are not desirable.
Teeth—Strong, without any defect. Scissors bite.

HARRIER

Advantages
- Good hunter

Disadvantages
- Noisy
- Needs exercise

The Harrier bears some similarity to the Beagle, but most resembles the Foxhound. Harriers and Foxhounds have been so interbred that few purebred Harriers exist today. It is slower than the Beagle or Foxhound. It is used to hunt rabbit and for foxhunting.

SIZE
Height—18 to 22 in
(46 to 56cm)
Weight—No requirement

EXERCISE
This dog needs a lot of exercise.

GROOMING
Use a hound glove for grooming.

FEEDING
Same as for the American Foxhound.

ORIGIN AND HISTORY
The word *harrier* is French for hunting dog. The Harrier is a popular animal. It is an ancient British breed; the first pack, the Penistone, was established by Sir Elias de Midhope in 1260 and existed for over 500 years. At one time, all hunting dogs in Britain were known as Harriers.

The breed is similar in appearance to the Foxhound. Primarily used for fox and rabbit hunting, it is also used for hunting leopards in South America and Ceylon. Harriers are exhibited in dog shows.

SHOW REQUIREMENTS
General Appearance—Active, balanced and strong. Shoulders slope in to the muscles of the back. Clean, not loaded on the withers or point. Back level and muscular. No dipping behind the withers or arching over the loin. Elbows point away from the ribs, running parallel with the body, not turning outward. Deep, well-sprung ribs and a deep chest. Straight legs with bone running down to toes. Hind legs and hocks stand square, with a good sweep and muscular thigh to take weight off the body. Not overburdened. Knuckles-over slightly, but not exaggerated.
Head And Skull—Medium size with bold forehead and expression. Head set on a neck of ample length. Not heavy. Stern long and controlled.
Feet—Round, catlike feet. Closed toes turn inward.

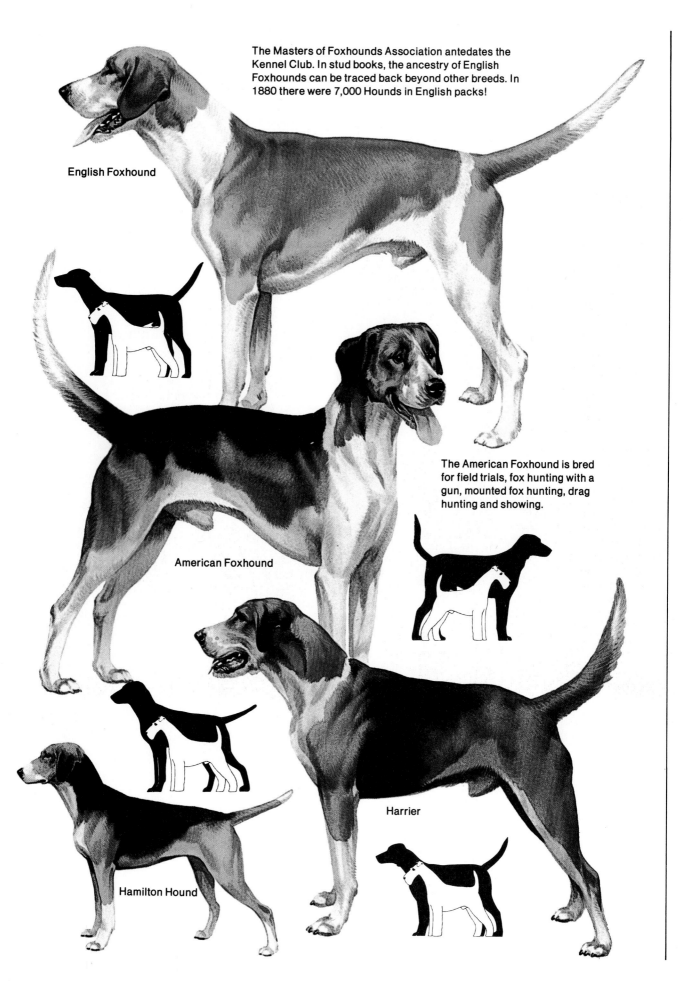

The Masters of Foxhounds Association antedates the Kennel Club. In stud books, the ancestry of English Foxhounds can be traced back beyond other breeds. In 1880 there were 7,000 Hounds in English packs!

English Foxhound

The American Foxhound is bred for field trials, fox hunting with a gun, mounted fox hunting, drag hunting and showing.

American Foxhound

Harrier

Hamilton Hound

HYGEN HOUND
Hygenhund

Advantages
● *Good hunter*

Disadvantages
● *Not a suitable pet*
● *Not common in the United States*

The Hygen Hound excels in tracking and retrieving. It is a fine hunting dog, dignified and even-tempered, but little known outside Scandinavia.

SIZE
Height—24 in (61cm)
Weight—No requirement

GROOMING
Use a hound glove daily.

FEEDING
For daily feeding, 3 cups of balanced dry dog food is recommended. Some dogs may prefer 1/2 cup water mixed with each cup of dog food. Add canned dog food for flavor.

ORIGIN AND HISTORY
This breed takes its name from a Norwegian named Hygen. In 1830, he bred the now-extinct Ringerike Hounds. The Hygen Hound emerged as a separate variety and was crossed with the Dunker Hound. An attempt was made to register the offspring under the name of Norwegian Beagles. This failed. Similarities remain but the Hygen Hound is heavier and less poised than the Dunker. It also retains the color of the Ringerikes.

Color—Red, yellow, black-brown or white with red or yellow spots.

SMALANDS HOUND
Smalandsstovare

Advantages
● *Good hunter*
● *Strong and sturdy*

Disadvantages
● *Not a suitable pet*
● *Not common in the United States*

The Smalands Hound is one of the three oldest hunting varieties in Sweden. Smaller than other hunting varieties, it is strong and sturdy. It copes well with the dense forest that covers a large area of Smaland in southern Sweden. It is a hunter and not recommended as a pet.

SIZE
Height—19-1/2 in (49.5cm)
Weight—No requirement

GROOMING
Use a hound glove for grooming.

FEEDING
For daily feeding, 3 cups of balanced dry dog food is recommended. Some dogs may prefer 1/2 cup water mixed with each cup of dog food. Add canned dog food for flavor.

ORIGIN AND HISTORY
Nearly unknown outside Scandanavia, the Smalands Hound is not recognized by the American Kennel Club. There are numerous historical references to the breed in Sweden. Many refer to the breed's naturally short tail, which is never docked.
Baron von Essen is credited with perfecting the breed at the beginning of the 20th century. He crossed the best Swedish hounds with the Schiller Hound. The Smalands Hound was recognized by the Swedish Kennel Club in 1921.

SHOW REQUIREMENTS
Color—Black with tan markings. White markings allowed on the chest and feet.
Tail—Short or reaching to the hocks. Naturally short is preferred. Never docked.

SCHILLER HOUND
Schillerstovare

Advantages
● *Good hunter*

Disadvantages
● *Not a suitable pet*
● *Not common in the United States*

The Schiller Hound is one of Sweden's most popular hunting dogs. It is shorter than the Hamilton Hound. The Schiller Hound evolved from crossing hounds from Germany, Austria and Switzerland. The Schiller Hound may be the fastest Scandinavian hound. It is used for tracking.

SIZE
Height—19-1/2 to 24 in (49.5 to 61cm)
Weight—No requirement

GROOMING
Use a hound glove daily.

FEEDING
For daily feeding, 3 cups of balanced dry dog food is recommended. Some dogs may prefer 1/2 cup water mixed with each cup of dog food. Add canned dog food for flavor.

Color—Black, with red-brown or yellow markings. White on the muzzle, neck, chest and legs.

FINNISH HOUND
Cuomenajokoira

Advantages
● *Good hunter*

Disadvantages
● *Not a suitable pet*
● *Not common in the United States*

The most popular dog in Finland, the Finnish Hound is used for hunting rabbit, fox, moose and lynx. The breed was established in the 19th century by a goldsmith named Tammelin. He crossed English, German, Swiss and Scandinavian hounds. The Finnish Hound is good-natured and friendly, but independent.

SIZE
Height—Male: 21-1/2 to 24 in (54.5 to 61cm)
Female: 20 to 22-1/2 in (51 to 57cm)
Weight—No requirement

FEEDING
For daily feeding, 3 cups of balanced dry dog food is recommended. Some dogs may prefer 1/2 cup water mixed with each cup of dog food. Add canned dog food for flavor.

GROOMING
Use a hound glove for grooming.

Color—Tricolor—Tan, black saddle and white marking on throat, breast, lower part of legs and tail.

HALDEN HOUND
Haldenstovare

Advantages
● *Good hunter*

Disadvantages
● *Not a suitable pet*
● *Not common in the United States*

This is a medium-size hound with stamina. It is little known outside Scandinavia. It is a Norwegian breed named after the town of Halden. This gentle, affectionate hound evolved by crossing Norwegian hounds with hounds from Britain, Germany, France and possibly Russia.

SIZE
Height—25 in (63.5cm)
Weight—No requirement

FEEDING
For daily feeding, 3 cups of balanced dry dog food is recommended. Some dogs may prefer 1/2 cup water mixed with each cup of dog food. Add canned dog food for flavor.

GROOMING
Use a hound glove daily.

Color—White with black patches and brown shadings on head, legs and surrounding the black. Small black or brown spots not preferred. Black must not predominate.

DUNKER HOUND
Norwegian Hound

Advantages
● *Good hunter*

Disadvantages
● *Not a suitable pet*
● *Not common in the United States*

The Dunker Hound is a Norwegian variety. It is a good tracker and retriever. It is popular in Sweden and throughout Scandinavia, but is not recognized by the American Kennel Club. It has stamina rather than speed, so it is used to hunt rabbit. The Dunker Hound is a strong dog, with a deep chest and long legs. It is affectionate and trustworthy, but is not recommended as a pet.

SIZE
Height—18-1/2 to 22 in (47 to 56cm)
Weight—No requirement

GROOMING
Use a hound glove for grooming.

FEEDING
For daily feeding, 3 cups of balanced dry dog food is recommended. Some dogs may prefer 1/2 cup water mixed with each cup of dog food. Add canned dog food for flavor.

ORIGIN AND HISTORY
The Dunker takes its name from Wilhelm Dunker. In the mid-1800s, he mated his hound, renowned as a tracker and retriever, with the best females, to carry on its hunting qualities. He crossed the Hygen Hound with the dog's offspring. An effort was made to register the offspring as Norwegian Beagles, but was rejected. The breeds have gone their separate ways, both retaining considerable tracking ability.
The Scandinavian hounds are not usually kept in packs. They hunt in forests and country where a tall hound with a good nose, able to call for the following huntsmen, is needed.

Color—Black or harlequin, with fawn and white markings. Deep chestnut objectionable. White with harlequin or liver markings disqualify the hound in competition.

Hygen Hound

Smalands Hound

Schiller Hound

Finnish Hound

Halden Hound

Dunker Hound

BLUETICK COONHOUND

Advantages
- **Good hunter**
- **Courageous**

Disadvantages
- **May chase smaller animals**
- **Voice can be annoying**

The Bluetick Coonhound was bred originally as a color variety of the English Coonhound. During the 1940s, a movement developed to form a separate breed. In 1946, the Bluetick Breeders of America agreed on breed standards.

SIZE
Height—Males: 22 to 24 in
     (55 to 60.5cm)
     Females: 21 to 25 in
     (53 to 63cm)
Weight—Males: 55 to 80 lbs
     (25 to 36kg)
     Females: 45 to 65 lbs
     (20 to 29kg)

EXERCISE
This working dog needs vigorous exercise.

GROOMING
Groom daily with a hound glove. Regular inspection of ears is necessary.

ORIGIN AND HISTORY
There were only three varieties of Coonhounds: Black and Tan, Redbone and English. In the early 1900s, a well-known, respected line of English Fox and Coonhounds known as the Old Galloway strain existed. One of the most famous was Tennessee Bill, a dog found in the pedigrees of many Bluetick Coonhounds.

English Coonhound breeders crossed the Galloway strain with others breeds known for producing trailing and treeing dogs. A definite trend toward a dog that was blue in color developed. Breeders began to selectively breed for the blue color, and the trailing and treeing ability that seemed to go with it. In 1946, the United Kennel Club approved separate breed status for the Bluetick.

SHOW REQUIREMENTS
General Appearance—Racy and muscular, with gradually sloping shoulders allowing freedom of movement. Body is neat with a glossy coat. Back moderately long, tapering to a high gather at the shoulders. Head is carried up. Eyes clear. Never wild or cowering. Active, ambitious and speedy on the trail. Voice is a medium bawl or bugle when striking or trailing, changing to a steady chop when running or treeing.

Bluetick Coonhounds are courageous and make excellent hunting dogs.

Color—Dark blue. Thickly mottled on the body and marked with black spots on the back, ears and sides. More blue than black on the body, but head and ears predominately black. Tan points appear above the eyes and on cheeks. Red ticking on feet and lower legs acceptable. A dog with red ticking may be eliminated. Off colors undesirable.
Head And Skull—Head has slightly domed skull. Broad between the ears. Muzzle is square, with deep flews. Ears placed slightly below the top of the skull, tapering to a point. Reach the end of the nose when measured. Eyes large and wide set with a houndlike expression. Dark brown or black; never lighter than hazel.
Coat—Medium texture. Lies close to the body. Smooth and glossy.
Feet—Round, with arched toes and thick pads.
Tail—Attached slightly below the back line, tapering to a moderate length. Not flagged or a rat tail.
Teeth—Even bite.

TREEING WALKER COONHOUND

Advantages
- **Intelligent**
- **Excellent trailing ability**
- **Good hunter**
- **A quick-working hound**

Disadvantages
- **Noisy**

The Treeing Walker Coonhound is considered to be the quickest working coonhound. It is often preferred as a field competitor because of its desire to be the first to the tree. Treeing Walkers are often more competitive than their owners or handlers.

SIZE
Height—22 to 27 in
     (55.5 to 68cm)
Slightly higher at shoulders than at hips.
Weight—No requirement

EXERCISE
This working dog needs vigorous exercise.

GROOMING
Groom daily with a hound glove. Check ears frequently.

ORIGIN AND HISTORY
The Treeing Walker Coonhound was considered a variety of the English Fox and Coonhound for many years. The Treeing Walker, as it is known today, developed in the Midwest through selective breeding. In 1947, it was given separate breed status by the United Kennel Club.

SHOW REQUIREMENTS
General Appearance—Energetic, intelligent, confident and strong, with graceful beauty. Sloping shoulders suggest strength and freedom of action. Deep chest.

True to its breeding, this Treeing Walker Coonhound has quickly treed its prey.

Moderately long, muscular back. Stifles strong. A bugle or a clear chop voice changes noticeably once its prey is treed.

Color—Tricolored, black, white and tan, preferred. White with either tan or black spots acceptable. In tricolors, white may be dominant with black spots and tan trim or black may be dominant with white markings, and tan trim. Any other colors are penalized.

Head And Skull—Head carried up. Skull broad and full with a prominent occiput. Stop moderate. Muzzle long and square. Flews taper.

Coat—Smooth, glossy and fine. Dense enough for protection.

Feet—Solid, compact and catlike. Arched toes and strong nails for quick action.

Tail—Strong, tapering, moderately long. Set high. Carried up and saberlike.

Teeth—Even bite.

PLOTT HOUND

Advantages
- *Courageous*
- *Bred to work large game*
- *Affectionate and friendly*
- *Quick to learn*

Disadvantages
- *Fights other dogs*

Selectively bred for over 200 years, the Plott Hound is one of the least-known American Hound breeds. A medium-size brindle dog with a do-or-die attitude, it is becoming more popular. The United Kennel Club has recognized the breed since 1946. The National Plott Hound Association has a large and growing membership.

SIZE
Height—Males: 22 to 27 in
      (53 to 68cm)
      Females: 21 to 25 in
      (53 to 63cm)
Weight—Males: 50 to 75 lbs
      (23 to 34kg)
      Females: 40 to 65 lbs
      (18 to 29kg)

EXERCISE
This working breed needs vigorous exercise. It takes readily to water.

GROOMING
Groom daily with a hound glove. Inspect ears regularly.

ORIGIN AND HISTORY
In 1750, the Plott brothers left Germany for America. With them were five brindle hunting dogs, which they had used to hunt wild boar. Johannes Plott, his family and his dogs settled in North Carolina. His son, Henry, founded the Plott Hound breed.

Using descendants of the imported hounds, Plott developed a breed with the courage and sagacity to work the region's black bears. The Great Smoky Mountain region was an excellent place to develop and train these dogs.

The hounds used by the Plott family were a private breed, shared only with family members and friends. The breed became known outside this remote area in the 1930s, when transportation and travel improved.

SHOW REQUIREMENTS
General Appearance—Active and bright, with confidence and courage. Head carried up. Muscular, sloping shoulders show speed and strength. Back slightly arched, muscular and strong. Possesses great strength and endurance.

Color—Shades of yellow, black or blue. Pattern must be brindle streaked. Background color may be lighter or darker than streaking.

Head And Skull—Head flat with medium width between and above the eyes. Muzzle moderately long but not square. Soft ears set high. Eyes brown or hazel with no drooping eyelids.

Coat—Hair is fine or medium in texture and appears glossy.

Feet—Padded, round, solid, catlike. Feet set directly under the leg.

Tail—Moderately heavy, strong at the root. Tapers. Carried up, free and saberlike.

These Plott Hound puppies will grow up to be affectionate and friendly, like their father.

This Plott Hound is a champion. Plott Hounds are quick learners and were bred to hunt large game.

ENGLISH COONHOUND

Advantages
- *Excellent trailing instinct*
- *Good hunter*

Disadvantages
- *Noisy*
- *Needs exercise*

This breed was first registered by the United Kennel Club in 1905 as the English Fox and Coonhound. As the breed developed for hunting raccoon, it became a treeing breed. This separated it from breeds used to hunt fox. The United English Breeders and Fanciers Association hosts bench shows and field trials under UKC sanction. It encourages sportsmanship and high ideals in breeding practices.

SIZE
Height—Males: 22 to 27 in (55.5 to 68cm)
Females: 21 to 25 in (53 to 63cm)
Height measured at the shoulder, never the hip.
Weight—No requirement

EXERCISE
This working breed needs vigorous exercise.

GROOMING
Use a hound glove for grooming. Check ears frequently.

ORIGIN AND HISTORY
The English Coonhound was originally known as the English Fox Hound. Its ancestors can be traced to the hounds of England and France, where breeding records have been maintained for centuries. In the United States, Fox Hounds were used to hunt a variety of game. Dogs adept at treeing their quarry, rather than running it to ground, were selectively bred to develop a line of hounds to hunt raccoon.

In 1905, the United Kennel Club recognized the English Coonhound. In the mid-1940s, the Bluetick Coonhound and the Treeing Walker Coonhound were given separate breed status by the UKC.

English Coonhounds were selectively bred to hunt raccoons. They developed into a treeing breed.

SHOW REQUIREMENTS
General Appearance—Broad-chested with a strong, slightly arched back. Muscular, with a strong, racy body. Voice must be a hound bawl.
Color—Red ticked.
Head And Skull—Skull wide and slightly domed. Muzzle is square and long. Stop medium. Ears hang low, are soft and reach nearly to the end of the nose.
Coat—Medium length and good hound type.
Feet—Strong, with arched toes and deep pads.
Tail—Carried up, but not hooked. Set high with a bit of brush.

REDBONE COONHOUND

Advantages
- *Courageous*
- *Good water dog*

Disadvantages
- *Noisy*

The Redbone Coonhound is known for its courage and ability to perform in the water. The beautiful Irish Setter-red color distinguishes it from its coonhound cousins. The National Redbone Coonhound Association, Inc. promotes the breed and sponsors events under United Kennel Club sanctions. The breed is gaining international popularity.

SIZE
Height—Males: 22 to 26 in (55.5 to 65.5cm)
Females: 21 to 25 in (53 to 63cm)
Higher at the shoulder than at the hip.
Weight—Proportionate to height.

EXERCISE
This working breed needs vigorous exercise.

GROOMING
Groom daily with a hound glove. Frequent ear checks are required.

ORIGIN AND HISTORY
Originally bred from Fox Hound stock, some breeders and fanciers preferred the solid red hound. The Redbone's instinct to tree his prey developed and it became known for its courage and ability to function in the water. Selective breeding for over 20 years set the breed's type. In 1902, the breed was recognized by the United Kennel Club.

SHOW REQUIREMENTS
General Appearance—Deep chest, with a strong, slightly arched back. Shoulders and thighs developed, denoting speed and strength.
Color—Solid red.
Head And Skull—Skull moderately broad and well-proportioned. Muzzle balanced, but not dished or upturned. Fine-textured ears set moderately low. Eyes brown to hazel, with darkness preferred.
Coat—Glossy red. A small amount of white on brisket or feet is acceptable.
Feet—Catlike, compact and padded.
Tail—Medium length with a slight brush.
Teeth—Even bite.

This Redbone Coonhound is bawling. Its deep chest and strong, slightly arched back are typical of the breed.

Bluetick Coonhound

English Coonhound

Plott Hound

Redbone Coonhound

Treeing Walker Coonhound

PHARAOH HOUND

Advantages
- **Affectionate**
- **Good hunter**
- **Good with children**

Disadvantages
- **Not suitable for city life**
- **Wary of strangers**

The Pharaoh Hound is the oldest-known domesticated dog. Two hounds hunting gazelle are depicted on a circular disk dating back to 4000 B.C. The dog played an important part in the daily life of kings and nobles in ancient Egypt. They are shown in reliefs carved on tomb walls.

The Pharaoh Hound is a medium-size hound, elegant, powerful and swift. It is intelligent, affectionate and full of fun. It is good with children, but diffident with strangers. When hunting, it is keen and fast, hunting by scent and sight.

This is a hardy, healthy breed. On the island of Gozo, where it was brought by Phoenicians, it was fed almost entirely on a meat-free diet of soup and goat's milk. Today, it enjoys a more traditional canine diet. It may become overweight.

SIZE
Height—Male: 22 to 25 in
(56 to 63.5cm)
Female: 21 to 24 in
(53 to 61cm)
Weight—No requirement

EXERCISE
This breed needs a lot of exercise.

An elegant and alert Pharaoh Hound female with her puppies. This breed is affectionate and likes to play. It is the oldest dog in recorded history and has changed little in 5000 years.

GROOMING
Its silky, smooth coat needs little attention.

FEEDING
For daily feeding, 3 cups of balanced dry dog food is recommended. Some dogs may prefer 1/2 cup water mixed with each cup of dog food. Add canned dog food for flavor. Increase rations if the dog is working.

ORIGIN AND HISTORY
The Phoenicians took these hounds with them when they settled on Malta and Gozo. Preservation of the breed, which has changed little in 5000 years, can be credited to the Maltese, who bred it for rabbit hunting.

In 1935, an American expedition led by Dr. George Reisner, found an inscription recording the burial of a dog named *Abuwtiyuw*. The burial was a ritual ceremony of a great man. When the dog died, the monarch ordered burial in a tomb of its own. Like humans buried in this fashion, its *ka* could enter the afterlife as an honored spirit. This assured its future existence as an attendant to the king.

SHOW REQUIREMENTS
General Appearance—Medium size with noble bearing and clean-cut lines. Graceful and powerful. Fast, with a free, easy movement and an alert expression.
Color—Tan, with white markings as follows: white tip on tail desirable; white on chest, called the star, white on toes, slim white blaze on center line of face permissible. Flecking, or white other than above, is undesirable.
Head And Skull—Skull long, lean and well-chiseled. Foreface slightly longer than the skull. Slight stop. Top of skull parallel with the foreface. Head represents a blunt wedge when viewed in profile and from above.

Tail—Fairly thick at the base and tapering. Whiplike. Reaches below the point of the hock in repose. Carried high and curved when the dog is in action. Not tucked between the legs. Screw tail is a fault.
Feet—Strong, knuckled and firm. Not turned in or out. Paws padded. Dewclaws may be removed.

IBIZAN HOUND

Advantages
- **Good with children**
- **Good gundog**
- **Kind dispositon**
- **Seldom fights**
- **Has acute hearing**

Disadvantages
- **Sensitive**
- **Feelings easily hurt**

The Ibizan Hound is a kind dog. It has acute hearing, so do not shout at it. It has stamina and can hunt by day or by night, alone or in pairs. This dog seldom fights and must be forced to do so. It willingly retrieves and can catch prey. It is said a pair can catch 1000 rabbits in a day. It is useful as a gundog and makes a wonderful pet.

SIZE
Height—Male: 22 to 28 in
(56 to 71cm)
Female: Slightly smaller
Weight—49 to 60 lbs
(22.2 to 22.7kg)

EXERCISE
Do not keep this hound in a confined space. It is a tireless dog, able to retrieve and jump great heights. It is an excellent companion for a sportsman.

GROOMING
The Ibizan needs a good brushing every day.

FEEDING
For daily feeding, 3 cups of balanced dry dog food is recommended. Some dogs may prefer 1/2 cup water mixed with each cup of dog food. Add canned dog food for flavor. The addition of raw fish and fruit to the diet of the Ibizan is beneficial.

ORIGIN AND HISTORY
Hounds like the Ibizan were owned by the pharaohs of Egypt. Hunting dogs of this type were drawn on rock, stone and papyrus as early as 3000 B.C. Bones of similiar hunting dogs have been found dating from 4770 B.C. The dogs probably traveled to neighboring lands with traders.

When the Romans invaded Egypt, the Carthaginians and the Phoenicians were driven to the island of Ibiza. They lived there for about a century. The strain of hound they brought with them remained on Ibiza for the next 3000 years. Although some fine hounds have been taken from Ibiza to Majorca, the purest hounds are still found on Ibiza. They retain all the colors shown in the Egyptian drawings, such as spotted red and gold on white or any of these as a single color.

The head of the noble Ibizan Hound. This ancient breed makes a sensitive, gentle pet.

SHOW REQUIREMENTS
General Appearance—Tall, narrow and finely built. Large, erect ears.
Color—White, chestnut, gold or any combination of these.
Head And Skull—Long, flat skull with prominent occipital bone. Stop not well-defined. Slightly convex muzzle. Length of muzzle from the eyes to the tip of the nose equal to the length from the eyes to the occiput. Nose flesh-color, protruding beyond the teeth. Jaw strong and lean.
Tail—Long, thin, low set reaching below the hock. When passed between the legs and around the flank, reaches the spine. May be carried high when excited.
Feet—Arched toes. Thick pads. Light-color claws. Front feet may turn slightly outward. Dewclaws not removed in front. No hind dewclaws.

At the beginning of this century, the Ibizan Hound was common as a hunting dog on the Spanish mainland. Although used for coursing rabbits, in some regions it hunted stag and bear. It was also used as a gundog. More recently, it has become popular in Southern Europe, and is frequently seen in large numbers at major shows. The modern Ibizan Hound closely resembles its ancestors of almost 50 centuries ago.

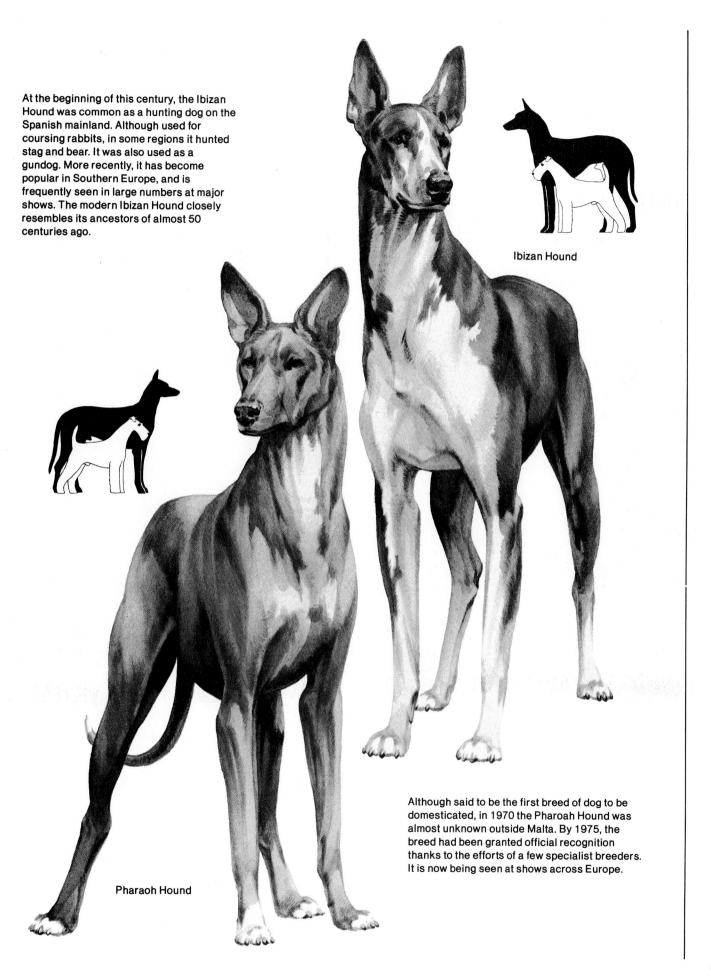

Ibizan Hound

Pharaoh Hound

Although said to be the first breed of dog to be domesticated, in 1970 the Pharoah Hound was almost unknown outside Malta. By 1975, the breed had been granted official recognition thanks to the efforts of a few specialist breeders. It is now being seen at shows across Europe.

SLOUGHI

Advantages
- **Good guard**
- **Good companion**
- **Healthy**
- **Intelligent**
- **Odorless**
- **Reliable with children**

Disadvantages
- **Has strong hunting instincts**
- **Not common in the United States**

The Sloughi is a rare hound that hunts by sight. Like the Saluki, which it closely resembles, it is capable of great speed. In the Mid-East, it is used for hunting gazelles.

This is an intelligent, gentle dog. Even though it retains strong hunting instincts, it adapts to life as a pet.

SIZE
Height—22 to 30 in (56 to 76cm)
Weight—No requirement

EXERCISE
This dog needs a large yard or suitable exercise area.

GROOMING
Brush daily with a soft brush and use a hound glove.

FEEDING
For daily feeding, 5 cups of balanced dry dog food is recommended. Some dogs may prefer 1/2 cup water mixed with each cup of dog food. Add canned dog food for flavor.

ORIGIN AND HISTORY
The Sloughi is frequently mistaken for a smooth Saluki. It is heavier

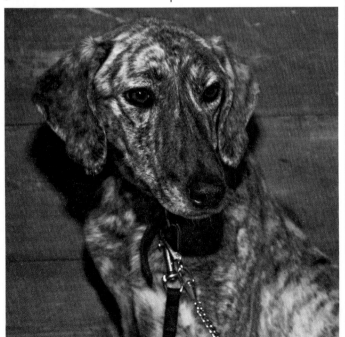

The Sloughi is capable of great speed and is used to hunt gazelle.

than the Saluki, often with black markings around the eyes. It evolved in Morocco.

The Sloughi and the Saluki are recognized by the Arabs as purebred. They call them *el hor,* the aristocrats. The Sloughi's sandy color helps it hunt gazelle because its quarry is unable to distinguish it from the background. This breed is recognized by the Federation Cynologique Internationale.

Color—Sand, all shades of fawn, with or without a black mask or black saddle. Also off-white, brindle or black with tan and brindle.

SALUKI
Gazelle Hound

Advantages
- **Good guard**
- **Good companion**
- **Healthy**
- **Intelligent**
- **Odorless**
- **Good with children**

Disadvantages
- **Strong hunting instincts**

The Saluki and the horse are prized by Arabs. The Saluki is capable of great speed and able to keep pace with Arab stallions. It is still used in the Middle East for hunting gazelle. In the West, it is kept mainly as a pet and show dog. It is intelligent and aloof, but is a faithful, gentle companion, trustworthy with children. The Saluki must be kept under control.

SIZE
Height—Male: 23 to 28 in (58.5 to 71cm)
Female: Slightly smaller
Weight—No requirement

A Saluki and her pup. These elegant, intelligent dogs make excellent pets.

EXERCISE
Salukis need plenty of exercise.

GROOMING
Brush daily with a soft brush and use a hound glove. It may be necessary to comb ear and tail fringes.

FEEDING
For daily feeding, 3 cups of balanced dry dog food is recommended. Some dogs may prefer 1/2 cup water mixed with each cup of dog food. Add canned dog food for flavor.

ORIGIN AND HISTORY
The Saluki is an ancient breed from the Middle East. Like the Afghan and Greyhound, it hunts by sight. It may be named after Saluk in the Yemen, but its likeness is found in the tombs of Egyptian Pharaohs.

The breed did not receive recognition by the American Kennel Club until 1927. It was known earlier in Great Britain because a litter bred in London Zoo in 1836 was shown as the Persian Greyhound. In 1896, the Amherstia Foundation Kennels started with two imported hounds. The breed was recognized by the British Kennel Club in 1922.

In 1927, the Saluki Club of America was formed. Later that year, the AKC granted registration status.

There are two coat types found in Saluki: the smoothcoat and roughcoat. The points are the same, except the smoothcoat has no feathering.

SHOW REQUIREMENTS
General Appearance—Graceful, with speed and endurance coupled with strength and activity. Expression is dignified and gentle with deep, far-seeing eyes.

Color—White, cream, fawn, gold, red, grizzle and tan, tricolor, white, black and tan, or variations of these colors.
Head And Skull—Head long and narrow. Skull moderately wide between ears, not domed. Stop not pronounced. Nose black or liver.
Tail—Long, set on low, carried naturally in a curve. Feathered on the underside with long silky hair. Not bushy.
Feet—Moderate length. Toes long and arched. Not splayed out, but not catfooted. Strong and supple. Feathered between toes.
Teeth—Strong and level.

The Saluki has strong hunting instincts and must be kept under control.

The Sloughi is a tall, elegant sighthound. It is similar to a Greyhound in appearance but has a flatter, shorter back. The breed was adopted by the Moroccan aristocracy and bred in their kennels. It has been allowed to intermingle with other breeds. A purebred Sloughi is now rare.

Sloughi

Although often regarded as a prize-winning show hound, the Saluki is the traditional hunting dog of the Bedouin tribes. Speedy, lithe, sturdy and tough, this dog has been a treasured possession of the tribesmen. It was often hidden from strangers and protected as a member of the family.

Saluki

AFGHAN HOUND

Advantages
- **Loyal and affectionate**
- **Good with older children**

Disadvantages
- **Independent**
- **Needs exercise**
- **Needs daily grooming**
- **Needs firm, loving handling**
- **Can be troublesome**

The Afghan is dignified, aloof and likes comfort. It likes to sit in a cosy armchair, but may not be the best choice for apartment dwellers or those with a small house and yard. The Afghan is a hunting dog. It is affectionate to its owners and usually trustworthy with children. It is also independent and can have a temper.

It is impossible to show an Afghan too much affection. Maintain superiority, especially during showing and training sessions.

SIZE
Height—Male: 27 to 29 in
(68.5 to 73.5cm)
Female: 24 to 27 in
(60.5 to 68cm)
Weight—No requirement

EXERCISE
Afghans need plenty of exercise to keep fit and happy. Their original task was to hunt wolves and gazelle in the deserts of Afghanistan. A walk in the park or a run in a yard may not be enough to expend their boundless energy. Allow a puppy unrestricted exercise in a safe, enclosed place. Give an adult a minimum of a half hour's free running a day, in addition to walking on a leash.

GROOMING
Daily grooming is necessary to prevent the thick coat from matting. A well-groomed Afghan is beautiful; a neglected dog looks terrible. This breed is not for those with little time for grooming and exercising.

The only brush for an Afghan's coat is one with an air cushion behind the tufts. The best kind is one made for humans. The nylon type is less expensive, but use a coat lubricant with it. Otherwise, static electricity builds up and causes the hair to become brittle. An air-cushioned brush with steel pins is excellent and inexpensive.

FEEDING
For daily feeding, 5 cups of balanced dry dog food is recommended. Some dogs may prefer 1/2 cup water mixed with each cup of dog food. Add canned dog food for flavor.

ORIGIN AND HISTORY
The Afghan is an ancient breed said to have been taken into the Ark by Noah. The book *Champion Dogs of the World* states, "Even if one rejects this claim it still remains virtually certain that some sort of Afghan existed thousands of years ago in the Middle East." Today, experts believe it was crossed with the Saluki.

It found its way to Afghanistan, where it grew a long, shaggy coat for protection against the harsh climate. Eventually, royal and aristocratic families became interested in it.

The first Afghan Hound Breed Club was formed in the United States in 1926.

SHOW REQUIREMENTS
General Appearance—Dignified and aloof. Gait is smooth, strong and dignified. It has speed and power. Head held proudly.
Color—All colors are acceptable, such as fawn, silver, gray and tan grizzle, and black and tan.
Head And Skull—Skull long. Not too narrow, with a prominent occiput. Foreface long, with punishing jaws and slight stop. Skull balanced, with a long topknot. Nose black.
Tail—Not too short. Set on low with a ring at the end. Raised when in action. Sparsely feathered.
Feet—Forefeet strong. Large in length and width. Covered with long thick hair. Toes arched. Pasterns long and springy, especially in front. Pads down on the ground. Hind feet long, but not as broad as forefeet. Covered with long thick hair.
Teeth—Level bite preferred, but a scissors not penalized. Undershot or overshot bite is faulted.

GREYHOUND

Advantages
- **Built for speed**
- **Adaptable**
- **Affectionate**
- **Good with children**
- **Loyal**

Disadvantages
- **Chases fast moving objects**
- **May get rheumatism**
- **May get arthritis**

The Greyhound is an ancient and misunderstood breed. Although built for speed, and used for racing, the Greyhound is lazy. It happily adapts to life as a pet. It is good-natured, friendly and affectionate. It is gentle with children.

The retired Greyhound racer is not an old animal. It is unlikely to be more than three or four years old. It may be as young as 18 months if it proves unsuitable for racing. There is no way to prevent a Greyhound from chasing cats and other small moving objects. It is a natural instinct. Outdoors, this dog must be kept on a leash at all times.

SIZE
Height—Male: 28 to 30 in
(71 to 76cm)
Female: 27 to 28 in
(68.5 to 71cm)
Weight—No requirement

EXERCISE
Three or four short walks a day is sufficient. Although the Greyhound must never be exercised off a leash, it enjoys a run. It is a sensitive creature and learns to respond quickly to your tone of voice, which is useful. The Greyhound has been clocked at up to 37mph (60 kph).

GROOMING
Daily use of a hound glove will keep the coat shining.

FEEDING
For daily feeding, 3 cups of balanced dry dog food is recommended. Some dogs may prefer 1/2 cup water mixed with each cup of dog food. Add canned dog food for flavor.

ORIGIN AND HISTORY
The Greyhound is a pure breed. It has not evolved from crossing with other types. It is unlikely it has changed since early Egyptian times, as proved by a carving of a Greyhound in a tomb in the Nile Valley from 4000 B.C.

SHOW REQUIREMENTS
General Appearance—Strong, with generous proportions. Muscular, symmetrical formation. A long head and neck. Well-laid shoulders, deep chest, roomy body. Arched loins, powerful quarters, sound legs and feet, supple limbs.
Color—Black, white, red, blue, fawn, fallow or brindle or any of these colors broken with white.
Head And Skull—Long and moderate width. Flat skull, slight stop. Jaws powerful and well-chiseled.
Tail—Long, set on low. Strong at the root, tapering to tip. Carried low and slightly curved.
Feet—Moderate in length, with compact, knuckled toes. Strong pads.

The Greyhound has been used for chasing game for many centuries, probably since Roman times. Its development has proceeded along three distinct lines: the larger and narrower show dog; the smaller, agile coursing hound; and the lean, muscular track-racing dog, the finest of which are now bred in Ireland.

Greyhound

Afghan Hound

The Afghan Hound is a glamorous dog. It stands out at any show with its long, flowing coat and sweeping grace.

LARGE MUNSTERLANDER

Advantages
- *Affectionate*
- *Learns quickly*
- *Good pet*
- *Loyal*
- *Trustworthy*

Disadvantages
- *Needs space to exercise*
- *Not common in the United States*

The Large Munsterlander has been known in Germany as long as other gundogs. It resembles a setter in build and coat, and has a head like a spaniel. It is a multipurpose gundog with a keen sense of smell and great stamina. It has equal ability on land or in water. It is an intelligent, amiable pet.

SIZE
Height—Male: 24 in (61cm)
　　　　Female: 23 in (58.5cm)
Weight—Male: 55 to 65 lbs
　　　　(25 to 29.5kg)
　　　　Female: 55 lbs (25kg)

EXERCISE
This energetic dog needs plenty of exercise.

GROOMING
A daily brushing will maintain its coat.

FEEDING
For daily feeding, 5 cups of balanced dry dog food is recommended. Some dogs may prefer 1/2 cup water mixed with each cup of dog food. Add canned dog food for flavor. Increase rations if your dog is working.

ORIGIN AND HISTORY
The best working males were mated to the best working females, with little regard to color, breeding or coat texture. Early in the 19th century, people became breed- and color-conscious, so records of the best dogs were kept. The Large

The keen expression of the intelligent Small Munsterlander.

The Large Munsterlander makes an ideal gundog. It has a keen sense of smell, plenty of energy and strong jaws.

Munsterlander was classed as a German Longhair Pointer.

When the German Kennel Club was founded, the general stud book came into being. Only brown and white German Longhair Pointers were registered. Odd-color puppies were often given away to farmers and gamekeepers, who were delighted to have well-bred dogs to work. They were not bothered by the dogs' lack of color or registration. This was fortunate, for it resulted in saving the breed now known as the Large Munsterlander.

SHOW REQUIREMENTS
General Appearance—Alert and energetic, with a strong, muscular body. Good movement with drive.
Color—Head solid black. White blaze, snip or star allowed. Body white with black patches, flecked, ticked or combination of these.
Head And Skull—Well-proportioned to the body. Skull broad, slightly round, with no pronounced occiput. Strong jaw muscles. Black nose, with wide soft nostrils. Slight rise from the nasal bone to the forehead but no pronounced stop. Lips slightly round and well-fitting.
Tail—Set on in line with the back. Base thick, tapering evenly toward the tip. Feathered. Carried horizontally or curved slightly upward. Docking optional.

Feet—Tight, moderately rounded and knuckled. Dense hair between toes. Padded. Nails black and strong.

The Small Munsterlander, or Moorland Spaniel, is a smaller, lighter dog, 17 to 22 inches (43 to 56cm) tall. Its coat is brown and white, usually with a brown head.

DRENTSE PARTRIDGE DOG
Drentse Patrijshond, Dutch Partridge Dog

Advantages
- *Affectionate*
- *Even-tempered*
- *Good gundog*
- *Intelligent*

Disadvantages
- *Not common in the United States*

The Drentse Partridge Dog is not well-known outside Holland. It is an attractive dog that looks like a Springer Spaniel. It combines the role of all-purpose gundog with affectionate pet. It points and retrieves, and has been a successful competitor in Field Trials in Holland.

SIZE
Height—23 to 24 in
　　　　(57.5 to 60cm)
Weight—No requirement

EXERCISE
This dog needs plenty of exercise.

GROOMING
Regular brushing maintains the coat.

FEEDING
For daily feeding, 3 cups of balanced dry dog food is recommended. Some dogs may prefer 1/2 cup water mixed with each cup of dog food. Add canned dog food for flavor.

ORIGIN AND HISTORY
The Drentse Partridge Dog, or *Partijshond,* comes from the Drentse district of Northeast Holland. It has existed there for 300 years. It evolved through early crossings with longhaired German sporting breeds. It is an accomplished bird dog.

SHOW REQUIREMENTS
General Appearance—Well-proportioned body, longer than height at the withers. Hair on the body gives the impression it is long because of the fringe on the neck, ears, legs and tail.
Color—White background, with brown or orange markings.
Head And Skull—Skull broad and flat. Stop scarcely defined. Passage from skull to muzzle gradual, with no sudden transition when seen from front or profile. Occipital protuberance not accentuated. Supraorbital ridges well-developed. Main jaw muscles slightly pronounced. Nose large and brown. Bridge straight, not arched or hollow. A slight arching allowed, but a pug nose is unacceptable. Lips thin and close fitting. Muzzle is wedge shape and cut blunt at the end.
Tail—Natural, not docked. Set on high. Reaches the point of the hock. Carried low or as a saber tail. When the dog is in action, tail is carried almost horizontally, with the final third turned up. Tail moves in a circle, especially when the dog has caught scent of game. Never carried over the back. Abundant fringes begin at the set-on of the tail, grow shorter toward the tip.
Feet—Round or oval. Closed toes, with developed pads.
Teeth—Strong, with an efficient bite.

A German breed, the Large Munsterlander has been known for many centuries. It was bred principally for work. Only the most proficient working dogs were used for breeding, so individual variation in type and size was considerable. Selective breeding since the beginning of the century has produced the typical setterlike gundog recognized today.

Large Munsterlander

Drentse Partridge Dog

Intelligent, easy to train and adaptable, the Drentse Partridge Dog has remained the same in appearance for at least 300 years. The dog resembles a cross between a setter and a spaniel. It may be the ancestor of many modern gundogs.

AIREDALE TERRIER

Advantages
- *Intelligent*
- *Good guard*
- *Loyal to owner*
- *Good with children*
- *Even-tempered*

Disadvantages
- *Can be overly protective*
- *Fights if provoked*

The Airedale is the largest terrier. It has stamina and makes a fine pet and guard. Before World War I, the Airedale worked as a patrol dog with dock and railway police. During the war, it served with the Russian and British armies. It also worked for the Red Cross, locating wounded and carrying messages. Its abilities as a messenger and guard were considered superior to those of the German Shepherd. The Airedale also took part in World War II, but was gradually replaced by the German Shepherd, Doberman, Boxer and other dogs.

SIZE
Height—Male: 24 in (60cm) at the shoulder
Female: Slightly smaller
Weight—55 lbs (25kg)

EXERCISE
This dog adapts to living in a small space. Give it two 20-minute walks a day. It also loves to run with horses. The Airedale can live outside in a heated kennel with an adequate run.

GROOMING
The Airedale needs daily grooming with a stiff-bristle brush. If you plan to show the dog, its coat must be stripped regularly. Ask the breeder to show you how to do it. You may want to have the job done by a skilled groomer. If you do not plan to show, strip your Airedale only in spring and summer for coolness and neatness. Allow it to keep its thick coat for winter protection.

FEEDING
For daily feeding, 3 cups of balanced dry dog food is recommended. Some dogs may prefer 1/2 cup water mixed with each cup of dog food. Add canned dog food for flavor.

Watch the Airedale's weight. If it becomes too heavy, reduce the amount of food.

ORIGIN AND HISTORY
The Airedale is named after the valley of Aire in England. It was originally called the Waterside or working terrier. Ancestors were kept for rodent control by Yorkshire gamekeepers. It was probably crossed with the Otterhound.

In the late 1800s, this bigger terrier was bred as an attractive and useful dog. It was soon adopted as a pet but is still an expert hunter.

SHOW REQUIREMENTS
General Appearance—Keen expression and quick movement. Character shown by expression of the eyes and the carriage of ears and tail.
Color—Head and ears tan, with the exception of dark markings on each side of the skull. Ears a darker shade. Legs tan to the thighs and elbows. Body dark grizzle.
Head And Skull—Skull long and flat. Not too broad between the ears. Skull free from wrinkles, with stop barely visible. Cheeks level. Jaws deep, powerful, strong and muscular. Strength of foreface essential. No excess development of jaws to give a round or bulging appearance to cheeks. Cheekiness not desired. Lips tight. Nose black.
Tail—Set on high and carried up. Not curled over the back. Strength and substance. Fair length.
Feet—Small, round and compact with depth of pad. Cushioned. Toes moderately arched, not turned in or out.
Teeth—Strong and white with a level or scissors bite.

DOBERMAN PINSCHER
Dobermann

Advantages
- *Alert*
- *Brave*
- *Loyal*
- *Good guard*
- *Intelligent*

Disadvantages
- *Not friendly with strangers*
- *Can be overly protective*

The Doberman is a strong, alert guard that enjoys the comforts of a home. It will protect its family with its life. The Doberman usually overcomes any opponent and is one of the best guard dogs in the world. It takes its responsibilities seriously, is skilled at tracking and makes a fine police or obedience dog.

SIZE
Height—Male: 27 in (68.5cm) at the withers
Female: 25-1/2 in (64cm)
Weight—No requirement

EXERCISE
Give a Doberman at least 40 minutes of exercise each day.

GROOMING
This dog needs little grooming other than daily rubbing with a towel to remove loose hairs.

FEEDING
For daily feeding, 5 cups of balanced dry dog food is recommended. Some dogs may prefer 1/2 cup water mixed with each cup of dog food. Add canned dog food for flavor.

ORIGIN AND HISTORY
Louis Dobermann was a tax collector during the 1880s, in Germany. He decided to breed a fierce dog to accompany him on his rounds. He wanted a medium to large dog, short-coated, easy to maintain, with courage, alertness and stamina. It was not a hard task for him because he was keeper of the local dog pound and had access to numerous strays.

The existing German Pinscher was aggressive and alert, so it was around this breed Dobermann founded his stock. He introduced the Rottweiler, a dog with great stamina and tracking ability, and the Manchester Terrier. It is probably from the Manchester that the Doberman obtained its gleaming coat and black and tan markings. The Pointer may also have been used.

A 10-week-old Doberman.

SHOW REQUIREMENTS
General Appearance—A well-set body. Muscular and elegant, with proud carriage and bold, alert temperament. Form compact and tough. Capable of speed. Gait light and elastic. Eyes show intelligence and firmness of character. Shyness or viciousness heavily penalized by show judges.
Color—Colors allowed are black; brown; blue, with rust red markings; red; blue or Isabella, with rust red markings. Markings sharply defined, appearing above each eye and on the muzzle, throat and forechest, on all legs, feet and below the tail. White markings undesirable.
Head And Skull—Proportionate to the body. Long, filled out under the eyes. Clean cut. Resembles a blunt wedge. Top of the skull flat with a slight stop. Muzzle line extends parallel to the top line of the skull. Cheeks flat and lips tight. Nose black in black dogs, dark brown in brown dogs and dark gray in blue dogs.
Tail—Docked at the first or second joint. Appears as a continuation of the spine, without material drop.
Feet—Forefeet arched, compact, not turning in or out. All dewclaws removed. Long, flat paws and weak pasterns penalized. Hind feet arched, compact and catlike.
Teeth—Scissors bite. Four or more missing teeth or an undershot or overshot jaw is disqualifying.

The Airedale has frequently been judged best of all breeds at major shows. This may be due to the perfection of type attained in this breed. To be shown to its full advantage, a potential champion requires long hours of brushing, trimming and shaping its thick, wiry coat.

Airedale

Doberman

In the past, the Doberman's public image has been marred by its sharp, fiery temperament. Generally, these traits have been bred out. Owners are encouraged to attend classes to train their dogs for obedience work, which reduces the dog's aggression.

BEARDED COLLIE

Advantages
- *Devoted pet*
- *Good with children*
- *Intelligent*
- *Natural herder*
- *Playful*

Disadvantages
- *Needs plenty of exercise*

The Bearded Collie, or Beardie, is not as well known as other collies. It almost became extinct after World War II. Today, numbers of this breed are increasing. It is a lovable dog, suited for family life. It retains its herding capabilities. It is easily trained, reliable with children and is a willing, lively playmate.

SIZE
Height—Male: 21 to 22 in (53.5 to 55cm) at the shoulder Female: 20 to 21 in (51 to 53.5cm)
Weight—No requirement

EXERCISE
This dog needs plenty of exercise.

GROOMING
Brush the dog daily. Bathing and chalking are necessary for show.

FEEDING
For daily feeding, 3 cups of balanced dry dog food is recommended. Some dogs may prefer 1/2 cup water mixed with each cup of dog food. Add canned dog food for flavor.

ORIGIN AND HISTORY
This breed bears a striking resemblance to the Old English Sheepdog. It is probably one of the oldest herding dogs in Scotland. It comes from purebred Polish Lowland Sheepdogs. Two females and a male were exchanged for a ram and a ewe on a trading voyage to Scotland in 1514. Some say it has Magyar or Hungarian blood.

Breed survival was assured when Mrs. G. Willison acquired a female Beardie puppy—then without pedigree—in 1944. After a search for a Beardie male, she found one playing with its owners on the beach. They were willing to sell and from this pair all of today's Beardies are descended.

SHOW REQUIREMENTS
General Appearance—Active, with a long, lean body. No stumpiness. Shows daylight under the body. Does not look too heavy. Face has an inquiring expression. Movement free and active.
Color—Slate-gray or red-fawn, black, all shades of gray, brown and sand, with or without white collie markings.

Head And Skull—Broad, flat skull with ears set high. Long foreface with moderate stop. Nose black except with brown or fawn coats, when brown is permitted.
Tail—Set low. Moderately long, with abundant hair or brush. Carried low when the dog is quiet, with an upward swirl at the tip. Carried up when the dog is excited, but not over the back.
Feet—Oval. Soles padded. Toes arched and close together. Covered with hair, including between the pads.

The Dutch Schapendoes.

A dog bearing a strong resemblance to the Bearded Collie is the Dutch Schapendoes, which has Beardie blood. It probably has Bergamasco, Puli and Briard blood, too. It is a popular sheepdog, guard and pet in Holland, but is little known in other countries.

SMOOTH COLLIE

Advantages
- *Affectionate*
- *Easily trained*
- *Excellent pet*
- *Good with children*
- *Loyal*

Disadvantages
- *Not friendly with strangers*

The Smooth Collie is like the Rough Collie in temperament. It makes an ideal pet, is hardy and simple to groom. It is identical to the Rough Collie except in coat. See *Show Requirements*.

SIZE
Height—Male: 24 to 26 in (60 to 65cm) at the shoulder Female: 22 to 24 in (55 to 60cm) Undersize or oversize penalized.
Weight—Male: 45 to 65 lbs (20.5 to 29.5kg) Female: 40 to 55 lbs (18.1 to 25kg)

EXERCISE
Give this dog normal daily exercise.

GROOMING
Brush daily to keep the coat in condition.

FEEDING
For daily feeding, 5 cups of balanced dry dog food is recommended. Some dogs may prefer 1/2 cup water mixed with each cup of dog food. Add canned dog food for flavor.

ORIGIN AND HISTORY
Most Collies can be traced to a tricolor dog called Trefoil, born in 1873. Although the Rough Collie has maintained international popularity, the Smooth Collie is seldom seen. It might have become extinct if not for the determined efforts of dedicated breeders.

The Smooth Collie is a variety of collie. It is judged separately and occupies a place in the working group.

SHOW REQUIREMENTS
General Appearance—Intelligent, alert and active. Dignified. Movements smooth and graceful. Appearance of a dog able to work.
Color—Sable, tricolor, blue merle and white, with sable or tricolor markings.
Head And Skull—Head in proportion to the size of the dog. When viewed from front and profile, looks like a blunt, clean wedge. Smooth outline. Nose black.
Tail—Long, with the bone reaching to the hock joint. Carried low when the dog is quiet, with a slight upward swirl at the tip. Carried up when the dog is excited, but never over the back.
Feet—Oval, with padded soles. Toes arched and close together. Hind feet slightly less arched.
Teeth—Scissors bite.

ROUGH COLLIE

Advantages
- *Affectionate*
- *Easily trained*
- *Good pet*
- *Loves children*
- *Loyal*

Disadvantages
- *Not friendly with strangers*

Identifying the type of Collie a person wants causes concern to buyers and breeders. People tend to have a fixed idea of what they want, whether it is a Rough, Smooth, Border, Old English or Bearded type. If you want a dog like Lassie, you are thinking of a Rough Collie. It is sometimes erroneously called a Scottish Collie. The Sheltie or Shetland Sheepdog is a miniature Lassie.

The Rough Collie makes an ideal family pet. It is affectionate, loyal, hardy and easy to groom despite its thick coat.

SIZE
Height—Male: 22 to 24 in (55 to 60cm) at the shoulder Female: 20 to 22 in (51 to 55cm)
Weight—Male: 45 to 65 lbs (20.5 to 29.5kg) Female: 40 to 55 lbs (18.1 to 25kg)

EXERCISE
Give this dog normal daily exercise.

GROOMING
Brush daily. Vacuum the dog, using the small brush if it gets muddy. Get the dog accustomed to the noise first.

FEEDING
For daily feeding, 5 cups of balanced dry dog food is recommended. Some dogs may prefer 1/2 cup water mixed with each cup of dog food. Add canned dog food for flavor.

ORIGIN AND HISTORY
The Rough Collie is considered a Scottish breed. Its ancestors were introduced in England and Scotland from Iceland 400 years ago. As guardians of the flock, they acquired their name in Scotland. Sheep with black faces and legs were known as colleys. In 1860, a breed member was exhibited in a British show.

SHOW REQUIREMENTS
General Appearance—Dignified. No part out of proportion to the whole.
Color—Same as for Smooth Collie.
Head And Skull—Head in proportion to the size of the dog. When viewed from the front or side, it looks like a blunt, clean wedge. Smooth in outline. Nose black.
Tail—Long, with the bone reaching to the hock joint. Carried low when the dog is quiet, with a slight upward swirl at the tip. Carried up when the dog is excited, but not over the back.
Feet—Oval in shape, with padded soles. Toes arched and close together. Hind feet slightly less arched.
Teeth—Scissors bite.

Although bred as a sheep herder, the Bearded Collie is not as popular with the shepherd as other collies. It is more suited to simple cattle driving than sheep herding.

Bearded Collie

Smooth Collie

Both Rough and Smooth Collies make good pets, but are probably happiest when given the freedom of fields and open country.

Rough Collie

GERMAN LONGHAIR POINTER
Langhaar

Advantages
- Easily trained
- Even-tempered
- Good gundog
- Good with children
- Obedient

Disadvantages
- Needs plenty of exercise
- Not common in the United States

The German Longhair Pointer, or *Langhaar*, is almost extinct. It is a healthy dog, with a good temperament, endurance and the swimming and hunting abilities of pointers. It is energetic and loyal to its master.

SIZE
Height—24 to 25 in (60 to 62.5cm) at the shoulder
Weight—No requirement

EXERCISE
This dog needs plenty of exercise.

GROOMING
Brush the coat regularly.

FEEDING
For daily feeding, 5 cups of balanced dry dog food is recommended. Some dogs may prefer 1/2 cup water mixed with each cup of dog food. Add canned dog food for flavor.

ORIGIN AND HISTORY
This dog looks different from other pointers. It resembles a setter because it evolved as the result of crossing Dutch and French spaniels and local German breeds with the Gordon Setter, which was favored by German hunters. It is an attractive dog with endurance. Its numbers are dwindling in favor of the Wirehair Pointer.

SHOW REQUIREMENTS
These are Federation Cynologique Internationale standards.
General Appearance—Robust, muscular build. Distinguished appearance. Intelligent and noble. Lively without nervousness.
Color—Self-colored or light brown. Red and black penalized.
Head And Skull—Long, lean and broad. Divided into equal length for skull and muzzle. Upper part of the head slightly round. Head gives distinction to general appearance. Nose flat and deep brown.
Tail—Carried horizontally. May slightly curve upward. Tail may be docked if too long or out of proportion with the rest of the body. Fringed long hair at the midpoint of the tail.
Feet—Closed and moderate length. Round.

GERMAN WIREHAIR POINTER
Drahthaar

Advantages
- Easily trained
- Even-tempered
- Excellent gundog
- Good with children
- Obedient

Disadvantages
- Needs plenty of exercise
- Aggressive

In Germany, the German Wirehair Pointer is known as the *Drahthaar*. Literally translated, it means *wirehair*. It is more spirited and aggressive than other pointers, with stronger guarding instincts and a hardy physique. It is an excellent gundog.

SIZE
Height—Male: 24 to 26 in (60 to 65cm) Female: Smaller, not less than 22 in (55cm)
Weight—No requirement

EXERCISE
This dog needs plenty of exercise.

GROOMING
Brush the coat regularly to keep it in condition.

FEEDING
Same as for the German Longhair Pointer.

ORIGIN AND HISTORY
The German Wirehair Pointer is almost identical to the Shorthair, except for the coat. They also have different backgrounds. The English Pointer contributed to the development of the Wirehair. It also came from other hunting breeds. It is mentioned in medieval German documents.

SHOW REQUIREMENTS
General Appearance—Medium size, with noble bearing. Rough hair. Intelligent expression. Devoted and energetic.
Color—Solid liver; liver and white spotted; liver and white spotted and ticked; liver and white ticked. Black penalized.
Head And Skull—Head medium length with a long, strong muzzle.
Tail—Starts high and thick, growing gradually thinner. Docked to two-fifths its original length. When quiet, tail carried down. When moving horizontally, never held high over the back or bent.
Feet—Compact, close knit, round or spoon shape. Padded. Toes arched. Heavily nailed.

GERMAN SHORTHAIR POINTER

Advantages
- Easily trained
- Even-tempered
- Good gundog
- Good with children
- Obedient

Disadvantages
- Needs plenty of exercise

The German Shorthair Pointer is a good all-around sporting dog. It is affectionate and good with children. It is happiest when hunting or swimming.

SIZE
Height—Male: 23 to 25 in (57.5 to 62.5cm) Female: 21 to 23 in (53.5 to 57.5cm)
Weight—No requirement

EXERCISE
This dog needs plenty of exercise.

GROOMING
Brush the coat regularly.

FEEDING
Same as for the German Longhair Pointer.

ORIGIN AND HISTORY
The German Shorthair Pointer originated in Spain. It was crossed with the English Foxhound for speed, the Bloodhound for nose and the English Pointer to retain its pointing ability.

SHOW REQUIREMENTS
General Appearance—Powerful, with speed. Alert and energetic, not nervous. Well-coordinated movements.
Color—Solid liver; liver and white spotted; liver and white spotted and ticked; liver and white ticked; liver roan. Black penalized.
Head And Skull—Clean cut. Not too light or too heavy. Proportionate to the body. Skull broad and slightly round. Nose brown. Nostrils open and soft.
Tail—Starts high and thick, growing gradually thinner. Docked two-fifths of its length. When quiet, tail carried down. When moving horizontally, never held high over the back or bent.
Feet—Compact, close knit, round or spoon shape. Padded. Toes arched. Heavily nailed.

POINTER

Advantages
- Even-tempered
- Obedient
- Good with children
- Easily trained
- Good gundog

Disadvantages
- Needs plenty of exercise

The Pointer is known for its classic pose—pointing with its nose and tail in the direction of game that has been shot. This friendly dog makes an ideal pet. It gets along with other animals and children. It needs a lot of exercise.

SIZE
Height—Male: 25 to 27 in (62.5 to 68.5cm) Female: 24 to 26 in (60 to 65cm)
Weight—No requirement

EXERCISE
This dog needs plenty of exercise.

GROOMING
Brush the coat regularly.

FEEDING
Same as for the German Longhair Pointer.

ORIGIN AND HISTORY
There is controversy as to whether the Pointer originated in Spain or was produced in Britain through crossing Bloodhounds, Foxhounds and Greyhounds. One authority on the breed, William Arkwright, spent his life traveling to discover the history and development of the breed. He believed it originated in the East, found its way to Italy, then Spain, where it developed its classic head. From there it traveled to England and South America.

SHOW REQUIREMENTS
Color—Lemon and white; orange and white; liver and white; and black and white. Self colors and tricolors acceptable.
Head And Skull—Skull medium breadth. In proportion to the length of the foreface. Stop well-defined. Pronounced occipital bone. Nose and eyerims dark, but lighter in a lemon and white dog. Nostrils wide, soft and moist. Muzzle concave, ending on a level with the nostrils, giving a slightly dish-face appearance. Cheekbones not prominent. Well-developed, soft lip.
Tail—Medium length. Thick at the root, growing thinner at the point. Covered with close hair and carried level with the back. No upward curl. When dog moves, tail lashes from side to side.
Feet—Oval. Well-knit, arched toes. Cushioned underneath.

Used originally for hawking and falconry, the German Longhair Pointer is a powerful animal and versatile gundog. Useful for work with gamebirds, it is also good in close coverts.

German Longhair Pointer

German Wirehair Pointer

German Shorthair Pointer

Pointer

Handsome rather than glamorous. With its deep chest, straight bones and beautifully proportioned body, the Pointer is the epitome of the working gundog.

IRISH SETTER
Red Setter

Advantages
- Affectionate
- Good with children
- Good hunter

Disadvantages
- Not a good guard

The Irish Setter is a first-class gundog, combining work with the role of family pet. It is happiest as a pet and needs affection. It is intelligent and reliable with children. High spirited and lively, it should not be confined or kept by those who cannot give it adequate exercise.

SIZE
Height—25 to 27 in (62.5 to 68.5cm)
Weight—No requirement

EXERCISE
This dog needs lots of exercise.

GROOMING
Brush the dog regularly, clip claws and inspect ears.

FEEDING
For daily feeding, 5 cups of balanced dry dog food is recommended. Some dogs may prefer 1/2 cup water mixed with each cup of dog food. Add canned dog food for flavor.

ORIGIN AND HISTORY
The Irish Setter evolved from crossing Irish Water Spaniels, Springer Spaniels, Spanish Pointers, and English and Gordon Setters. Its name came from the Ulster Irish Setter Club in 1876. Edward Laverack, an authority on the Irish Setter, spent his lifetime improving the breed.

SHOW REQUIREMENTS
General Appearance—Racy and full of quality.
Color—Chestnut, with no black. White on chest, throat, chin, toes. A small star on the forehead or a narrow streak or blaze on the nose or face will not disqualify.
Head And Skull—Head long and lean. Not narrow, snipy or coarse at the ears. Skull is oval from ear to ear. Well-defined occipital protuberance. Brows raised, showing stop. Muzzle moderately deep and fairly square at the end. Nostrils wide and jaws of equal length. Flews not pendulous. Nose black, dark mahogany or dark walnut.
Tail—Moderate length, proportionate to the size of the body. Set on low. Strong at the root, tapering to a fine point. Carried level with or below the back.
Feet—Small and firm. Toes strong, close together and arched.
Teeth—Scissors or level bite.

ENGLISH SETTER

Advantages
- Adaptable
- Can live in a house or kennel
- Good gundog

Disadvantages
- Needs company
- Needs a lot of exercise

The English Setter is the most distinctive of the three Setter varieties because of its spotted coat. It has a gentle nature, making it an ideal companion for children. It is also an excellent gundog. Because it needs lots of exercise, it is not a suitable dog for someone living in an apartment. It also requires a lot of grooming.

SIZE
Height—Male: 25-1/2 to 27 in (64 to 68.5cm)
Female: 24 to 25 in (60 to 62.5cm)
Weight—Male: 60 to 66 lbs (27.2 to 30kg)
Female: 56 to 62 lbs (25.4 to 28.1kg)

EXERCISE
Give this dog at least 10 minutes of exercise a day as a 3-month-old pup until it reaches adulthood. An adult needs an hour a day to keep it in condition.

GROOMING
Groom daily with a steel comb and a stiff-bristle brush. Be careful feathering on the legs does not become tangled. Remove silky hair under the ears, under the throat and below the ear down to the breast bone, and between the dog's pads. Straggly hair must be plucked from the body before the dog enters the show ring. The English Setter is always bathed before a show and the coat combed flat when it is dry. American competitors are trimmed more heavily than those in Britain.

FEEDING
For daily feeding, 5 cups of balanced dry dog food is recommended. Some dogs may prefer 1/2 cup water mixed with each cup of dog food. Add canned dog food for flavor.

ORIGIN AND HISTORY
The English Setter evolved from Spaniels. Credit for the breed is given to Edward Laverack. In his work *The Setter,* he wrote, "This breed is but a Spaniel improved." The Setting Spaniel, accepted by many as the forerunner of the English Setter, was used in the 16th century for setting partridges and quails. Through interbreeding, Laverack developed the strain on which the present-day English Setter was built.

The English Setter became popular at the turn of the century. Its reputation spread to the United States and Canada where it has dominated field trials for a quarter of a century.

SHOW REQUIREMENTS
General Appearance—Clean outline. Elegant appearance and movement.
Color—Color black and white; lemon and white; liver and white or tricolor—black, white and tan. Those without heavy patches of color on the body, but flecked all over, are preferred.
Head And Skull—Head long and lean, with a well-defined stop. Nose black or liver, according to coat color.
Tail—Set on almost in line with the back. Medium length, not curly or ropy. Slightly curved or scimitar-shape, but with no tendency to turn up. The flag or feather hangs long.
Feet—Close and compact. Protected by hair between the toes.

GORDON SETTER

Advantages
- Affectionate
- Even-tempered
- Good gundog
- Good with children

Disadvantages
- Not a good guard

The Gordon Setter is a good gun-and birddog, used for silent tracking. It will not accept strangers as readily as the Irish Setter, but it is still too friendly to be a good guard dog. The Gordon is an excellent family pet and is trustworthy with children. It enjoys an active working life and is not suited for apartment life.

SIZE
Height—Male: 26 in (65cm) at the shoulder
Female: 24-1/2 in (61cm)
Weight—Male: 65 lbs (29.5kg)
Female: 56 lbs (25.4kg)

EXERCISE
This dog needs plenty of exercise.

GROOMING
Regular brushing and monthly nail clipping is necessary.

FEEDING
For daily feeding, 5 cups of balanced dry dog food is recommended. Some dogs may prefer 1/2 cup water mixed with each cup of dog food. Add canned dog food for flavor.

ORIGIN AND HISTORY
The Gordon is a true Scot, bred at Gordon Castle, the seat of the Duke of Richmond and Gordon. It is the only native Scottish gundog and was originally known as the Gordon Castle Setter. Credit goes to the 4th Duke of Richmond and Gordon for establishing the breed in the 1770s. Ancestors were probably the Collie and Bloodhound.

SHOW REQUIREMENTS
General Appearance—Symmetrical conformation, showing true balance. Strong. Short, level back. Short tail. Head long, clearly lined, with an intelligent expression. Long, flat coat.
Color—Black, with no sign of rustiness. Lustrous tan markings of chestnut red. Black penciling allowed on toes and under jaw. Tan markings: two clear spots over the eyes, not over 4/5 inch (2cm) in diameter.
Head And Skull—Head deep rather than broad. Broader than the muzzle. Nose big and broad, with open nostrils. Nose black.
Tail—Fairly short, straight or slightly scimitar-shape. Not reaching below the hocks. Carried horizontally or below the line of the back. Thick at the root, tapering to a fine point. The feather, which starts near the root, is long, straight and grows shorter to the point.
Feet—Oval, with close-knit, arched toes. Plenty of hair between toes. Full toepads and deep heel cushions.
Teeth—Strong and white, meeting in a scissors bite. A level bite not faulted.

Setters are elegant, efficient gundogs. The name arises from the practice of training dogs to sit when they locate game by scent and sight, hence the term *sitting* or *setting* dogs.

Irish Setter

English Setter

Gordon Setter

GERMAN SHEPHERD
Alsatian

Advantages
- **Devoted to owner**
- **Good worker**
- **Obedient**
- **Loyal**
- **Intelligent**
- **Protective**

Disadvantages
- **Tendency to overguard**

The German Shepherd is one of the most popular breeds. It arouses strong emotions in people. The German Shepherd is a courageous, intelligent dog. The breed has fought bravely in two world wars. They are excellent seeing-eye dogs and work well as police dogs, military and guard dogs. Their strong guarding instinct can be their undoing; a German Shepherd protecting a toddler may menace a stranger. The German Shepherd deserves a job to do, whether in public service or competing in obedience and working trials. It could also turn vicious through boredom, if kept only as a pet.

SIZE
Height—Male: 24 to 26 in (60 to 65cm) at the shoulder
Female: 22 to 24 in (55 to 60cm)
Weight—No requirement

EXERCISE
This dog needs plenty of exercise and obedience training. It will excel in scent and retrieve competitions.

GROOMING
Daily brushing is recommended.

FEEDING
For daily feeding, 5 cups of balanced dry dog food is recommended. Some dogs may prefer 1/2 cup water mixed with each cup of dog food. Add canned dog food for flavor.

A German Shepherd puppy with soft undercoat.

HEALTH CARE
This is a healthy, hardy breed. Its popularity in recent years has encouraged indiscriminate breeding, resulting in loss of temperament and form. When purchasing a German Shepherd, buy it only from registered *HD-free* stock. *HD* is an abbreviation for hip dysplasia, a malformation of the hip joint resulting in crippling before middle age. Reliable sellers do not breed from affected stock.

ORIGIN AND HISTORY
German Shepherd lineage is attributed to the Bronze Age wolf by some people. This may be an unfortunate suggestion because it wrongly implies the breed has wolflike tendencies. Around 700 A.D., a sheepdog of this type with a lighter coat existed in Germany. By the 16th century, the coat had darkened.

The breed was first exhibited at a dog show in 1882. Credit for the development of the breed is given to a German named von Stephanitz, who improved its temperament and physical appearance through breeding following World War I. The German Shepherd was introduced in the United States by fanciers who had seen the breed working in Germany.

SHOW REQUIREMENTS
General Appearance—Well-proportioned. Shows suppleness of limb. Not massive or heavy. Body long, strongly boned, with plenty of muscle. Capable of endurance, speed and quick movement. Gait smooth and long, carrying the body along with the minimum of up-and-down movement. Free from stiltiness.
Color—Most colors acceptable. Strong, rich colors preferred. A white dog or a dog with a nose not predominantly black will be disqualified from show competition.
Head And Skull—Head proportionate to the size of the body. Long, lean and clean cut. Broad at the back of the skull, without coarseness. Tapers to the nose with a slight stop between the eyes. Skull slightly domed. Top of

An agile German Shepherd successfully climbs a special barrier at a working trial.

the nose parallel to the forehead. Cheeks not full or prominent. The whole head, when viewed from the top, in the form of a V, filled in under the eyes. Muzzle strong and long, tapering to the nose, but not overshot. Lips tight fitting and clean. Nose black.
Tail—At rest, hangs in a slight curve, reaching as far as the hock. Raised during movement and excitement. Not carried past a vertical line drawn through the root.
Feet—Round and closed toe. Toes strong and slightly arched. Pads firm. Nails short and strong. Dewclaws removed from hind legs.
Teeth—Scissors bite.

BELGIAN SHEPHERD
Belgian Sheepdog, Belgian Malinois, Belgian Tervuren, Laekenois

Advantages
- **Alert and agile**
- **Good guard**
- **Intelligent**
- **Physically robust**

Disadvantages
- **Needs space and exercise**
- **Needs firm, kind handling**

There are four types of Belgian Shepherd—the Belgian Sheepdog, the Laekenois, the Belgian Malinois and the Belgian Tervuren. All are similar to the German Shepherd. They are hunting and herding dogs, but have also served as Red Cross messengers in wartime. They are vigilant guards and protectors of children.

SIZE
Height—Male: 24 to 26 in (60 to 65cm)
Female: 22 to 24 in (55 to 60cm)
Weight—No requirement

EXERCISE
The Belgian Shepherd needs plenty of exercise and a job to do. If it is bored, it will entertain itself, often at the owner's expense. It is a working dog and excels in defending master and property. Oblivious to bad weather, it enjoys being outdoors so adequate exercise is necessary.

The dog does well in working trials and obedience competitions. A Belgian Shepherd in the hands of an experienced trainer learns quickly.

GROOMING
Little grooming is needed other than surface brushing. Bathing is not recommended, even for exhibition, unless the dog is filthy. Because of its double coat, combing out the undercoat results in a dog with only half a coat.

FEEDING
For daily feeding, 5 cups of balanced dry dog food is recommended. Some dogs may prefer 1/2 cup water mixed with each cup of dog food. Add canned dog food for flavor.

ORIGIN AND HISTORY
At the end of the 19th century, there were shepherd varieties of all colors and sizes in Belgium. In 1890, Monsieur Rose of the Cafe du Groenendael discovered a black, longcoated female among one of its litters. He later bought a similar dog and by selective breeding eventually produced the Groenendael.

In 1891, a collection of shepherd dogs of all colors and sizes was gathered at the Brussels Veterinary University. Three varieties were recognized: roughcoat black, smoothcoat fawn with black mask and wirehair dark gray.

The Belgian Shepherd is divided into three separate breeds by the American Kennel Club. They are shown separately and each occupies a place in the Working Group. The Belgian Sheepdog is the longcoat black variety, also known as the Groenendael. The Belgian Tervuren is the longcoat fawn or mahogany and black, known in Europe as the Tervueren. The Belgian Malinois is the shortcoat fawn and black variety, and is not recognized by the American Kennel Club. Although the Laekenois is rare, a few have been imported. Interest in the dog is growing.

The characteristic expression of the German Shepherd gives the impression of vigilance, liveliness and watchfulness. It is alert to every sight and sound, with nothing escaping attention. The German Shepherd has highly developed senses.

German Shepherd

Belgian Shepherd

The Belgian Shepherd has received high praise for its working abilities in the United States, where it first appeared in 1907.

The following apply to the Belgian Sheepdog only.

General Appearance—Hardy, well-proportioned, intelligent. Bred to tolerate bad weather. Alert and attentive with a lively, inquiring air.

Color—Black or black with limited white as follows: small to moderate patch or strip on chest, between the pads of the feet and on the tops of the hind toes. White or gray frosting on the muzzle.

Head And Skull—Head finely chiseled. Skull and muzzle roughly equal in length, with a slight bias in favor of the muzzle. Skull medium width in proportion to the length of the head, with a flat, rather than round forehead. The center line not pronounced. Muzzle medium length, tapering gradually toward the nose. Black nose with flared nostrils.

Coat—Topcoat long, straight and abundant. Not silky or wiry. Medium-rough texture. Undercoat dense. Hair shorter on the head, outside of the ears and lower part of the legs. Ear opening protected by hair. Hair long and abundant around the neck, like a ruff, particularly in the male. A fringe of long hair down the back of the forearm and long, abundant hair on hindquarters and tail. Males have a longer coat than females.

Tail—Firmly set, strong at the base and medium length. At rest, carried hanging down with the tip slightly bent backward at the level of the hock. On the move, lifted, accentuating curve toward the tip. Not curled up or bent to one side.

Feet—Round cat feet. Padded and closed toe.

Teeth—Scissors or level bite.

The four varieties of Belgian Shepherd vary only in coat and color. These are the standards for the other three varieties:

Laekenois

Coat—Rough, dry, untidy looking. Not curly. Any sprinkling of fluffy fine hair in locks disqualifies the dog. Coat length about 2.4 inches (6cm) on all parts of the body. Hair around eyes and on the muzzle fairly long. Hair around the muzzle does not make the head look square or heavy. Tail not plumed.

Color—Red-fawn with black shading, mainly on muzzle and tail.

Belgian Malinois

Coat—Hair short on the head, outside the ears and on the lower parts of the legs. Longer on the rest of the body. Thicker on the tail and around the neck, where it resembles a ridge or collar, beginning at the base of the ear and extending to the throat. Hindquarters fringed with longer hair. Tail thick and bushy. Coat thick, close and firm textured with a woolly undercoat.

Color—Dark fawn with black overlay. Washed-out fawn or gray is undesirable, as is patchy black overlay or the total absence of black overlay. Black shading on muzzle and ears desirable.

Belgian Tervuren

Coat—Topcoat long, straight and abundant. Not silky or wiry. Texture medium-rough. Undercoat dense. Hair shorter on the head, outside the ears and on the lower part of the legs. Ear opening protected by hair. Hair long and abundant around the neck, like a ruff, particularly in the male. A fringe of long hair down the back of the forearm and long, abundant hair on the hindquarters and tail. Male has a longer coat than the female.

Color—All shades of red, fawn and gray with black overlay. Grays and silvers are not shown. Coat double pigmented; the tip of each light-color hair is blackened. On mature males this blackening is pronounced on shoulders, back and rib section. Face has black mask, not extending above the line of the eyes. Ears mostly black. Tail has darker or black tip. A small to moderate white patch or strip permitted on the chest, between the pads and on the tips of the hind toes. White or gray frosting on the muzzle. Beyond the age of 18 months, washed-out color or a color that is too black is a fault.

HOLLANDSE HERDER
Dutch Shepherd

Advantages
- **Good guard**
- **Hardy**
- **Intelligent**
- **Even-tempered**

Disadvantages
- **Not common in the United States**

The Hollandse Herder was bred in Holland as a sheepdog. Today, it is kept as a companion and guard. It is almost unknown outside Holland, where it is used as a police dog, a seeing-eye dog and as a farm worker. It comes in three coat types—shorthair, longhair and wirehair. The longhair variety is almost extinct and the wirehair is not favored. The shorthair type is most common.

SIZE
Shorthair and *Wirehair*
Height—Male: 23 to 25 in
(57.5 to 62.5cm)
Female: 21-1/2 to
24-1/2 in
(54.5 to 61cm)
at the withers
Longhair
Height—Male: 21-1/2 in (54.5cm)
Female: 21 in (53cm)
at the withers
Weight—No requirement

EXERCISE
This dog needs plenty of exercise.

GROOMING
Regular brushing will keep the coat in condition.

FEEDING
For daily feeding, 5 cups of balanced dry dog food is recommended. Some dogs may prefer 1/2 cup water mixed with each cup of dog food. Add canned dog food for flavor.

ORIGIN AND HISTORY
The Hollandse Herder is closely related to the Belgian Shepherd. They are of similar origin. It has developed as a separate breed in Holland, where it is popular.

General Appearance—Medium size, muscular, strong and symmetrical. Intelligent expression, showing aptitude for working with sheep.

Color—
Shorthair: Yellow, chestnut, brown, gold and silver streaked. Streaks sharp and distributed over the body, on back of thighs and tail. Streaking involves hair from root to tip. Too much black in the topcoat is a fault. Black mask.
Wirehair: Yellow, red-brown, blue, streaked, gray-blue, salt and pepper.
Longhair: Chestnut, gold or silver streaked.

Head And Skull—In proportion to the body, without being coarse. Lean. Moderate length, narrow, but not the greyhound type. Conical shape. Muzzle longer than the skull. Bridge is straight and parallel to the skull line. Stop barely perceptible. Head of the wirehair variety is squarer than the shorthair. Top of the nose black. Lips closed over gums.

Tail—In repose, carried low with a slight curve. Tip does not reach the hocks. In action, carried high but not rolled and without tending to either side.

Feet—Arched toes. Nails black. Pads soft, elastic and black.

Teeth—Strong, regular and meet in a scissors bite.

A Hollandse Herder, showing its streaked coat. Originally bred as a sheepdog, it is now used as a companion and guard.

Belgian Shepherds are similar in size and appearance to the German Shepherd. The four varieties take their names from villages in Belgium.

Belgian Malinois

Laekenois

Belgian Tervuren

DALMATIAN

Advantages
- **Even-tempered**
- **Loyal**
- **Reliable with children**

Disadvantages
- **Needs lots of exercise**
- **Coat sheds**

The Dalmatian has a happy nature. It is loyal, devoted to its owners and rarely fights. It is easily trained and easy to show. It is long-lived and has a lively youth. Because it was bred to run with horse and carriage, it needs a lot of exercise.

SIZE
Height—Male 23 to 24 in (57.5 to 60cm) Female 22 to 23 in (55 to 57.5cm)
Weight—No requirement Overall balance is important.

EXERCISE
Do not buy a Dalmatian unless you can give it plenty of exercise.

GROOMING
Daily brushing and occasional bathing are required.

FEEDING
For daily feeding, 5 cups of balanced dry dog food is recommended. Some dogs may prefer 1/2 cup water mixed with each cup of dog food. Add canned dog food for flavor.

ORIGIN AND HISTORY
The Dalmatian is often thought of as a British dog, but it originated in Yugoslavia. It was popular as a carriage dog in the 18th century. The breed became more popular after 1959, when Walt Disney made a film of Dodie Smith's book, *A Hundred and One Dalmatians*. It is a competitive breed and has won many Group and Best in Show ribbons.

SHOW REQUIREMENTS
General Appearance—Balanced, strong and muscular. Active, symmetrical in outline, free from coarseness and extra flesh. Capable of endurance with a fair amount of speed.
Color—Ground color pure white. Dogs may be black-spotted or liver-spotted. Spots do not run together, but are round and defined. Spots on extremities smaller than those on the body. Spots well-distributed and range in size from a dime to a dollar.

Head And Skull—Skull flat, broad between the ears, but refined. Black nose in the black-spotted dog; brown in the liver-spotted.
Tail—Reaching to the hocks. Strong at the insertion, gradually tapering to the end. Not inserted too low or too high. Free from coarseness. Carried with a slight upward curve, never curled. Preferably spotted.
Feet—Round, compact, catlike feet. Tough, elastic pads. Nails black or white in the black-spotted dog; brown or white in the liver-spotted variety.

WEIMARANER
Silver Ghost

Advantages
- **Does not shed**
- **Obedient**
- **Good gundog**
- **Even-tempered**

Disadvantages
- **Likes to work**
- **Do not keep in a kennel**

The Weimaraner, or Silver Ghost, is an excellent gundog that originally hunted big game. It is obedient and trainable, and excels in obedience competitions. It has been used as a police dog and guard. It makes a good pet, but is happiest when given a job to do.

SIZE
Height—Male: 25 to 27 in (62.5 to 68.5cm) at the withers Female 23 to 25 in (57.5 to 62.5cm)
Weight—No requirement

EXERCISE
This dog needs plenty of exercise.

FEEDING
For daily feeding, 5 cups of balanced dry dog food is recommended. Some dogs may prefer 1/2 cup water mixed with each cup of dog food. Add canned dog food for flavor.

ORIGIN AND HISTORY
The Weimaraner was bred as a gundog in Weimar, Germany. Toward the end of the 18th century Bloodhounds, Pointers and St. Hubert Hounds were crossed with the Weimaraner to improve the breed. Its silver-gray color is distinctive.

The Weimaraner is popular as a family pet, show dog and contender in obedience competitions. The best stock is available in the United States and the United Kingdom.

SHOW REQUIREMENTS
General Appearance—Medium-size gray dog with light eyes. Appears to have driving power, stamina, alertness and balance.
Color—Preferably silver-gray. Shades of mouse or roe-gray admissible. Color blends to a lighter shade on head and ears. A dark eel stripe frequently occurs along the back. Coat gives appearance of metallic sheen.
Head And Skull—Long, with moderate stop and slight median line extending back over the forehead. Expression keen and intelligent.
Tail—Docked. At maturity, it measures about 6 inches (15cm). Thickness of the tail is in proportion to the body. Carried in a manner expressing confidence and sound temperament.
Feet—Firm and compact. Toes arched. Pads thick. Nails short and gray or amber in color.

BOXER

Advantages
- **Brave**
- **Good guard**
- **Good with children**
- **Loyal**

Disadvantages
- **Enjoys a fight**

The Boxer takes longer than most dogs to grow up. It loves children and is a good protector of the family. It is an exuberant, powerful dog, needing a large home and yard. Owners must be prepared to spend time exercising and training their dog. The Boxer has served as a seeing-eye dog and in the armed forces. Its tail is docked, so when pleased it tends to wag its whole body.

SIZE
Height—Male: 22-1/2 to 25 in (56 to 62.5m) at the withers Female: 21 to 23-1/2 in (53.5 to 58cm)
Weight—Male: 66 lbs (30kg) Female: 62 lbs (28.1kg)

EXERCISE
Give this dog daily walks and runs in a large fenced area.

GROOMING
Daily brushing will keep the coat in condition.

FEEDING
For daily feeding, 5 cups of balanced dry dog food is recommended. Some dogs may prefer 1/2 cup water mixed with each cup of dog food. Add canned dog food for flavor.

ORIGIN AND HISTORY
The Boxer can be traced to the Molossus dogs or mastiff types, which the Cimbrians took into battle against the Romans. Like the Bulldog, its jaw is undershot, a trait common in bull-baiters. The Brabant Bull-baiter, from which the English Bulldog evolved, also played its part in the evolution of the Boxer. The Boxer retains its fighting spirit to this day.

SHOW REQUIREMENTS
General Appearance—Medium size, sturdy and smooth-haired. Short, square figure and strong limb. Muscles clean and powerfully developed, standing out under the skin. Movement alive with energy. Gait is elastic. Stride free and roomy. Carriage proud and noble.
Color—Brindle and fawn in various shades from light yellow to dark red. Brindle variety has black stripes on a golden yellow or red-brown background. Stripes clearly defined. White markings on fawn or brindle dogs limited to one-third of ground color and not on back. Entirely white or black disqualified.
Head And Skull—Head in perfect proportion to the body. Head never too fine. Muzzle in proportion to the skull. Nose broad and black, slightly turned up. Nostrils broad with a naso-labial line between them. Jawbones not terminated in a perpendicular level in front. Lower jaw protrudes beyond the upper jaw and bends slightly upward. Upper jaw broad, maintaining this breadth except for a slight tapering to the front.
Tail—Attachment high. Tail docked and carried upward. Not more than 2 inches (5cm) long.
Feet—Small, cat feet with hard soles. Rear toes longer than front toes, but similar in all other respects.
Teeth—Normally undershot.

Weimaraner

The Weimaraner should show ability to work hard in the field. Movement should be effortless, ground covering and coordinated.

Dalmatian

Boxer

Boxers in America have their ears cropped. This practice makes them ineligible for competition in some areas of the world.

GOLDEN RETRIEVER

Advantages
- *Good gundog*
- *Gentle with children*
- *Even-tempered*

Disadvantages
- *No drawbacks known*

The Golden Retriever will suit the entire family. It can play with the children and enjoy a day's shooting. This trustworthy breed can be kenneled, but dogs are happiest in the home. They love to retrieve and enjoy carrying the newspaper home or wandering around the house with an old slipper. They are often used as seeing-eye dogs.

SIZE
Height—Male: 23 to 24 in
(57.5 to 60cm)
at the shoulder
Female: 21-1/2 to
22-1/2 in
(54 to 56cm)
Weight—Male: 65 to 70 lbs
(30 to 33kg)
Female: 60 to 70 lbs
(27 to 33kg)

EXERCISE
This dog needs an hour's exercise every day in a large yard.

GROOMING
Regular brushing will keep the coat in condition.

FEEDING
For daily feeding, 5 cups of balanced dry dog food is recommended. Some dogs may prefer 1/2 cup water mixed with each cup of dog food. Add canned dog food for flavor.

ORIGIN AND HISTORY
There is a question as to the origin of the breed. Some believe it developed from a troupe of Russian shepherd dogs found by Lord Tweedmouth performing in a Brighton circus in 1860. He was so greatly impressed with Russian shepherd dogs, he bought the entire troupe and bred from them, adding Bloodhound to develop the nose. Others think the breed began with a litter of golden-hair pups of retriever-spaniel ancestry born on Tweedmouth's Scottish estate.

SHOW REQUIREMENTS
General Appearance—Active, symmetrical and powerful. Sound and well-put together, not clumsy or long in the leg.
Color—Lustrous gold of various shades. A few white hairs on the chest permissible. White collar, feet, toes or blaze penalized. Nose black.
Head And Skull—Broad skull on a clean, muscular neck. Muzzle wide and powerful, not weak jawed. Good stop.
Tail—Not carried up or curled at the tip.
Feet—Round and catlike. Not open or splay.
Teeth—Scissors bite.

A Golden Retriever with pups. It is an ideal family pet.

Yellow Labrador Retrievers, now more popular than Black Labradors.

LABRADOR RETRIEVER

Advantages
- *Even-tempered*
- *Good gundog*
- *Good family pet*
- *Good with children*

Disadvantages
- *No drawbacks known*

The Labrador Retriever is recommended for the whole family. It is an excellent retriever, can be trusted with children and will do well in obedience competitions. The Labrador Retriever is used as a seeing-eye dog.

SIZE
Height—Male: 22-1/2 to 24 in
(56 to 60cm)
Female: 21-1/2 to
22-1/2 in
(54 to 56cm)
Weight—Male: 60 to 75 lbs
(27 to 34kg)
Female: 65 to 70 lbs
(29 to 32kg)

EXERCISE
This breed needs an hour a day of exercise and a large yard to play in.

GROOMING
Regular brushing will keep the coat in condition.

FEEDING
For daily feeding, 5 cups of balanced dry dog food is recommended. Some dogs may prefer 1/2 cup water mixed with each cup of dog food. Add canned dog food for flavor.

ORIGIN AND HISTORY
The Labrador Retriever was brought to Great Britain from Newfoundland, not Labrador, in the 1830s. The dog's task was to land the nets of the fishermen. Its ability to swim has survived. A popular gundog, it is also desired as a pet.

SHOW REQUIREMENTS
General Appearance—Strongly built, short coupled and active. Broad skull, deep chest and ribs. Strong over the loins and hindquarters. Coat is close and short, with a dense undercoat, free from feather. Must not move too wide or too close in front or behind. Stands and moves true all around on legs and feet.
Color—Black, yellow or chocolate. Coat free from white markings but a small white spot on the chest permitted. Coat one color, not flecked.
Head And Skull—Skull broad with a slight stop. Head clean cut without flashy cheeks. Jaws medium length, powerful and free from snipiness. Nose wide and nostrils well-developed.
Tail—Thick toward the base, gradually tapering toward the tip. Medium length and almost free from feathering. Clothed thickly with short, thick, dense coat, giving the peculiar round appearance described as the otter tail. Carried up, but not curling over the back.
Feet—Round and compact, with arched toes and developed pads.
Teeth—Level mouth.

Golden Retrievers were first registered in 1925.
Since then, the breed has undergone a growth in
popularity, both as pets and as reliable, intelligent
working dogs.

Golden Retriever

The Labrador Retriever has
been celebrated around the
world for its intelligence, even
temperament and all-around
ability.

Labrador Retriever

CHESAPEAKE BAY RETRIEVER

Advantages
- **Excellent retriever**
- **Usually good with children**

Disadvantages
- **Occasionally aggressive**
- **Oily coat and odor**

The Chesapeake Bay is a favorite with American sportsmen. It is an excellent swimmer and retriever of wild duck. It is usually good with children, but can be headstrong and difficult to train. The breed's yellow-orange eyes and web feet are distinguishing features. Its coat is water resistant.

SIZE
Height—Male: 23 to 26 in (57.5 to 65cm)
Female: 21 to 24 in (53.5 to 60cm)
Weight—Male: 65 to 75 lbs (29.5 to 34kg)
Female: 55 to 65 lbs (25 to 29.5kg)

EXERCISE
This dog needs plenty of exercise to stay in condition.

GROOMING
Normal brushing is sufficient.

FEEDING
For daily feeding, 5 cups of balanced dry dog food is recommended. Some dogs may prefer 1/2 cup water mixed with each cup of dog food. Add canned dog food for flavor.

ORIGIN AND HISTORY
This is an American retriever of British origin. An English brig went aground off the coast of Maryland in 1807, and was rescued by an American ship, the *Canton*. Aboard the brig were two Newfoundland pups. They were named Canton, after the rescue ship, and Sailor. They were trained to retrieve duck. They were later crossed with Otterhounds and the Curly Coated and Flat-Coated Retriever. Americans want to retain the breed as a sporting dog. It has not become popular as a pet. Some people do not like their oily coats, slightly oily odor or yellow-orange eyes.

SHOW REQUIREMENTS
General Appearance—Bright and happy, with an intelligent expression. General outlines indicate a good worker.
Color—Any color from dark brown to faded tan or dead-grass color, or any shade from tan to dull straw.

Head And Skull—Broad and round, with medium stop. Nose medium. Muzzle pointed but not sharp. Lips thin, not pendulous.
Tail—Medium length. Male 12 to 15 inches (30 to 38cm), female 11 to 14 inches (28 to 35.5cm). Heavy at the root. Moderate feathering on tail and stern permissible.
Feet—Webbed harefeet. Toes round and closed. Pasterns slightly bent.

CURLY COATED RETRIEVER

Advantages
- **Even-tempered**
- **Good guard**
- **Fine swimmer**
- **Good hunter**

Disadvantages
- **No drawbacks known**
- **Needs a lot of exercise**

The Curly Coated Retriever is an excellent worker on land and in water. It will retrieve any game, is a hardy dog, is even-tempered and has a fine appearance.

SIZE
Height—25 to 27 in (62.5 to 68.5cm)
Weight—70 to 80 lbs (34 to 36kg)

EXERCISE
This dog needs a lot of exercise.

GROOMING
Do not brush or comb this breed. Dampen the coat and massage with circular movements. Seek advice on trimming.

FEEDING
Same as for the Chesapeake Bay Retriever.

ORIGIN AND HISTORY
The Curly Coated Retriever was one of the earliest British retrievers. It was exhibited at dog shows in England as early as 1860, and was shown in sporting pictures before then. Its popularity has waned since World War I. The early Labrador played a part in its makeup. The Water Spaniel may also have been an ancestor.

SHOW REQUIREMENTS
General Appearance—Strong and upstanding. Shows activity, endurance and intelligence.
Color—Black or liver.
Head And Skull—Long, well-proportioned, flat skull. Jaws strong and long, but not inclined to snipiness. Nose black, with wide nostrils. Coarse head faulted.
Tail—Moderately short. Carried straight and covered with curls. Tapering toward the point.
Feet—Round and compact, with arched toes.

HOVAWART

Advantages
- **Good guard**
- **Home-loving**
- **Good with children**
- **Loyal**
- **Obedient**

Disadvantages
- **Slow maturing**
- **One-person dog**
- **Will fight if challenged**
- **Not common in the United States**

The Hovawart is an old German breed not bred for a specific purpose. It is a loyal companion and protector. It is obedient, loves children and is loyal to its master. Although it is a one-person dog, it will defend the family with its life. It will fight if challenged.

SIZE
Height—Male: 25 to 27 in (62.5 to 68.5cm)
Female: Slightly smaller
Weight—Male: 65 to 90 lbs (30 to 41cm)
Female: Slightly smaller

EXERCISE
Give this dog normal regular exercise.

GROOMING
Regular brushing keeps the coat in top condition.

FEEDING
For daily feeding, 4 cups of balanced dry dog food is recommended. Some dogs may prefer 1/2 cup water mixed with each cup of dog food. Canned dog food may be added for flavor.

ORIGIN AND HISTORY
The Hovawart was a popular companion dog in Germany during the Middle Ages. The name Hovawart means *house guard*. It resembles the Kuvasz in stature and looks like a large Collie. The dog was unpopular for awhile. After World War I it was crossed with Leonbergers and Newfoundlands.

SHOW REQUIREMENTS
General Appearance—Robust working dog of medium weight. A good runner and jumper. Brave, attentive, strong and quick to react. Excellent guard. Sexual characteristics clearly evident. Voice deep, full and powerful.
Color—Black; black and tan, with small white ticking; flaxen, with a dark shade preferred. Eyes, nose and nail color consistent with the basic coloring of the coat, but not too light.
Head And Skull—Strong, with a broad, convex forehead. Muzzle straight, not too long or short. Maximum muzzle length equal to the distance from the occipital bone to the stop. Tight lips.
Tail— Reaches beyond the hocks but not to the ground. Feathered.

Carried low in repose and high when the dog is excited.
Feet—No dewclaws. Hard pads on forefeet.
Teeth—Scissors bite. A level bite is allowed but counted as a fault in a show.

FLAT-COATED RETRIEVER

Advantages
- **Can live in a kennel or house**
- **Easy to train**
- **Good with children**
- **Hardy**
- **Natural retriever**

Disadvantages
- **No drawbacks known**

The Flat-Coated Retriever will probably become popular again since winning the Best in Show award. It is a natural retriever, used for picking up game. It is hardy, easily trained and makes a good pet. It is excellent with children.

SIZE
Height—No requirement
Weight—60 to 70 lbs (27 to 33kg)

EXERCISE
This dog needs plenty of exercise.

GROOMING
Regular brushing keeps the coat in condition.

FEEDING
For daily feeding, 4 cups of balanced dry dog food is recommended. Some dogs may prefer 1/2 cup water mixed with each cup of dog food. Canned dog food may be added for flavor.

ORIGIN AND HISTORY
The Flat-Coated Retriever probably evolved from the Labrador Retriever, the Collie and certain spaniels. At one time it was known as the Wavy-Coated Retriever. It was crossed with Collies to produce the flat coat. Before World War I, the Flat-Coat was the best-known gundog in Britain. It was overshadowed after the war by the Golden Retriever and Labrador Retriever.

SHOW REQUIREMENTS
General Appearance—Bright and active, with an intelligent expression. Shows power without lumbering and raciness without weediness.
Color—Black or liver.
Head And Skull—Head long. Skull flat and moderately broad. A depression or stop between the eyes. Nose has open nostrils. Jaws long and strong, with the capacity for carrying a rabbit or pheasant.
Tail—Short and straight. Carried up, but never above the level of the back.
Feet—Round, strong and arched, with closed toes. Soles thick and strong.

Curly Coated Retriever

Chesapeake Bay Retriever

Flat-Coated Retriever

Hovawart

AKITA

Advantages
- *Easily trained*
- *Good guard*
- *Even-tempered*
- *Intelligent*

Disadvantages
- *Can be ferocious*

The Akita is the best known Japanese Spitz, but has only recently come on the international scene. The breed has been exhibited in the United States. The Japanese are attempting to improve their purebred stock.

The Akita was bred as a hunter of wild boar, deer and black bear. It can be ferocious, but is easily trained and generally has an even temper.

SIZE
Height—Male: 26 to 28 in (65 to 71cm) Female: 24 to 26 in (60 to 65cm)
Weight—85 to 110 lbs (38 to 50kg)

EXERCISE
The Akita does not require a lot of exercise.

GROOMING
Give this dog normal daily brushing.

FEEDING
For daily feeding, 5 cups of balanced dry dog food is recommended. Some dogs may prefer 1/2 cup water mixed with each cup of dog food. Canned dog food may be added for flavor.

ORIGIN AND HISTORY
The Akita resembles a Chow. It is the largest Japanese Spitz. Bred in Japan as a hunter of wild boar and deer, it is related to the Icelandic breeds. It has been bred in Japan's Akita Province for more than 300 years. Its exact origin is obscure.

SHOW REQUIREMENTS
This is the Federation Cynologique Internationale standard.
General Appearance—Solid, well-proportioned, with an appearance of great distinction. Prudent, docile, intelligent without sacrificing an impetuous temperament.
Color—Any color. Brilliant colors preferred.
Head And Skull—Skull large, with a broad forehead. Medial furrow is well-marked. Stop defined and cheeks well-formed. Muzzle broad and full, the bridge straight and short. Nose large and black. Lips thin, fitting over the gums.

Tail—Stout and strong, reaching to the hocks when straight. Carried over the back in a ring, which can be shifted from one side to the other. May be a screwtail or a spiral curl. Curl should be a complete turn.
Feet—Catlike feet, knuckled, with thick pads. Nails hard and dark. Pads hard and rugged.
Teeth—Scissors bite preferred, but level acceptable.

CHOW CHOW

Advantages
- *Loyal*
- *Odorless*

Disadvantages
- *Formidable opponent*
- *Needs firm, gentle handling*
- *Strong-willed*

The Chow Chow is a member of the Spitz family. Its name may be derived from the Chinese Choo Hunting Dog. Known for over 2000 years, it looks like a lion and is known for its black tongue. It is odorless and is a loyal companion. It will devote itself to one person, but can accept and return the affection of family members. It needs quiet, but firm handling. With an aloof temperament, it is unlikely to walk at your heel without persuasion. It does not like strangers and is fierce if provoked.

SIZE
Height—18 in (46cm)
Weight—No requirement

EXERCISE
Most Chows manage with regular walks, with runs in enclosed areas.

GROOMING
Brushing 5 to 10 minutes a day during the week and an hour each weekend with a wire brush should maintain the Chow's coat.

FEEDING
For daily feeding, 3 cups of balanced dry dog food is recommended. Some dogs may prefer 1/2 cup water mixed with each cup of dog food. Canned dog food may be added for flavor.

ORIGIN AND HISTORY
Although there are other black-mouthed dogs, the Chow is the only dog with a black tongue. Reputed to be the original Lama's Mastiff, the Chow Chow may be one of the oldest members of the Spitz family. It was bred for its fur and its meat, which in many parts of Asia is considered a delicacy. In

early Chinese writings, it was known as the Tartar Dog or Dog of Barbarians. The first breed members imported to England in 1760 were exhibited in a zoo. The Chow has a reputation for ferocity, yet it is an affectionate, devoted animal. It is unlikely to fight unless provoked, then it is a formidable opponent.

The first Chow was exhibited in 1890 in the United States. Since then the breed has become popular.

SHOW REQUIREMENTS
General Appearance—Active, compact and balanced. Well-knit frame, with tail carried over the back.
Color—Usually any solid color.
Head And Skull—Skull flat and broad, with little stop. Filled out under the eyes. Muzzle short when compared to length of skull. Broad from the eyes to the point. Not

The beautiful, lionlike Chow is a one-person dog that will be friendly with the rest of the family. Delightful as a puppy, the adult Chow can be single-minded and aloof. It is a stunning sight in the show ring.

pointed at the end like a fox. Nose large and wide. In creams and whites, a light-colored nose is permissible; in blues and fawns a self-colored nose. In all colors, a black nose preferred.
Tail—Set high and carried over the back.
Feet—Small, round and catlike.

The Japanese Akita is popular in the United States. Many were brought back from Japan by American servicemen at the end of World War II.

Japanese Akita

Now appreciated in the Western world as a successful show dog, the Chow is an ancient breed with scenting and hunting ability. It was first exhibited in 1890.

Chow Chow

ALASKAN MALAMUTE

Advantages
- **Affectionate**
- **Fast and strong**
- **Fine sled dog**
- **Loves children**

Disadvantages
- **No drawbacks known**

The Alaskan Malamute is an Arctic Spitz dog. It is not well-known outside the United States. It likes people and is highly prized as a sled dog, capable of immense speed. Do not be put off by its wolfish appearance.

SIZE
Height—Male: 25 to 28 in
(62.5 to 71cm)
Female: 23 to 26 in
(57.5 to 65cm)
Weight—85 to 125 lbs
(38 to 57kg)

EXERCISE
This dog needs plenty of exercise.

The Alaskan Malamute is a sociable breed.

GROOMING
Regular brushing will keep the coat in condition.

FEEDING
For daily feeding, 5 cups of balanced dry dog food is recommended. Some dogs may prefer 1/2 cup water mixed with each cup of dog food. Canned dog food may be added for flavor.

ORIGIN AND HISTORY
The Alaskan Malamute is named after a native tribe called the Mahlemuts. The origin of the dog is obscure, but the breed is closely related to other Spitz types, such as the Samoyed.

SHOW REQUIREMENTS
General Appearance—Heavily boned and powerfully built. Not too compact and never appearing low on the leg.
Color—From light gray to black. Or from gold to liver. White always on the underbody, feet, part of legs and part of mask markings. Face markings caplike or masklike. Combination of cap and mask is not unusual. A white blaze on the forehead, a white collar or a spot on the nape acceptable. Heavy

Strong and beautiful, two Greenland Dogs in sled harness.

mantling of unbroken color acceptable, but broken color extending over the body in spots or uneven splashings is undesirable. The only allowable solid color is white.
Head And Skull—Head broad and powerful, not coarse. Head in proportion to the size of the dog. Skull broad between the ears, gradually narrowing to the eyes. Moderately round between the ears, flattening on top as it approaches the eyes. Rounds off to moderately flat cheeks. Slight but perceptible stop. Muzzle large in proportion to the size of the skull, scarcely diminishing in width or depth from the stop. Nose black except in red-and-white dogs, when it is brown.
Tail—Set high, following the line of the spine. Furry and carried over the back when the dog is not working. Not tightly curled. Carried like a fox brush, with the appearance of a waving plume.
Feet—Large and compact. Tight-fitting arched toes. Thick, tough pads. Toenails short and strong, with a protective growth of hair between toes.

ESKIMO DOG
Greenland Dog

Advantages
- **Devoted**
- **Excellent sled dog**
- **Strong**
- **Good guard**

Disadvantages
- **Rarely lives indoors**
- **Suspicious of strangers**
- **Needs a lot of exercise**
- **Not common in the United States**

The Eskimo Dog is one of several regional sled dogs. Few are known outside the polar area. It is hardy and will take care of itself, living outdoors and often finding its own food.

The Greenland Dog is similar; there is controversy as to whether they should be separately classified.

Usually the Eskimo Dog is shorter in the back than the Greenland and weightier but without extra height.

SIZE
Height—Male: 23 to 27 in
(57.5 to 68.5cm)
Female: 20 to 24 in
(51 to 60cm)
Weight—Male: 75 to 105 lbs
(34 to 48kg)
Female: 60 to 90 lbs
(27 to 41kg)

EXERCISE
This dog needs a lot of exercise. It is accustomed to pulling sleds and hauling fishing boats ashore. It will quickly get bored without a job to do.

GROOMING
Regular brushing keeps the coat in condition.

FEEDING
For daily feeding, 5 cups of balanced dry dog food is recommended. Some dogs may prefer 1/2 cup water mixed with each cup of dog food. Canned dog food may be added for flavor.

ORIGIN AND HISTORY
The sled dogs, also known as Polar Spitzes, originated in Eastern Siberia and share a common ancestry with the Alaskan Malamute, Siberian Husky and Samoyed. To quote the American explorer Peary, "There is, in fact, only one sled dog."

SHOW REQUIREMENTS
Color—Any color or combination.
Head And Skull—Head proportioned, broad and wedge shape. A moderate stop. Strong, flat skull and powerful jaws. Black or brown nose and lips. Muzzle medium length, gently tapering to the nose.
Tail—Large and bushy. Set high and curled loosely over the back, falling to one side or the other.
Feet—Large, well-spread and strong. Thick pads intersected with fur. Strong nails.

The Eskimo Dog is recognized by the Canadian Kennel Club as a separate breed. The Federation Cynologique Internationale recognizes the closely related Greenland Dog. Both are Arctic hauling dogs.

Eskimo Dog

The Alaskan Malamute is a powerful sled dog, known for generations in its native Alaska. It has survived as a pure breed and is popular for winter sports.

Alaskan Malamute

OTTERHOUND

Advantages
- *Easy to groom*
- *Friendly*
- *Gentle with children*
- *Waterproof coat*

Disadvantages
- *Not suited to city life*

When otter hunting was outlawed in England, this breed could have become extinct. The last master of the Kendal and District otterhounds set up the Otterhound Club to ensure survival of the breed. Without continued interest of breeders and the show world, the Otterhound would certainly die out.

It is an amiable, friendly animal. It is gentle with children and responsive to affection. However, this was a packhound, bred to kill. Its background may not make it a good pet.

SIZE
Height—Male: 24 to 27 in
(60 to 68.5cm)
Female: 22 to 24 in
(55 to 60cm)
Weight—Male: 75 to 115 lbs
(34 to 52kg)
Female: 65 to 100 lbs
(30 to 45kg)

EXERCISE
The Otterhound needs a lot of exercise.

GROOMING
Brushing and combing once a week will keep the Otterhound's coat in top condition. There is natural oil in the coat. If bathing the animal for a show, do it a week before, to allow the coat to regain its correct texture. Head hair can be bathed the day before a show because it is a finer texture. The Otterhound requires no trimming for show.

Pay attention to the ears. They collect wax and can become irritated. Inspect them regularly.

FEEDING
For daily feeding, 5 cups of balanced dry dog food is recommended. Some dogs may prefer 1/2 cup water mixed with each cup of dog food. Canned dog food may be added for flavor.

ORIGIN AND HISTORY
The Otterhound is an old breed, and its origins are not clear. It may be descended from the Southern Hound. The Bloodhound may be an ancestor. It is similar to French hounds, such as the Griffon Nivernais or Griffon Vendeen. It is possible the Otterhound has the same origins as these French breeds.

Otter hunting was one of the earliest field sports in Great Britain. King John, Henry II and Elizabeth I kept Otterhound packs before foxes were hunted. Monasteries kept Otterhounds to protect their fish ponds from otters. Otterhounds made their first appearance in the United States at a bench show in 1907.

SHOW REQUIREMENTS
General Appearance—Strong, with straight limbs and rough coat. Large head, strong body and loose, long-striding action. For work in water, the rough double coat and large feet are essential. Free moving.
Color—Any recognized hound color is permissible, with the exception of liver and white. Whole-colored grizzle, sandy, red, wheat or blue may have white markings on head, chest, feet and tail tip. White hounds may have slight lemon, blue or badger pied markings. Also black and tan; blue and tan; black and cream; or liver and tan. Pigment should harmonize, though not necessarily blend, with coat color.
Head And Skull—Clean and imposing. Deeper than wide, with clean cheekbones. Skull domed, not coarse or overdone, rising from a distinct stop to a slight peak at the occiput. No trace of scowl or bulge in the forehead. Expression open and amiable. Muzzle strong and deep with nose bone ending in wide nostrils. Distance from nose end to stop slightly shorter than from stop to occiput. Plenty of lip and flew, though not exaggerated. Head covered with rough hair, ending in slight moustache and beard. Both are part of the natural face hair.
Feet—Forelegs strongly boned, straight from elbow to ground. Strong, slightly sprung pasterns. Feet not turned in or out. Large, round, well-knuckled and thickly padded with web in evidence. Compact when standing but capable of spreading. Hind feet slightly smaller than forefeet.
Tail—Set high and carried up when alert or on the move. Never curling over the back, though it may droop when standing. Thick at the base, tapering to a point. Reaching to the hock. Carried straight or in a slight curve. Hair under the stern is longer and more profuse than on the topside.
Teeth—Scissors bite.

The Otterhound is a good retriever and an excellent swimmer.

SPINONE ITALIANA

Advantages
- *Affectionate*
- *Good retriever*
- *Hardy*

Disadvantages
- *No drawbacks known*

The Spinone Italiana is a gundog, appreciated by Italian horsemen for its ability to work in marshy and wooded country. It has a soft mouth, will point and retrieve, and is good-natured.

SIZE
Height—Male: 23-1/2 to 25-1/2 in
(59 to 63cm)
Female: 21-1/2 to
23-1/2 in
(54 to 59cm)
Weight—No requirement

EXERCISE
This dog needs plenty of vigorous exercise.

GROOMING
Daily brushing keeps the coat healthy.

FEEDING
For daily feeding, 5 cups of balanced dry dog food is recommended. Some dogs may prefer 1/2 cup water mixed with each cup of dog food. Canned dog food may be added for flavor.

ORIGIN AND HISTORY
The Spinone originated in the French region of Bresse, but later found its way to Italy. Its evolution is attributed to French Griffon, French and German Pointers, the Porcelaine, Barbet and Korthals Griffon. The result is a reliable gundog with the appearance of a Pointer and a Foxhound. This breed is shown in the Miscellaneous Class at American Kennel Club-sanctioned shows.

SHOW REQUIREMENTS
General Appearance—Square body, solid and vigorous. Strong bones and developed muscles. A fast trotting gait. Facial expression is intelligent, showing power and courage. Eyes are expressive with a sweet, almost-human expression. Thick skin and hard, thick coat protect it from stickers and cold water.
Color—White, white with orange markings, solid white peppered with orange, white with brown markings, white speckled with brown hairs, and brown roan, with or without larger brown markings.
Head And Skull—Large with broad, domed skull. Stop not accentuated. Muzzle well-developed and square.
Tail—Thick at the base and set on as a continuation of the croup line. Carried horizontally or down. Docked 6 to 10 inches (16 to 25cm) from the root.
Feet—Compact and round. Arched, closed toes covered with short, thick hair.

Otterhound

Spinone Italiana

The Spinone Italiana's coat is rough to the touch. It protects the dog when it retrieves game from densely wooded areas.

ROTTWEILER

Advantages
- **Even-tempered**
- **Intelligent**
- **Good companion**
- **Reliable working dog**
- **Good guard**

Disadvantages
- **Needs firm handling**

The Rottweiler is a German working dog with high intelligence and an even temperament. It has been a draft dog and herder, and is still used as a guard, police dog, sled dog and mountain rescue dog. In many countries it is sought after as a pet and guard. It is popular in the show ring and does well in obedience tests.

SIZE
Height—Male: 23-3/4 to 27 in (60 to 68.5cm)
Female: 21-3/4 to 25-3/4 in (54 to 64cm)
Weight—No requirement

EXERCISE
Regular walks and runs are necessary.

GROOMING
Daily brushing keeps the coat in condition.

FEEDING
For daily feeding, 5 cups of balanced dry dog food is recommended. Some dogs may prefer 1/2 cup water mixed with each cup of dog food. Canned dog food may be added for flavor.

ORIGIN AND HISTORY
The Rottweiler is a butcher's dog. It comes from the West German town of Rottweil. There it is known as the Rottweiler Metzgerhund or Rottweil butcher's dog.

In the middle ages it was used to hunt wild boar. Later, it was used as a cattle and draft dog to draw carts for butchers and cattle dealers. Before World War I, its abilities were recognized as a police dog and guard.

The breed was recognized by the American Kennel Club in 1935. It has seen a remarkable growth in popularity.

The breed was introduced in the United Kingdom in 1936. It was developing a following until World War II, when breeding ceased. When a British captain serving in Germany brought home a male and female, a sound breeding program was re-established. Since then many offspring have been produced.

SHOW REQUIREMENTS
General Appearance—Stalwart. Correctly proportioned. Compact, powerful form. Strength, maneuverability and endurance. Boldness and courage.
Color—Black, with clearly defined markings on cheeks, muzzle, chest and legs, over both eyes and beneath the tail. Markings range from tan to mahogany brown.
Head And Skull—Head medium length. Skull broad between ears. Forehead line moderately arched when seen from the side. The occipital bone not conspicuous. Cheeks muscular but not prominent. The zygomatic arch well-formed. Skin on the head not loose, although it wrinkles moderately when the dog is attentive. Muzzle deep with topline level and length not more than that from stop to occiput.
Tail—Carried horizontally. Short, strong and not set too low. Docked at the first joint.
Feet—Strong, round and compact. Toes arched. Hind feet longer than forefeet. Pads hard. Toenails short, dark and strong. Rear dewclaws removed.

RHODESIAN RIDGEBACK

Advantages
- **Affectionate**
- **Rarely barks**
- **Obedient**
- **Good with children**
- **Intelligent**

Disadvantages
- **May be overprotective**

The Rhodesian Ridgeback is a handsome, muscular dog of the hound group. It has a short tan coat, pendulous ears and a long, uncropped tail. The breed is named after the line of hair, shaped like the blade of a broadsword, which grows in the reverse direction along the back. It has two crowns at the shoulder and a point toward the tail. The ridge is a distinctive marking not found in any other breed. Although the ridge may appear to be a superficiality, it has come down through the centuries by way of the African Hottentot Hunting Dog.

The Rhodesian Ridgeback has a quiet temperament and rarely barks. It enjoys spending hours lazily curled up. Although its exploits as an African game hunter first brought it recognition, the breed was developed as a dual-purpose dog. Its purposes were to serve as a hunter and as a guardian of families of white settlers. People are becoming more aware of the tranquil temperament and affectionate disposition of this breed.

A Rhodesian Ridgeback and her pup.

SIZE
Height—Male: 25 to 27 in (62.5 to 68.5cm)
Female: 24 to 26 in (60 to 65cm)
Weight—Male: 70 to 80 lbs (32 to 36kg)
Female: 60 to 70 lbs (27 to 32kg)

EXERCISE
This large, sleepy, slow-moving animal contrasts sharply with its action when alerted. It becomes a streak of rhythmic motion. It is a pleasure to watch as it quickly overtakes a rabbit or squirrel in full flight. This pet needs a large yard to run in and must have a walk every day. Correct feeding and plenty of exercise keep the Ridgeback in healthy condition.

GROOMING
Groom daily with a hound glove.

FEEDING
For daily feeding, 5 cups of balanced dry dog food is recommended. Some dogs may prefer 1/2 cup water mixed with each cup of dog food. Canned dog food may be added for flavor.

ORIGIN AND HISTORY
Members of the South African Hottentot tribe had a dog they took on hunting expeditions with them, the Hottentot Hunting Dog. A distinct characteristic of the animal was the ridge of hair growing in the reverse direction along its back.

During the 16th and 17th centuries, Europeans migrated to South Africa. They pioneered an uncivilized country inhabited by fierce wild animals. They brought with them their own European working and hunting dogs. The settlers' dogs crossed with the tough Hottentot Hunting Dogs. The superior offspring were quickly recognized, the ridge identifying the most desirable dogs.

This blending over 200 years of the best qualities of European breeds with the Hottentot Hunting Dog formed the immediate ancestor of today's Ridgeback. It has many characteristics usually associated with other hounds. Rhodesian Ridgebacks arrived in the United States in 1950 and were recognized by the American Kennel Club in 1955.

SHOW REQUIREMENTS
General Appearance—Strong, muscular and active. Symmetrical in outline. Capable of endurance with speed. Movement similar to the Foxhound gait.
Color—Light wheat to red-wheat. Head, body, legs and tail a uniform color. A little white on the chest permissible but excessive white on chest, belly or above the paws penalized. White toes undesirable. Dark muzzle and ears permissible.
Head And Skull—Skull flat and broad between the ears. Free from wrinkles when in repose. Stop defined, not one straight line from nose to the occiput bone. Nose black or brown, depending on the color of the dog. No other-color nose permissible. Black nose accompanied by dark eyes, a brown nose by amber eyes.
Tail—Strong at the insertion, tapering toward the end. Free from coarseness. Not inserted too high or too low. Carried with a slight curve upward.
Feet—Compact, with arched toes. Round, tough elastic pads protected by hair between toes and pads.

The Rottweiler was used by German butchers to drive cattle to market and guard its master when the cattle had been sold. It became known as the Rottweiler Metzgerhund or Rottweil butcher's dog. It was recognized by the American Kennel Club in 1935. It is increasing in international popularity.

Rottweiler

The characteristic ridge of hair along the back of the Rhodesian Ridgeback should be clearly defined, tapering and symmetrical. It extends from immediately behind the shoulders to the haunches. It has an average width of 2 inches (5cm) and contains two identical crowns. The lower edges must not extend down the ridge farther than one-third its length.

Rhodesian Ridgeback

BOUVIER DES FLANDRES

Advantages
- **Good pet**
- **Easily trained**
- **Good guard**
- **Loyal**
- **Trustworthy**

Disadvantages
- **Fierce appearance**
- **One-person dog**

The Bouvier des Flandres is a Belgian cattle dog. It is hardy and trustworthy. Its cropped ears can make it look fierce. It makes a fine pet, but tends to be a one-person dog. It is a good guard dog.

SIZE
Height—Male: 23-1/2 to 27-1/2 in (57 to 69cm)
Female: 22-3/4 in (57cm) minimum
Weight—Male: 77 to 88 lbs (34 to 40kg)
Female: 59-1/2 to 77 lbs (27 to 35kg)

EXERCISE
This dog needs plenty of exercise. It is not suited to city life.

GROOMING
Regular brushing keeps the coat in condition.

FEEDING
For daily feeding, 5 cups of balanced dry dog food is recommended. Some dogs may prefer 1/2 cup water mixed with each cup of dog food. Canned dog food may be added for flavor.

ORIGIN AND HISTORY
The Bouvier came from working Belgian dogs. It was bred to produce an animal capable of hunting, herding and draft work. In 1912, a meeting was held to discuss a standard for the Bouvier but no agreement was reached. It was not until after World War I that a standard was drawn up by the Club National Belge du Bouvier des Flandres.

Efforts were also made to improve future stock of the breed. According to the *American Kennel Club Complete Dog Book,* the first official standard was drawn up in August 1912. The breed was making rapid progress when World War I broke out. The parts of Belgium where the Bouvier was bred suffered great losses during the war. Many of the dogs were abandoned and died.

SHOW REQUIREMENTS
General Appearance—Short legged, with muscular, strong legs. Strength without clumsiness.
Color—Black, fawn or gray, often brindled or shaded. No color preferred. Chocolate-brown with white spots is a fault.
Head And Skull—Head large. Moustache and beard make it appear larger in proportion to the body. Well-chiseled. Skull developed and flat, broader than long. The underside and the top of the skull parallel. Proportion of the length of the skull to the muzzle should be a ratio of 3 to 2. Slight furrow in the forehead. Stop not deep, but appears so, due to heavy eyebrows. Muzzle broad, strong and bony, gradually narrowing toward the nose. Never pointed. The circumference, measured just in front of eyes, almost equal to the length of the head. Nose round at its edges and always black. Nostrils wide. Cheeks flat and clean.
Tail—Docked to about 4 inches (10cm). Continues the normal line of the vertebral column. Carried up when moving. Dogs born tailless not faulted.
Feet—Short, round and compact. Toes tight and arched. Nails black, strong. Thick, hard pads.

BRIARD

Advantages
- **Easy to train**
- **Good pet**
- **Good worker**
- **Gentle**

Disadvantages
- **No drawbacks known**

The Briard is the most well-known of four French sheepdogs. The others are the Beauceron, Picardy and the Great Pyrenees Dog. Briards are good-natured and can be kept as a pet or for farm work. Many are shown.

SIZE
Height—Male: 23 to 27 in (57.5 to 68.5cm)
Female: 22 to 25-1/2 in (55 to 63.5cm)
Weight—No requirement

EXERCISE
Give this dog regular exercise.

GROOMING
Brush the dog regularly. The Briard cleans itself.

FEEDING
For daily feeding, 5 cups of balanced dry dog food is recommended. Some dogs may prefer 1/2 cup water mixed with each cup of dog food. Canned dog food may be added for flavor.

ORIGIN AND HISTORY
The Briard comes from the area of Brie, France, where it is also known as the *Berger de Brie* or *Chien de Brie*. It has been known there since the 12th century.

SHOW REQUIREMENTS
General Appearance—Rugged, supple, well-proportioned and muscular.
Color—All uniform colors permitted except white. Black, tawny and shades of gray. Deeper shades of each color preferred. Combinations of these colors permitted, if there are no marked spots. Transition from one color to another takes place gradually and symmetrically. White permissible only as white hairs scattered throughout the coat or a white spot on the chest. Spots not to exceed 1 inch (2.5cm) in diameter at the root of the hair.
Head And Skull—Head strong and long. A defined stop is placed midway in the length of the head. Head has a moustache, beard and eyebrows that slightly veil the eyes. Muzzle not narrow or pointed. Nose large, square and always black. Forehead slightly rounded. Skull rectangular.
Tail—Long, covered with hair, with an upward hook at the tip. Carried low, not deviating to one side or the other. Bone of the tail reaches at least to the point of the hock.
Feet—Strong and slightly round. Nails always black. Pads firm and hard. Closed toes.

A Briard suckles her pups. This French sheepdog is used for herding. It is also an affectionate pet, good-natured, easy to train and successful as a show dog.

The name of the Bouvier des Flandres comes from the French word for a cowherd or oxherd. This reflects its function as a working dog in the 19th century. The Bouvier's rough, tousled and unkempt coat requires regular brushing. This is reflected in another early name for the breed: Vuibaard, or dirty beard.

Bouvier des Flandres

It is believed the Briard was first brought to America by the Marquis de Lafayette or Thomas Jefferson. No litter was registered with the American Kennel Club until 1922. The Briard Club was founded in 1928.

Briard

VIZSLA

Advantages
- *Good gundog*
- *Good family pet*
- *Keen sense of smell*

Disadvantages
- *No drawbacks known*

The Vizsla is Hungary's national dog and one of the purest breeds in the world. It is an excellent gundog, with a keen sense of smell, the ability to point, set and retrieve. Despite its hunting abilities, it adapts to life as a family pet because of its even temperament.

SIZE
Height—Male: 22 to 24 in (55 to 60cm) Female: 21 to 23 in (53.5 to 57.5cm)
Weight—48-1/2 to 66 lbs (22 to 30kg)

EXERCISE
This dog needs plenty of vigorous exercise.

GROOMING
Regular brushing keeps the coat in condition.

FEEDING
For daily feeding, 5 cups of balanced dry dog food is recommended. Some dogs may prefer 1/2 cup water mixed with each cup of dog food. Canned dog food may be added for flavor.

ORIGIN AND HISTORY
The Vizsla was developed by Magyar nobles. Care has been taken to avoid introducing new blood. It is a pure breed of ability and quality.

SHOW REQUIREMENTS
General Appearance—Medium size, robust, not heavily boned. **Color**—Russet-gold. Small white marks on chest and feet, though acceptable, are not desirable. **Head And Skull**—Head lean and muscular. Skull moderately wide between the ears, with a median line down the forehead and a moderate stop. Muzzle a little longer than the skull and tapering. Squared at the end. Nostrils developed, broad and wide. Jaws strong and powerful. Lips cover jaws completely, not loose or pendulous. Nose brown. **Tail**—Moderately thick, set low, with one-third docked off. Held horizontally while moving. **Feet**—Round. Toes short, arched and closed. A cat foot is desirable. A hare foot is objectionable. Nails short, strong and a shade darker in color than the coat. Dewclaws removed.

The Vizsla is one of the purest breeds in the world.

SLOVAKIAN KUVASZ
Tsuvatch

Advantages
- *Brave*
- *Intelligent*
- *Good watchdog*

Disadvantages
- *Not common in the United States*

The Slovakian Kuvasz is a lively, intelligent dog. It is watchful and has acute hearing. It is similar to the Kuvasz.

SIZE
Height—Male: 24 to 28 in (60 to 71cm) Female: 24 to 26 in (60 to 65cm)
Weight—No requirement

EXERCISE
This dog needs plenty of vigorous exercise.

GROOMING
Regular brushing is necessary to keep the coat in condition.

FEEDING
For daily feeding, 5 cups of balanced dry dog food is recommended. Some dogs may prefer 1/2 cup water mixed with each cup of dog food. Canned dog food may be added for flavor.

ORIGIN AND HISTORY
The Slovakian Kuvasz is not well-known outside of Hungary. It is similar to the Kuvasz. It bears a resemblance also to the Tatry Mountain Polish Sheepdog, a Polish herding breed. Bengstson and Wintzell in *Dogs of the World* suggest the three breeds could be local varieties of the same herding breed. The Polish and Slovakian types are sometimes known as Tatry dogs, after the mountain range stretching through both countries.

SHOW REQUIREMENTS
There is no recognized standard for this breed. The most desirable color is pure white. White animals have always been desired by huntsmen, because their color distinguished them from their prey.

KUVASZ

Advantages
- *Good guard*
- *Loyal*

Disadvantages
- *One-person dog*

The Kuvasz is a loyal and devoted guard. It is an intelligent dog. The name Kuvasz comes from a Turkish word meaning *guardian of the peace*. A natural herder, it has been used for big game hunting.

SIZE
Height—Male: 28 to 30 in (71 to 75cm) Female: 26 to 28 in (65 to 71cm)
Weight—Male: 100 to 115 lbs (45 to 52kg) Female: 66 to 93 lbs (30 to 44kg)

EXERCISE
This dog needs plenty of exercise.

GROOMING
Regular brushing will keep the coat in condition.

FEEDING
For daily feeding, 5 cups of balanced dry dog food is recommended. Some dogs may prefer 1/2 cup water mixed with each cup of dog food. Canned dog food may be added for flavor.

ORIGIN AND HISTORY
The Kuvasz has existed in Hungary for centuries. As early as the 1490s, it was used to protect Hungarian nobility against assassins. It became known as the guard dog of the privileged. Only high-born people were permitted to keep one. Today, it has become popular.

SHOW REQUIREMENTS
General Appearance—Big and powerful. Body not too long or too compact. Outline is square. Joints and muscles lean. Bone structure strong without coarseness. Position of the limbs, the deep chest and the slightly hollowed croup allow the Kuvasz to work tirelessly. Coat rough and wavy. **Color**—White. Ivory is accepted. **Head And Skull**—Nose pointed and black. Black inner lips and eyerims. Bridge is long, broad and straight. Lips fit close to the gums and have a saw-tooth closure. Muzzle tapers from base to nose. Not too pointed at the tip. Forehead medial furrow continues to the muzzle. Stop slopes gently. Broadly curved. Skull long but not pointed, medium width with a broad occiput. Ears set on high, close to the flat skull. Supraorbital ridges moderately developed. **Tail**—Set on low, a continuation of the croup. It hangs down to the height of the hocks. Tip is curved slightly upward, without forming a ring. When excited or alerted, tail is elevated to loin level. **Feet**—Hind feet are longer than forefeet but as strong. Pads tight and elastic. Nails slate-gray. Dewclaws removed. **Teeth**—Regular and strong. Scissors bite.

The Kuvasz is a natural herder and makes an excellent guard. It has also been used for big-game hunting.

A dog resembling the Vizsla is shown on a Magyar rock carving dating from around 1000 A.D. The Vizsla became known outside Hungary only after World War II, when many dogs left with refugees.

Vizsla

Slovakian Kuvasz, or Tsuvatch

A decline in the Kuvasz breed, caused by two world wars and a Communist takeover, has been outweighed by increased interest abroad.

Kuvasz

BERNESE MOUNTAIN DOG

Bernese Sennenhund

Advantages
- *Easily trained*
- *Good watchdog*
- *Good with animals and people*
- *Good pet*
- *Docile*

Disadvantages
- *Not common in the United States*

The Bernese Mountain Dog is the most well-known of four Swiss Mountain Dogs. The others are the Great Swiss Sennenhund, the Appenzell Sennenhund and the Entlebuch Sennenhund. The Bernese Mountain Dog is a draft dog and a pet in Switzerland. It is gaining popularity as a pet and show dog, because it is easy to train. It is affectionate and docile.

SIZE
Height—Male 23 to 27-1/2 in (57.5 to 69cm)
Female: 21 to 26 in (53.5 to 65cm)
Weight—No requirement

EXERCISE
This dog needs moderate exercise.

GROOMING
Regular brushing keeps the coat in condition.

FEEDING
For daily feeding, 5 cups of balanced dry dog food is recommended. Some dogs may prefer 1/2 cup water mixed with each cup of dog food. Canned dog food may be added for flavor.

ORIGIN AND HISTORY
The Bernese has been used as a herder and draft dog for centuries.

The types of Sennenhund are named after the regions in which they were found. The St. Bernard, Mastiff, Rottweiler and Newfoundland are also related.

SHOW REQUIREMENTS
General Appearance—Strong, active, alert and well-boned.
Color—Black, with red-brown on the cheeks, over eyes, on all four legs and on the chest. Symmetrical white blaze on head and white cross on chest essential. Preferred, but not essential, are white paws. White reaches no higher than the pastern. A white tip to the tail. A few white hairs at the nape of the neck and a white anal patch undesirable but tolerated.
Head And Skull—Strong with flat skull and slightly developed furrow. Well-defined stop. Strong, straight muzzle. Lips slightly developed.
Tail—Bushy, reaching just below the hock. When alert may be carried up, but not curled or carried over the back.
Feet—Short, round and compact. Dewclaws removed.
Teeth—Undershot or overshot is a disqualification.

The Bernese, used as a draft dog for centuries.

Two Bernese puppies, showing white tips on their tails.

The Great Swiss Sennenhund stands as high as 28 inches (70.5cm). It is shorthair and black with a red brand and white markings. The shorthair Appenzell Sennenhund is smaller, maximum 23 inches (58cm) but identical except for a curled tail. The Entlebuch Sennenhund stands no higher than 18 inches (45.5cm), has short hair, a stump tail and its coat is black with yellow to brown and white markings.

The Great Swiss Mountain Dog was bred to herd cattle.

Appenzell
Sennenhund

Entlebuch
Sennenhund

Great Swiss
Sennenhund

Bernese Mountain Dog

POLISH SHEEPDOG

Owczarek Podhalanski, Owczarek Nizinny

Advantages
- *Good guard*
- *Hardy*
- *Good-natured*
- *Intelligent*

Disadvantages
- *Not common in the United States*

There are two varieties of Polish Sheepdog. The Lowlands Shepherd, *Owczarek Nizinny,* looks something like the Old English Sheepdog. The Tatry Mountain Sheepdog, *Owczarek Podhalanski,* is larger and looks something like the Retriever or Kuvasz. They are intelligent, good-natured, docile and have a keen memory.

SIZE
Height—23 in (57.5cm)
Weight—No requirement

EXERCISE
This dog needs a lot of exercise.

GROOMING
Brush the coat regularly. The Lowlands type must be combed with a steel comb.

FEEDING
For daily feeding, 2 cups of balanced dry dog food is recommended. Some dogs may prefer 1/2 cup water mixed with each cup of dog food. Canned dog food may be added for flavor.

ORIGIN AND HISTORY
The Tatry Mountain Sheepdog bears a strong resemblance to the Hungarian Kuvasz. Both varieties of Polish Sheepdog were introduced to Poland in the 4th or 5th century. They are not well-known outside their homeland.

OLD ENGLISH SHEEPDOG

Bobtail

Advantages
- *Good with children*
- *Gets along with other animals*
- *Even-tempered*

Disadvantages
- *No drawbacks known*

The Old English Sheepdog is a popular breed. It is a devoted friend and guardian of children, with a sound, even temperament. Despite its large size, it is content in a small house.

SIZE
Height—Male: 22 in (55cm)
　　　　　Female: Slightly smaller
Weight—No requirement

EXERCISE
Give this dog two 20-minute walks each day. Keep it in a fenced yard.

GROOMING
Brush daily and comb weekly with a steel comb. Hair is brushed forward to cover the eyes. White parts are powdered for showing.

FEEDING
For daily feeding, 5 cups of balanced dry dog food is recommended. Some dogs may prefer 1/2 cup water mixed with each cup of dog food. Canned dog food may be added for flavor.

HEALTH CARE
Check ears for cankers. Be careful matted hair does not accumulate around the feet. Some Bobtails are born with a stumpy tail; otherwise, it is docked to 2 inches (5cm).

ORIGIN AND HISTORY
Because of its short tail, the Old English Sheepdog is also known as the Bobtail. The breed evolved by crossing a Briard with a large Russian Owtscharka, a dog related to Hungarian sheepdogs. It was used in England as a cattle dog and guard, but today is kept mainly as a pet.

The first breed club for the Old English Sheepdog was established in Britain in 1888. The standard has changed little since then.

SHOW REQUIREMENTS
General Appearance—Strong and free of legginess. Profuse coat. Elastic in a gallop, but in walking or trotting has an ambling or pacing movement. Loud bark. It is thickset, muscular and able bodied, with an intelligent expression. Free of Poodle or Deerhound character.

Color—Any shade of gray, grizzle, blue or blue-merle, with or without white markings. Any shade of brown or sable is objectionable.
Head And Skull—Skull squarely formed. Arched over the eyes and covered with hair. Jaw long, strong, square and truncated. Stop defined. Nose black, large and capacious.
Tail—Not to exceed 1-1/2 to 2 inches (3.8 to 5cm). Docked tail.
Feet—Small. Toes arched. Pads thick and round.
Teeth—Evenly placed, in level opposition.

It is easy to see why Old English Sheepdogs make popular pets. This pup will grow into a playful dog, excellent with children and happy to live in a small house with a yard.

Polish Sheepdog

The coat of the Old
English Sheepdog
should be profuse and
hard textured. It should
not be straight, but
shaggy and free from
curl.

Old English Sheepdog

ANATOLIAN KARABASH
Anatolian Sheepdog, Turkish Shepherd's Dog

Advantages
- **Affectionate**
- **Hardy**
- **Intelligent**
- **Loyal**
- **Easily trained**

Disadvantages
- **Not suited to city life**
- **Can be possessive**
- **Not common in the United States**

The Anatolian Karabash is a shepherd's guard dog of ancient lineage. It is a large, fast, vigorous outdoor working dog with a self-sufficient temperament. These dogs come from the Anatolian plateau of Turkey. Shepherds of Central Asia give them massive iron-spiked collars to help defend the flocks from predators.

The Anatolian Karabash can live outside all day. If let in the house, it becomes a good companion. This dog will identify with one person as its owner, but will accept other members of the family and friends. It needs a lot of love. It should be socialized at an early age or it may become too possessive. It is friendly with other animals.

SIZE
Height—Male: 29 to 32 in
(73.5 to 80cm)
Female: 28 to 31 in
(71 to 77.5cm)
Weight—Male: 110 to 141 lbs
(50 to 64kg)
Female: 90 to 130 lbs
(42 to 59kg)

EXERCISE
As a pet, the Karabash is not suited to city life. It needs plenty of space to work off energy. It will do this on its own, so there is usually no need to take it for long walks. The breed is naturally active and playful, and is happy in a large, fenced yard.

For such a large dog, the Anatolian Karabash moves quickly and gracefully. It has been clocked at speeds of 34mph (55kh).

GROOMING
Its coat is clean, odorless and free of parasites. Regular brushing is all that is needed.

FEEDING
For daily feeding, 6 cups of balanced dry dog food is recommended. Some dogs may prefer 1/2 cup water mixed with each cup of dog food. Canned dog food may be added for flavor.

ORIGIN AND HISTORY
A breed of large, strong dogs with a heavy head has existed in Turkey since ancient times. They were used as fighters and for hunting big game such as lions and horses. Drawings can be seen on preserved bas-reliefs in the Assyrian room of the British Museum in London.

Today, the dogs do not herd the sheep, but patrol around them. They often seek higher ground to get a better view. The dogs patrol the ground ahead of the flock, checking for trouble. If they notice anything, they silently split up and converge on it at great speed.

SHOW REQUIREMENTS
General Appearance—Steady and bold without undue aggression. Naturally independent. Intelligent and trainable.
Color—All shades of fawn. White socks and chest blaze commonly occur. Black mask varies from a black head and ears, to a slight blackness around the muzzle.
Head And Skull—Large and broad between the ears with slight stop. Mature males have a broader head, the females a more narrow head. Square profile. Foreface one-third of total head length. Slightly pendulous black lips. Nose black.
Tail—Long bone reaches at least to hock joint. Set on high. When relaxed, carried low with slight curl. When alert, carried high with end curled over back, especially by males.
Feet—Strong, with arched toes. Nails blunt. Gray or black, depending on coat color.

ESTRELA MOUNTAIN DOG
Rafeiro do Alentejo

Advantages
- **Excellent sheepdog**
- **Even-tempered**
- **Useful draft animal**

Disadvantages
- **Not common in the United States**

The Estrela Mountain Dog is a hardy animal with great power. It is used for herding sheep and pulling carts. It is a popular show dog in Portugal.

SIZE
Height—Male: 26 to 29 in
(65 to 73.5cm)
Female: 25 to 27-1/2 in
(62.5 to 69cm)
Weight—Male: 88 to 110 lbs
(40 to 50kg)
Female: 34 to 44 lbs
(16 to 20kg)

EXERCISE
This dog needs plenty of exercise.

GROOMING
Regular brushing keeps the coat in condition.

FEEDING
For daily feeding, 5 cups of balanced dry dog food is recommended. Some dogs may prefer 1/2 cup water mixed with each cup of dog food. Canned dog food may be added for flavor.

ORIGIN AND HISTORY
This dog has existed for centuries in the Estrela mountains of Portugal. It resembles the St. Bernard, but is lighter. It has some Mastiff in its development. It was originally bred as a herding dog.

SHOW REQUIREMENTS
General Appearance—Large and powerfully built, with stout configuration.
Color—Black; tawny or yellow, mixed with white; bicolored; roan or dappled. Often streaked or grizzled.
Head And Skull—Bearlike head, in proportion to the overall body structure. Skull broad, with a slight medial furrow above and between eyes. Stop not accentuated. Upper longitudinal axes of muzzle and skull are divergent. Occipital protuberance not pronounced. Muzzle round, with a straight profile. Not as long as the skull. Moderately broad. Lips slightly round in front and overlapping. Lips thin and solid, with a slight curve to the lower profile. Jaws strong, muscular and well-opposed. Dark nose oval, tip blunted from above to below and from forward back.

Tail—Set on moderately high. Slightly curved at the end. When the dog is at rest, tail is carried between the hocks, reaching below them. It may curl moderately when the dog is moving.
Feet—Must not be flat. Closed and long, with stout toes barely arched. Color varies with the color of the coat. Pads thick and tough.

TIBETAN MASTIFF

Advantages
- **Good guard**
- **Even-tempered**

Disadvantages
- **No drawbacks known**

The Tibetan Mastiff has a strong resemblance to the St. Bernard. It is an excellent guard dog and is good-natured unless provoked. The dog can be happy as a companion or guard.

SIZE
Height—Male: 25 to 27 in
(62.5 to 68.5cm)
Female: 22 to 24 in
(55 to 60cm)
Weight—No requirement

EXERCISE
This dog needs regular vigorous exercise.

GROOMING
Daily brushing keeps the coat in condition.

FEEDING
For daily feeding, 5 cups of balanced dry dog food is recommended. Some dogs may prefer 1/2 cup water mixed with each cup of dog food. Canned dog food may be added for flavor.

ORIGIN AND HISTORY
The Tibetan Mastiff is regarded as a British breed, but it originated in Central Asia. Its job was to guard flocks of sheep. Like other Mastiffs, it is descended from the Roman Molossus. It is a purebred, but not registered by the American Kennel Club. There is growing interest in the breed; there are two national clubs in the United States.

SHOW REQUIREMENTS
General Appearance—Powerful and heavy boned. Docile and aloof.
Color—Gold or black and tan.
Head And Skull—Broad, massive head and smooth face. Powerful jaws. Muzzle of Mastiff type, but lighter than the English Mastiff.
Tail—Set on high, curled over back to one side. Thick and bushy.
Feet—Smooth, large, strong and compact.
Teeth—Level bite.

The Anatolian Karabash developed its hardiness as a result of centuries of herding on the rough and arid plateau, which extends over most of Turkey.

Anatolian Karabash

Estrela Mountain Dog

Tibetan Mastiff

Although now seldom seen in Britain, the Tibetan Mastiff was known during the 19th century, when King George IV imported the breed.

BORZOI

Advantages
- **Intelligent**
- **Faithful**

Disadvantages
- **Not a children's pet**
- **Needs a lot of exercise**

The Borzoi is an animal of great beauty and grace. It was used in Russia in the 17th century for wolf hunting and coursing. Today, it is often considered fashionable to own one. These good-natured, dignified animals may be aloof. They do not like children.

SIZE
Height—Male: 29 in (73.5cm)
Female: 27 in (68.5cm)
Weight—No requirement

EXERCISE
The Borzoi needs a lot of exercise. This dog was originally a hunter, so it needs to run.

FEEDING
For daily feeding, 5 cups of balanced dry dog food is recommended. Some dogs may prefer 1/2 cup water mixed with each cup of dog food. Canned dog food may be added for flavor.

ORIGIN AND HISTORY
The Borzoi was kept by the Czars and noblemen of Imperial Russia for wolf hunting. During the 15th and 16th centuries, it was crossed with the sheepdog to provide strength. Later, it was crossed with hounds for speed. From the strain developed by the Grand Duke Nicolai Nicolayevitch, the present-day standard evolved. Up-to-date information on Borzois in Russia is sketchy. Today, there are many Borzois in New York, London and Paris.

SHOW REQUIREMENTS
General Appearance—Graceful, aristocratic and elegant. Possesses courage, power and speed.
Head And Skull—Head long and lean. Filled in below the eyes. Measurement equal from the occiput to the inner corner of the eye and from the inner corner of the eye to the tip of the nose. Skull slightly domed and narrow. Stop not perceptible. Inclining to Roman nose. Head fine so the direction of the bones and principal veins can be clearly seen. Female's head finer than a male's. Jaws long, deep and powerful. Nose large and black, not pink or brown. Round, not sharp. Viewed from above, the skull looks narrow, converging gradually to tip of nose.
Tail—Long and set low. Feathered. Carried low, not up. In action may be used as a rudder, but not rising above back level. From the level of the hocks, may be sickle-shape, but not ringed.
Feet—Front feet long. Arched, closed toes. Never flat. Hind feet harelike.
Teeth—Strong, clean and even or scissors bite.

BLACK AND TAN COONHOUND

Advantages
- **Keen sense of smell**
- **Even-tempered**
- **Strong**
- **Hardy**

Disadvantages
- **No drawbacks known**

The Black and Tan Coonhound is a fast, hardy, strong working hound. Like the Bloodhound, it does not kill its prey. It is similar to the Bloodhound in appearance, but does not have wrinkles.

SIZE
Height—Male: 25 to 27 in
(62.5 to 68.5cm)
Female: 23 to 25 in
(57.5 to 62.5cm)
Weight—No requirement

EXERCISE
This dog needs plenty of vigorous exercise.

GROOMING
Groom this dog daily with a hound glove. Regular ear inspection is necessary.

FEEDING
For daily feeding, 5 cups of balanced dry dog food is recommended. Some dogs may prefer 1/2 cup water mixed with each cup of dog food. Canned dog food may be added for flavor.

ORIGIN AND HISTORY
The Black and Tan Coonhound is an American breed and a close relation of the Bloodhound. Both are identical in size and often in color. Its line traces back from the Talbot Hound to the Bloodhound and Virginia Foxhound. The Black and Tan is one of six breeds recognized by the United Kennel Club. It is used for hunting opossum and raccoon but is being seen more frequently at shows.

SHOW REQUIREMENTS
The Black and Tan Coonhound is a working dog. It is capable of withstanding cold, heat and difficult terrain over which it may be required to work. Judges are asked to place great emphasis on these factors when evaluating merits of the dog.
General Appearance—Powerful, agile and alert. Expression friendly, eager and aggressive. Covers ground with powerful rhythmic strides.
Color—Black, with tan markings above eyes, on the sides of muzzle and on chest, legs and breeching. Black pencil markings on toes.
Head And Skull—Head cleanly modeled, with medium stop midway between occiput bone and nose. Head measures 9 to 10 inches (23 to 25.5cm) in males and 8 to 9 inches (20.5 to 23cm) in females. Viewed in profile, line of skull is almost on a parallel plane to the foreface or muzzle. Skin should not have folds or excess dewlap. Flews developed, with typical hound appearance. Nostrils open and black. Skull an oval outline.
Tail—Strong, with base slightly below level of back line. Carried free. When in action, carried at right angle to the back.
Feet—Catlike, with compact, arched toes and thick, strong pads.
Teeth—Fit evenly with a slight scissors bite.

BLOODHOUND

Advantages
- **Keen sense of smell**
- **Good with children**
- **Good tracking ability**
- **Good pet**

Disadvantages
- **Feelings easily hurt**
- **Use only voice control**

The Bloodhound is a delightful animal with a keen sense of smell. It follows its quarry, but does not kill it. It is loved by children, so it is often kept as a family pet. Bloodhounds are popular show dogs. They are still often used by police for tracking purposes.

SIZE
Height—Male: 25 to 27 in
(62.5 to 68.5cm)
Female: 23 to 25 in
(57.5 to 62.5cm)
Weight—Male: 90 lbs (42kg)
Female: 80 lbs (37kg)

EXERCISE
This dog needs plenty of exercise. Consider joining a Bloodhound Club to take part in organized events.

GROOMING
Groom this dog daily with a hound glove. Regular ear inspection is necessary.

HEALTH CARE
Bloodhounds are subject to *torsion*, stomach gases building into a bloat. It can prove fatal if not treated by a vet within minutes. Be aware of this and be ready to seek immediate help.

FEEDING
For daily feeding, 5 cups of balanced dry dog food is recommended. Some dogs may prefer 1/2 cup water mixed with each cup of dog food. Canned dog food may be added for flavor.

ORIGIN AND HISTORY
The Bloodhound was brought to England by William the Conqueror in 1066. It is one of the oldest and purest hound breeds. Bloodhounds have been shown since the first dog shows.

SHOW REQUIREMENTS
General Appearance—Noble, dignified and solemn expression. Gait is elastic, swinging and free. Stern carried high and curved.
Color—Black and tan; liver and tan; tawny and tan; tawny. Darker colors sometimes interspersed with lighter or badger-color hair. Sometimes flecked with white.
Head And Skull—Head narrow, relative to its length. Long, relative to the body. It tapers only slightly from temples to muzzle. When viewed from above and in front, it appears flat at the sides. Nearly equal in width throughout its length. In profile, the upper outline of the skull is on the same plane as the foreface. Length from the end of the nose to the stop not less than from the stop to the occipital protuberance. Brows not prominent, although they may have that appearance because of deep-set eyes. Foreface long, deep and of even width with a square outline when seen in profile. Head has some loose skin, which appears superabundant. Skin falls into loose folds, especially over the forehead and sides of the face. Nostrils large and open. Lips make a right angle with the upper line of the foreface, forming deep hanging flews and continue into the pendant folds of loose skin about the neck. Dewlap pronounced.
Tail—Stern long and thick, tapering to a point. Set on high with a moderate amount of hair underneath. Carried curved, but not curled over the back or corkscrew at any time.
Feet—Strong and knuckled up.

Borzoi

Black And Tan Coonhound

Bloodhound

The Bloodhound's long ears must be given regular attention. Thin and soft to the touch, they are set on low and fall in graceful folds. The lower parts curl inward and backward.

IRISH WOLFHOUND

Advantages
- **Good with children**
- **Good guard**
- **Happiest as a housedog**

Disadvantages
- **Fierce when provoked**
- **Needs discipline**

The Irish Wolfhound, also known as the Wolfdog, the Irish Greyhound and the Great Dog of Ireland, is a gentle giant. It is fierce only when provoked. It is loyal, intelligent and slow to anger. Irish Wolfhounds have minds of their own, so firm, gentle discipline is necessary in puppyhood.

SIZE
Height—Minimum
Male: 31 in (77.5cm)
Female: 30 in (75cm)
Weight—Minimum
Male: 120 lbs (54kg)
Female: 105 lbs (48kg)

EXERCISE
Despite its size, the Irish Wolfhound does not require more exercise than smaller breeds. Give it room to run. Let it have unrestricted play during puppyhood, but do not force it to take long walks. Allow it to develop by its own activity. Irish Wolfhounds are usually taught to walk and move at a trot while being led.

GROOMING
Brush regularly and remove long, straggly hairs from ears, neck and underside with finger and thumb. This natural-looking breed is not difficult to groom.

Irish Wolfhound puppies need firm, gentle discipline.

FEEDING
For daily feeding, 5 cups of balanced dry dog food is recommended. Some dogs may prefer 1/2 cup water mixed with each cup of dog food. Canned dog food may be added for flavor.

ORIGIN AND HISTORY
The Irish Wolfhound is the national dog of Ireland. Its original role was to kill wolves. It is mentioned in many legends, but probably came from Greece with the invading Celts, around 279 B.C.

The best-known story of an Irish Wolfhound is of the dog Gelert, given to Llewellyn, Prince of Wales, in 1210. Prince Llewellyn went hunting, leaving Gelert in charge of his son. On his return he could only see Gelert, with blood on its mouth. Thinking it had killed the child, he drew his sword and killed the dog. It was only then he saw the body of a wolf nearby and heard the child. Gelert had killed the wolf and saved the child. Full of remorse, Prince Llewellyn ordered a statue be erected in memory of Gelert. The dog's memory has lived on through the centuries.

SHOW REQUIREMENTS
General Appearance—Large, muscular and strongly built. Movement easy and active. Head and neck carried high. Tail carried with an upward sweep, a slight curve toward the end
Color—Gray, brindle, red, black, white or fawn.
Head And Skull—Long. Frontal bones of the forehead slightly raised, with little indentation between the eyes. Skull not too broad. Muzzle long and pointed.
Tail—Long and slightly curved. Moderately thick, covered with hair.
Feet—Large and round. Not turned in or out. Toes arched and closed. Nails strong and curved.

DEERHOUND
Scottish Deerhound

Advantages
- **Likes people**
- **Loving**
- **Even-tempered**

Disadvantages
- **Needs lots of space**

The Deerhound is graceful and beautiful, mentioned frequently in the novels of Sir Walter Scott. The dog is strong, healthy and anxious to please. It enjoys being a devoted companion.

SIZE
Height—Minimum
Male: 30 in (75cm)
Female: 28 in (71cm)
Weight—Male: 85 to 110 lbs (38 to 50kg)
Female: 65 to 80 lbs (29 to 36kg)

EXERCISE
This dog needs a lot of exercise.

GROOMING
A Deerhound requires little trimming. Remove extra shaggy hairs for show and brush regularly. Its coat is weather resistant so this breed rarely feels the cold.

FEEDING
For daily feeding, 5 cups of balanced dry dog food is recommended. Some dogs may prefer 1/2 cup water mixed with each cup of dog food. Canned dog food may be added for flavor.

ORIGIN AND HISTORY
The Deerhound was bred to hunt with its master by day and be a companion by night. With the invention of breech-loading rifles, the need for the hunting Deerhound ceased. So did its popularity. It is now kept by a few people. Many believe once you own a Deerhound you will never want to own another breed. It is a gentle giant.

The breed has Greyhound in its make-up. Until the 19th century, the Irish Wolfhound and the Deerhound were similar. Today, it is easy to distinguish between the two. The Deerhound is a sleeker, lighter dog.

The graceful Deerhound makes a devoted companion.

SHOW REQUIREMENTS
Color—Dark blue-gray preferred, darker and lighter grays or brindles, the darkest preferred. Yellow, sandy red or red-fawn, especially with black points. White is disliked. A white chest and white toes, which occur in many of the darkest dogs, are not objectionable, but the less the better. A white blaze on the head or a white collar heavily penalized. A white tip on the stern may occur in the best strains.
Head And Skull—Head broadest at the ears, tapering slightly to the eyes. The muzzle tapers more to the nose. Muzzle pointed, but lips level. Head long. Skull more flat than round, with a slight rise over the eyes. No stop. Skull covered with long hair, softer than the rest of the coat. Nose black. In some blue-fawns, the color is blue and slightly aquiline. In lighter color dogs, a black muzzle is preferred. Dog should have a moustache and beard.
Tail—Long. Thick at the root. Tapering, reaching about 1-1/2 inches (4cm) from the ground. When the dog is still, dropped straight down or curved. When in motion, curved. Never lifted out of the line of the back. Covered with hair on the inside. Thick and wiry. Longer on the underside. Toward the end, a slight fringe is not objectionable. Curl or ring tail undesirable.
Feet—Close and compact, with well-arranged toes. Nails strong.

After a history spanning 2,000 years, the Irish Wolfhound was almost extinct by the mid-19th century. It was restored by a captain in the British Army. In 1885, the first standard for the breed was established.

Irish Wolfhound

The Deerhound is shaggy but not overcoated and never woolly. The hair on the body, neck and quarters should be rough and wiry, about 3 to 4 inches (7.5 to 10 cm) long. Hair on the head, chest and belly is softer.

Deerhound

LEONBERGER

Advantages
- *Good swimmer*

Disadvantages
- *Not common in the United States*

The Leonberger is a strong, sound dog. It is used for protecting livestock and as a draft dog in Western Germany and other European countries. The dog loves the water and is a good swimmer. It comes from animals of sound temperament and is creating interest internationally.

SIZE
Height—Minimum
Male: 30 in (75cm)
Female: 27-1/2 in (69cm)
Weight—No requirement

EXERCISE
This dog needs adequate space and exercise.

GROOMING
Normal daily brushing is sufficient.

FEEDING
For daily feeding, 5 cups of balanced dry dog food is recommended. Some dogs may prefer 1/2 cup water mixed with each cup of dog food. Canned dog food may be added for flavor.

ORIGIN AND HISTORY
The Leonberger is German, derived through crossing the Landseer-type Newfoundland with the Great Pyrenees Dog. The result is an attractive, light-colored animal little known except in Germany and bordering countries.

SHOW REQUIREMENTS
General Appearance—Large, muscular and well-proportioned, with a lively temperament.
Color—Light yellow, gold-yellow to red-brown, with a black mask highly desirable, but not necessary. Dark or black points on the coat. Some coats are sandy, silver-gray or yellow-red with dark points . White inadmissible. A small white star on the chest and a little light or white hair on toes allowed. Tail color same as the rest of the coat.
Head And Skull—The upper part of the head is moderately domed, but not the length and depth of a St. Bernard's. Longer than wide. Lips not pendulous. No slobbering. Skin on head and muzzle close fitting, with no wrinkles on the forehead. Muzzle moderately deep, well-proportioned and never pointed. Cheeks not greatly developed. Stop not pronounced. Bridge broad, continuous and slightly arched.

Tail—Bushy. Always carried at half mast. Not too high and never curled over the back.
Feet—Closed and rounded. Hare feet not acceptable. Toes webbed.
Teeth—Strong, with good adaptation between lower and upper jaws.

GREAT PYRENEES DOG
Pyrenean Mountain Dog

Advantages
- *Can be kept outdoors*
- *Easily trained*
- *Good guard*
- *Good with other animals*
- *Intelligent*

Disadvantages
- *Needs a job*
- *Does not like strangers*
- *Needs plenty of space*

The Great Pyrenees Dog is a natural shepherd bred to guard flocks in the Pyrenees. It is a good pet for those who have the space and income to keep such a large dog.

It is hardy, good-natured and becomes devoted to the family. It is not friendly with strangers. Strangers who have tried to pet the dog have been bitten.

SIZE
Height—Male: 27 to 32 in
(68.5 to 80cm)
Female: 25 to 29 in
(62.5 to 73.5cm)
Weight—Male: 100 to 125 lbs
(45 to 58kg)
Female: 90 to 115 lbs
(41 to 52kg)

EXERCISE
Normal exercise is sufficient. The dog adapts to city or country living and is content with walks of average length.

GROOMING
Regular brushing will keep the coat in condition.

FEEDING
For daily feeding, 5 cups of balanced dry dog food is recommended. Some dogs may prefer 1/2 cup water mixed with each cup of dog food. Canned dog food may be added for flavor.

ORIGIN AND HISTORY
The Great Pyrenees was a favorite in the French court before the French Revolution. Since then it has never regained the same popularity, though it is widely known and frequently exhibited. It was once used to guard sheep and fortresses, wearing a spiked collar like a Mastiff. The breed became known when tourists began buying puppies from shepherds.

SHOW REQUIREMENTS
General Appearance—Large and powerful. Well-balanced. Nervousness or unprovoked aggression heavily penalized by judges.
Color—All white or white with patches of badger, wolf-gray or pale yellow. Areas of black hair, where black goes to the roots, are a serious fault. Colored markings on head, ears and at the base of the tail permitted. A few patches on the body permitted. Nose and eyerims black. Liver or pink-color pigmentation is a serious fault.
Head And Skull—Head strong with no sign of coarseness. Not heavy in proportion to the size of the dog. Top of the skull, as viewed from front and side, shows a definite curve and slight dome. Breadth of the skull at its widest point about equal to the length from occiput to stop. Sides of the head nearly flat. No obvious stop.

Only a slight furrow so skull and muzzle are joined by a gentle slope. Muzzle strong, medium length, with a slight taper near its tip. Nose black. When viewed from above, head forms a blunt V, filled in below the eyes.
Tail—Thick at the root. Tapers gradually toward the top, with a slight curl. Reaches below hocks. Long hair forms an attractive plume. In repose, tail carried low with the tip turned slightly to one side. As the dog becomes excited, the tail rises. When animal is fully alert tail curls high above the back in a circle.
Feet—Short and compact. Toes slightly arched. Nails strong.

The large and elegant Pyrenean Mountain Dog, seen here with a pup, will happily adapt to city living.

The Leonberger takes its name from a town in Germany. It was bred to produce a dog resembling the lions on the town's coat of arms. It was first shown in Paris in 1907.

Leonberger

In keeping with its large size and dignity, the gait of the Pyrenean Mountain Dog should be unhurried. It should give the impression of a powerful animal moving steadily and smoothly, yet able to produce bursts of speed.

Pyrenean Mountain Dog

MAREMMA SHEEPDOG
Italian Sheepdog

Advantages
- Has stamina
- Intelligent
- Natural guarding instinct

Disadvantages
- Not obedient
- Not common in the United States

The Italian Sheepdog, also known as the Maremma, has a double name in Italy. Two regions claim it: *Maremma*—the land following the coast from Cecina down to Rome—and *Abruzzi*, a mountainous area. In the past, some people called the breed Pastore Abruzzese, others Pastore Maremmano, thinking there was a difference between them.

In 1962, in Florence, Giuseppe Solaro drew up the present breed standard. Because both regions were proud of their sheepdog it was given the double name *Pastore Maremmano Abruzzese.* This satisfied everyone.

The task of this breed was not to work sheep but to defend the flocks from wolves, bears and thieves. The Maremma does not tolerate discipline. It does not forget kindness or forgive injury. It is a good family protector.

SIZE
Height—Minimum
Male: 25-1/2 in (63cm)
Female: 23-1/2 in (58.5cm)
Weight—No requirement

EXERCISE
Exercise is necessary for the breed in puppyhood. It does not need a lot of exercise. Daily walks should be varied and interesting. Walking on a hard surface keeps the dog's nails in condition.

GROOMING
Grooming should be done regularly, with a wire brush and a cleansing powder. Give it a bath once a year. Check ears for infection. Rain does not affect the Maremma's coat. It needs a rubdown after a soaking. The dog will clean itself.

FEEDING
For daily feeding, 5 cups of balanced dry dog food is recommended. Some dogs may prefer 1/2 cup water mixed with each cup of dog food. Canned dog food may be added for flavor.

ORIGIN AND HISTORY
The Maremma Sheepdog may have evolved from the ancient white working dog of the Magyars. It has been bred true by Tuscan farmers. The first known Maremma was a white dog mentioned by Columbella about 2000 years ago.

SHOW REQUIREMENTS
General Appearance—Large, lithe and strongly built. Majestic, distinguished, sturdy, courageous without being aggressive, lively and intelligent. Nervousness is penalized. Movement free and active, giving the impression of a nimble dog, able to move easily and turn quickly.
Head And Skull—Head large and conical, in proportion to the body. Skull wide between the ears, narrowing toward the facial area. The occipital ridge slightly less than the cranial area. Muzzle converges without showing snipiness. Jaws powerful. Plenty of substance in the foreface. Lips close fitting and not pendulous. Lips and nose black.
Tail—Set low and carried low in repose. Curls into the horizontal at hock level in normal carriage. Carried above back level in excitement. Covered with thick hair.

Little known outside its country of origin is another Italian Sheepdog, the Bergamasco or Bergamaschi Herder. It is a working dog descended from the herding dogs of Roman times. It has lived and worked for centuries in the mountains of Northern Italy.

KOMONDOR

Advantages
- Hardy
- Loyal
- Good guard
- Seldom sheds
- Odorless
- Good with other animals

Disadvantages
- Will not tolerate teasing
- Wary of strangers

The Komondor is a large white dog of imposing stature. It is strong and agile for its size. No one will mistake a grown Komondor for any other breed. It is covered with a full coat falling in tassels or cords and looks like a string mop.

This loyal dog will guard property and people. It does not attack without being provoked, but trespassers will not be tolerated.

SIZE
Height—Male: 26 to 30-1/2 in (65 to 76cm)
Female: 25 to 27-1/2 in (62.5 to 69cm)
Weight—Male: 110 to 135 lbs (50 to 62kg)
Female: 80 to 110 lbs (36 to 50kg)

EXERCISE
Puppies are large and active, and require a lot of exercise for development. A grown dog maintains good condition with a moderate amount of exercise.

GROOMING
The Komondor has a thick, heavy, double coat. The shorter undercoat is woolly and soft. The topcoat is longer, coarse and wavy. The combination of the two types of hair forms into tassellike cords. The cords are a type of controlled matting. The coat feels felty to the touch. The adult coat is a pleasure to maintain and live with. It is never brushed or combed. It forms into cords naturally, with the owner aiding by controlling the size of the cords in areas where matting is heavy. This must be done on the ears and the area behind them, especially in areas where limbs join the body.

Bathe the Komondor when it gets dirty. Wet the coat and use a canine shampoo. Rinse thoroughly and wring with towels. A grown dog will take a long time to dry. Cords do not come out when you wash the dog. They will tighten with age and washing. The dog requires standard care for eyes, pads and nails. If the eyes or ears run, it can stain the coat.

FEEDING
For daily feeding, 5 cups of balanced dry dog food is recommended. Some dogs may prefer 1/2 cup water mixed with each cup of dog food. Canned dog food may be added for flavor.

ORIGIN AND HISTORY
The Komondor was bred to guard sheep and property from thieves and predators on the Hungarian plains. It has worked alone and with other dogs. It first herded Hungarian sheep and later protected herds and property. Bred into the dog is an instinct to guard and make decisions. The Komondor protects whatever is entrusted to it.

SHOW REQUIREMENTS
General Appearance—Large and muscular, with plenty of bone and substance. Powerful in conformation.
Color—Always white. Skin gray. Pink skin is acceptable if there is no evidence of albinism.
Head And Skull—Head short in comparison to the wide forehead. Skull slightly arched when viewed from the side. Stop moderate. Muzzle slightly shorter than the length of the skull. Broad, coarse muzzle, not pointed. Nostrils wide. Nose black, though a dark gray or dark brown nose is acceptable, but not desirable.
Tail—Continuation of rump line. Reaches to the hocks, slightly curved at tip. When excited, raised in line with body.
Feet—Strong, large and compact. Arched toes. Claws strong, gray or black. Toes slightly longer on hind feet. Pads hard, elastic and dark.

The Maremma Sheepdog is an ancient Italian breed, believed to have first been recorded 2000 years ago. It is an excellent guard, intelligent and fearless. But it is independent and difficult to discipline. It was shown in the 19th century, but then disappeared from the show ring until the 1930s.

Maremma Sheepdog

Although still rare outside Hungary, the Komondor is being shown more often. Its unique corded coat grows slowly. The adult coat starts to replace the soft, fluffy puppy coat at 6 to 9 months, but may not be fully grown until the age of two.

Komondor

BULLMASTIFF

Advantages
- **Affectionate**
- **Good guard**
- **Good with children**

Disadvantages
- **Must be trained**

The Bullmastiff is a strong breed, obtained through crossing the Mastiff with the Bulldog. At one time it had an almost unequaled reputation for ferocity. But today's specimens are lovable and trustworthy, despite their power and size. The large dog needs skillful handling.

SIZE
Height—Male: 25 to 27 in
(62.5 to 68.5cm)
Female: 24 to 26 in
(60 to 65cm)
Weight—Male 110 to 130 lbs
(50 to 59kg)
Female: 100 to 120 lbs
(45 to 54kg)

EXERCISE
This dog needs regular exercise. A child or lightweight adult may not be able to handle it.

GROOMING
Regular brushing keeps the coat in condition.

FEEDING
For daily feeding, 5 cups of balanced dry dog food is recommended. Some dogs may prefer 1/2 cup water mixed with each cup of dog food. Canned dog food may be added for flavor.

ORIGIN AND HISTORY
The Bullmastiff evolved 300 years ago by crossing the Mastiff with the Bulldog. It was bred as a guard against poachers. With its weight, the dog could hold down intruders without harming them. It was not until later they attained their reputation for ferocity. Today, the breed has become a gentle animal whose appearance alone deters aggression.

SHOW REQUIREMENTS
General Appearance—Powerfully built and symmetrical, showing strength. Not cumbersome.

Color—Any shade of brindle, fawn or red. Color pure and clear. A slight white marking on the chest is permissible but not desirable. Other white markings are a fault. A dark muzzle is essential, toning off toward the eyes. Dark markings around eyes give expression. Dark toenails desirable.

Head And Skull—Skull large and square, viewed from every angle. Fair wrinkle when interested, but not when in repose. Circumference of the skull may equal the height of the dog measured at the top of the shoulder. Broad and deep with good cheeks. Muzzle short. The distance from the tip of the nose to the stop about one-third of the length from the tip of the nose to the center of the occiput. Broad under the eyes and nearly parallel in width to the end of the nose. Blunt and square, forming a right angle with the upper line of the face. Proportionate with the skull. Underjaw broad to the end. Nose broad with widely spreading nostrils when viewed from the front. Flat, not pointed or turned up in profile. Flews not pendulous or hanging below the bottom of the lower jaw. Stop definite.

Tail—Set high. Strong at the root and tapering. Reaching to the hocks, carried straight or curved, but not hound fashion. Crank tail a fault.

Feet—Not large. Round toes. Arched, catlike feet. Pads hard. Splay feet a fault.

NEAPOLITAN MASTIFF

Advantages
- **Good guard**
- **Friendly**

Disadvantages
- **May have physical problems**

The Neapolitan Mastiff is a large, imposing dog, usually depicted wearing a spiked collar. It is an excellent guard, but has a docile, friendly temperament when trained. It is unlikely to attack except on command. The dog may have limb-joint problems.

SIZE
Height—Male: 25-1/2 to 28-1/2 in
(63 to 72cm)
Female: 23-1/2 to 27 in
(58 to 68.5cm)
Weight—110 to 150 lbs
(50 to 64kg)

EXERCISE
This dog needs room to exercise. It is happiest when given a task.

GROOMING
Regular grooming keeps the coat in condition.

FEEDING
For daily feeding, 5 cups of balanced dry dog food is recommended. Some dogs may prefer 1/2 cup water mixed with each cup of dog food. Canned dog food may be added for flavor.

ORIGIN AND HISTORY
A scientific classification of the Neapolitan Mastiff puts it in the Molossoid group. It is a guard and defense dog, a police dog and a tracker. It is not known if the Mastiff fought in the arenas of Rome, but geographical evidence suggests this. It is a purebred, but not recognized by the American Kennel Club. The breed is growing in popularity.

SHOW REQUIREMENTS
General Appearance—Strongly built, vigorous and majestic. Robust and courageous. Intelligent expression and good mental balance, with a docile, unaggressive character. Body longer than height at the withers.

Color—Black, lead, mouse-gray or streaked. Sometimes with small white spots on the chest or on the tip of the toes.

Head And Skull—Massive, with a broad, short skull. Total length of the head is about 35% of height at the withers. Muzzle length one-third of total head length. Skin abundant, forming wrinkles and folds.

Tail—Thick at the root, robust and slightly tapered toward the tip. In repose, tail carried as a saber. It hangs for the first two-thirds of its length and is slightly curved in the lower third. Never carried straight up or curled over the back, but horizontal or slightly above the backline when the dog is in action. Length is equal to or slightly more than the distance to the hock. Docked to two-thirds of its length.

Feet—Oval, hare feet. Arched toes. Pads lean, hard and dark. Nails strong, curved and dark.

MASTIFF

Advantages
- **Brave**
- **Good guard**
- **Intelligent**
- **Loyal**
- **Quiet**

Disadvantages
- **Needs a job to do**

The Mastiff is a large, powerful dog that makes a formidable guard and loyal companion. It becomes devoted to its owners.

SIZE
Height—Male: 30 in (75cm)
Female: 27-1/2 in (69cm)
Weight—No requirement

EXERCISE
This dog needs normal exercise, preferably with task to do.

GROOMING
Daily grooming keeps the coat in condition.

HEALTH CARE
Size can contribute to limb-joint problems. Check with a vet if you suspect trouble.

ORIGIN AND HISTORY
The Mastiff is an ancient breed that fought in the arenas of Rome. It has lived in Great Britain since the time of Julius Caesar. In the Middle Ages, the Mastiff was used as a guard dog and for hunting. St. Bernard blood has been introduced in an effort to restore the Mastiff to its earlier size.

SHOW REQUIREMENTS
General Appearance—Large, massive, powerful, symmetrical and well-knit. A combination of even temperament, courage and docility. Head is square when viewed from any point. Breadth is desired, to the length of the whole head and face in the ratio of 2 to 3. Body massive, broad, deep, long and powerfully built, on legs wide apart and squarely set. Muscles sharply defined. Size prized, if combined with quality.

Color—Apricot, silver, fawn or dark fawn-brindle. Muzzle, ears and nose black, with black around the orbits, extending upward between them.

Head And Skull—Skull broad between the ears. Forehead flat, but wrinkled when excited. Brows slightly raised. Muscles of the temples and cheeks developed. Arch across the skull round. A depression up the center of the forehead. Face or muzzle short, broad under the eyes, nearly parallel in width to the end of the nose. Blunt and cut off squarely, forming a right angle with the upper line of the face. Great depth from the point of the nose to underjaw. Underjaw broad to the end. Nose broad, with widely spreading nostrils when viewed from the front. Flat, not pointed or turned up. Lips diverging at obtuse angles with the septum. Slightly pendulous to show a square profile. Length of muzzle to whole head and face in the ratio of 1 to 3. Circumference of muzzle to the head in the ratio of 3 to 5.

Tail—Set on moderately. Reaching to the hocks or below them. Wide at the root and tapering to the end. Hangs straight in repose. Forms a curve with the end pointing upward, but not over the back when the dog is excited.

Feet—Large and round. Toes arched. Nails black.

Teeth—Scissors bite preferred, but moderately undershot permissible.

Bullmastiff

The Neapolitan Mastiff is rarely seen outside Italy. There, it has a strong, enthusiastic following and is regularly shown. In spite of its forbidding appearance, it is a gentle, friendly animal.

Neapolitan Mastiff

Mastiff

The Mastiff should have a wide chest, deep and well-let-down between the forelegs, with arched, well-rounded ribs. The dog's girth should be one-third greater than its height at the shoulder. Its back and loins are wide and muscular.

GIANT SCHNAUZER

Advantages
- *Easily trained*
- *Good with children*
- *Fearless*
- *Good guard*
- *Playful*

Disadvantages
- *Slow to mature*
- *Wary of strangers*

The Giant Schnauzer is the largest Schnauzer. It is intelligent and devoted. It has been used as a guard and as a messenger by the military. It does well in obedience competitions and is a good rodent catcher. This giant variety is not seen as often as the Miniature variety.

SIZE
Height—Male: 25-1/2 to 27-1/2 in
(64 to 69cm)
Female: 23-1/2 to
25-1/2 in
(58 to 63cm)
Weight—No requirement

EXERCISE
This dog needs plenty of vigorous exercise.

GROOMING
This breed requires care. Daily grooming with a wire brush or glove is necessary. Whiskers must be combed. Strip the coat. Pluck out dead hairs with finger and thumb. Ask the breeder for a grooming chart or a demonstration before tackling the job yourself. Do this if you want to show the dog.

FEEDING
For daily feeding, 5 cups of balanced dry dog food is recommended. Some dogs may prefer 1/2 cup water mixed with each cup of dog food. Canned dog food may be added for flavor.

ORIGIN AND HISTORY
Descended from German sheepdogs and cattle dogs, this Schnauzer evolved through interbreeding with smaller Schnauzer varieties. It was first shown in Munich in 1909, under the name *Russian Bear Schnauzer*. The breed was classified as a working dog in Germany in 1925.

The moustache and chin whiskers of the Giant Schnauzer need daily combing.

SHOW REQUIREMENTS
General Appearance—Powerfully built, robust and vigorous. Length of body equal to height at shoulder. Temperament combines high spirits, reliability, strength, endurance and vigor. Expression is keen and attitude alert. Correct conformation more important than color or other purely aesthetic points.
Color—Black or pepper-and-salt colors in even proportions.
Head And Skull—Head strong and elongated, gradually narrowing from ears to eyes and forward toward the tip of the nose. Occiput to base of forehead moderately broad between the ears. Flat, creaseless forehead. Muscular but not too-strongly developed cheeks. Medium stop accentuates prominent eyebrows. Powerful muzzle formed by the base of forehead to tip of nose, ends in a moderately blunt line. Bristly, stubby moustache with chin whiskers. Ridge of nose straight, running almost parallel to the extension of the forehead. Nose black and full. Lips tight and not overlapping. Ears cropped, with tips pointed. When uncropped, V-shape button ears acceptable.
Tail—Set on and carried high. Cut to three joints.
Feet—Short, round and compact. Toes arched, nails dark, with hard soles. Feet deep or thickly padded, pointing forward.
Teeth—Scissors bite. Overshot or undershot bites are disqualifying.

GREAT DANE

Advantages
- *Devoted to owners*
- *Friendly with other animals*
- *Good-natured*
- *Easily trained*
- *Family dog*

Disadvantages
- *Not long-lived*

The Great Dane is a wonderful companion. It is devoted to the family, slow to anger and accepts other pets. Despite its size, it does not object to apartment life if it has plenty of exercise outdoors. You will find the dog easy to train. This breed is not known for longevity.

SIZE
Height—Minimum
Male: 30 in (75cm)
Female: 28 in (71cm)
Weight—Minimum
Male: 120 lbs (54kg)
Female: 100 lbs (46kg)

EXERCISE
This dog needs regular exercise on hard ground.

GROOMING
Groom this dog daily with a body brush.

FEEDING
For daily feeding, 5 cups of balanced dry dog food is recommended. Some dogs may prefer 1/2 cup water mixed with each cup of dog food. Canned dog food may be added for flavor.

ORIGIN AND HISTORY
The Great Dane has existed for many centuries. It is a descendant of the Molossus hounds of Roman times. In the Middle Ages it was used as a body guard and to chase wild boar.

Interest in the breed increased in Germany in the 1800s. Bismarck worked with Great Danes. By crossing the Mastiff of Southern Germany and the Great Dane, he produced a Dane similar to the type known today. It was first exhibited at Hamburg in 1863. In 1876, it was decided to show it under the heading of *Deutsche Dogge*. It was acclaimed as the national dog of Germany. This breed is sometimes referred to as the Apollo of the dog world.

SHOW REQUIREMENTS
General Appearance—Large, muscular and strongly built. Head and neck carried high. Tail in line with the back or slightly upward, but not curled over the hindquarters. Elegant outline essential. Large size is necessary.

Must be an alertness of expression and briskness of movement. Action lithe, springy and free. Hocks move freely. Head carried high except when galloping.
Color—Brindle, blue, black and harlequins. Brindles are striped. Ground color from the lightest yellow to the deepest orange. Stripes always black. Eyes and nails dark. Fawns vary from light buff to deep orange. Darker shadings on muzzle, ears and around eyes not objectionable. Eyes and nails dark. Blues vary from light gray to deep slate. White admissible only on the chest and feet. It is not desirable even there. Nose always black, except in blues. Eyes and nails dark. Harlequins are a white ground preferably with black patches. In harlequins, wall eyes, pink noses or butterfly noses permissible but not desirable.
Head And Skull—Head shows great length and strength of jaw. Muzzle or foreface broad. Skull narrow so head has the appearance of equal breadth throughout. Length of head varies with the height of the dog. From the tip of the nose to the back of the occiput 13 inches (33cm) is a good measurement for a dog 32 inches (85cm) at the shoulder. Length from the end of the nose to the point between the eyes equal to or greater than from this point to the back of the occiput. Skull flat, with a slight indentation running up the center. Occipital peak not prominent. A rise or brow over the eyes but no abrupt stop between them. Face well-chiseled and filled-in below the eyes, with no appearance of being pinched. Cheeks show as little lumpiness as possible, compatible with strength. Underline of the head runs in a straight line from the corner of the lip to the corner of the jawbone, allowing for the fold of the lip. No loose skin hangs down. Bridge of the nose wide, with a slight ridge where cartilage joins bone. Nostrils large, wide and open, giving a blunt look to the nose. Lips hang squarely in front, forming a right angle with the upper line of the foreface.
Tail—Thick at the root. Tapers toward the end, reaching to or just below the hocks. Carried in a straight line level with the back. When the dog is in action slightly curved toward the end, but not curled or carried over the back.
Feet—Catlike. Not turned in or out. Toes arched. Dark nails strong and curved.
Teeth—Scissors bite.

As a German herd dog in the late 19th century, the Giant Schnauzer was known as the Munchener. The finest dogs were found in the Munich-Augsburg region. Its progress as a show dog has been slowed by the popularity of the German Shepherd. It is not common.

Giant Schnauzer

Great Dane

The coat of the Great Dane is short, dense and sleek looking. It should never be rough. The dog's ears are small, set high on the skull and carried erect with the tips falling forward.

ST. BERNARD

Advantages
- *Loves children*
- *Easily trained*
- *Intelligent*

Disadvantages
- *Not long-lived*

The St. Bernard is powerful, but gentle. It adores children and is loyal and affectionate. It is intelligent and easy to train. It is not long-lived.

SIZE
The taller the better, provided symmetry is maintained and the dog is well-proportioned.

EXERCISE
Do not give a young St. Bernard too much exercise. Short, regular walks are better than long, tiring ones.

GROOMING
Daily brushing keeps the coat in condition.

FEEDING
For daily feeding, 5 cups of balanced dry dog food is recommended. Some dogs may prefer 1/2 cup water mixed with each cup of dog food. Canned dog food may be added for flavor.

ORIGIN AND HISTORY
The St. Bernard is a descendant of the Roman Molossian dogs. It is named after the St. Bernard Hospice in the Swiss Alps, where it was introduced between 1660 and 1670. It became famous for rescuing climbers in the Alps. One dog, Barry, is credited with saving 40 lives between 1800 and 1810. The first St. Bernard arrived in Great Britain in 1865. The breed became popular in the 1950s, when a St. Bernard played a prominent role in the film, *Genevieve*.

SHOW REQUIREMENTS
General Appearance—Dignified and intelligent. Movement important. Hind legs prone to faults.

Color—Orange, red-brindle, mahogany-brindle, white with patches on the body of any of the colors mentioned. Markings: white muzzle, white blaze up the face, white collar around the neck, white chest, white forelegs, feet and end of tail. Dark shadings on face and ears.

Head And Skull—Large and massive. Circumference of skull more than double the head length from nose to occiput. Muzzle short, full in front of the eye and square at nose end. Cheeks flat. Great depth from eye to lower jaw. Lips deep, but not too pendulous. From nose to stop straight and broad. Stop abrupt and well-defined. Skull broad, slightly round at the top, with prominent brow. Nose large and black.

Tail—Set on high. Long and feathered. Carried low when in repose. When excited or in motion, not curled over the back.

Feet—Large and compact, with arched toes. Dewclaws may be removed.

Teeth—Scissors or even bite.

A young St. Bernard needs regular exercise but should not be taken for long, tiring walks.

NEWFOUNDLAND

Advantages
- *Good guard*
- *Fierce only when provoked*
- *Good swimmer*
- *Good with animals*
- *Good with children*

Disadvantages
- *No drawbacks known*

The Newfoundland is a gentle giant and a protector of the family. It gets along with other animals and is a reliable companion and guard. The dog will not attack unless provoked.

SIZE
Height—Male: 28 in (71cm)
Female: 26 in (65cm)
Weight—Male: 140 to 150 lbs (64 to 68kg)
Female: 110 to 120 lbs (50 to 54kg)

EXERCISE
This dog needs regular exercise on hard ground.

GROOMING
Daily brushing with a hard brush keeps the coat in condition.

FEEDING
For daily feeding, 5 cups of balanced dry dog food is recommended. Some dogs may prefer 1/2 cup water mixed with each cup of dog food. Canned dog food may be added for flavor.

ORIGIN AND HISTORY
The Newfoundland is the traditional lifesaving dog. It is an animal with the overpowering instinct to carry anything in the water safely ashore. It originated in Northeastern Canada where fishing boats have come for many years to avoid bad weather. It is believed ships' dogs mated with local working dogs, whose ancestors probably included Red Indian dogs and Basque sheepdogs. The Newfoundland is a lifesaving dog and will rescue almost anything from the water.

SHOW REQUIREMENTS
General Appearance—Strong. Moves freely, with the body swung loosely between legs. A slight roll in gait not objectionable. Bone is massive, but not enough to give a heavy, inactive appearance.

Color—Dull black. A slight tinge of bronze or a splash of white on chest and toes acceptable. Black dogs with only white toes, white chest and white top of tail exhibited in classes for blacks. Brown can be chocolate or bronze. A splash of white on chest and toes acceptable. Brown dogs exhibited in classes for blacks. The Landseer type has a black head with a narrow blaze, a saddle and a black rump extending to the tail. Ticking not desirable.

Head And Skull—Head massive. Occipital bone well-developed. Slope from the top of the skull to the top of the muzzle a definite stop. Muzzle short, clean cut and square, covered with short, fine hair.

Tail—Moderate length, reaching a little below the hocks. Covered with hair, but not forming a flag. When the dog is standing still and not excited, the tail hangs down with a slight curve at the end. When the dog is in motion, carried up. When excited, straight out with only a slight curve at the end. Tails with a kink or curled over the back are objectionable.

Feet—Large. Splayed or turned-out feet objectionable.

Teeth—Scissors or level bite.

In the United States, the St. Bernard Club is among the oldest established specialty clubs. The club was founded in 1888, the year after the Zurich Congress set an international standard for the breed.

St. Bernard

Newfoundland

PRACTICAL GUIDE

CHOOSING A DOG

by Joan Palmer and Bruce Sessions

Buying a puppy can be an enjoyable experience. Unfortunately, many puppies end up in animal control facilities because buyers give little advance thought to their purchase.

There are times when a dog cannot remain with a family. Owners may be divorced or sick, or financial circumstances may change and they cannot keep their pet. When you choose a dog, you assume responsibility for its life. It will need feeding, exercise, comfort, care and love.

THINK BEFORE YOU BUY

There are many points to consider when choosing a dog. A small or large breed? A shorthair or longhair breed? An active or quiet dog?

The Golden Retriever is an all-purpose dog for a family. An Airedale Terrier, despite its size, does not need a great deal of space. The Dachshund hides a big bark in a small body.

Toy dogs make devoted companions and defend their owners bravely. They are good choices for town dwellers, the elderly and people who do not

like much exercise. Toy dogs are not suitable for young children, who may be too rough with them.

Boxers love children and so do St. Bernards, Old English Sheepdogs and spaniels. Most dogs are compatible, especially if they are brought up with children from puppyhood. Trouble may occur when a breed with a strong protective instinct begins to overguard the children.

PET OR SHOW DOG?

Having decided on a breed, you next want to consider quality. If you want a purebred dog with a pedigree, you must decide whether you want a healthy, attractive dog or a show dog. Many people often think any dog with a pedigree can be a show dog. This is not true. People are disappointed when they enter their pet in a show and discover it falls below the show standard for the breed. This does not mean the breeder cheated them. It just means they bought an animal of *pet* rather than *show* quality. They probably paid a lower price than they would pay for

a show-quality dog.

A pet-quality dog is not unsound. The animal falls below the standard of *perfection* for its breed. It may be slightly taller or shorter than it should be. It may have a small defect that has no bearing on its suitability as a healthy, lovable pet.

The earliest age at which a pup should leave its mother is between 8 and 10 weeks. This is when most litters are sold. It is hard to determine at this early age which animals have show potential. Breeders often breed promising pups to develop show lines. If you want to be sure of purchasing a show dog, you may have to wait and choose a dog 6 months of age or older.

No reputable breeder will object to a veterinary check as a condition of purchase. You should receive a certificate of pedigree with the pup. If the dog is to be registered with the American Kennel Club (AKC), the new owner must receive an Individual Registration Application. He also receives a blue slip, or an

official Registration Certificate, signed in full on the back by the seller.

If the dog has changed owners and the change has not been recorded by the AKC, you must receive an accompanying supplemental transfer statement. It is necessary to obtain these documents. Without proper registration, your dog can only be exhibited in exemption

The dainty Papillon is an ideal toy breed for someone with limited space who wants a lively pet.

shows and its offspring cannot bring purebred prices.

Most breeders provide the buyer with a diet sheet. They also give information on whether the pup has been wormed or received inoculations. Often a breeder will offer a guarantee of a puppy's health, quality, temperament or all three.

MALE OR FEMALE?

An important decision is whether to buy a male or female. The female is preferred for competitive obedience work because she is usually more obedient than the male. Unlike the male, she is usually uninterested in the sex act except during her *season,* or period of fertility. Some people enjoy the company of a male dog and prefer it to a female.

On the positive side of owning a female is her ability to reproduce. But it may be difficult to cope with her 21-day season every six months. It is possible to have her spayed to avoid unwanted matings. Spaying is irreversible.

WHERE TO BUY A PUPPY

Puppies are advertised in the classified sections of newspapers, in pet magazines and elsewhere. They can also be found in pet shops.

It is usually best to buy from a breeder who specializes in the breed you choose. The breeder can select a pup to fit your requirements and give you advice on its care. If you are able to see the pup's parents, you may have an idea of the puppy's future appearance and health.

Unless the breed you choose is popular, there may not be a breeder in your area. It is better to wait for a puppy than to buy a dog you might be unhappy with.

Every breed has its own breed club. The club secretary will put you in touch with members who may have stock for sale and give you details of membership. Addresses of these clubs and breeders can be obtained from the American Kennel Club, 51 Madison Ave., New York, NY 10010 or the United Kennel Club (UKC), 100 E. Kilgore, Kalamazoo, MI 49001. The AKC and UKC are national organizations.

The AKC came into existence in 1874. The UKC began in 1898.

HOW MUCH DOES A PUPPY COST?

It is impossible to give a price you should pay for each breed. Price depends on the popularity or rarity of a breed, location, and supply and demand. Generally, prices of purebred dogs range from $75 to $300 for popular breeds. Prices of $200 and up for show dogs and rare breeds are not unusual. One breeder will tell you, ''The price is whatever you can get!'' Another will say, ''Soon the expensive dog will no longer be a rarity.''

Many serious breeders are interested in seeing show-quality puppies placed in good homes, so the pup will receive time and attention. Occasionally a breeder may consider a smaller price if a puppy is placed on a co-ownership basis. This arrangement can benefit the

Above: If you want to show your dog, start training early. Here a West Highland White Terrier learns how to stand.

Below: This girl loves her Schnauzer, a breed that is good with children.

breeder and person interested in a quality dog. It can also lead to complications if not specifically outlined in a contract signed by both parties. If you are interested in a show-quality puppy, do not be discouraged by the price. Be honest with the breeder about your interest in the breed and your financial situation.

TAKING YOUR PUPPY HOME

When taking your puppy home, it must not be put down in the street or come in contact with other dogs until it has its shots. Carry it on this trip. Be sure the puppy has a comfortable basket of unchewable substance at home. Have an identity tag engraved and put it on a collar, in case your puppy wanders off.

Be certain everyone in the family wants a pet. Never buy a dog as a present unless you are sure the recipient will appreciate the gift. Make sure you are permitted to keep a dog where you live.

The decision to buy a dog should not be taken lightly. Much as you may admire an Afghan Hound, it may not adapt to life in a small apartment. An energetic terrier is probably not a suitable pet for an elderly lady. A Chihuahua is not the ideal dog for a hunter.

There are probably a number of breeds to suit your home and way of life. It is important to make the right choice, for your sake and the dog's!

Feeding And Exercise

by Kay White

Today's dog is fortunate. The introduction of well-balanced dog food has revolutionized canine nutrition. Meat is not essential with today's nutritionally balanced dog food. Meat may be added for flavor. Like humans, dogs need fats and carbohydrates, proteins, water and small amounts of vitamins and minerals to stay healthy. These can be found in both dry and canned dog food.

A new puppy should be fed a diet recommended by the breeder. Follow the diet for at least two weeks after the puppy's arrival. Milk is not essential for weaned puppies. Many are unable to digest the lactose in milk after early puppyhood. A bowl of milk given to a dog may cause a loose bowel movement. Mother's milk is richer in fats than cow's or goat's milk. If puppies must be bottlefed, use a commercial substitute according to directions.

In an emergency, homemade formula for puppies can be made from 7 ounces (800ml) of cream and one egg yolk. Add two drops of multivitamins and store in the refrigerator. Warm small amounts slowly and feed every two hours for the first week if the mother is not available. If the mother has some milk, small amounts of formula may be offered to puppies needing more. Formula should be given in a bottle designed for premature babies, with a nipple appropriate to the size of the puppy. A dropper is unsuitable because it injects too much air.

The pregnant female does not need to drink milk to make milk for her puppies. Extra protein is the best food to promote maximum lactation.

Water is necessary for all dogs. From 3 weeks old, puppies should be given water several times a day, even if they are being fed milk. Older dogs should always have access to water.

WHAT KIND OF FOOD?

Meat provides protein in a dog's diet. A balanced dry dog food supplies this necessary protein at a much lower price.

Any meat fed to a pet should be *cooked*. Liver should be limited in the dog's diet

Puppies feed most easily from a flat plate. Use a disposable one, so dogs do not share plates with the family.

because it is a laxative. Cooked lamb, chicken and turkey may be fed to dogs, but pork is unsuitable. Cooked fish, eggs and hard cheese are other valuable sources of protein.

BALANCING THE DIET

The amount of protein necessary varies with the growth stage and activity of the dog. Protein should account for about 18% of the diet for fully grown pets receiving little exercise. Large-breed puppies growing rapidly may require twice as much. A nursing female may need four times the usual ration when puppies are taking large quantities of milk.

Fruit and vegetables are not essential for dogs with access to grass. Some dogs may enjoy fruit, such as fresh raspberries or apples.

Use the same diet every day for your dog, except when physical illness requires modification. Dogs do best on food their system is accustomed to. Addition of occasional nutritious household scraps provides enough variety.

Think of your dog's food in terms of calories. A growing puppy will need 100 calories a day per pound (0.45kg) of body weight. An elderly dog needs only 25 calories per pound. A 13.3-ounce can (376g) of dog food contains about 300 calories.

BONES

Large, unsplintered bones may be given to puppies when they cut teeth, between 6 weeks and 5 months of age. Later, when the teeth and jaws are powerful, do not give bones. Many emergencies have been caused by swallowed bone splinters.

FEEDING AN OLDER DOG

Decaying teeth often affect the appetite of an older dog. General health may be improved by removing bad teeth. Older dogs sometimes suffer from indigestion. Small, light meals, served often, may help.

FEEDING AN INVALID DOG

A dog in pain or physically uncomfortable will stop eating, which may make it more comfortable. A dog recovering from illness may respond to slivers of cooked chicken, sardines, cheese or creamed cheese. Canned dog food made for a convalescent dog is good. After surgery, the dog's throat may be sore from tubes put down its throat. Ice cream or pureed baby food may be fed for a day or two. A milk-based food may create a loose-bowel problem. A lamb-and-boiled-rice menu is the standard diet for any dog recovering from disease of the stomach or intestine.

DOG FOOD

A great deal of research goes into making commercial dog food. Products are tested for quality and taste. Most dog food is nutritionally balanced. It contains cereal, protein, vitamins and minerals. An owner can be confident that commercial dog food is tasty, nutritious and well-balanced.

Dry dog food may be fed dry or presoaked. If given dry, fresh water must always be available. Dogs need to drink at night if they are fed in the evening. Dog food contains roughage and other necessary components of a dog's diet. Roughage passing through the intestines keeps a dog active and healthy. A smoothcoated dog thrives on a high-fat diet. Add extra vegetable oil to its dog food.

Taking dogs for a walk can become a family outing. Keep adult dogs on a leash and carry young puppies.

VITAMINS

Your dog's food should contain vitamins A, B and D, with trace minerals. Most dog food contains essential vitamins. Vitamin E for fertility must be bought separately. Few dogs need extra vitamin C. If necessary, it can be given in the form of rosehip syrup. A dog's vitamin C requirements are normally synthesized from sunlight.

Supply basic vitamins if you feed a diet of fresh meat. Do this by buying a complete vitamin supplement formulated for dogs, made in tablet form. Dogs may find the tablets tasty. Tablets ensure accurate doses.

When additional vitamins are needed, such as during rapid growth or pregnancy, the number of tablets given can be increased according to directions. The female needs extra calcium during pregnancy and nursing. Special tablets are available to meet her needs.

ALLERGIES

A few dogs have *carbohydrate intolerance* or *gluten sensitivity.* Remove cereals and bread from the diet of dogs with gluten intolerance. Dogs may also be allergic to milk, beef, horsemeat, liver, kidney or heart. If your dog has persistent loose bowel movements, discuss allergies with your veterinarian.

Above: If puppies are fed from separate dishes, make sure each gets a fair share and there is no stealing.

Right: A tall dog will find it more comfortable to eat from a plate on a low bench. A sick dog will also appreciate not having to bend.

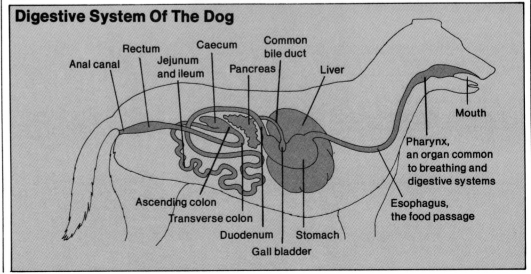

Digestive System Of The Dog

Anal canal
Rectum
Jejunum and ileum
Caecum
Pancreas
Common bile duct
Liver
Mouth
Pharynx, an organ common to breathing and digestive systems
Esophagus, the food passage
Ascending colon
Transverse colon
Duodenum
Stomach
Gall bladder

Types Of Dog Food

Above left: Holding the food bowl is good for long-legged pups. But it may cause the puppy not to eat unless its owner is in attendance.

Above: These dogs have been given tidbits too often. They are now fat. Overweight dogs do not live as long as normal-weight ones.

1. Plain biscuit meal. Mix with meat or fish to provide essential carbohydrates.

2. Meaty canned dog food. Made with animal products and meatlike chunks of vegetable protein.

3. Meat-and-cereal canned food. Costs less, but you will need to use twice as much.

4. Canned puppy food. Made for puppies. It gives them excellent nutrition. No extra vitamins are needed.

5. Large dog biscuits. Provide jaw exercise for medium and large dogs.

6. Bone-shape biscuits. Ideal for dogs to carry. Not as hard as large ones. Useful to satisfy fast-growing dogs between meals.

7. Small dog biscuits. Available in various shapes and flavors. Good for rewards.

8. Expanded complete food. Dry chunks containing all essential nutrients. Can be fed mixed with milk, water, broth, or dry with water available.

9. Flaked complete food. Add gravy, milk or hot water.

10. Soft-moist complete food. Made of partly dehydrated chunks of meat substitute. Feed straight from the package. Easy to carry and convenient to use when away from home.

11. Water. Essential. Dogs with free access to water adjust drinking according to the moisture content of their food. Provide water at all times, especially for dogs feeding on dry diets that have not been presoaked. The best container for water is a plastic bowl. It can be cleaned easily.

AMOUNT TO FEED

Obesity is a problem for some dogs. Activity, environment, size and metabolism determine a dog's food needs.

A working dog, active during the day and sleeping in an unheated kennel at night, will need more food than a pet that takes only a short walk. A growing dog needs more food than an adult dog of the same weight. A Labrador puppy weighing 40 pounds (18kg) needs twice as much food as an adult Bull Terrier of the same weight.

The well-fed dog has a shiny coat, glowing eyes, alert carriage and happy demeanor. Sluggishness may indicate an overfed dog. A haggard look with sharply outlined ribs—except where breed standards call for it—suggests the dog needs extra food. A dry, scruffy coat may indicate a need for extra oil in the diet.

Sometimes food intake varies with external factors. A male obsessed by nearby females in season will lose weight. A sensitive dog may lose weight in a boarding kennel or when there is sadness or disharmony in the family. Dogs in these situations need increased rations, supplied in two or three meals. Discontinue extra feeding when the stress is over.

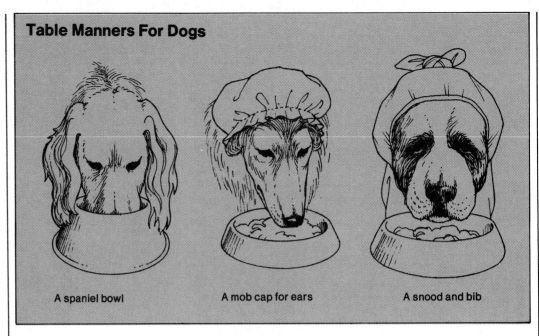

Table Manners For Dogs

A spaniel bowl   A mob cap for ears   A snood and bib

EXERCISE

Dogs are as adaptable as humans in their exercise requirements. They need activity in their lives, but they do not need mileage. A dog will be more fit if it gets exercise. Many people do not exercise a great deal and remain healthy. The same applies to dogs.

A dog can survive on little or no exercise. In quarantine, it may spend several months in a kennel. Exercise is confined to a kennel run smaller than a small yard. Yet the dog comes out of quarantine in good condition. The dog's day is not boring. That is the secret of good health in less-than-ideal circumstances.

Even the smallest dog should have the freedom to go inside or outside occasionally. If a dog does not have some freedom, it spends all its time under human domination. A yard provides an element of choice and the opportunity to be independent. Free outdoor access is essential to the physical and mental health of your dog.

Dogs like to keep busy, especially small terriers and guarding breeds. They enjoy having access to the house and

dashing from one door to another. Two dogs will exercise each other.

Adaptable, dogs can walk for miles one day and relax the rest of the week. Young puppies and older dogs must not be overexercised. Boxers, Bullmastiffs, Bulldogs, Boston Terriers and other *brachycephalic* dogs—those with high foreheads, broad skulls and shortened faces—must not be given too much exercise in hot, humid conditions. These breeds faint easily under stress.

Many people believe it is irresponsible to walk a dog where it can urinate and defecate on the sidewalk. In many places, owners are fined if they allow their pets to soil pavements. Elimination should take place on the owner's property or some place convenient for cleaning up. A walk is for pleasure if the dog is taught to eliminate in its own yard.

These two Yorkshire Terriers from the same owner are allowed to share their quarantine. A friendly kennel attendant keeps them active.

Animals signal playtime to one another by distinctive body movements and possibly by scent. Humans have to make their purpose clear by tone of voice. Use your dog's power of scent by playing hunt-the-slipper in increasingly difficult places. Or have a treasure hunt with dog biscuits. You can also train your dog to choose which hand holds the treat.

BEGINNING TRAINING

Simple obedience tasks are best taught indoors. A dog can learn the commands *sit, beg, down, stand again, down and roll* from someone sitting in a chair. First, the animal must be taught to pay attention to one person. Do this by having one person talk to the dog, call it and offer a small food reward.

You can play many games with your dog in a large yard. This kind of exercise involves more interaction with the dog than walking on a leash. More behavior control is possible when a dog is part of a football game in your yard with you than when it is ambling along. Playing in a confined area develops attachment.

A chairbound person can do a lot for a dog. A young puppy or an old or arthritic dog can benefit from attention. A person can gently stroke the dog's body. Hand contact will provide the opportunity to detect lumps, find knots in the coat or see fleas. Massaging the muscles of the limbs of an older dog can help increase circulation. Examining feet, nails, teeth and ears is a pleasurable grooming activity. You may discover conditions that need attention. Stroking also will accustom a puppy to having sensitive areas handled, making future vet visits easier for dog and doctor.

In a growing puppy, you should massage the jaw or ears to help develop shape. Use your fingers to clear knots in the coat.

EXERCISING PUPPIES

Young puppies should not be exercised a lot. Children may be tempted to take out a new pet to show it off. There is a risk to growing limbs. Tugging a puppy along on a leash can be the quickest way to instill bad habits. Teach puppies leash control in the yard. Your puppy should not go out on public ground until it has its shots.

Unfortunately, this advice conflicts with the need to accustom a puppy to traffic noise and meeting people. The best compromise is to carry the puppy for short journeys through busy places. Road walking will be less terrifying when the dog is old enough to be on a leash.

Avoid formal exercise for large-breed puppies until they are 6 months old. It is better for their development if you keep them from jumping and climbing. Their shoulders can become overdeveloped through too much early exercise.

OTHER ACTIVITY

There are several kinds of special exercise. Swimming is excellent, especially to help a female regain her figure after giving birth. Familiarity with water may save a dog's life.

Agility tests can be devised by older children. Teaching a dog to crawl, climb short ladders, jump through a tire and catch a ball will fill many hours. Humans and dogs can have fun together.

On stormy or rainy days, play indoor activities. Play hide-and-seek with your dog. Call it to come to you, then praise it when it tracks you down. Be sure you play all games with laughter and a happy voice to help the dog learn the difference between play situations and those calling for aggression and guarding.

Grooming And Health Care

by Michael Findlay

Grooming is an essential part of a dog's daily routine. It should be done from the day you acquire your dog or puppy. It is important to groom enthusiastically. Use the right brushing and combing techniques. Know what equipment is required and be informed about preparations such as shampoos.

Daily grooming removes old, dead hair and reduces the amount of shedding. Frequent grooming also prevents matting of the coat in longcoated breeds. It simplifies the work of a clipper or groomer in breeds such as Poodles, which require clipping or stripping. Proper brushing and combing also removes dirt and parasites from fur. Stimulating the blood supply to the skin by brushing produces a healthier coat.

Regular grooming helps the owner detect skin problems and other conditions. This makes early veterinary treatment possible. It may be cured after a short treatment and save you money. Many dogs are brought to a vet with matted fur or overgrown nails because routine grooming was neglected by owners.

Dogs can be divided into longcoat dogs such as Old English Sheepdogs, Afghans and Yorkshire Terriers, and shortcoat dogs such as Boxers, Dachshunds and Labrador Retrievers.

GROOMING EQUIPMENT

Buy grooming equipment designed for dogs. Do not use combs or hairbrushes made for human hair. Tool requirements depend on the hair type of the dog. A pet shop can tell you about proper equipment. Also, the breeder who sells you your puppy can tell you what he uses.

Shortcoat dogs should usually be brushed daily with a firm brush. Do this in long sweeping strokes, following the lay of the fur. It is easiest if you follow a sequence. Do the back, belly, chest, limbs and tail. Be careful when grooming the head or around other sensitive areas such as the reproductive organs.

Brushing alone is not enough with longcoat dogs. Only the topcoat will benefit. The undercoat, which usually becomes matted, will remain untouched. For these dogs, use a stiff-bristle brush and a wire brush or a metal comb to

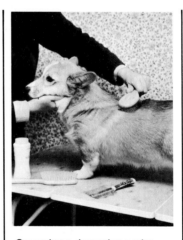

Grooming a dog using a wire brush. A comb, a bristle brush for finishing and powder are also used.

penetrate to the skin.

Do not use a dematting comb, designed to remove mats. If used incorrectly, these combs could cut the animal's skin. Vets and groomers use dematting combs only as a last resort. They are used in cases of neglect, often with the animal sedated.

Groom longhair dogs systematically. Use the comb for the soft fur behind ears, the feathered fur down the back of the limbs, the tail, armpits and other places where fur tangles and knots.

Rub with a a silk or velvet pad to produce a brilliant shine when brushing and combing is complete. You will see this used at dog shows, especially on shortcoat dogs, immediately before they enter the ring.

CLEANING YOUR DOG

Regular bathing with shampoo removes oils in the coat, taking away natural waterproofing. This often makes the animal more sensitive to colds and rheumatism. But there are times when you must bathe a dog.

Many shortcoat dogs may go through their lives without a bath, particularly if daily grooming is adequate. Breeds such as Poodles, which are clipped at 6- to 8—week intervals, are bathed to assist the clipper. They rarely require supplementary baths.

Longcoat dogs, especially show dogs, benefit from baths about once a month to reduce odor. But bathing a longcoat dog with matting may make matting worse. Frequent

Basic Grooming Equipment

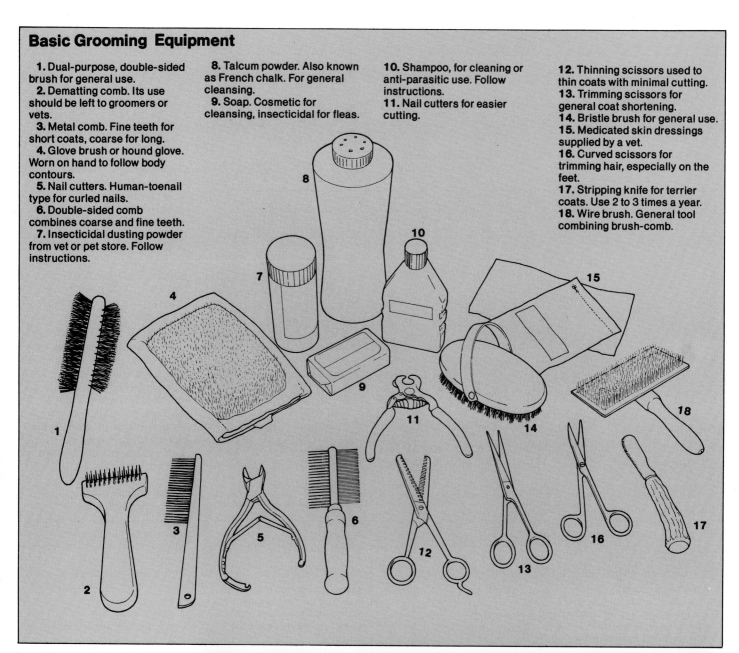

1. Dual-purpose, double-sided brush for general use.
2. Dematting comb. Its use should be left to groomers or vets.
3. Metal comb. Fine teeth for short coats, coarse for long.
4. Glove brush or hound glove. Worn on hand to follow body contours.
5. Nail cutters. Human-toenail type for curled nails.
6. Double-sided comb combines coarse and fine teeth.
7. Insecticidal dusting powder from vet or pet store. Follow instructions.

8. Talcum powder. Also known as French chalk. For general cleansing.
9. Soap. Cosmetic for cleansing, insecticidal for fleas.

10. Shampoo, for cleaning or anti-parasitic use. Follow instructions.
11. Nail cutters for easier cutting.

12. Thinning scissors used to thin coats with minimal cutting.
13. Trimming scissors for general coat shortening.
14. Bristle brush for general use.
15. Medicated skin dressings supplied by a vet.
16. Curved scissors for trimming hair, especially on the feet.
17. Stripping knife for terrier coats. Use 2 to 3 times a year.
18. Wire brush. General tool combining brush-comb.

---

bathing will also depend on the size and cooperation of the dog and your bathing facilities.

Brush or comb the dog, section by section, while it is drying under a hair dryer. Most domestic hair dryers are not powerful enough for this purpose. You may need a commercial one.

A medicated or insecticidal shampoo is needed when parasites such as fleas are present or in summer when risk of getting them is high. Ask your vet to recommend a shampoo. Aerosol sprays or dusting powder may be

Grooming a dog using a hound glove. It shapes to the contours of the dog comfortably.

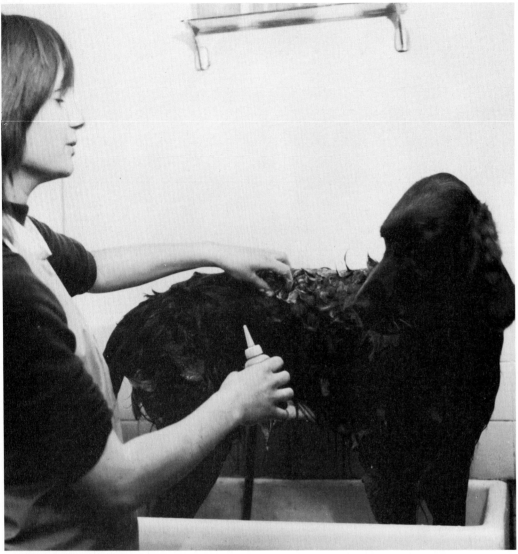

substituted. For general cleaning purposes, many dog shampoos are available. A mild baby shampoo can also be used. This is often less expensive than special dog preparations.

Your vet may prescribe other types of shampoo for skin problems. Use these according to instructions and throw them away when the treatment is complete. It is dangerous to keep and use leftover shampoos.

An alternative to bathing, useful for pale dogs, is dusting with talcum powder. The process is messy. Brush out all powder after it has been in the coat for 15 to 30 minutes. Be careful the dog does not inhale the powder.

REGULAR INSPECTIONS

Set aside time each week to check other parts of your dog. Check whether anal glands, or scent glands, need to be emptied. Some dogs require this frequently. Your vet can show you how to do this. It can be unpleasant, so you may prefer to have it done by a vet or groomer.

Checks nails weekly. They should not grow so long they risk snapping off or so curved that they stick into the flesh. Pay attention to dewclaws. They never come into contact with the ground so they are not worn down like other nails. Active dogs' nails seldom need trimming.

Teeth should also be checked. Small amounts of tartar can be removed with cotton swabs dipped in toothpaste. Teeth with severe tartar deposits require veterinary attention, usually under anesthetic.

Check ears at least once a week. Do not poke inside the ear. Do not use ear drops, except as prescribed by a veterinarian. It is safe to put a drop of olive oil in each ear the day before the ears are to be cleaned. This will help soften and loosen wax.

Eyes usually require no attention, except in certain breeds such as the Pekingese. They may have an overflow of tears that cause streaks down the cheeks. Cleanse these tear streaks once or twice daily. Use cotton moistened with eyewash.

A pair of curved, blunt-end scissors are useful. Use them to

Above: Bathing. Shampoo in plastic, unbreakable container. Large dogs should be bathed in a bathtub, unless you have a big sink, or bathing will be messy.

Below: Drying. Have adequate towels on hand before bathing. Remove excess water and finish with hot-air dryer or exercise until dry.

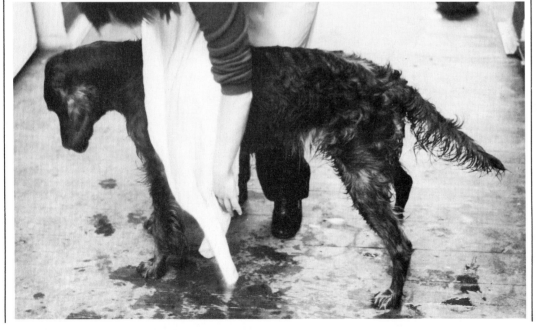

trim fur, especially on the soles of the feet between pads.

HEALTH CARE

Dogs are healthy animals. But they may have accidents and injuries. There are also problems specific to certain breeds. These problems include respiratory disease in short-nose dogs such as Pugs and Bulldogs. Lameness can affect large breeds, such as German Shepherds, Labradors and St. Bernards. Heart disease is found in Pekingese and Cavalier English Toy Spaniels. Inherited conditions are found in specific breeds.

Before you buy a dog, ask a breeder or vet about the risks. Have a new puppy checked for signs of illness within a few days of purchase. Make your purchase conditional on the animal's being free from congenital disorders.

Many puppy problems can be discovered and corrected quickly. Some serious conditions are inherited. They cannot be diagnosed with certainty in young animals. A dog must be at least 6 months old before it can be examined for signs of progressive retinal atrophy and hip dysplasia. You can lessen the likelihood of buying a dog with these problems by buying from breeding stock certified as clear.

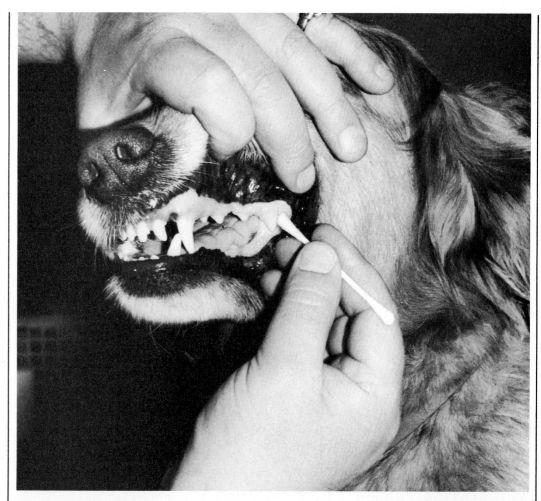

Above: Regular dental care is necessary. Small deposits of tartar may be removed with a cotton swab moistened and dipped in toothpaste.

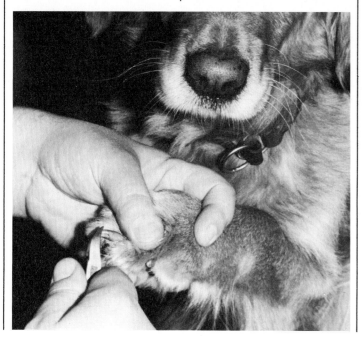

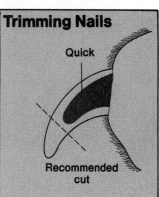

Left and below: Cutting nails. Hold foot firmly and cut safely below the quick to avoid bleeding and pain. The quick can be seen in white nails, but is masked in black nails.

Trimming Nails

Quick

Recommended cut

VACCINATIONS

When possible, prevention is better than cure. Vaccines protect against illnesses such as *distemper* and *canine infectious hepatitis,* a liver inflammation. Two serious diseases affecting the kidneys and liver can also be prevented by vaccination. These are *leptospirosis canicola* and *leptospirosis icterohaemorrhagia,* or Weil's disease. Weil's desease can be transmitted to humans, so dog owners should have their pets vaccinated against it.

Vaccination against rabies is necessary for the dog and family. Rabies does not occur in certain parts of the world, such as Australia and the United Kingdom.

Vaccination against distemper, hepatitis and leptospirosis is common at about 9 to 10 weeks of age. Two injections, with an interval of two to three weeks between them, are required for full protection. Booster shots should be given as suggested by your veterinarian, usually yearly.

Most authorities believe booster vaccinations should be given throughout a dog's life. There is no reliable evidence to show age makes dogs less susceptible to these diseases. Vaccinations are usually free from side effects.

WORMS

Worming is an important aspect of health care. Dogs can have various worms, such as

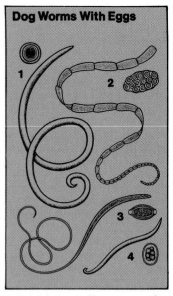

Dog Worms With Eggs

1. Roundworm— *Toxocara canis*
2. Tapeworm— *Dipylidium caninum*
3. Whipworm— *Trichuris vulpis*
4. Hookworm— *Ancylostoma caninum*

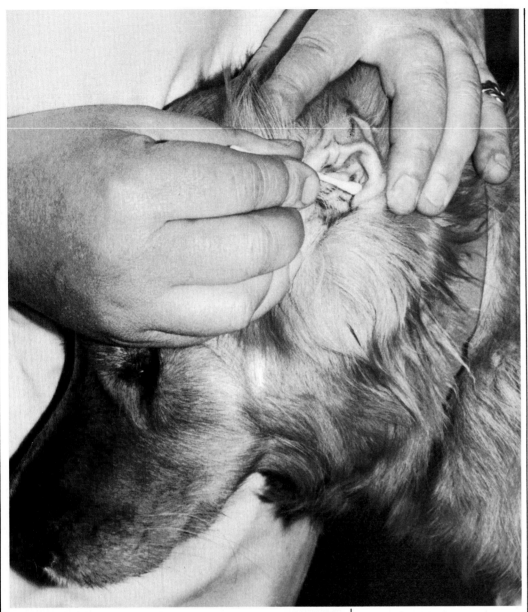

Above: Cleansing the ear with a slightly moistened cotton swab. Never probe into ear recesses you cannot see.

Left: Use scissors to remove material sticking to the long fur between toes. Be careful not to cut the web or pad.

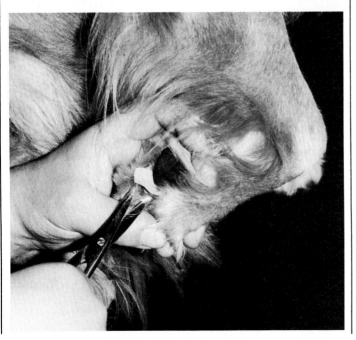

Use common-sense hygiene, such as removing feces, washing children's hands and giving the dog its own feeding and drinking dishes. Medicine for roundworms is available from your vet. Regular dosing of dogs in contact with children is necessary. A dose is in proportion to the animal's weight. The dog must be weighed to determine the proper dose.

Young puppies, and females before whelping and while nursing their litter, are particularly at risk. Many vets recommend worming at two-week intervals for these dogs. Otherwise, worming once every three to six months may be enough.

Tapeworms are less a problem, except for beef and sheep tapeworm, *Echinococcus granulosus*. The beef and sheep tapeworm is a problem in dogs fed raw, waste meat. The remedy is simple. Exclude raw waste meat from the diet. Worm regularly, about every 6 to 12 months. A more common tapeworm in dogs is *Dipylidium caninum*, acquired by swallowing fleas while grooming. This tapeworm produces few ill effects. It can be cleared out by using a drug to kill tapeworms. There are drugs effective against both tapeworms and roundworms.

In some areas of the world,

roundworms, tapeworms, hookworms, whipworms and heartworms.

The common dog roundworm, *Toxocara canis,* is a big problem in some areas. The sticky eggs in the stools of infected dogs may be ingested by people, especially children. When eggs hatch and larvae travel through the human body, the results are unpleasant, serious symptoms.

hookworms are a problem. They respond to roundworm medications. Whipworms are a parasite of foxes, but are occasionally found in dogs. They are easily treated.

Dogs may suffer from heartworms, which can cause circulatory problems. Treatment is by a drug available only from veterinarians.

DIET

Dietary deficiencies from commercial dog food are rarely encountered today. Nearly all dog food companies provide tasty, nourishing products. These foods have essential minerals and vitamins, as well as protein and carbohydrates. Getting the best from such foods means following feeding instructions on the can or package.

Prepared food can be divided into canned, semimoist and dry. The type used depends largely on the owner and dog. Some dogs with digestive problems do better on semimoist or dry food. The content of some food may cause diarrhea because the protein level is too high.

Feeding fresh meat is not as common as it once was. This is because of the high cost and perishability of fresh meat. You may need to add vitamin and mineral supplements to fresh meat. Vitamins and minerals are usually unnecessary when animals are fed prepared foods.

Young growing dogs, especially large breeds, may need extra calcium, phosphorus and vitamin D until 6 months old, preferably until 9 months or a year. Similar recommendations are frequently made for females during the last half of pregnancy and during nursing. Supplements reflect an increased need for calcium, either for bone formation or to replace calcium drawn from mother's milk.

Old animals and those recovering from a major illness or operation will also benefit from vitamins and minerals. There are many brands on the market in liquid, powder or tablet form.

Feeding can affect coat condition. Owners often complain of a dog's poor coat. Reasons include frequency of swimming, bathing or grooming, and the temperature of the dog's environment. If it is too warm, coat quality can be poor. This may be remedied by feeding unsaturated fatty acids. The best sources are vegetable oils, available as liquids, and soft margarine. Too much may cause diarrhea, so give doses every other day, according to the dog's size. Vegetable oils improve coat oil and overall condition. Animal fats such as butter and milk will not have this effect.

EXERCISE

All dogs need exercise, some more than others. The amount of exercise needed does not vary with the size of the dog, but according to the original purpose of the breed. Great Danes are happy with less exercise than terriers. Some breeds, such as the Jack Russell Terrier, are often not recommended for the city dweller. Do not keep them unless they have large exercise areas.

Game dogs such as spaniels and retrievers were bred for a 12-hour working day. They need plenty of exercise. Boxers were originally bred as guard dogs and now enjoy a quieter life. It is a mistake to carry toy breeds everywhere. Chihuahuas, Pekingese and Yorkshire Terriers enjoy walking and need the exercise.

It is possible to overexercise dogs, especially large-breed puppies up to 6 months of age. It can result in permanent deformity of tendons and ligaments. Females in the last half of pregnancy should be allowed whatever exercise they choose. Old dogs may suffer from rheumatism or arthritis. They should be exercised cautiously. But they stiffen up if they are allowed to rest all the time. Most seem better after short walks, which can be given frequently during the day.

In summer heat, dogs with heart conditions, such as Pugs and Bulldogs, have difficulty breathing. They should be exercised only in the cool early morning or late evening. Allow them to rest during the hottest part of the day.

Swimming can be an integral part of exercise for many breeds. It should be

Exercise is essential for all dogs. Exercise requirements vary for each dog.

encouraged if the dog is interested. Avoid dirty ponds or polluted water. Domestic swimming pools can be dangerous because dogs can get in easily but often cannot get out without help.

REGULAR HEALTH CHECKUPS

Dogs need regular checkups. Grooming time is a convenient time for health checkups, especially for longcoat dogs. Paws should be checked for length of nails and glass or thorns sticking in the pads. Grass seeds found in the web or between the toes should be removed. Foreign material such as gum or cigarette wrappers should be removed

Weigh the dog on a bathroom scale. Subtract your weight from the combined weight. Check weekly.

from between the pads. If you think your dog walked through a substance such as soft road tar, immerse the feet in oil or butter to soothe and soften the irritant. Wash thoroughly with soap.

Examine teeth for signs of discoloration. Tartar frequently builds up on teeth, especially in dogs reluctant to chew and those with narrow bites. Yorkshire Terriers and Toy Poodles have narrow bites. Watch for signs of broken teeth, teeth with holes, receding or inflamed gums or loose teeth. The exception is in puppies between 4 and 6 months, when baby teeth are lost to make room for adult teeth. Teeth problems require veterinarian treatment before the animal develops a toothache or mouth pain.

Check the dog's eyes regularly for inflammation and opacity in the cornea. Severe inflammation will cause the eye to be half closed and to water profusely. A dog with this problem will often rub the inflamed eye.

When checking ears, look for signs of drainage. Examine each flap for excessive wax. If you find this, have the ears checked by your vet. If ear canals smell unpleasant, the dog may have a problem. If either ear seems irritated, see your vet.

Pay attention to the areas around the anus and urinary region when grooming. Problems here include diarrhea and cystitis. They are often found by an observant owner.

Notice the general condition of the coat. Watch for bald patches and parasites, fleas, lice and ticks.

SIGNS TO WATCH FOR

There are signs of poor health that may help your veterinarian reach a diagnosis. Sudden weight gain or loss may indicate a problem. Weigh your dog regularly, perhaps once a week. This can be done by holding the dog while you stand on a bathroom scale. The difference in your weight and the total is the dog's weight. For small dogs and puppies, kitchen scales may be easier. For large dogs, find a scale with higher limits.

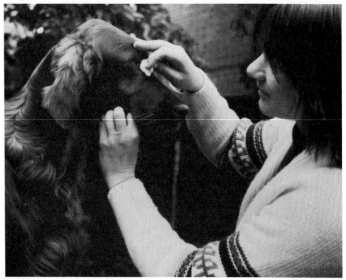

Cleansing the eye area with moistened cotton. Use a new pad for each eye. Cleanse carefully, with a gentle eyewash.

Appetite and thirst changes should be noted. If in doubt about fluid consumption, measure water or milk daily. Keep a record of how much is consumed. Letting your dog drink puddle or pond water will change the amount.

Signs of vomiting and diarrhea should be carefully watched. These can be a valuable indicator of illness. All animals have an occasional upset stomach. If this is persistent or combined with laziness and a loss of appetite, veterinary help is needed.

Intolerance or unwillingness to exercise may indicate heart disease. This could be true if combined with a persistent soft, dry cough.

Any departure from normal behavior should be carefully watched. If in doubt, call your vet and describe the signs that are worrying you. He will answer your questions or ask to see the animal.

SIMPLE FIRST AID

Assemble a simple first-aid kit. You may never need the items, but keep them handy.

The kit illustrated on the next page does not include splints. They are rarely required. If you suspect a limb fracture, make splints from wooden boards, dowels, tightly rolled newspaper or other similar materials.

Simple First-Aid Kit

1. Eye ointment. If in doubt, ask your vet what to use.
2. Cream or ointments for cuts and burns.
3. Sedative tablets. These should be supplied by a vet with dosage details.
4. Aspirin tablets, the type that dissolve. One tablet treats a 20-pound (9kg) dog.
5. Alcohol for cleansing and sterilizing.

6 and 7. Bandage rolls.
8. Bandage for sprains and injured limbs.
9. Antiseptic to use on dogs, such as an antiseptic designed to use on babies.
10. Mixture for sickness and diarrhea.
11. Antiseptic powder for cuts, scrapes or after operations. Easy to apply from plastic bottle.

12, 13 and 14. White open-weave cotton bandages for dressing cuts and wounds.
15. Sterile dressings for cuts and scrapes.
16. Nail clippers.
17. Blunt-end tweezers, such as eyebrow tweezers, to remove thorns, ticks and other foreign matter from the skin.

18. Cotton for dressings and bandages.
19. Curved, blunt-end scissors for trimming fur and removing foreign materials from between the pads.
20. Cotton swabs for cleansing purposes.

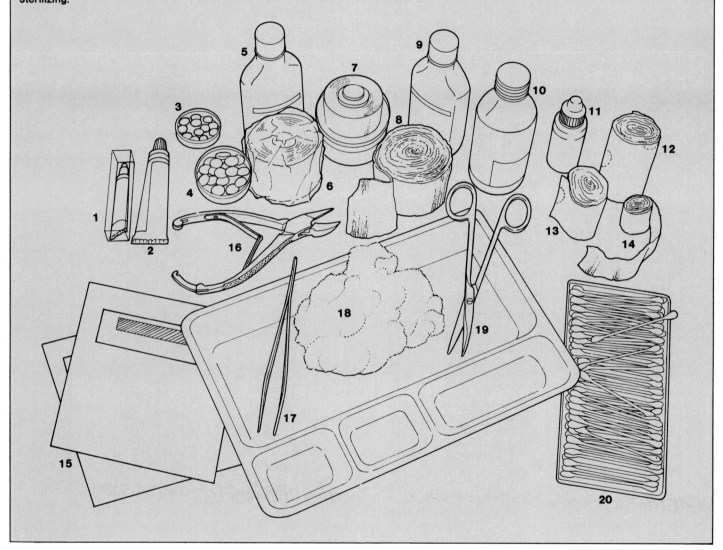

AILMENTS

The following information deals with problems grouped according to parts of the body. This may help you recognize whether veterinary treatment is required and how urgently. First-aid measures are outlined where appropriate. It is often impossible for the vet to diagnose over the telephone.

Skin—Many problems are the direct result of parasites. Fleas are the most common. Usually found on the back of a dog,

they leave their droppings, but not their eggs, in the coat. The droppings appear as small black particles in the fur. Fleas are easily seen with the naked eye. They are brownish and flattened from side to side. They scatter quickly through the hair. If you see fleas, give prompt treatment with a special shampoo, powder or aerosol. Repeat if the dog becomes infested again.

If left untreated, dogs may become allergic to flea bites.

They may scratch or bite themselves until a patch of wet eczema appears. This patch can vary from 1/2 inch (1.2cm) in diameter to almost a quarter of the body if left untreated. Eczema has a shiny, moist-looking surface. Take your dog to the vet if you think it may have eczema. Treat wet eczema by applying a soothing cream. Give the dog an aspirin tablet, which helps curb scratching and biting.

Lice are gray-blue and

usually found on ear flaps. They barely move. They attach their eggs to the fur. Insecticidal treatment is essential. Many lice on one dog can cause anemia because they suck large quantities of blood.

Common Dog Parasites

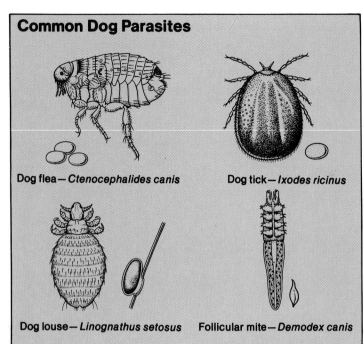

Dog flea— *Ctenocephalides canis*

Dog tick— *Ixodes ricinus*

Dog louse— *Linognathus setosus*

Follicular mite— *Demodex canis*

Four common types of external parasite. Lice and their eggs are found mostly on the head. Fleas, ticks and mites may be found on the body.

Ticks embedded in the skin may cause problems by transmitting disease. If there are many ticks, insecticidal treatment will clear them. If there are just one or two, they can be smothered with petroleum jelly and removed with tweezers after a few minutes.

Scratches cause few problems and should be cleaned with an antiseptic. Follow this with an application of medicated ointment. If the dog persists in licking, seek treatment. Cuts vary in depth, length and position. If you apply a firm bandage, it will usually control bleeding. Stitching is required for cuts longer then 4/5 inch (2cm). Bathe cuts with disinfectant, but do not apply any ointment.

Ears—Ear troubles usually require a vet's diagnosis and treatment. Home treatment does not work satisfactorily. One condition is *aural hematoma,* a blood blister in the ear flap. This must be drained surgically and bandaged to protect it while healing. Aural hematomas are usually caused by an animal excessively shaking or scratching an ear flap.

Eyes—It is safe to bathe the dog's eyes in lukewarm water or with an eyewash. Seek professional advice if your dog has serious problems. A delay could result in permanent loss of vision.

Nails—You may need to cut these occasionally, especially dewclaws, which do not wear down. If left unchecked they can curve and dig into the flesh. They can also catch in undergrowth and wire fencing. All nails contain a blood vessel and nerve. Leave cutting to experienced people unless you are sure what you are doing. Broken nails usually need to be removed by a vet.

Digestive System—Watch animals regularly while they eat. Signs of mouth pain usually show in the way an animal eats its food. A temporary pain reliever such as aspirin can be given. Seek professional attention.

Uncomplicated vomiting is common in dogs. The vomit is usually fluid, often described as a froth, which may be white or yellow. If solid food is returned, it may indicate inflammation of the stomach, called *gastritis,* or food poisoning. If vomiting persists, especially in young dogs that swallow stones, there may be an obstruction. Seek veterinary attention as soon as possible. With gastritis, withhold food from the dog for a period of 24 hours. Allow small, frequent

drinks of boiled water.

Liver failure is common in dogs. It usually requires veterinary treatment. It is aggravated by fats, so special diets may be needed.

Failure of the pancreatic gland to work efficiently may result in a dog that eats a lot but loses weight. Avoid fats and seek veterinary help. An enzyme deficiency often causes these symptoms.

Diarrhea may be one of the most common signs of illness. There are many possible causes. An unsuitable diet or a bowel infection are most common. Withholding food for 24 hours, followed by a light diet of white meat, such as chicken, veal or fish, will cure mild cases. If the condition persists or recurs, treatment by a vet is indicated.

Anal Glands—These are a source of irritation to some dogs. They are situated on either side of the anus. If they become overfilled, they cause

irritation. If not relieved, the glands can become infected and form abscesses, like a boil. Anal glands can be emptied by the owner if a vet shows how to do it. Attention will help avoid prolonged treatment. Immediate care will lessen the risk of the animal causing other lesions, such as wet eczema, while trying to soothe the discomfort.

Dogs have two scent or anal glands, each about the size of a cherry. They may enlarge if overfilled with secretion or if infected. If left untreated, they will burst like a boil. They can be surgically removed.

Anal Glands

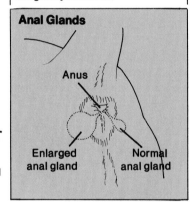

Anus

Enlarged anal gland

Normal anal gland

Anal or scent glands may be emptied by applying gentle pressure with thumb and second finger just below and to either side of the anus.

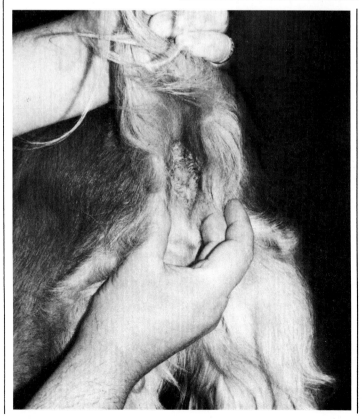

Heart And Circulation—These cause few problems in young animals, except for rare cases of inherited heart disease. Some breeds develop heart murmurs, exercise intolerance, a dry cough of increasing frequency and severity, and progressive lethargy or exhaustion. Veterinary treatment is necessary. Owners can help by exercising dogs at the coolest time of day in hot weather. Provide adequate ventilation indoors and prevent pets from becoming overweight.

Respiratory System—Most dogs have a good respiratory system. There are few cases of bronchitis and pneumonia except when associated with the distemper virus. Kennel cough, or *tracheitis,* is an inflammation of the windpipe. Usually it is not serious except in young, ill or old animals. The owner can help veterinary treatment by giving cough preparations. Even the old-fashioned honey and lemon remedy seems to help.

Muscles And Bones—A common condition is pain in a limb, which causes limping. There are many causes. Inspect pads for signs of an imbedded piece of glass or thorn. Allow the animal to rest until help is obtained. Support the affected limb with a bandage if necessary.

Dogs can tear muscles, ligaments and tendons by tripping or jumping awkwardly. In an older animal, joint disease such as arthritis or muscular rheumatism can cause limping. The degree of lameness is often linked with climatic conditions. Damp, cold weather aggravates the problem. Drugs will help. In early stages, many vets prescribe aspirin.

Broken limbs are uncommon and usually the result of a major trauma, such as a car accident. Until professional help is obtained, do the following:

1. Give nothing by mouth.
2. Move the animal as little as possible.
3. Try to immobilize the broken limb by a splint or use a bandage to tie it to the limb on the opposite side of the body. A stretcher helps reduce pain while the animal is taken to a veterinary

Bandaging Limbs

After applying a dressing to the foot injury, place a double layer of bandage around the top and bottom of the foot.

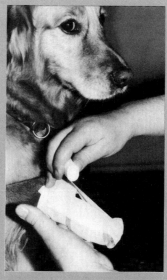

Continue winding the same bandage around the leg from the bottom up. Overlap each turn.

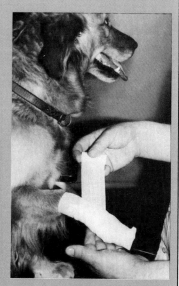

Apply at least two layers for comfort and protection. Do not wrap the limb too tightly.

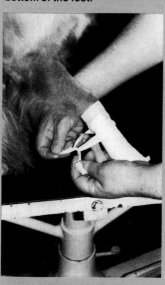

Split the end of the bandage. Tie a double knot around the leg. It is not safe to use pins.

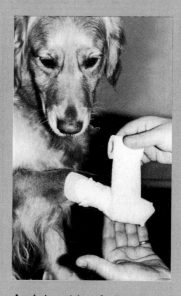

Apply two strips of adhesive tape crosswise over the foot, then up the bandage, sticking ends of tape to fur.

The bandage is neat, strong and relatively waterproof. It should be firm, comfortable and not too tight.

hospital. A jacket or coat can be used as an emergency stretcher.

The vet will set the limb, using stainless steel pins or a cast. This depends on the place of fracture and the preference of the doctor.

A common injury to a back leg is tearing a small but important ligament in the knee. Rest may help, but usually the ligament must be replaced. This is done with nylon or a skin graft to strengthen the knee.

Abnormal hip development—called *hip dysplasia*—is widespread in large breeds. The abnormality seldom shows up in young dogs. As the dog ages, it becomes stiffer, probably as a result of arthritis in the joint. It has difficulty rising, jumping or walking far. Often it is possible to remove the malformed hip joint. Various techniques are used to relieve pain, depending on the vet's preference.

Another bone condition is *spondylitis,* a progressive disease

affecting the spinal cord. It produces progressive paralysis of the hindquarters, sometimes linked with incontinence. It is incurable.

Urinary System—If kidneys do not work effectively, the whole body system collapses. Leptospirosis vaccination has become widespread and kidney disease has grown rarer.

The kidneys can become damaged and renal disease develops in many dogs as they age. There is no cure, but veterinary help may ensure

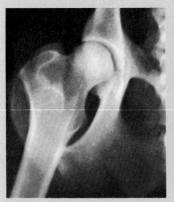

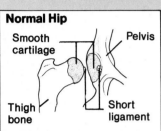

Normal Hip

Smooth cartilage — Pelvis

Thigh bone — Short ligament

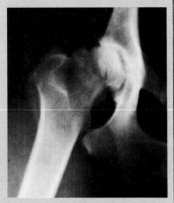

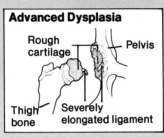

Advanced Dysplasia

Rough cartilage — Pelvis

Thigh bone — Severely elongated ligament

years of useful, happy, pain-free life. Symptoms are usually an increase in water intake, loss of weight, decreasing appetite and a tendency to vomit, especially after drinking a lot of water. Diagnosis is usually by urine and blood tests. Veterinary treatment and dietary advice are helpful.

Cystitis, inflammation of the bladder, is a more acute condition. It must be treated promptly to prevent discomfort. It can start with a simple infection or in combination with bladder tumors, polyps or stones. Diagnosis and treatment must be done by a vet. Symptoms include increased frequency of urination. Difficult and painful urination are usual.

Veterinarians can sometimes feel stones in females. Those in males are often detected with a catheter. If stones are present, they must be removed for long-term relief. Blood passed in urine is also a sign. Total inability to pass urine, especially in a male, requires immediate treatment.

Reproductive System—This system gives little trouble in males but can cause serious problems in females. The only organ likely to trouble a male is the prostate. This gland enlarges, causing difficulty in passing urine or feces. The

The normal hip is a perfectly smooth fit between the top of the thigh bone and the pelvis, like a ball and socket. In dysplasia, close contact is lost and the edges of the ball and socket become rough and uneven. This cause uneven gait, pain and weakness.

problem responds to drug treatment.

An inflammation of the female's womb is a condition referred to as *metritis*. The result may be sterility. A severe attack can endanger the animal's life. This condition may respond to antibiotics. It is often safest to have an entire ovario-hysterectomy. Danger signs include a progressive vulvar discharge along with increasing thirst, decreasing appetite and vomiting.

One of the most common and annoying conditions encountered in females is false pregnancy. About two months after season, a female behaves as if she had been mated. She will nest, lactate and foster mock pups such as socks, cushions and toys. Treatment is required in some cases. Remove all make-believe pups and prevent licking of milk glands, which will stimulate milk production. Do this by painting the teats with vinegar.

Nervous System—Infection of the brain by distemper virus may result in fits sometimes controllable by medication.

Epilepsy also occurs. This is usually treated with an anti-convulsant drug. Spinal disc injuries are common, especially in long dogs such as Dachshunds. They may be treated by drugs or surgery. Discourage these dogs from jumping or climbing stairs.

Tumors—Some owners have a horror of all tumors. An experienced vet can dismiss some swellings as harmless. Most lumps are benign, such as fatty lumps, warts and cysts. These do not spread and many can be removed without trouble if desired. Skin masses and female tumors of the mammary glands are also common. Some benign growths are inoperable because of their position. It is impossible to remove them from surrounding vital tissues.

Cancerous tumors may present a similar problem. These may not be worth removing if cells have spread through the body to other organs. It is pointless to remove the primary growth only to find growths elsewhere. A doctor may use X-rays and laboratory tests to determine the type of tumor and chance of surgical success. He may also take a small sample for a pathologist's

assessment. This is often done after removal to confirm the nature of the tumor.

Shock—Dogs may suffer shock after an accident, following surgery or in any condition involving extensive bleeding. Prompt, skilled veterinary care is necessary. Never give anything by mouth to an unconscious dog. It may choke.

Poisoning—Toxic substances may be swallowed accidentally or given deliberately. Probably the greatest risk is from garden chemicals, such as weedkillers. When using these, read safety instructions.

If you know a dog has been poisoned, make it vomit by forcing it to swallow a strong salt solution or mustard in water. This helps only if done minutes after the dog eats the poison. Take the poison container to the vet. It may help him choose the right antidote quickly.

COMMON DOG DISEASES

Distemper—Caused by a virus that can attack almost all of a dog's body tissues. It can affect

German Shepherds may have hip dysplasia. Be sure your dog is certified HD-free.

Applying Tape Muzzle

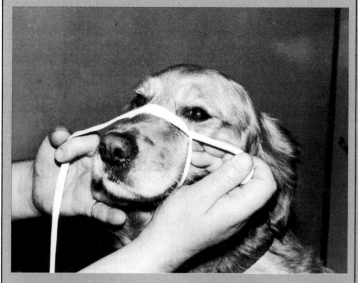

A tape muzzle ensures safety with a vicious, nervous or injured dog. Using a length of

bandage or cord, make a wide loop. Pass this over the snout and pull tight.

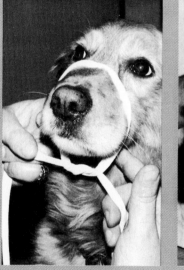

Knot the ends once and retie under the muzzle. Again, pull tight to ensure effectiveness.

Finally, take the ends behind the dog's crown and tie in a bow. The muzzle should not dislodge.

Improvising Splint And Stretcher

A dog with limb injuries can be made more comfortable if you tie the damaged leg to the opposite

one. Use strips of bandage to limit movement. Tie it firmly to the lower limb at 3 or 4 points.

A coat, jacket or blanket held at all four corners by two people is a useful means of transportation.

This minimizes struggling, which could cause further injury. Roll the dog gently onto this stretcher.

---

the eyes and nose, causing discharges; the bowel, causing diarrhea; the lungs, causing a cough; and the brain, resulting in twitches, paralysis or fits. Distemper can cause crusting of the nose and pads, hence its old name *hard pad*. Vaccination has reduced the incidence of this disease.

Viral Hepatitis—Can affect all ages but is particularly dangerous to pups. Signs vary from persistent vomiting, lack of appetite and possibly jaundice, to Fading Puppy Syndrome and sudden death. As with distemper, the dog is obviously ill and prompt treatment must be sought.

Leptospirosis—Caused by either of two microorganisms. Both will damage kidneys and liver, causing collapse, vomiting, high fever, coma or a yellowing of the whites of the eyes. One form of leptospirosis can be contracted from rats. It can affect humans.

Rabies—Dogs or people bitten by a rabid animal are likely to die in pain if not treated. Dogs must be vaccinated against it. Never befriend stray dogs. Keep pets isolated from possible sources of infection.

Signs range from *dumbness,* when an affected dog is subdued and its mouth hangs open dribbling saliva, to *furiousness,* which is less common. The affected dog becomes aggressive and attacks live or inanimate objects, even its owners. *Hydrophobia,* or fear of swallowing water, is not a symptom among dogs.

Kennel Cough—Caused by a variety of germs spread from dog to dog, especially when they are confined together. Despite a persistent cough, there are rarely other or more serious symptoms.

Canine Parvovirus—Causes sudden death in puppies up to 8 to 9 months old. It is an infection of the heart muscle. Infected adult dogs vomit and have diarrhea, often with blood present. Protection is given using cat panleucopaenia vaccine.

Tonsilitis—May be uncomplicated or occur with other illness, such as gastritis. Signs may be gulping, difficulty in swallowing, a soft cough, a tendency to eat grass and retching. Response to antibiotics is usually good. It is

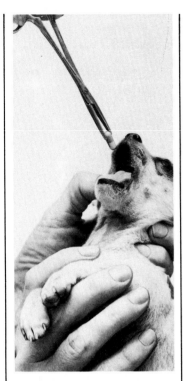

Small dogs can be given tablets with forceps or tweezers. This reduces the chance of your getting bitten or choking the dog.

Keep the mouth closed when giving liquids. Pour liquid into flap formed by the lips. Allow dog to swallow before releasing.

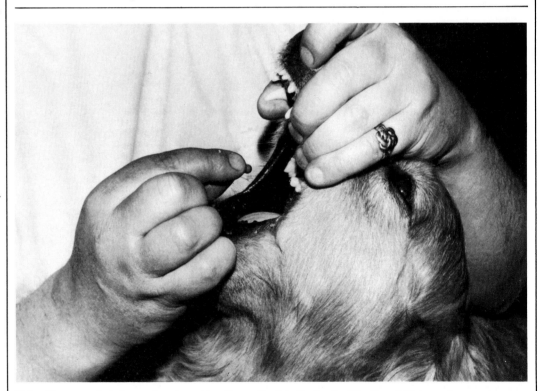

Grip pill or capsule between thumb and forefinger. Push to the back of the throat. Release jaws and allow dog to swallow.

rarely necessary to remove the tonsils.

Hormone Disease—Not transmitted to other animals. Signs depend on the gland affected, but weight gain, hair loss and change in the coat are frequent. These are especially evident in older animals and females during the active part and immediately following the estrus cycle. Sometimes surgery is required. Often gland extracts will cure these diseases.

Diabetes—Affected dogs show increased thirst and appetite, with a weight loss. Treatment of diabetes may involve giving the dog daily insulin injections.

Pancreatic Disease—A failure to digest food properly, caused by inability to produce a digestive enzyme. Signs are ravenous appetite, marked decline in weight and general condition, and bulky, pale, puttylike feces.

Anal Gland Disease—Frequently troublesome. It is due to overfilling, infection or abscess formation affecting anal glands. Irritation of the anal region occurs, resulting in pain. Surgical removal of the glands may be needed if the problem recurs after treatment.

GIVING MEDICINES

Most owners must give their pets medicines at some time. This can be accomplished easily. Medicines given by mouth should not be mixed with food. The dog may be too ill to eat all the food or may know its food has been altered and leave it. If fed with other animals, the ill dog may swap bowls. It is better to give it a direct dose to be certain it is swallowed.

Few medicines come in powder form except those that are tasty and designed to be mixed with food. When giving powders, do not pour them into the mouth. The dog will cough them up again. Instead, mix

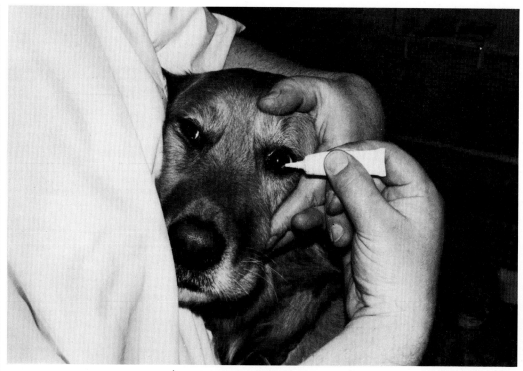

To apply eye medications, hold the dog's head against your body. Keep lids open and put ointment on the eye. Hold tube away.

Never give drugs not made for animal use without the advice of your vet. Drugs for humans may cause suffering to your dog and could harm or even kill the animal. Check with a vet before giving your dog *any* medicine.

Always store dog medicine in a safe place away from other medication. Dispose of drugs when treatment is completed. Your vet may give you some drugs you can safely keep for future use with a specific medical condition. Mark these clearly with the dosage, frequency and particular condition for which the drugs are to be used.

them with water, milk, butter, jam or honey. Smear the paste on the tongue or lips. The dog will swallow it.

Tablets, pills or capsules should be given by pushing them to the back of the throat and holding the mouth closed until you see the dog swallow. If the dog protests, get someone to hold the dog during dosage. Dipping the medicines in oil or butter may make them easier for the dog to swallow.

Liquid medicines usually do not exceed 1 teaspoon (5ml) per dose. Sit the dog down and hold the jaws closed with the head tilted back. Pull out the flap of the lip on one side to form a funnel. Pour the liquid in. Do not release the head or jaws until you see the dog swallow.

Ointments, creams and lotions must be applied to affected areas when prescribed. Rub the preparations into the skin unless otherwise directed. There is a natural tendency for animals to lick off these applications immediately. This is reduced if little remains on the skin surface. Apply these medicines just before taking the dog for a walk. Your pet's attention will be distracted while the ointment does its work. If you have to rub it on at bedtime when you cannot keep the dog from licking, apply a protective bandage or sock.

Eardrops should be put down the largest visible opening to the vertical canal. They will work their way into the ear to reach the troubled area. A gentle external massage of the ear will help. Frantic head shaking by the dog will not dislodge the drops. Ear powders clog the ear. A vet will have to remove them by syringing or other cleansing. Do not pour powder inside a dog's ears unless prescribed by your vet.

Application of eyedrops or ointments requires special handling. Always steady the dog in a sitting position with its head slightly raised. If necessary, get someone to help. Eyes are delicate and will not take rough treatment. Hold the head firmly with one hand. Use the thumb and index finger to keep the lids open. With the dropper bottle or tube in the other hand, put the medicine in the open eye. Squeeze ointment from a tube but be sure the tube nozzle does not touch the eye. The natural blinking that follows treatment will spread the preparation over the eye. Do not allow the dog to rub its eye for a few minutes after application.

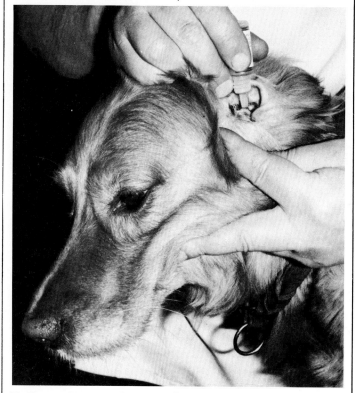

To give eardrops, steady the head, lift the earflap and aim the drops down the widest canal. Close the flap and massage the ear.

Words in italics refer to separate listings in the Glossary.

A

Action—The way a dog moves.

AKC—American Kennel Club.

Albino—Animal with pigmentation deficiency.

All-Rounder—A judge qualified to judge all recognized breeds.

Almond eyes—Oval shape, like an almond, slanted at corners.

Amble—A relaxed, easy *gait* in which the legs on either side move almost, but not quite, as a pair. Often seen as the transitional movement between the *walk* and a faster gait.

Angulation—The angles formed by a meeting of the bones. Mainly, the shoulder, upper arm, *stifle* and *hock*.

Ankylosis—The abnormal adhesion of bones, especially those forming a joint. Stiffening of a joint.

Anorchid—A male dog without testicles.

Anticipating—In obedience training, acting before receiving a command.

Apophysis—An outgrowth or projection, especially one from a bone.

Apple-head—Having a round skull. Not desirable in most breeds.

Apron—The long hair on the throat and below the neck on longcoat dogs.

ARF—Animal Research Foundation.

B

B (or b)—Abbreviation for female, also called *bitch.*

Babbler—A hound that barks when not on the *trail.*

Back—Variable meaning, depending on breed standard. In some standards, defined as the vertebrae between the *withers* and the *loin.*

Bad mouth—Teeth crooked or misaligned. *Overshot* or *undershot* bite.

Balanced—A consistent whole. Symmetrical. Proportioned as a whole or its separate parts, such as balance of head or body or balance of head and body.

Bandy legs—Legs bent outward.

Barrel—Rounded rib section.

Barrel hocks—*Hocks* that turn out, causing the toes to turn in. Also called spread hocks or divergent hocks.

Basewide—Having a wide footfall, resulting from *paddling* movement. Causes body to rock from side to side.

Bat ears—Large, stiff, open ears pointing outward, like a French Bulldog's.

Bay—The long drawn-out sound made by a hound in pursuit.

Beard—The profuse, bushy *whiskers* of the Griffon Bruxellois, as opposed to terrier whiskers.

Beauty spot—A distinct spot, usually round, of colored hair, surrounded by a white *blaze,* on the top of the skull between the ears, such as the Boston Terrier.

Beefy—Overheavy development of the *hindquarters.*

Belton—The lemon- or blue-flecked color of certain English Setters, notably the Laverack strain. Also orange or liver belton.

Bench show—A dog show at which the dogs competing for prizes are leashed on benches.

Best in Show—The animal judged to be the best of all the breeds in a show.

Bevy—A flock of birds.

Bilateral cryptorchid—See *Cryptorchid.*

Bird dog—A sporting dog trained to hunt birds.

Bitch—A female dog.

Bite—The position of the teeth when the mouth is shut.

Blanket—The coat color on the back and upper part of the sides, between the neck and on the tail.

Blaze—A white stripe running up the middle of the face, generally between the eyes.

Blenheim—A variety of spaniel with white and red markings.

Blinker—A dog that points to a bird and then leaves it, or on finding a bird, avoids making a definite *point.*

Blocky—Having a square or cubelike formation of the head.

Blooded—Of good breeding. Pedigreed.

Bloom—The glossiness of a *coat* in the best condition.

Blue merle—Blue and gray mixed with black. Marbled.

Bluies—Colored portions of the coat with a distinct blue or smoky cast. This coloring is associated with extremely light or blue eyes and liver or gray eyerims, nose and lip pigment, such as the Pembroke Welsh Corgi.

Board—To kennel and care for a dog in its owner's absence, for a fee.

BOB—Abbreviation for Best of Breed.

Bobtail—A naturally tailless dog or a dog with a tail *docked* short. Also, common name for the Old English Sheepdog.

Bodied up—Mature and well-developed.

Bolt—To drive or start an animal out of its earth or burrow.

Bone—A well-boned dog is one with limbs giving an appearance and feel of strength and spring without *coarseness.*

Bossy—Overdevelopment of the shoulder muscles.

Braccold—Belonging to the *hound* family of dogs.

Brace—A pair of dogs of the same type.

Breastbone—*Sternum.* Bone running down the middle of the chest, to which all but the *floating rib* is attached.

Breeching—The tan hairs on the inside and back of the thighs, as seen in Manchester Terriers.

Breed—A variety of *purebred* dog. A male or female with a *pedigree.*

Breeder—Someone who breeds dogs.

Breeding particulars—*Sire, dam,* date of birth, sex, color, club registration details.

Brindle—A mixture of light and dark hairs, usually darker streaks on a gray, tawny or brown background.

Brisket—The part of the lower chest including the breastbone.

Brock—A badger.

Broken color—*Self-color* relieved by a color.

Broken-haired—A roughed-up wirecoat.

Broken-up face—A receding nose, together with a deep stop, *wrinkle* and *undershot* jaw, such as a Bulldog or Pekingese.

Brood bitch—A female kept for breeding.

Brush—A bushy tail. A tail heavy with hair, such as an Alaskan Malamute.

Brushing—A *gaiting* fault. When parallel *pasterns* are so close, the legs brush in passing.

Bull-baiting—A sport of the past in which a dog or dogs baited a bull.

Bull neck—A heavy neck, well-muscled.

Burr—The irregular inner part of the pinna of the ear.

Butterfly nose—A nose of two colors, usually dark brown or black spotted with flesh color.

Buttocks—The rump or hips.

Button ear—Ear that folds over in front, with tip drooping forward, as in the Fox Terrier.

Bye—At *field trials,* an odd dog remaining after the dogs entered in a *stake* have been paired in *braces* by *drawing.*

C

Camel back—Arched back, like a one-hump camel.

Canine—Applies to dogs, foxes, wolves and jackals.

Canines—The two upper and two lower sharp-pointed teeth next to the *incisors.*

Canter—A *gait* with three beats to each stride, two legs moving separately and two as a diagonal pair. Slower than the *gallop* and not as tiring.

Carinated—Keel shape. Having a prominent central line like the bottom of a ship.

Carpals—Bones of the *pastern* joints.

Carp back—Arched back.

Castrate—To remove the testicles of a male dog.

Catch dog—A dog used to catch and hold a hunted animal so the huntsman can take it alive.

Cat feet—Short, compact and round feet common to terriers, as opposed to *splay feet.*

Cephalic index—The ratio, multiplied by 100, of the greatest breadth of the dog's head from side to side, to the length from above the root of the nose to the occiput.

Champion—The title awarded based on points won at major shows.

Character—Expression, individuality, general appearance and deportment considered typical of a *breed.*

Check-chain—A chain collar fitted to a dog's neck so that pulling on the dog's leash tightens or loosens the collar. Also referred to as a *choker.*

Cheeky—With cheeks prominently rounded, thick or protruding.

Chest—The part of the body or trunk enclosed by the ribs.

Chicken-breasted—With a short, protruding *breastbone.*

China eye—A clear blue eye.

Chippendale front—Named after the Chippendale chair. Forelegs out at *elbows, pasterns* close and feet turned out. See *Fiddle front.*

Chiseled—Clean cut head, particularly beneath the eyes.

Chops—The thick upper lips that hang below the lower jaw, such as in the Bloodhound.

Chorea—A nervous jerking caused by involuntary contraction of the muscles, usually affecting the face or legs.

Clip—A type of cut, as used on the Poodle.

Clipping—The back foot striking the front foot during the *gait*.

Cloddy—Low, thickset, heavy.

Close coupled—Having a short back or a short body.

Coarse—Without refinement.

Coat—The dog's hair covering.

Cobby—Short bodied, compact.

Collar—A marking around the neck, usually white. Also, a circle of leather or chain around the neck used to direct and control a dog when a leash is attached.

Companion Dog (CD)—A suffix used with the name of a dog as recorded by the American Kennel Club as a result of winning minimum scores at three obedience trials under three different judges.

Companion Dog Excellent (CDX)—A suffix used with the name of a dog as recorded by the American Kennel Club as a result of winning minimum scores in three open classes at obedience trials.

Condition—Health, shown by coat, weight, general appearance and deportment.

Conformation—Form and structure, makeup and shape. Arrangement of the parts in conformance with breed *standard* requirements.

Corky—Active, lively, alert.

Couple—A pair of hounds.

Couplings—The length of the body between the last rib and the pelvis.

Coursing—The sport of chasing rabbits by Greyhounds.

Covering ground—The ratio of the distance between the ground and the *brisket* and the distance between the front and rear legs.

Cow hocked—With *hocks* turned toward one another.

Crabbing—Moving with the body at an angle to the line of travel.

Crank tail—A tail carried down with the tip held outward in the shape of a crank.

Crest—The upper, arched portion of the neck, as in the Chinese Crested.

Crop—To cut off the tops of the ears so they stand erect.

Not allowed for shows in some countries.

Crossbred—The progeny of *purebred* parents of different *breeds*.

Crossing over—Unsound *gaiting* action starting with twisting elbows ending with crisscrossing and toeing out.

Croup—The rear part of the back, above the hind legs.

Crown—The highest part of the head. The top of the skull.

Cry—The *baying* of hounds.

Cryptorchid—An adult male whose testicles have not descended into the scrotum. A dog of this type cannot be exhibited. *Bilateral cryptorchids* are affected on both sides. *Unilateral cryptorchids* are affected on one side only.

Cull—A pup that is an inferior specimen of its *breed*.

Culotte—The feathery hair on the backs of the legs.

Cur—A mongrel.

Cushion—Fullness or thickness of the upper lip.

Cynology—The study of canines.

D

Dam—The mother of a *litter* of puppies.

Dappled—A mottled color, generally patches of silver and tan, black and silver or black and tan.

Dead grass—Tan or dull straw color.

Depigmentation—Partial or complete loss of coloration.

Derby—*Field trial* competition for novice sporting dogs, usually between 1 and 2 years of age.

Dewclaw—A claw on the inside of the leg, often removed in early puppyhood but retained by some breeds.

Dewlap—Loose hanging skin under the throat and chin, as in the Bloodhound.

Diagonals—Right front and left rear legs constitute the right diagonal. Left front and right rear legs constitute the left diagonal. In the *trot,* the diagonals move together.

Diehard—Nickname for Scottish Terrier or Aberdeen Terrier.

Dish-face—Having the nasal bone higher at the nose than at the *stop.*

Disqualification—A ruling made by a *judge* or show committee that a dog has a condition making it ineligible

for further competition under the *dog show* rules or the *standard* for its breed.

Distemper teeth—Teeth that are marked, pitted, ringed and often stained. Due to distemper or other severe infection.

Divergent hocks—See *Barrel hocks.*

Dock—To shorten the tail by cutting. Usually done in early puppyhood if breed *standards* demand.

Dog—Any member of the species *Canis familiaris.* Also, a male dog.

Dog show—An exhibition at which dogs are judged in accordance with an established *standard* of perfection for each breed.

Dollchocephalic—Having a disproportionately long head, long skull and *muzzle* long and the *bite* even. A skull with a *cephalic index* below 75.

Dome—The rounded part of the skull, as in spaniels.

Double coat—An *undercoat* of soft, thick hair to warm the body and an outercoat of coarse, strong hair to keep out dampness and cold.

Down face—The *muzzle* inclining downward from the skull to the tip of the nose.

Down in pastern—Weak or faulty *pastern* set at a pronounced angle from the vertical.

Drag—A trail prepared by dragging a bag impregnated with scent along the ground.

Drawing—Selection of dogs to be run, in a *field trial stake.*

Drive—A solid thrusting of the *hindquarters,* denoting sound movement.

Drop eared—When the ears are pendant and hang close and flat to the side of the cheeks.

Dropper—A *bird-dog* cross.

Dry neck—The skin taut. Not loose or wrinkled.

Dual champion—Dog that has won championships in both *dog shows* and *field trials.*

Dudley nose—Flesh-colored nose.

E

Elbow—The joint between the upper arm and the forearm.

Elbows out—Elbows pointing away from the body.

Entropion—A condition in which the eyelid turns inward and the lashes irritate and may eventually penetrate the eyeball.

Even bite—Meeting of front teeth at edges with no overlap of upper or lower teeth.

Ewe neck—Concave curvature of the top neckline.

Expression—The general appearance of all features of the head as viewed from the front and typical of the *breed.*

Eyeteeth—The upper *canines.*

F

Faking—Changing the appearance of a dog by artificial means to deceive its real merit to an onlooker.

Fall—Long hair overhanging the face.

Fancier—Someone active in the sport of breeding, showing and judging *purebred* dogs.

Fangs—See *Canines.*

Fawn—A rich, light, golden tan.

FCI—Federation Cynologique Internationale.

Feathering—Long, fine fringe of hair seen on the ears, legs, tail and body of breeds such as spaniels.

Feet east and west—With the toes turned out.

Femoral-tibial joint—The joining of the thigh and shin bones.

Fetch—The retrieval of *game* by a dog. Also, the command to retrieve.

Fiddle face—An elongated, pinched-in *foreface.*

Fiddle front—The front of a dog with bandy or crooked forelegs.

Field trial—A competition for certain *hound* or sporting breeds in which dogs are judged on their ability and style in finding or retrieving *game* or following a game trial.

Field Trial Champion—(Field Ch.)—A prefix used with the name of a dog as recorded by the American Kennel Club as a result of beating other dogs in specified competitions at AKC licensed *field trials.*

Flag—The fringe or *feathering* found under the tails of setters and some retrievers. Long at the base and shorter at the tip.

Flank—The side of the body between the last rib and hip.

Flare—A *blaze* that widens as it approaches the top of the skull.

Flat bone—The leg bone whose girth is elliptical rather than round.

Flat-sided—Ribs insufficiently rounded as they approach the *breastbone.*

Flat withers—An unattractive fault. The result of short upright shoulder blades that join the *withers* abruptly.

Flecked—Lightly *ticked* with other colors, as in the English Setter. Not *roan* or spotted.

Flesh nose—Pink or tan nose.

Flews—Hanging upper lips, like those of a Bulldog. Usually refers to the lateral parts of the lips.

Flexor-cubital muscle—A muscle that flexes the joint at the elbow.

Flicking pasterns—Extremely loose movement of the lower forelegs.

Floating rib—The last, or 13th, rib, which is unattached to other ribs.

Fluffies—A coat of extreme length with exaggerated *feathering* on ears, chest, feet, legs, underparts and *hindquarters.*

Flush—To drive birds from cover. To force them to take flight.

Fly-eared—Ears that fall or tilt at the tips when they should be erect. Usually a blemish.

Flying lips—Unsettled lips, not assuming the correct position.

Flying trot—A fast *gait* in which all four feet are off the ground for a brief second during each half stride. Because of the long reach, hind feet step beyond the imprint left by the front.

Forearm—The bone of the foreleg between the *elbow* and *pastern.*

Foreface—The front part of the head, before the eyes. The muzzle.

Foster mother—A female used to nurse another animal's pups.

Foul color—Uncharacteristic color or marking.

Foxlike—Having a pointed nose and short *foreface.*

French front—See *Fiddle front.*

Frill—Long hair under the neck and on the forechest.

Fringes—*Featherings* of longcoat breeds.

Frog face—Extending nose accompanied by a receding jaw, usually *overshot.*

Front—The whole front part of the body.

Frontal bone—The skull bone over the eyes.

Furnishings—The long hair on the *foreface* of certain breeds.

Furrow—A groove running down the center of the skull, as in the Bulldog.

Futurity stake—A class at *dog shows* or *field trials* for young dogs that have been nominated at or before birth.

G

Gait—A style of movement, such as running or *trotting.*

Gallop—Fastest of the dog *gaits* or *paces.* A four-beat rhythm often with an extra period of suspension when the body is propelled through the air with all four feet off the ground.

Game—Birds and animals that are hunted.

Gay tail—A tail carried straight up.

Gazehound—A hound that hunts by sight.

Geld—See *Castrate.*

Genealogy—Recorded family descent.

Giving tongue—*Baying* on the trail of *game.*

Graioid—Belonging to the Greyhound family.

Grizzle—Blue-gray color.

Groom—To brush, comb, trim and otherwise prepare a dog's coat for show or pleasure.

Groups—Breeds put together to facilitate judging.

Guard hairs—The longer, smoother, stiffer hairs growing through and usually concealing the *undercoat.*

Gundog—Dog trained to assist the hunter in the field, such as retrievers, setters, spaniels and pointers.

Guns—Those who shoot at *field trials.*

Gun-shy—Frightened by the sound of a gun being fired.

H

Hackles—Hair on the neck and back raised involuntarily in fright or anger.

Hackney gait—A vigorous, proud, high-stepping *gait.*

Ham—Well-developed hind leg muscles just above the knee.

Handler—A person who handles or shows a dog at *dog shows, field trials* or obedience tests.

Hard-mouth—Given to biting down hard on *retrieved game.* A serious fault.

Harefeet—Long, narrow, closed-toe feet, as in the rabbit.

Harlequin—A combination of colors in patches on a solid ground, as in the coat of a Great Dane. Usually blue on white.

Harness—A leather strap shaped around the shoulders and chest, with a ring at its top over the *withers.*

Haunches—Back part of the thighs, on which the dog sits.

Haw—A third eyelid in the inside corner of the eye.

Heat—Seasonal fertility period of the female, normally every six months.

Heel—Command by *handler* to keep the dog close to his heel.

Heel free—Command where the dog must walk to heel without a *leash.*

Height—Dog's height measured from the ground to the withers.

Heterometropia—A condition in which the degree of refraction is different in the two eyes.

Hie on—A command to urge the dog on. Used in hunting or *field trials.*

High standing—Tall and upstanding with plenty of leg.

Hindquarters—Rear part of dog: pelvis, thighs, *hocks* and paws.

Hip dysplasia—Malformation of the ball of the hip joint. Usually hereditary.

Hocking out—Having *barrel hocks.*

Hock—Joint in the hind limb below the true knee or *stifle* joint.

Hocks well-let-down—*Hock* joints close to the ground.

Holt—The lair of an animal in a bank, drain or other hideout.

Honorable scars—Scars from injuries suffered as a result of work.

Hound—A dog commonly used for hunting by scent or sight.

Hound colors—White, tan and black, in order of predominant color.

Hound jog—The usual pace of the *hound.*

Hound marked—Fox Terriers are described as hound marked if their body patches conform to the pattern of hound markings.

Hucklebones—The top of the hip bones.

I

Inbreeding—*Mating* within the same family; a female to her sons or a male to his daughters.

Incisors—The upper and lower front teeth, between the *canines.*

Great Dane. Usually blue on white.

In season, in heat—Ready for mating.

In-shoulder—Shoulders pointing in, not parallel with the backbone. A fault found in dogs with shoulder blades too far forward on the chest.

Interbreeding—The breeding together of different varieties.

Isabella—Fawn or light bay color.

Ischium—Hip bone.

J

Jabot—A white stripe down the chest, like a shirtfront.

Jowls—Flesh of lips and jaws.

Judge—An evaluator of dogs in *dog shows,* obedience tests and *field trials.*

K

KC—Kennel Club in the United Kingdom.

Kennel—Enclosure where dogs are kept, with room to move about.

Kink tail—A sharply bent tail.

Kiss marks—Tan spots on the cheeks and over the eyes.

Knee joint—*Stifle* joint.

Knuckling over—Condition in which the front legs bend forward at the wrist or carpus.

Kyphosis—An abnormal curvature of the spine, with convexity backward.

L

Lack of type—Deficiency in traits that define the fundamental makeup of a *breed.*

Landseer—A Newfoundland that is not all black, but white with black, as depicted by the painter Sir Edward Landseer.

Layback—The angle of the shoulder blade as compared with the vertical.

Leash—A strap, cord or chain attached to the *collar* or *harness,* for the purpose of restraining or leading a dog. A lead.

Leather—The flap of the ear.

Leggy—Having legs too long for the body.

Level back—A back that makes a straight line from *withers* to tail, but not necessarily parallel to the ground.

Level bite—When the front teeth, the *incisors,* of the upper and lower jaws meet exactly edge to edge. *Pincer bite.*

Level gait—Dog moves without a rise or fall of the *withers.*

License—Formal permission granted by the American Kennel Club to a non-member club to hold a *dog show,* obedience test or *field trial.*

Light eyes—Yellow eyes.

Line breeding—The mating of related dogs of the same breed, within the line or family to a common ancestor.

Lion—Tawny color.

Lippy—Having thick, hanging lips.

Litter—The pups from one birth.

Liver—A dark red-brown color.

Loaded shoulders—Shoulders that are too thick and heavy.

Loin—The part of the body between the last rib and back legs.

Lordosis—Hollow back. *Saddle back:* Curvature of the spine.

Lower thigh—See *Second thigh.*

Lumber—Extra flesh.

Lumbering—Awkward *gait.*

Lupoid—Belonging to the wolf family.

Lurcher—A *crossbred hound.*

Lymer—A *hound* of ancient times led on a *leash.*

M

Mad dog—A dog with rabies.

Mane—Long and profuse hair on the top and sides of the neck.

Mantle—Dark-shaded portion of the coat on the shoulder, back and sides.

Manubrium—The portion of the malleus, the hammer bone in the ear, which represents the handle.

Mark—Dark shading on the *foreface.*

Masseter—A powerful chewing muscle.

Match show—Usually an informal *dog show* at which no championship points are awarded.

Mate—To breed a male and female.

Mealy—Covered or flecked with spots.

Median line—See *Furrow.*

Merle—A blue-gray mixture streaked or ticked with black. A coat color seen in some Shetland Sheepdogs and Collies.

Milk teeth—First teeth. Puppies lose these at 4 to 6 months.

Miscellaneous class—A competitive class at *dog shows* for dogs of certain specified breeds for which no regular show classification is provided.

Mismarks—Self-colors with any area of white on the back between *withers* and tail, on the sides between *elbows* and back of *hindquarters* or on the ears. Black with white markings and no tan present.

Molars—Dogs have two molars on each side of the upper jaw and three on each side of the lower jaw. Upper molars have three roots, lower have two roots.

Molera—Incomplete, imperfect or abnormal formation of the skull.

Molossoid—Belonging to the Mastiff family of dogs.

Mongrel—A dog whose parents are both of mixed breeding.

Monorchid—A male dog, one of whose testicles has not descended into the scrotal sac. Also called a *unilateral cryptorchid.*

Mort—A flourish on the hunting horn at the death of *game.*

Moving close—When the *hocks* turn in and the *pasterns* drop straight to the ground and move parallel to one another. Action places strain on ligaments and muscles.

Moving straight—Term descriptive of balanced *gaiting.* The angle of inclination begins at the shoulder or hip joint and the limbs remain relatively straight from these points to the *pads* of the feet, even as the legs flex or extend in reaching or thrusting.

Music—The *baying* of hounds.

Mute—To be silent on the trail, to *trail* without *baying* or barking.

Muzzle—The part of the head containing the mouth and nose. Also, a device to prevent biting.

Muzzle band—White marking around the *muzzle.*

N

Neck well-set on—Neckline merging gradually with strong *withers,* forming a pleasing transition into *topline.*

Nick—A breeding producing desirable puppies.

Nictitating membrane—See *Haw.*

Non-slip retriever—The dog that walks at heel, marks the fall and *retrieves* game on command. Not expected to find or *flush.*

Nose—The ability to scent.

O

Oblique shoulders—Shoulders well-laid back. The ideal shoulder slants at a 45° angle to the ground, forming an approximate right angle with the humerus at the shoulder joint.

Occipital protuberance—A prominently raised *occiput* characteristic of some *gundog* breeds.

Occiput—Upper, back point of the skull.

Open class—For all dogs of the *breeds* or varieties for which a class is provided and eligible for entry at the show.

Otter tail—Thick at the root, round and tapering, with the hair parted or divided on the underside.

Out at elbows—*Elbows* turning out from the body, as opposed to being held close.

Out at shoulder—Shoulder blades loosely attached to the body, leaving shoulders jutting out in relief and increasing the breadth of the front.

Out at walk—To lease or lend a puppy to someone for raising.

Outcrossing—The mating of unrelated individuals of the same breed.

Oval chest—Chest deeper than it is wide.

Overhang—A heavy or pronounced brow.

Over-nose wrinkle—A fold of loose skin dropping forward from the skull onto the bridge of the nose. Seen in Pugs, Pekingese and some other short-nose breeds.

Overreaching—Fault in the *trot* caused by more angulation and drive from behind than in front. The rear feet are forced to step to one side of the forefeet to avoid interfering or *clipping.*

Overshot—When the upper teeth project beyond the lower. Also called *pigjaw.*

P

Pace—A *gait* that tends to promote a rolling motion of the body. The left foreleg and left hind leg advance together, then the right foreleg and right hind leg.

Pack—Several *hounds* kept together in one *kennel.* A mixed pack is composed of males and females.

Paddling—A *gaiting* fault. It resembles the swing and dip of a canoeist's paddle. Pinching in at the elbows and shoulder joints causes the front legs to swing forward on a stiff outward arc. Also referred to as being tied at the elbows.

Pads—The tough, cushioned soles of the feet.

Paper foot—A flat foot with thin *pads.*

Particolor—A term used for a dog of two colors in equal proportion, usually red and white or black and white.

Pastern—The region of the foreleg between the carpus, wrist and digits.

Patellar luxation—When the kneecap, also called the stifle, slips or dislocates. An abnormality, said to be hereditary, found in several small breeds.

Peak—An unusually prominent *occiput.*

Pedigree—Written record of the names of a dog's ancestors going back at least three generations.

Pencilling—The dark lines on the surface of the toes in some breeds, notably the Manchester Toy Terrier.

Pepper and salt—Coat color consisting of an even mixture of gray and black hair, as in the Schnauzer.

Pied—When two colors occur in irregular patches, one more than the other.

Pigeon breast—A chest with a short protruding *breastbone.*

Pigeon toe—Toes pointing in.

Pigjaw—See *Overshot.*

Pile—Dense *undercoat* of soft hair.

Pily—A coat containing both soft and coarse hair.

Pincer bite—See *Level bite.*

Pitching—Severe rocking of the *haunches* as the rear legs swing forward in a wide arc, rather than flexing normally at the *stifle* and *hocks.*

Plumes—The soft hair on the tail of the Pekingese and Pomeranian.

Poach—When hunting, to trespass and kill *game* on private property.

Point—The immovable *stance* of the hunting dog indicating the presence and position of *game.*

Points—Color on face, ears, legs and tail when correlated, usually white, black or tan.

Poke—To carry the neck stretched forward in an abnormally low, ungainly position, usually when moving.

Police dog—A dog trained for police work, often a German Shepherd.

Pompon—Ball of hair left on the end of a Poodle's tail after it has been *clipped*.

Pounding—*Gaiting* fault. A dog's stride is shorter in front than in the rear. Forefeet strike the ground hard before the rear stride is expended.

Prick ear—Carried erect, usually pointed at the tip.

Professional handler—A person who shows dogs for a fee.

Progressive Retinal Atrophy (PRA)—Sometimes incorrectly called night blindness. A hereditary defect of the eyes, found in several breeds. Causes early loss of sight.

Pump handle—Long tail, carried high.

Puppy—A dog under 1 year old.

Purebred—A dog whose *sire* and *dam* belong to the same *breed* and are themselves of unmixed descent since the recognition of the breed.

Purling—See *Crossing over*.

Put down—To prepare a dog for the *show ring*. Also, unplaced in competition. Also, to humanely destroy an old or terminally sick animal.

Q

Quality—Refinement, fineness.

Quarters—Any leg of a four-legged animal, with adjoining parts.

Quick—The sensitive flesh at the end of the dog's nail.

R

Racy—Lean, long legged, slightly built.

Ragged—Muscles appear ragged rather than smooth, as in the English Foxhound.

Ram's nose—See *Roman nose*.

Rangy—Long bodied, usually lacking depth in chest.

Rat tail—Long pointed tail, with short thin hair.

Reach of front—Length of forward stride taken by forelegs without wasted or excessive motion.

Register—To record details of a dog's breeding with the respective kennel club.

Retrieve—To bring back shot *game* for a hunter.

Ribbed up—Having long ribs that angle back from the spinal column: 45° is ideal.

Ringer—A substitute for another dog. A dog closely resembling another.

Ring tail—Carried up and around almost in a circle.

Roached—A back that arches convexly, as in the Dandie Dinmont, Italian Greyhound and Whippet.

Roan—Mixture of white with another color, usually blue or red, in equal proportions, as in the Cocker Spaniel.

Rocking horse—Stance with both front and rear legs extended out from the body as in a toy rocking horse.

Rolling gait—Swaying, ambling *action* of the *hindquarters* when moving.

Roman nose—A nose with a bridge so high it forms a slightly convex line from forehead to nose tip. Also called *ram's nose*.

Rose-eared—When the ear, not *pricked* or *dropped*, folds or twists over showing the inside, as in a Bulldog.

Rounding—To cut or trim the end of the ear *leather*, as in English Foxhounds.

Rubber hocks—See *Twisting hocks*.

Rudder—The tail.

Ruff—Thick, longer hair growth around the neck.

S

Sable—The color of a light coat shaded with black, as in a Collie.

Saber tail—Carried in a semicircle.

Saddle—A black marking over the back, like a horse's saddle.

Saddle back—Overlong back, with a dip behind the *withers*.

Scapula—The shoulder blade.

Scent—Odor left by an animal on the *trail*, a ground scent, or wafted through the air, an airborne scent.

Scissor bite—A *bite* in which upper front teeth slightly overlap lower front teeth.

Screw tail—A short, twisted tail tapering to a point.

Second thigh—The part of the *hindquarter* from the *stifle* to the *hock*, corresponding to the human shin and calf.

Seeing-eye dog—A guide dog for the blind.

Self-color—One color except for lighter shadings.

Self-marked—A dog is self-marked when it is one color, with white or pale markings on the chest, feet and tail tip.

Semiprick ears—Ears carried erect with only the tips leaning forward.

Septum—Thin dividing wall between the nostrils.

Set on—Insertion or attachment of tail or ears.

Set up—Posed to make the most of the dog's appearance for the show ring.

Shelly—Having a long, narrow body like a Borzoi.

Shoulder height—Height of dog's body as measured from the *withers* to the ground.

Sicklehock—Unable to straighten the *hock* joint on the back reach of the hind leg.

Sickle tail—Carried out and up in a semicircle.

Side-wheeling—See *Crabbing*.

Side-winding—See *Crabbing*.

Sighthound—A hound that hunts by sight rather than scent. Also called a gazehound.

Single tracking—All footprints falling on a single line of travel. When a dog breaks into a *trot*, its body is supported by only two legs at a time, which move as alternating diagonal pairs. To achieve balance, the legs angle inward toward a center line beneath the body. The greater the speed, the closer they come to tracking on a single line.

Sire—The father of a *litter* of puppies.

Skully—Thick, coarse-looking skull.

Slab sided—Having flat ribs with too little spring from spinal column.

Sled dogs—Dogs used in teams to pull sleds.

Slew feet—Feet turned out.

Slipping stifle—See *patellar luxation*.

Sloping shoulders—Shoulders laid back on the body.

Smooth coat—Short, sleek hair lying close to the skin.

Snatching hocks—A *gaiting* fault indicated by a quick outward snatching of the *hock* as it passes the supporting leg and twists the rear *pastern* far in beneath the body. The action causes noticeable rocking in the hindquarters.

Snipy—Narrow and weak in the *muzzle*.

Soft-mouth—Able to carry retrieved *game* in the mouth without damaging it.

Soundness—The state of mental and physical health when all organs and faculties are complete and functioning normally, each in its rightful relation to the others.

Spay—To perform a surgical operation, a hysterectomy, on the female's reproductive organs to stop conception.

Speak—To bark.

Spectacles—Shadings or dark markings over or around the eyes or from eyes to ears.

Spike tail—Straight short tail tapering rapidly along its length.

Spitz—A *breed* of dog with a tapering *muzzle*.

Splashed—Irregularly patched. Color on white or white on color.

Splay feet—Feet with toes spread wide.

Spread—Width between the forelegs, when accentuated, as in the Bulldog.

Spread hocks—See *Barrel hocks*.

Spring—See *Flush*.

Spring of ribs—Curvature of ribs for heart and lung capacity.

Squirrel tail—Tail carried up and curving more or less forward.

Stake—A competition held at a *field trial*.

Stance—Manner of standing.

Standard—The level of perfection for each *breed*.

Stand-off coat—Rough, coarse hair that stands away from the body.

Staring coat—Coarse, hard hair, curling at the end.

Station—Height of a dog from the ground.

Stern—Tail of a sporting dog or *hound*.

Sternum—See *Breastbone*.

Stifle—Joint in the hind leg of a dog like a knee in man, particularly relating to the inner side.

Stilted—A stiff, awkward way of walking.

Stop—The depression between and in front of the eyes, roughly corresponding to the bridge of the nose.

Strabismus—Cross-eyed.

Straight hocks—*Hocks* that are vertically straight.

Straight in pastern—With little or no bend between joint and foot.

Straight shoulders—Shoulder blades running almost straight up and down, without any *angulation*.

Stripping—To clip or cut off the dog's hair so it is a short, uniform length all over the body.

Stud—Male used for breeding.

Stud book—A record of the breeding particulars of dogs of recognized *breeds*.

Substance—Bone.

Superciliary arch—The ridge, projection or prominence of the frontal bone of the skull over the eye. The brow.

Suspension trot—See *Flying trot*.

Sway back—A sagging back.

Symmetry—Pleasing *balance* between all parts of the dog.

T

Tail set—How the base of the tail sets on the rump.

Terrier—A group of dogs used originally for hunting vermin.

Terrier front—Straight front, as found on the Fox Terrier.

Thigh—The *hindquarter* from hip to *stifle*.

Throaty—Having too much skin around the throat.

Thumb marks—Circular black marks around the ankles.

Ticked—Small, isolated areas of black or colored hairs on a white ground.

Timber—Bone, especially of the legs.

Tongue—Noise made by *hounds* when on the *trail of game*.

Topknot—The longer, finer hair on the top of the head, as in the Dandie Dinmont.

Topline—The dog's outline from just behind the *withers* to the tail set.

Toy dog—A dog of small size.

Trace—A dark line of hair running down the back, like on the Pug.

Trail—To hunt by following ground scent.

Triangular eye—An eye set in surrounding tissue of triangular shape. A three-cornered eye.

Tricolor—Three colors more or less proportionate. Usually black, tan and white, as in *hounds*.

Trim—To groom by plucking or clipping.

Trot—A rhythmic two-beat diagonal *gait* in which the feet at diagonally opposite ends of the body strike the ground together—the right hind with left front and left hind with right front.

Trousers—Hair on the *hindquarters*.

Trumpet—The slight depression or hollow on either side of the skull just behind the orbit or eye socket. The region comparable with the temple.

Truncated—Cut off. The Old English Sheepdog standard calls for a jaw that is square and cut off.

Tucked-up—When the *loins* are lifted up but the *chest* is deep, giving a *racy* appearance, as in Borzois, Greyhounds and Whippets.

Tulip ears—Ears carried stiffly, straight, slightly open and leaning forward.

Turn-up—An up-tilted *foreface*.

Twisting hocks—A *gaiting* fault in which the *hock* joints twist both ways as they flex or bear weight.

Type—The characteristic qualities distinguishing a *breed*. The embodiment of a *standard's* essentials.

U

Undercoat—The soft, furry wool beneath the outer hair of some *breeds*. Gives protection against cold and wet.

Undershot—Having the lower jaw projecting. Opposite of *overshot*.

Underslung—Low to the ground, with short legs.

Unilateral cryptorchid—See *Cryptorchid*.

UKC—United Kennel Club.

Up-face—A *foreface* slanting upward, as in the Bulldog.

Upper arm—The humerus or bone of the foreleg, between the shoulder blade and *forearm*.

V

Varminty—A bright, searching, alert expression. Usually seen in terriers.

Vent—Both the anal opening and small area of light hair directly beneath the tail.

W

Walk—*Gaiting* pattern in which three legs are in support of the body at all times. Each foot lifts from the ground one at a time in regular sequence.

Wall eyes—Eyes *particolored* white and blue, seen in merle-colored collies and sheepdogs. Often valued.

Weaving—See *Crossing Over*.

Weedy—Having a light, scrawny build.

Well-boned—See *Bone*.

Well-let-down—Having short *hocks*.

Well-sprung ribs—Roundness or curvature of the rib cage.

Wet neck—Loose or extra skin, with *dewlap*.

Wheat—Pale-yellow color.

Wheel back—A back that is arched or convex.

Whelping—Giving birth to puppies.

Whelps—Newly born puppies.

Whip tail—A tail stiff and straight, as in the Pointer when the dog is *pointing*.

Whiskers—The *beard* of a dog, like the Miniature Schnauzer.

Whitelies—Color type that is white with red or dark markings, such as the Pembroke Welsh Corgi.

Wind—To catch the *scent* of *game*.

Winging—A *gaiting* fault. One or both front feet twist outward as the limbs swing forward.

Winners—Awards given at *dog shows* to the Best Dog (Winners Dog) and Best Female (Winners Bitch) competing in regular class.

Wirehair—Having a tough, dense, harsh coat.

Withers—The highest point of the shoulders, just behind the neck.

Wolf color—Black, brown and gray distributed in equal amounts.

Wrinkle—The loose folds of skin puckered up on the brows and sides of the face. In Bloodhounds, St. Bernards, Basenjis, Pugs and others.

Wry mouth—Lower jaw does not line up with the upper.

X

Xiphoid—Sword-shape.

Y

Yawing—See *Crabbing*.

INDEX

ACKNOWLEDGMENTS

COVER PHOTOGRAPHS
Anne Cumbers, Bill Kohler, Sally Anne Thompson.

TEXT PHOTOGRAPHS
Anne Cumbers, Paddy Cutts, Ploon de Raad, Michael Findlay, Marc Henrie, Roger Hyde, Bill Kohler, Christina Payne, Bernard Rebouleau, Joe Rinehart, Anne Roslin-Williams, Angela Sayer, Sally Anne Thompson, Ron Willbie, Trevor Wood.

COVER AND LINE ARTWORK
John Francis, John Green, Alan Hollingbery, Gordon Riley, Clive Spong, Glenn Steward, Harold White.